Microsoft

MCSE Self-Paced Training Kit (Exam 70-297): Designing a Microsoft® Windows Server™ 2003 Active Directory® and Network Infrastructure

Walter Glenn with Michael T. Simpson

PUBLISHED BY
Microsoft Press
A Division of Microsoft Corporation
One Microsoft Way
Redmond, Washington 98052-6399

Copyright © 2004 by Microsoft Corporation

Library of Congress Cataloging-in-Publication Data pending.

Printed and bound in the United States of America.

1 2 3 4 5 6 7 8 9   QWT   8 7 6 5 4 3

Distributed in Canada by H.B. Fenn and Company Ltd.

A CIP catalogue record for this book is available from the British Library.

Microsoft Press books are available through booksellers and distributors worldwide. For further information about international editions, contact your local Microsoft Corporation office or contact Microsoft Press International directly at fax (425) 936-7329. Visit our Web site at www.microsoft.com/mspress. Send comments to *tkinput@microsoft.com*.

Active Directory, Microsoft, Microsoft Press, Windows, the Windows logo, Windows Server, and Windows NT are either registered trademarks or trademarks of Microsoft Corporation in the United States and/or other countries. Other product and company names mentioned herein may be the trademarks of their respective owners.

The example companies, organizations, products, domain names, e-mail addresses, logos, people, places, and events depicted herein are fictitious. No association with any real company, organization, product, domain name, e-mail address, logo, person, place, or event is intended or should be inferred.

Acquisitions Editor: Kathy Harding
Project Manager: Julie Pickering
Technical Editor: Tony Northrup

Body Part No. X10-09386

32.93

...ered *Microsoft Study Guide.*

...guide delivers in-depth preparation for the exam along with great new study ...de: SJ 5104

- Relevant exam... chapter

- "Why This Chap...
how you can ap...

- Case scenario ...
step, real-world...

...by using the Active Directory Users and

...y using automation.

...user profiles

...outs.

...d to user account properties.

3-14   Chapter 3   User Accou...

Lesson 2: Creatin...

There occasionally...
such as a new cl...
organization. In th...
mate user object ...
account basis. In ...
Active Directory U...
and tools to inclu...
and command line...

After this lesson,...
- Create and ...
- Import user...
- Leverage ne...
Estimated lesson...

Creating and Using ...

It is common for ...
tives may belong...
during the same ...
server. In such ca...
populated with o...
user object—often...

To generate a use...
appropriate grou...

Security Alert
account is not us...

To create a new u...
the Action menu...
a new user: first ...
When the object ...
based on the foll...

- **General** N...
- **Address** A...

...begin to access resources they require,
...ndividuals. Of course, the primary com-
...s identity, maintained as an account in
...review and enhance your knowledge
...d troubleshooting of user accounts and

...h it a unique set of challenges related to
...nfigure for a standard user account are
...y to the account of a Help Desk team
...ose configured on the built-in Adminis-
...create or modify a single user account
...a are working with masses of accounts,
...s for a number of new hires.

...g of account management scenarios, we
...ent skills and tools including the Active
...d powerful command-line utilities.

3-1

Lesson 3   Managing User Profiles   3-29

...s allowing Everyone Full Control. The Windows
...Read, which is not sufficient for a roaming pro-

...dialog box, type the Profile Path in the for-
...e. The *%username%* variable will automat-
...ne.

...on to their system, the system will identify

...g more than a shared folder and a path to the
...into the user object's profile path property.
...y of a computer object.

...will upload the profile to the profile server.
...or any other system in the domain, and the
...r RUP will be applied.

...w policy: Only allow local user profiles. This pol-
...nts, will prevent roaming profiles from being
...l, maintain local profiles.

When a user with an RUP logs on to a new system for the first time, the system does
not copy its Default User profile. Instead, it downloads the RUP from the network location. When a user logs off, or when a user logs on to a system on which they've
worked before, the system copies only files that have changed.

Real World   Roaming Profile Synchronization
Unlike previous versions of Microsoft Windows, Windows 2000, Windows XP,
and Windows Server 2003 do not upload and download the entire user profile at
logoff and logon. Instead, the user profile is *synchronized*. Only files that have
changed are transferred between the local system and the network RUP folder.
This means that logon and logoff with RUPs are significantly faster than with earlier Windows systems. Organizations that have not implemented RUPs for fear of
their impact on logon and network traffic should reevaluate their configuration in
this light.

- "Off the Recor...
things *should* ...

- Security Alerts ...
world

- Exam highlights—key points and terms you should know

- Exam tips written by industry insiders

Exam 70-297: Designing a Microsoft Windows Server 2003 Active Directory and Network Infrastructure

Objective	Pages
Creating the Conceptual Design by Gathering and Analyzing Business and Technical Requirements	
Analyze the impact of Active Directory on the existing technical environment.	2-3 to 2-10, 2-12 to 2-17, 2-18 to 2-24
■ Analyze hardware and software requirements.	
■ Analyze interoperability requirements.	
■ Analyze current level of service within an existing technical environment.	
■ Analyze current network administration model.	
■ Analyze network requirements.	
Analyze DNS for Active Directory directory service implementation.	6-3 to 6-9
■ Analyze the current DNS infrastructure.	
■ Analyze the current namespace.	
Analyze existing network operating system implementation.	2-18 to 2-24
■ Identify the existing domain model.	
■ Identify the number and location of domain controllers on the network.	
■ Identify the configuration details of all servers on the network. Server types might include primary domain controllers, backup domain controllers, file servers, print servers, and Web servers.	
Analyze security requirements for the Active Directory directory service.	2-18 to 2-24
■ Analyze current security policies, standards, and procedures.	
■ Identify the impact of Active Directory on the current security infrastructure.	
■ Identify the existing trust relationships.	
Design the Active Directory infrastructure to meet business and technical requirements.	3-2 to 3-12, 4-3 to 4-20, 5-22 to 5-32
■ Design the envisioned administration model.	
■ Create the conceptual design of the Active Directory forest structure.	
■ Create the conceptual design of the Active Directory domain structure.	
■ Design the Active Directory replication strategy.	
■ Create the conceptual design of the organizational unit (OU) structure.	
Design the network services infrastructure to meet business and technical requirements.	6-10 to 6-40, 7-15 to 7-21, 8-29 to 8-40, 10-3 to 10-17
■ Create the conceptual design of the DNS infrastructure.	
■ Create the conceptual design of the WINS infrastructure.	
■ Create the conceptual design of the DHCP infrastructure.	
■ Create the conceptual design of the remote access infrastructure.	
Identify network topology and performance levels.	2-12 to 2-23
■ Identify constraints in the current network infrastructure.	
■ Interpret current baseline performance requirements for each major subsystem.	
Analyze the impact of the infrastructure design on the existing technical environment.	2-12 to 2-23, 5-10 to 5-21
■ Analyze hardware and software requirements.	
■ Analyze interoperability requirements.	
■ Analyze current level of service within the existing technical environment.	
■ Analyze network requirements.	
Creating the Logical Design for an Active Directory Infrastructure	
Design an OU structure.	4-3 to 4-20
■ Identify the Group Policy requirements for the OU structure.	
■ Design an OU structure for the purpose of delegating authority.	
Design a security group strategy.	4-26 to 4-31
■ Define the scope of a security group to meet requirements.	
■ Define resource access requirements.	
■ Define administrative access requirements.	
■ Define user roles.	
Design a user and computer authentication strategy.	4-25 to 4-26
■ Identify common authentication requirements.	
■ Select authentication mechanisms.	
■ Optimize authentication by using shortcut trust relationships.	
Design a user and computer account strategy.	4-21 to 4-25
■ "Specify account policy requirements.	
■ "Specify account requirements for users, computers, administrators, and services.	
Design an Active Directory naming strategy.	3-16 to 3-28
■ Identify Internet domain name registration requirements.	
■ Specify the use of hierarchical namespace within Active Directory.	
■ Identify NetBIOS naming requirements.	

Objective	Pages
Design migration paths to Active Directory.	5-33 to 5-35
■ Define whether the migration will include an in-place upgrade, domain restructuring, or migration to a new Active Directory environment.	
Design a strategy for Group Policy implementation.	4-32 to 4-42
■ Design the administration of Group Policy objects (GPOs).	
■ Design the deployment strategy of GPOs.	
■ Create a strategy for configuring the user environment with Group Policy.	
■ Create a strategy for configuring the computer environment with Group Policy.	
Design an Active Directory directory service site topology.	5-22 to 5-32
■ Design sites.	
■ Identify site links.	
Design an OU structure.	4-3 to 4-20
■ Identify the Group Policy requirements for the OU structure.	
■ Design an OU structure for the purpose of delegating authority.	

Creating the Logical Design for a Network Services Infrastructure

Objective	Pages
Design a DNS name resolution strategy.	6-10 to 6-24
■ Create the namespace design.	
■ Identify DNS interoperability with Active Directory, WINS, and DHCP.	
■ Specify zone requirements.	
■ Specify DNS security.	
■ Design a DNS strategy for interoperability with UNIX Berkeley Internet Name Domain (BIND) to support Active Directory.	
Design a NetBIOS name resolution strategy.	7-22 to 7-30
■ Design a WINS replication strategy.	
Design security for remote access users.	10-25 to 10-35
■ Identify security host requirements.	
■ Identify the authentication and accounting provider.	
■ Design remote access policies.	
■ Specify logging and auditing settings.	
Design a DNS service implementation.	6-25 to 6-28
■ Design a strategy for DNS zone storage.	
■ Specify the use of DNS server options.	
■ Identify the registration requirements of specific DNS records.	
Design a remote access strategy.	10-3 to 10-17
■ Specify the remote access method.	
■ Specify the authentication method for remote access.	
Design an IP address assignment strategy.	8-3 to 8-17, 8-29 to 8-35
■ Specify DHCP integration with DNS infrastructure.	
■ Specify DHCP interoperability with client types.	

Creating the Physical Design for an Active Directory and Network Infrastructure

Objective	Pages
Design DNS service placement.	6-29 to 6-40
Design an Active Directory implementation plan.	5-10 to 5-21
■ Design the placement of domain controllers and global catalog servers.	
■ Plan the placement of flexible operations master roles.	
■ Select the domain controller creation process.	
Specify the server specifications to meet system requirements.	5-10 to 5-21
Design Internet connectivity for a company.	9-2 to 9-26
Design a network and routing topology for a company.	8-3 to 8-17, 8-18 to 8-23
■ Design a TCP/IP addressing scheme through the use of IP subnets.	
■ Specify the placement of routers.	
■ Design IP address assignment by using DHCP.	
■ Design a perimeter network.	
Design the remote access infrastructure.	10-18 to 10-24
■ Plan capacity.	
■ Ascertain network settings required to access resources.	
■ Design for availability, redundancy, and survivability.	

Note Exam objectives are subject to change at anytime without prior notice and at Microsoft's sole discretion. Please visit Microsoft's Training & Certification Web site (*www.microsoft.com/traincert*) for the most current listing of exam objectives.

For my wife, Susan

Walter Glenn

Walter Glenn, MCSE and MCT, has been a part of the computer industry for more than 17 years and currently works in Huntsville, Alabama, as a consultant, trainer, and writer. He is the author or coauthor of nearly 20 computer titles, including *Exchange Server 2003 Administrator's Companion* (Microsoft Press, 2003), *MCSE: Exchange 2000 Server Administration Study Guide* (Sybex, 2000), and *Mike Meyers' MCSA Managing a Microsoft Windows Server 2003 Network Environment Certification Passport* (Osborne, 2003). He has also written a number of Web-based courses geared toward Microsoft certification training.

Michael T. Simpson

Michael Simpson is president/senior consultant of MTS Consulting, Inc., which specializes in supporting, configuring, and designing networks and is based in Hawaii. He conducts vulnerability assessment and penetration testing for businesses and also gives network security seminars in the private sector and to government audiences. Mike's certifications include MCSE, MCSA, MCT, CNE, CCNP, Security+, and Certified Ethical Hacker (CEH). He has coauthored four books and has more than 17 years of industry experience, including 12 years with the Department of Defense, where he designed and configured computer networks and served as Information Systems Security Officer (ISSO).

Contents at a Glance

Practices

Tables

Case Scenario Exercises

Contents

3   Planning an Active Directory Structure   3-1

4   Designing an Administrative Security Structure   4-1

9   Designing Internet Connectivity   9-1

Acknowledgments

It always makes me feel a little strange to say that I have written a book because it takes the combined effort of a lot of people to put a book like this into your hands. Foremost, I'd like to thank my coauthor, Mike Simpson, for all his work. He signed on late in the project and did a great job. I'd also like to thank Tony Northrup for a wonderful technical review.

I'd also like to thank the folks at Microsoft Press for guiding this book through its various stages. Kathy Harding, our acquisitions editor, showed her faith in the project and in me. Julie Pickering, our project manager, worked hard to make sure that this book is of the best quality and that it was published on schedule. I'd also like to thank Rajni Gulati, Karen Szall, and Lori Kane for their help at various stages.

Finally, as always, I'd like to thank Neil Salkind and everyone else at StudioB for helping put this project together.

Walter Glenn

About This Book

Welcome to *MCSE Self-Paced Training Kit (Exam 70-297): Designing a Microsoft Windows Server 2003 Active Directory and Network Infrastructure.* This book teaches you how to gather the network requirements for a business, how to analyze an existing network, and how to design an Active Directory directory service and networking infrastructure.

The first chapter of this book provides an overview of the technologies that you work with on a Windows Server 2003 network. In subsequent chapters, you learn how to design an Active Directory structure, which includes creating a forest and domain plan, an organizational unit and administrative plan, and a site topology plan. The remaining chapters teach you how to design a network infrastructure and focus on Domain Name System, Windows Internet Naming System, routing, and remote access.

Note   For more information about becoming a Microsoft Certified Professional, see the section titled "The Microsoft Certified Professional Program" later in this introduction.

Intended Audience

This book was developed for information technology (IT) professionals who plan to take the related Microsoft Certified Professional exam 70-297, "Designing a Microsoft Windows Server 2003 Active Directory and Network Infrastructure," as well as for IT professionals who design, develop, and implement software solutions for Microsoft Windows environments using Microsoft tools and technologies.

Note   Exam skills tested are subject to change without prior notice and at the sole discretion of Microsoft.

Prerequisites

This training kit requires that students have a solid understanding of the networking technologies in Windows Server 2003. Although Chapter 1 provides an overview of those technologies, you should have 12 to 18 months of experience administering Windows technologies in a network environment.

About the CD-ROM

For your use, this book includes a Supplemental Course Materials CD-ROM that contains a variety of informational aids to complement the book content, including:

- The Microsoft Press Readiness Review Suite Powered by MeasureUp. This suite of practice tests and objective reviews contains questions of varying degrees of complexity and offers multiple testing modes. You can assess your understanding of the concepts presented in this book and use the results to develop a learning plan that meets your needs.

- An electronic version of this book (eBook). For information about using the eBook, see the section "The eBook" later in this introduction.

- eBooks of the *Microsoft Encyclopedia of Networking*, Second Edition, and the *Microsoft Encyclopedia of Security.*

- Sample chapters from several Microsoft Press books. These chapters give you additional information about Windows Server 2003 and introduce you to other resources that are available from Microsoft Press.

A second CD-ROM contains a 180-day evaluation edition of Microsoft Windows Server 2003, Enterprise Edition.

Caution   The 180-day evaluation edition provided with this training kit is not the full retail product and is provided only for the purposes of training and evaluation. Microsoft Technical Support does not support this evaluation edition.

For additional support information regarding this book and the CD-ROM (including answers to commonly asked questions about installation and use), visit the Microsoft Press Technical Support Web site at *http://www.microsoft.com/mspress/support/*. You can also e-mail tkinput@microsoft.com or send a letter to Microsoft Press, Attention: Microsoft Press Technical Support, One Microsoft Way, Redmond, WA 98052-6399.

Features of This Book

Chapter and Appendix Overview

Each chapter identifies the exam objectives covered within the chapter, provides an overview of why the topics matter by identifying how the information applies in the real world, and lists any prerequisites that must be met to complete the lessons presented in the chapter.

The chapters are divided into lessons. Lessons end with a summary of important concepts and a set of review questions to test your knowledge of the material presented in the lesson. Many lessons also include a practice exercise.

After the lessons, you are given an opportunity to apply what you've learned in a case scenario exercise. In this exercise, you work through a multistep solution for a realistic case scenario. Each chapter concludes with a summary of important concepts and a short section listing key topics and terms that you need to know before taking the exam. A glossary of key terms used in the book follows the chapters.

Real World **Helpful Information**

You will find sidebars similar to this one that contain related information you might find helpful. "Real World" sidebars contain specific information gained through the experience of IT professionals just like you.

Reader Aids

Several types of reader aids appear throughout the training kit.

Tip   contains methods of performing a task more quickly or in a less obvious way.

Note   contains supplemental information.

Caution   contains valuable information about possible loss of data; be sure to read this information carefully.

Warning   contains critical information about possible physical injury; be sure to read this information carefully.

See Also   contains references to other sources of information.

Security Alert   highlights information you need to know to maximize security in your work environment.

Exam Tip   flags information you should know before taking the certification exam.

Notational Conventions

The following conventions are used throughout this book.

- *Italic* in syntax statements indicates placeholders for variable information. Italic is also used for book titles.

- Names of files and folders appear in title caps, except when you are to type them directly. Unless otherwise indicated, you can use all lowercase letters when you type a file name in a dialog box or at a command prompt.

- File name extensions appear in all lowercase.

- Acronyms appear in ALL UPPERCASE.

- **Bold** type represents entries that you might type at a command prompt or in initialization files.

Getting Started

This training kit provides many chances for you to practice the design concepts it teaches. The practices throughout this book are guided design activities and do not require you to work on a computer. However, if you plan to use the evaluation software, you can use this section to prepare the computer environment.

Hardware Requirements

The test computer must have the following minimum configuration. All hardware should be on the Microsoft Server 2003 Hardware Compatibility List and should meet the requirements listed at *http://www.microsoft.com/windowsserver2003/evaluation/sysreqs/*. The following requirements apply to Windows Server 2003 Enterprise Edition.

- **Minimum CPU:**   133 MHz for x86-based computers (733 MHz recommended) and 733 MHz for Itanium-based computers

- **Minimum RAM:**   128 MB (256 MB recommended)

- **Disk space for setup:**   1.5 GB for x86-based computers and 2.0 GB for Itanium-based computers

Software Requirements

A 180-day evaluation edition of Windows Server 2003, Enterprise Edition, is included on the CD-ROM.

Caution The 180-day evaluation edition provided with this training kit is not the full retail product and is provided only for the purposes of training and evaluation. Microsoft Technical Support does not support these evaluation editions. For additional support information regarding this book and the CD-ROMs (including answers to commonly asked questions about installation and use), visit the Microsoft Press Technical Support Web site at *http://mspress.microsoft.com/mspress/support/*. You can also e-mail tkinput@microsoft.com or send a letter to Microsoft Press, Attention: Microsoft Press Technical Support, One Microsoft Way, Redmond, WA 98502-6399.

Setup Instructions

Set up your computer according to the manufacturer's instructions. The following items are included in the Windows Server 2003 Evaluation Kit:

- Windows Server 2003, Enterprise Edition, CD-ROM
- Windows Server 2003 Resource CD-ROM
- A unique Product Key (required for installation)
- Links to additional Web-based documentation

After you install Windows Server 2003 evaluation software, you have 14 days to activate the product. If you do not activate the product within 14 days of installation, you will not be able to continue your evaluation until you activate it. None of your data will be lost.

The Readiness Review Suite

The CD-ROM includes a practice test made up of 300 sample exam questions. Use these tools to reinforce your learning and to identify any areas in which you need to gain more experience before taking the exam.

▶ **To install the practice test**

1. Insert the Supplemental CD-ROM into your CD-ROM drive.

Note If AutoRun is disabled on your machine, refer to the Readme.txt file on the CD-ROM.

2. Click Readiness Review Suite on the user interface menu.

The eBook

The CD-ROM includes an electronic version of the Training Kit. The eBook is in portable document format (PDF) and can be viewed using Adobe Acrobat Reader.

▶   **To use the eBook**

1. Insert the Supplemental CD-ROM into your CD-ROM drive.

> **Note**   If AutoRun is disabled on your machine, refer to the Readme.txt file on the CD-ROM.

2. Click Training Kit eBook on the user interface menu. You can also review any of the other eBooks that are provided for your use.

The Microsoft Certified Professional Program

The Microsoft Certified Professional (MCP) program provides the best method to prove your command of current Microsoft products and technologies. The exams and corresponding certifications are developed to validate your mastery of critical competencies as you design and develop, or implement and support, solutions with Microsoft products and technologies. Computer professionals who become Microsoft certified are recognized as experts and are sought after industry-wide. Certification brings a variety of benefits to the individual and to employers and organizations.

> **See Also**   For a full list of MCP benefits, go to *http://www.microsoft.com/traincert/start/itpro.asp*.

Microsoft Certification Benefits

The Microsoft Certified Professional program offers multiple certifications, based on specific areas of technical expertise:

■ **Microsoft Certified Professional (MCP)**   Demonstrates in-depth knowledge of at least one Microsoft Windows operating system or architecturally significant platform. An MCP is qualified to implement a Microsoft product or technology as part of a business solution for an organization.

■ **Microsoft Certified Solution Developer (MCSD)**   Professional developer qualified to analyze, design, and develop enterprise business solutions with Microsoft development tools and technologies including the Microsoft .NET Framework.

■ **Microsoft Certified Application Developer (MCAD)**   Professional developer qualified to develop, test, deploy, and maintain powerful applications using Microsoft tools and technologies including Microsoft Visual Studio .NET and XML Web services.

■ **Microsoft Certified Systems Engineer (MCSE)**   Qualified to effectively analyze the business requirements, and design and implement the infrastructure for business solutions based on the Microsoft Windows and Microsoft Server 2003 operating systems.

- **Microsoft Certified Systems Administrator (MCSA)**   Individual with the skills to manage and troubleshoot existing network and system environments based on the Microsoft Windows and Microsoft Server 2003 operating systems.

- **Microsoft Certified Database Administrator (MCDBA)**   Individual who designs, implements, and administers Microsoft SQL Server databases.

- **Microsoft Certified Trainer (MCT)**   Instructionally and technically qualified to deliver Microsoft Official Curriculum through a Microsoft Certified Technical Education Center (CTEC).

Requirements for Becoming a Microsoft Certified Professional

The certification requirements differ for each certification and are specific to the products and job functions addressed by the certification.

To become a Microsoft Certified Professional, you must pass rigorous certification exams that provide a valid and reliable measure of technical proficiency and expertise. These exams are designed to test your expertise and ability to perform a role or task with a product, and are developed with the input of professionals in the industry. Questions in the exams reflect how Microsoft products are used in actual organizations, giving them "real-world" relevance.

- Microsoft Certified Professional (MCP) candidates are required to pass one current Microsoft certification exam. Candidates can pass additional Microsoft certification exams to further certify their skills with other Microsoft products, development tools, or desktop applications.

- Microsoft Certified Solution Developers (MCSDs) are required to pass three core exams and one elective exam. (MCSD certification for Microsoft .NET requires candidates to pass four core exams and one elective.)

- Microsoft Certified Application Developers (MCADs) are required to pass two core exams and one elective exam in an area of specialization.

- Microsoft Certified Systems Engineers (MCSEs) are required to pass five core exams and two elective exams.

- Microsoft Certified Systems Administrators (MCSAs) are required to pass three core exams and one elective exam that provide a valid and reliable measure of technical proficiency and expertise.

- Microsoft Certified Database Administrators (MCDBAs) are required to pass three core exams and one elective exam that provide a valid and reliable measure of technical proficiency and expertise.

- Microsoft Certified Trainers (MCTs) are required to meet instructional and technical requirements specific to each Microsoft Official Curriculum course they are certified to deliver. The MCT program requires ongoing training to meet the requirements for the annual renewal of certification. For more information about becoming a Microsoft Certified Trainer, visit *http://www.microsoft.com/traincert/ mcp/mct/* or contact a regional service center near you.

Technical Support

Every effort has been made to ensure the accuracy of this book and the contents of the companion disc. If you have comments, questions, or ideas regarding this book or the companion disc, please send them to Microsoft Press using either of the following methods:

E-mail: tkinput@microsoft.com

Postal Mail: Microsoft Press
                Attn: MCSE Self-Paced Training Kit (Exam 70-297):
                Designing a Microsoft Windows Server 2003
                Active Directory and Network Infrastructure, Editor
                One Microsoft Way
                Redmond, WA 98052-6399

For additional support information regarding this book and the CD-ROM (including answers to commonly asked questions about installation and use), visit the Microsoft Press Technical Support Web site at *http://www.microsoft.com/mspress/support/*. To connect directly to the Microsoft Press Knowledge Base and enter a query, visit *http:// www.microsoft.com/mspress/support/search.asp*. For support information regarding Microsoft software, please connect to *http://support.microsoft.com/*.

Evaluation Edition Software Support

The 180-day Evaluation Edition provided with this training is not the full retail product and is provided only for the purposes of training and evaluation. Microsoft and Microsoft Technical Support do not support this evaluation edition.

Caution   The Evaluation Edition of Windows Server 2003, Enterprise Edition included with this book should not be used on a primary work computer. The evaluation edition is unsupported. For online support information relating to the full version of Windows Server 2003, Enterprise Edition that *might* also apply to the Evaluation Edition, you can connect to *http:// support.microsoft.com/*.

Information about any issues relating to the use of this evaluation edition with this training kit is posted to the Support section of the Microsoft Press Web site (*http:// www.microsoft.com/mspress/support/*). For information about ordering the full version of any Microsoft software, please call Microsoft Sales at (800) 426-9400 or visit *http:// www.microsoft.com*.

1 Introduction to Active Directory and Network Infrastructure

Exam Objectives in this Chapter:

- This first chapter serves as an overview of the technologies involved in designing a network infrastructure and does not specifically cover any exam objective.

Why This Chapter Matters

Designing a network is a challenge. Throughout this book, you will learn how to evaluate your networking needs, analyze the existing business and network configuration, and design an appropriate networking solution based on Microsoft Windows Server 2003 technologies. Much of this book deals with the practical aspects of designing a network.

This chapter introduces you to the theory behind it all. It starts with an overview of Microsoft Active Directory directory service and Domain Name System (DNS), which together dictate the basic design of your network. This chapter also provides overviews of designing a TCP/IP infrastructure and providing for remote access. Although no single chapter can make you an expert in these technologies, you should come away with a grounding that allows you to understand the design principles explored in the rest of this book. The knowledge provided in this chapter is essential for understanding both how a network works and how Microsoft Windows Server 2003 addresses the needs of a working network.

Lessons in this Chapter:

Before You Begin

To complete this chapter, you should be familiar with the basic administration of Microsoft Windows 2000 Server or Windows Server 2003.

Lesson 1: Active Directory Overview

Active Directory provides a means of coordinating the resources on a network and presenting them as a centralized source of information. This lesson introduces the principal functions and architecture of Active Directory.

After this lesson, you will be able to

- Explain the purpose of Active Directory on a network.
- Describe the logical and physical structure of Active Directory.
- Describe the interactions of the different components of Active Directory.
- Explain the importance of the Active Directory Schema.

Estimated lesson time: 45 minutes

What Is Active Directory?

A directory is really just an easy way to look things up. There are directories everywhere. When you look up a number in your phone book, you are using a directory. When you organize the files and folders on your computer, you are also using a directory. Like these, the Active Directory is a collection of information—in this case, a collection of information about the resources available on a Windows Server 2003 network.

The Need for Directory Services

The traditional method for keeping up with the enormous amount of information about network resources is to store it in separate directories that are typically managed from within the application or operating system component that uses the information.

A perfect example of this lies just a few years back in versions of Windows prior to Windows 2000. On a typical Windows NT 4.0–based network, for example, you might find several directories of information scattered across servers on a network. Users and access-controls lists were kept within a directory called the Security Accounts Manager (SAM) database. Exchange Server mailboxes and their user associations were stored in the Exchange directory. Other services and applications maintained their own directories. Although there was some interaction between these directories, they were largely separate.

Directories were most often developed for a particular application. Developers of these directories had no real incentive to provide integration with other systems. However, administrators and users who were faced with ever-increasing amounts of work did have a real need for all these separate databases to be able to work together and be managed as a single unit.

What Directory Services Bring to the Table

Directory services go beyond the functionality of scattered, proprietary directories by providing a unified source of information. Active Directory is not the first directory service. In fact, there are several directory services and standards used on networks today. These include (but are not limited to):

- **X.500 and the Directory Access Protocol (DAP)**   X.500 is an Internet Standards Organization (ISO) specification that defines how global directories should be structured. X.500 specifies the use of DAP to provide communication between clients and directory servers.

- **Lightweight Directory Access Protocol (LDAP)**   LDAP was developed in response to criticism that DAP was just too complicated for use on most directory service implementations. LDAP has quickly become the standard directory protocol used on the Internet.

- **Novell Directory Services (NDS)**   NDS is the directory service used for Novell Netware networks and complies with the X.500 standard.

- **Active Directory**   Active Directory is integral to Windows 2000– and Windows Server 2003–based networks. It was designed to comply with the LDAP standard.

> **See Also**   For more technical information on the X.500, DAP, and LDAP standards (and any other Internet standards), go to *www.ietf.org*, the official site of the Internet Engineering Task Force (IETF). Run a keyword search using the terms "X.500," "DAP," or "LDAP."

For a complex network, a directory service should provide an efficient way to manage, find, and access all the resources on a network—resources such as computers, users, printers, shared folders, and many others. A good directory service implementation should provide a number of core benefits:

- **Centralization**   The idea behind centralization is to reduce the number of directories on a network. Bringing information about all network resources into a centralized directory provides a single point of management, easing the administration of resources and allowing you to more effectively delegate administrative tasks. It also provides a single point of entry for network users (or their computers or applications) when searching for resources.

- **Scalability**   A directory service should also be able to accommodate the growth of a network without incurring significant additional overhead. This means that there needs to be a way of breaking up (or partitioning) the directory database so that it does not grow too large to be usable, while still maintaining the benefits of centralization.

- **Standardization**   A directory service should also provide access to its information through open standards. This ensures that other applications can make use of resources in Active Directory (and publish their own resources there) rather than having to maintain their own directories.

- **Extensible**   A directory service should also provide a way for administrators and applications to extend the information contained in the directory to meet an organization's needs.

- **Separation of physical network**   A directory service should make the physical network topology transparent to users and administrators. A resource should be identified and accessed without any knowledge required of how or where it is connected to the network.

- **Security**   A directory service would be very useful to a malicious attacker because it would contain detailed information about the organization. Therefore, a directory service must provide a secure means to store, manage, retrieve, and publish information about network resources.

How Active Directory Addresses the Issue

Active Directory is designed to meet all of the needs of a directory service outlined in the previous section.

- Active Directory is centralized, providing a single database of network resources that is easy to search and administer.

- Active Directory is scalable because it allows the database to be partitioned and distributed across the domains that make up the network, yet still be managed as a single directory.

- Active Directory is standardized because it is made accessible through LDAP, an open Internet standard overseen by the IETF.

- Active Directory is extensible, allowing developers to use the directory to store information for their own applications.

- Active Directory is secure, since it is tightly integrated with Windows Server 2003 security.

- Active Directory abstracts the logical organization of the network and identification of network resources from the physical structure of the network.

> **Exam Tip**   It is important to remember how Active Directory fits into Windows Server 2003. Active Directory is both a database of information about network resources *and* a service run by a domain controller that provides access to that database.

The Logical Active Directory Structure

What makes Active Directory so configurable, and so scalable, is that it separates the logical structure of the Windows Server 2003 domain hierarchy—which is made up of domains, trees, forests, organizational units, and objects—from the physical structure of the network itself. The logical structure of Active Directory does not rely on the physical location of servers or the network connectivity throughout the domain. This provides the powerful ability to structure domains according to your administrative and organizational needs.

Because Active Directory separates the logical structure of network resources from the physical structure of the network itself, it is useful to break the discussion of Active Directory along those same lines. The logical components of the Active Directory structure include the following:

- Objects
- Domains
- Trees
- Forests
- Organizational Units

Objects

Resources are stored in the Active Directory as objects. Since the object is the most easily understood component of the Active Directory (being that it usually represents a tangible resource), it is a good place to start.

Objects are stored in the Active Directory in a hierarchical structure of containers and subcontainers, making the objects easier to find, access, and manage—much like organizing files in a set of Windows folders. You can tailor a directory structure to meet the needs of your organization, and scale that structure to easily accommodate a network of any size.

- **Object Classes**   An object is really just a collection of attributes. A user object, for example, is made up of attributes such as name, password, phone number, group membership, and so on. The attributes that make up an object are defined by an object class. The user class, for example, specifies the attributes that make up the user object.

   Object classes help organize objects by their similarities. All user objects fall under the object class Users. When you create a new object, it automatically inherits attributes from its class. Microsoft defines a default set of object classes (and the attributes they define) used by Active Directory in Windows Server 2003. Of course, because Active Directory is extensible, administrators and applications can modify the object classes available and the attributes that those classes define.

■ **The Active Directory Schema**   The classes and the attributes that they define are collectively referred to as the Active Directory Schema—in database terms, a schema is the structure of the tables and fields and how they are related to one another. You can think of the Active Directory Schema as a collection of data (object classes) that defines how the real data of the directory (the attributes of an object) is organized and stored.

Just about everything in the Active Directory is an object and that includes the schema itself. As with all other objects, the schema is protected by access control lists (ACL) that are managed by the Windows Server 2003 security subsystem. Users and applications with the appropriate permissions can read, use, and even modify the schema.

Domains

The basic organizational structure of the Windows Server 2003 networking model is the domain. A domain represents an administrative boundary. The computers, users, and other objects within a domain share a common security database.

Using domains allows administrators to divide the network into security boundaries. In addition, administrators from different domains can establish their own security models; security from one domain can then be isolated so that other domains' security models are not affected. Primarily, domains provide a way to logically partition a network along the same lines as an organization. Organizations large enough to have more than one domain usually have divisions that are responsible for maintaining and securing their own resources.

A Windows Server 2003 domain also represents a namespace that corresponds to a naming structure that most network administrators are already familiar with: the same DNS used on the Internet (and covered in detail in the next lesson). A domain, when created, is given a name that follows the DNS structure.

For example, a server named msnews in a domain named microsoft.com would have the fully qualified domain name (FQDN) msnews.microsoft.com.

> **Exam Tip**   The word namespace is used often. You will do well to remember that, at its simplest, a namespace is a structure (often a database) in which all objects are named similarly, but are still uniquely identified.

Trees

Multiple domains are organized into a hierarchical structure called a tree. Actually, even if you have only one domain in your organization, you still have a tree. The first domain you create in a tree is called the root domain. The next domain that you add becomes a child domain of that root. This expandability of domains makes it possible to have many domains in a tree. Figure 1-1 shows an example of a tree. Microsoft.com was the first domain created in Active Directory in this example and is therefore the root domain.

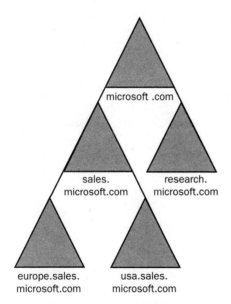

Figure 1-1   A tree is a hierarchical organization of multiple domains.

All domains in a tree share a common schema and a contiguous namespace. In the example shown in Figure 1-1, all of the domains in the tree under the microsoft.com root domain share the namespace microsoft.com. Using a single tree is fine if your organization is confined within a single DNS namespace. However, for organizations that use multiple DNS namespaces, your model must be able to expand outside the boundaries of a single tree. This is where the forest comes in.

Forests

A forest is a group of one or more domain trees that do not form a contiguous namespace but may share a common schema and global catalog. There is always at least one forest on a network, and it is created when the first Active Directory–enabled computer (domain controller) on a network is installed. This first domain in a forest, called the forest root domain, is special because it holds the schema and controls domain naming for the entire forest. It cannot be removed from the forest without removing the entire forest itself. Also, no other domain can ever be created above the forest root domain in the forest domain hierarchy.

Figure 1-2 shows an example of a forest with two trees. Each tree in the forest has its own namespace. In the figure, microsoft.com is one tree and contoso.com is a second tree. Both are in a forest named microsoft.com (after the first domain created).

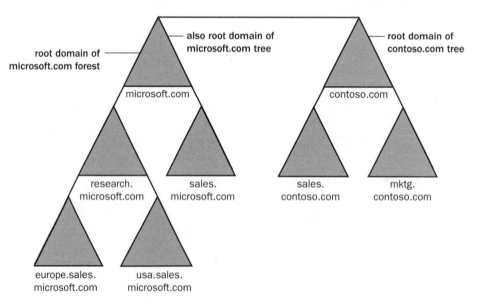

Figure 1-2   Trees in a forest share the same schema, but not the same namespace.

A forest is the outermost boundary of Active Directory; the directory cannot be larger than the forest. However, you can create multiple forests and then create trust relationships between specific domains in those forests; this would let you grant access to resources and accounts that are outside of a particular forest.

Organizational Units

Organizational Units (OUs) provide a way to create administrative boundaries within a domain. Primarily, this allows you to delegate administrative tasks within the domain. Prior to the introduction of the Active Directory, the domain was the smallest container to which you could assign administrative permissions. This meant that giving a group of administrators administrative control over particular resources was difficult or impossible to do without giving them sweeping permissions throughout the domain.

OUs serve as containers into which the resources of a domain can be placed. You can then assign administrative permissions on the OU itself. Typically, the structure of OUs follows an organization's business or functional structure. For example, a relatively small organization with a single domain might create separate OUs for departments within the organization.

You can even nest OUs (create OUs inside other OUs) for further control. However, an overly complicated OU structure within a domain has its drawbacks. For one thing, the simpler you keep your structure, the simpler the implementation and management of that structure. For another, once you go beyond about 12 OUs deep in a nesting structure, you start running into significant performance issues.

Trust Relationships

Since domains represent security boundaries, special mechanisms called trust relationships allow objects in one domain (called the trusted domain) to access resources in another domain (called the trusting domain).

Windows Server 2003 supports six types of trust relationships:

- Parent and child trusts
- Tree-root trusts
- External trusts
- Shortcut trusts
- Realm trusts
- Forest trusts

Parent and Child Trusts and Tree-Root Trusts

Active Directory automatically builds transitive, two-way trusts between parent and child domains in a domain tree. When a child domain is created, a trust relationship is automatically configured between that child domain and the parent domain. This trust is two-way, meaning that resource access requests can flow from either domain to the other. In other words, both domains trust one another.

The trust is also transitive, meaning that domain controllers in a trusted domain pass along authentication requests to domain controllers in trusting domains. The transitive nature of these trusts is illustrated in Figure 1-3. A transitive, two-way trust exists between Domain A and Domain B. Another exists between Domain B and Domain C. Since Domain A trusts Domain B and Domain B trusts Domain C, then Domain A automatically trusts Domain C.

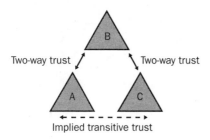

Figure 1-3   Parent and Child trusts allow authentication requests throughout a domain tree.

Two-way transitive trusts are also created automatically between the root domains of all domain trees you create in a single forest. Two-way transitive trusts simplify domain administration greatly over the method used in versions of Windows prior to Windows 2000. No longer must you configure separate one-way trusts between domains. For the most part, you can rely on the automatic trust relationships of Windows Server 2003 to do what you need them to. However, there are times when you will want to create other types of trust relationships.

External Trusts

An external trust is used when you need to create a relationship between a Windows Server 2003 domain and a Windows NT 4.0 domain. Since down-level domains (domains that do not use Active Directory) cannot participate in two-way transitive trusts, you must use external trusts. External trusts are not bidirectional. The trusting domain allows access to its objects by users in the trusted domain, but the trust does not flow the other way. You can, however, create two separate external trusts (going in opposite directions) between two domains to simulate a two-way trust.

External trusts are also not transitive, meaning that the relationship created by the trust exists only between the two domains involved and is not passed along to other domains.

Shortcut Trusts

Shortcut trusts provide a way to create a direct trust relationship between two domains that may already be linked using a chain of transitive trusts, but which you need to respond more quickly to one another. Consider the domain tree shown in Figure 1-4. In a complex tree like this, all domains are connected via transitive trust relationships.

However, assume that a user in Domain B needed to access a resource in Domain K. Since the resource is not located in the user's domain, the request is referred to the next domain and then to the next and then the next, and so on—each referral relying on the transitive trusts built up between the initial and final domain.

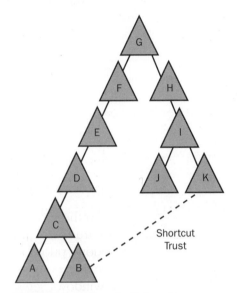

Figure 1-4   Although all domains are connected via transitive trusts, resolution can take time.

If users in Domain B needed more than occasional access to resources in Domain K, the delays caused by the referral process would quickly become an annoyance. The solution is to create a shortcut trust directly between Domain B and Domain K. This allows authentication requests to pass directly between the two domains.

Realm Trusts

New to Windows Server 2003, the realm trust is used to connect a Windows Server 2003 domain with a non-Windows realm that uses the Kerberos V5 security protocol. Realm trusts can be transitive or non-transitive, one-way or two-way.

Forest Trusts

Also new to Windows Server 2003, the forest trust makes it easier to manage multiple forests and provide a better security relationship between them. This type of trust allows users to access resources in a different forest while still using the single user identification (ID) provided by the user's own forest.

Partitioning the Active Directory Database

As you know by now, Active Directory is a collection of all the objects in a forest. As the forest grows, so does the directory. One challenge in designing the directory was in making sure that the directory database could grow along with an organization without being limited by the performance of a single server or location on the network. The answer to this problem is to partition the directory into distributed pieces.

Because domains represent the primary building block of a network, it makes sense that the partitioning of the directory occurs along domain boundaries. Each domain contains a partition of the directory that holds information about the objects in that domain. Each domain contains exactly one partition and the combination of partitions from domains across the forest results in the complete Active Directory.

The important advantage of partitioning the directory by domains is that new domains can be added to a forest without causing an undue burden on existing domains. This is because a new partition is created for the new domain and the new domain controllers in that domain will handle most work involved in managing the new partition.

> **Real World   Keeping it Simple**
>
> What with domains, trees, forests, and organizational units, you can see how enticing it could be to try to use all these components to organize your Active Directory implementation. However, you are best served by keeping your design as simple as your organizational needs allow. The details involved in designing and implementing an Active Directory setup are challenging enough without unnecessary complication. If you can work with a single domain, and a couple of OUs to help organize administrative tasks, then do it. The whole purpose of Active Directory is to ease the burden of administration. A simple, well-thought-out design goes a long way toward achieving this purpose.

The Physical Network Structure

The physical structure of an Active Directory network is fairly simple compared to its logical structure. The physical components are domain controllers and sites.

Domain Controller

A domain controller is a server running Windows Server 2003 that has Active Directory services installed and running. You can create any number of domain controllers in a domain. Each domain controller in a given domain has a complete replica of that domain's directory partition. Domain controllers locally resolve queries for information about objects in their domain and refer queries regarding information they do not hold to domain controllers in other domains. Domain controllers also manage changes to directory information and are responsible for replicating those changes to other domain controllers.

Since each domain controller holds a full replica of the directory partition for their domain, domain controllers follow what is known as a *multimaster model*. This simply means that every domain controller holds a master copy of the partition and can be used to modify that information.

However, there are certain roles that can be taken on by domain controllers for which the chosen domain controller is the only one allowed to perform that task. These domain controllers fill what are called operations master roles.

Forest-Wide Roles   There are two operations master roles that are taken on by only one domain controller in a forest. These forest-wide roles include:

■ **Schema Master**   The first domain controller in the forest holds the role of the Schema Master and is responsible for maintaining and distributing the schema to the rest of the forest. It maintains a list of all the possible object classes and attributes that define the objects found in Active Directory. If the schema needs to be updated or changed, the Schema Master must be available.

■ **Domain Naming Master**   This domain controller records the additions and deletions of domains to the forest and is vital in maintaining the integrity of the domain. The Domain Naming Master is queried when new domains are added to the forest. Keep in mind that if the Domain Naming Master is not available, then new domains cannot be added; however, this role can be moved to another system if necessary.

Domain-Wide Roles   There are three operations master roles that can only be taken on by one domain controller in each domain. These domain-wide roles include:

■ **Relative Identifier (RID) Master**   This domain controller is responsible for assigning blocks of RIDs to all domain controllers in a domain. A security identifier (SID) is a unique identifier for each object in a domain. SIDs in Windows Server 2003 are made up of two parts. The first part is common to all objects in the domain; a unique identifier (the RID) is then suffixed to create the unique SID for each object in a domain. They uniquely identify the object and specify where it was created.

■ **Primary Domain Controller (PDC) Emulator**   This domain controller is responsible for emulating a Windows NT 4.0 PDC for clients who have not migrated to Windows 2000, Windows Server 2003, or Windows XP, and do not have the Directory Services Client installed. One of the PDC emulator's primary responsibilities is to log on legacy clients. The PDC emulator will also be consulted if a client fails to authenticate. This gives the PDC emulator a chance to check for any last-minute password changes for legacy clients in the domain before it rejects the logon request.

- **Infrastructure Master**   This domain controller records changes made concerning objects in a domain. All changes are reported to the Infrastructure Master first, and then they are replicated out to the other domain controllers. The Infrastructure Master deals with groups and group memberships for all domain objects. It is also an Infrastructure Master's role to update other domains with changes that have been made to objects.

Global Catalog Server   Another server function that can be assigned to a domain controller is the Global Catalog server. The Global Catalog server maintains a subset of Active Directory object attributes that are most commonly searched for by users or client computers, such as a user's logon name. Global Catalog servers provide two important functions. They allow users to log on to the network and they allow users to locate objects anywhere in a forest.

The Global Catalog contains a subset of information from each domain partition and is replicated among Global Catalog servers in the domain. When a user attempts to log on or to access a network resource from anywhere in the forest, the Global Catalog is consulted for the resolution to the request. Without the Global Catalog, that request for access would have to be fielded by each domain controller in the forest until a resolution could be found. If your network uses a single domain, this function of the Global Catalog isn't really necessary because all domain controllers in the domain would have information on all users and objects on the network. With multiple domains, however, this function of the Global Catalog is essential.

The other function that the Global Catalog provides, which is useful whether you have one or many domains, is to assist in the authentication process when a user logs on to the network. When a user logs on, the name is checked against the Global Catalog before the user is resolved. This provides the ability for users to log on from computers in domains other than where their user accounts are located.

The first domain controller installed in a forest becomes the Global Catalog server by default. Unlike operations master roles, however, you can assign multiple domain controllers to serve as Global Catalog servers. You can create as many Global Catalog servers as you want to achieve load balancing and redundancy of services. Microsoft recommends placing at least one Global Catalog server in each site.

Although you can make any domain controller a Global Catalog server, you should be careful when deciding which servers should fill the role. To start with, you should not make the same domain controller an Infrastructure Master and a Global Catalog server if you have more than one domain controller. Also, being a Global Catalog server uses a significant amount of resources on the domain controller. For this reason, you would probably not want to make a Global Catalog server out of a domain controller that was fulfilling other demanding roles.

Site

A Windows Server 2003 site is a group of domain controllers that exist on one or more IP subnets (see Lesson 3 for more on this) and are connected by a fast, reliable network connection. Fast means connections of at least 1Mbps. In other words, a site usually follows the boundaries of a local area network (LAN). If different LANs on the network are connected by a wide area network (WAN), you'll likely create one site for each LAN.

Sites are primarily used to control replication traffic. Domain controllers within a site are pretty much free to replicate changes to the Active Directory database whenever changes are made. Domain controllers in different sites compress the replication traffic and operate based on a defined schedule, both of which are intended to cut down on network traffic.

Sites are not part of the Active Directory namespace. When a user browses the logical namespace, computers and users are grouped into Domains and OUs without reference to sites. Sites contain only two types of objects. The first type is the domain controllers contained in the site. The second type of object is the site links configured to connect the site to other sites.

Site Link   Within a site, replication happens automatically. For replication to occur between sites, you must establish a link between the sites. There are two components to this link: the actual physical connection between the sites (usually a WAN link) and a site link object. The site link object is created within Active Directory and determines the protocol used for transferring replication traffic (Internet Protocol [IP] or Simple Mail Transfer Protocol [SMTP]). The site link object also governs when replication is scheduled to occur.

Replication in Active Directory

The Active Directory replication process is fascinating. All objects and attributes need to be replicated to all the domain controllers in a domain to ensure that each domain controller has an up-to-date master copy of that domain's directory partition. That is a tremendous amount of data moving around, and with it comes the huge task of keeping track of that data.

Windows Server 2003 uses a replication model called *multimaster replication*, in which all replicas of the Active Directory database are considered equal masters. You can make changes to the database on any domain controller and the changes will be replicated to other domain controllers in the domain.

Domain controllers in the same site replicate on the basis of notification. When changes are made on a domain controller, it notifies its replication partners (the other domain controllers in the site); the partners then request the changes and replication occurs. Because of the high-speed, low-cost connections assumed within a site, replication occurs as needed rather than according to a schedule.

Unless you configure your own sites in Active Directory, all domain controllers are automatically made a part of a single site—a default site named "Default-First-Site-Name" that is created when you create the first domain.

You should create additional sites when you need to control how replication traffic occurs over slower WAN links. For example, suppose you have a number of domain controllers on your main LAN and a few domain controllers on a LAN at a branch location, as shown in Figure 1-5. Those two LANs are connected to one another with a slow (256K) WAN link. You would want replication traffic to occur as needed between the domain controllers on each LAN, but you would want to control traffic across the WAN link to prevent it from affecting higher priority network traffic. To address this situation, you would set up two sites—one site that contained all the domain controllers on the main LAN and one site that contained all the domain controllers on the remote LAN.

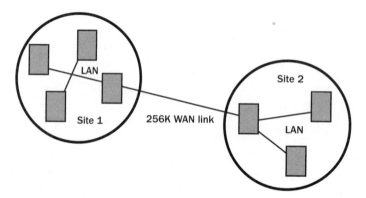

Figure 1-5   Sites allow you to control how replication traffic occurs over slower connections.

To clarify this, look first at replication within a single site (called intrasite replication) and then compare that with replication between sites (intersite replication).

- **Intrasite Replication**   Intrasite replication sends replication traffic in an uncompressed format. This is because of the assumption that all domain controllers within the site are connected by high-bandwidth links. Not only is the traffic uncompressed, but replication occurs according to a change notification mechanism. This means that if changes are made in the domain, those changes are quickly replicated to the other domain controllers.

- **Intersite Replication**   Intersite replication sends all data compressed. This shows an appreciation for the fact that the traffic will probably be going across slower WAN links (as opposed to the LAN connectivity intrasite replication assumes), but it increases the server load because compression/decompression is added to the processing requirements. In addition to the compression, the replication can be scheduled for times that are more appropriate to your organization. For example, you may decide to allow replication only during slower times of the day. Of course, this delay in replication (based on the schedule) can cause inconsistency between servers in different sites.

Lesson Review

The following questions are intended to reinforce key information presented in this lesson. If you are unable to answer a question, review the lesson materials and try the question again. You can find answers to the questions in the "Questions and Answers" section at the end of this chapter.

1. Which of the following represents the outermost boundary for a single schema?

    a. A domain tree

    b. A domain forest

    c. A domain

    d. A domain controller

2. You are planning to add global catalog servers to your site. What is the recommended placement?

    a. You should place at least one global catalog server in each domain tree.

    b. You should place at least one global catalog server in each domain.

    c. You should place at least one global catalog server in each site.

    d. You should make each domain controller a global catalog server.

3. What are the advantages of using a cross-link trust?

    _____

    _____

Lesson Summary

■ Directory services, including Active Directory, provide access to information about resources across a network. The centralization and scalability offered by Active Directory ease the burden of administrating large networks.

■ Active Directory is divided into logical structures—which include objects, domains, trees, forests, and organizational units—and physical structures, which include domain controllers and sites.

- In the logical structure, domains are the primary security boundaries of a network. Multiple domains sharing a contiguous namespace are organized into trees. Multiple trees make up a forest. The forest is the outermost boundary of an organization. Organizational Units (OUs) are used to create administrative boundaries within a domain.

- Domain controllers and sites make up the physical structure. Domain Controllers are Windows Server 2003 systems running Active Directory services; each domain controller holds a full replica of the directory partition for that domain. Sites are collections of domain controllers that are connected by fast, reliable connections. Site boundaries are used to control replication traffic.

Lesson 2: Domain Name System Overview

Domain Name System (DNS) provides a method for mapping computer names to Internet Protocol (IP) addresses in a distributed database. This lesson introduces you to DNS and how it is used on a Windows Server 2003 network.

After this lesson, you will be able to

- Explain the need for name resolution and DNS.
- Identify the major components necessary in creating a DNS structure.
- Describe the name resolution process.
- Explain how DNS is used by Active Directory.

Estimated lesson time: 30 minutes

Name Resolution

As you'll learn in Lesson 3, computers on a Transmission Control Protocol/Internet Protocol– (TCP/IP-) based network are uniquely identified using an IP address. IP addresses are decimal representations of long binary numbers; a typical IP address is 192.168.132.103. Even though the decimal representations are easier to deal with than the binary numbers they represent, they are not so easy for people to remember and work with.

Computers on a TCP/IP network are called hosts and are also given unique, simple-language host names to identify them. An example might be the host name mailserver. People find it much easier to work with names, but the routing protocols in TCP/IP work with IP addresses. Name resolution is a process that brings host names and IP addresses together.

Name resolution is the process of resolving a host name to an IP address. When a user or application searches for a host name, the name resolution service used on the network is queried. The service looks up the host name, matches it to an IP address, and returns the IP address to the computer where the user or application needs it. IP routing takes over from there and make sure the data goes where it needs to go.

There are a number of name resolution services in use today, including:

- **HOSTS files**   Still in use on some networks, HOSTS files are a predecessor to DNS and are files with static mappings of hostnames to IP addresses.

- **LMHOSTS files**   In the early days of Microsoft networking, a different computer name called a NetBIOS computer name was used to name computers on the network. NetBIOS names represented an alternative to hostnames. LMHOSTS files tracked NetBIOS names and IP address mappings.

- **Domain Name System (DNS)**   DNS is the standard name resolution service used on the Internet. It has also become the resolution service of choice on Windows 2000 and Windows Server 2003 networks and is tightly integrated with Active Directory Services.

- **Windows Internet Naming Service (WINS)**   WINS is a database-driven service that tracks NetBIOS names and IP addresses. WINS was in prominent use in versions of Windows prior to Windows 2000, but its use has dropped sharply due to the adoption of DNS as the primary name resolution service in Windows.

Exam Tip   Understand the evolution of name resolution services in Windows. HOSTS files were largely replaced by DNS for mapping host names. LMHOSTS files were largely replaced WINS for mapping NetBIOS names. DNS is now the system of choice (being tightly integrated with Windows Server 2003 and Active Directory) and is supplanting WINS.

Understanding DNS

When the Internet was young—so young, in fact, that it was known as ARPANET—it consisted of only a few hundred computers. The task of tracking what host names went with what IP addresses was a relatively easy one. All of these mappings were located in a file named HOSTS, which was kept on a central computer on the network and perhaps mirrored on a few additional computers. Whenever a computer needed to resolve a host name, it consulted that file (occasionally copying it to the local computer). As the network grew, however, it became impossible to use a single file to hold all the mappings. There were three problems with the existing setup:

- The file became too big to manage effectively and required administration many times per day.

- All name resolution traffic had to be routed through the computer that held the HOSTS file and the file could not be copied enough to be continually up to date.

- The file used a flat data structure, so every computer on the network had to have a unique host name.

Domain Name System (DNS) was created to solve these three problems. The DNS database is distributed across many computers on the Internet, all these computers sharing the burden of name resolution. The DNS namespace is also hierarchical and broken down into different domains. A particular host name has to be unique only within its domain instead of within the whole network. Each domain is considered the authority on names within its boundaries.

Domain Namespace

A namespace is a defined realm in which the names of all like components must be similarly structured, but uniquely identifiable. The Internet is the most readily understood DNS namespace. All hosts on the Internet must be uniquely identifiable; their full DNS name must point to a particular address.

The domain namespace is organized into a hierarchy that works much like the folder structure on a computer. You cannot have two files named readme.txt in the same directory. However, there are probably dozens of files by this name scattered across different directories on your computer. That's how DNS works, too. You could not have two hosts named mailserver within the same domain, but every different domain out there could have one host named mailserver. Figure 1-6 illustrates the hierarchical nature of domain name space.

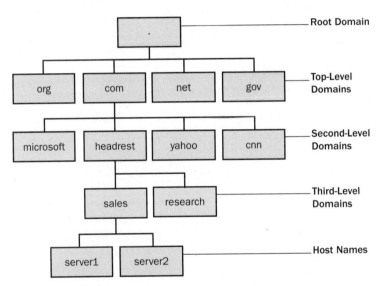

Figure 1-6   DNS domains are organized hierarchically.

The Root Domain   At the top of the DNS hierarchy, there is a single domain called the root domain. The root domain is represented by a single period.

Top-Level Domains   Top-level domains are controlled by the Internet Activities Board (IAB), an Internet authority controlling the assignment of domain names, among other things. Top-level domains have names like com (for business) and gov (for government). Table 1-1 lists common top-level domains, starting with the most frequently used domains.

Table 1-1   Common Top-Level Domain Names

Top-Level Domain	Type of Organization
com	Commercial organizations
edu	Educational institutions
org	Nonprofit organizations, although this is not strictly enforced
net	Network service providers, although this is not strictly enforced
gov	Government institutions
mil	Military institutions
num	Telephone numbers
arpa	Used for reverse DNS lookups. See the section "DNS Reverse Lookup" later in the chapter
xx	Two-letter country codes; every country has its own top-level domain name
info	Available for all uses
name	Used for personal sites

Second-Level Domains   Beneath the top-level domains, there is a second level of domains that is registered to individual organizations. For example, microsoft.com and contoso.com are second-level domains within the top-level domain com. Once a second-level domain is registered, control of the namespace for that domain is passed to the registering organization to manage. The organization can even further divide the namespace into another level of domains. For example, a company with the domain contoso.com might divide the domain into the third-level domains sales.contoso.com and research.contoso.com.

Fully Qualified Domain Names   A fully qualified domain name (FQDN) is the full description of a particular host's place in the DNS hierarchy—think of it like the full path of a file in your computer's file system. The following is an example of an FQDN:

mailserver.sales.contoso.com

The name refers to a host named mailserver in a subdomain named sales, which is under a second-level domain named contoso, which in turn is under the top-level domain com, which of course is in the root domain (.).

Zones and Name Servers

In addition to being segmented into domains, the DNS namespace is also broken up into partitions called zones. Each zone is a file representing a contiguous portion of the namespace for which a particular name server (or group of servers) is responsible. A zone actually corresponds to a series of resource records stored on a DNS server that map IP addresses to various hosts and services in the zone. This database of records is considered authoritative for all the domains contained in that zone.

A zone encompasses at least one domain, which is referred to as the zone's root domain. The zone may also contain subdomains of that root domain but does not necessarily have to hold all the subdomains of the root domain. Consider the example shown in Figure 1-7, which shows a second-level domain named contoso.com that contains two subdomains, sales.contoso.com and research.contoso.com. In this case, contoso.com is the root domain of zone1 and sales.contoso.com is also contained in this zone. A separate zone, zone2, has been configured for the subdomain research.contoso.com.

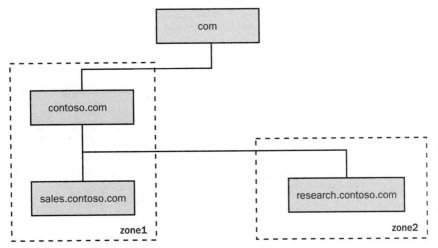

Figure 1-7   A domain is divided into nested zones of authority.

Zones must contain contiguous domains within the namespace. This means that a single zone could contain a domain and its subdomains, but a zone could not contain two different subdomains without also containing the parent domain. Take another look at the example in Figure 1-7. Zones could be configured the way they are shown in the figure. Or a single zone could be configured that contained contoso.com and its two subdomains. You could not, however, create a zone that contained the contoso.com domain and then create a separate zone that contained just the two subdomains.

Each zone has at least one name server responsible for knowing the address information for each device within that zone, and a single name server can be configured to manage more than one zone. Each name server also knows the address of at least one parent name server. If a particular name server cannot resolve a host name, it can pass the query on to another name server that may have the information.

Using Multiple Name Servers in a Zone   You can also create multiple name servers for a single zone. One of these name servers contains a master copy of the zone database file, which is referred to as the primary zone file. Other name servers created for a zone act as secondary servers, and each contains a secondary zone file. When records in the zone are updated, they are updated on the primary server and then replicated to the secondary servers. Using multiple servers in a zone provides a number of important benefits, including:

- Redundancy—If a primary name server fails, secondary servers can provide DNS services to your network.

- Load Balancing—On large networks, creating multiple servers distributes the load of client requests among the primary and secondary servers, decreasing response time.

- Remote Access—Creating secondary servers on remote subnets prevents client requests from having to cross remote access links, decreasing response time.

Types of Zones   Windows Server 2003 supports three distinct types of zones. These zones include:

- **Active-Directory Integrated**   In this type of zone, the DNS database is stored within Active Directory. All DNS servers in an Active Directory–integrated zone are considered primary servers because the DNS information actually becomes part of the Active Directory database; any DNS server can be updated and any of them can resolve client requests. Active Directory is responsible for replicating zone information between DNS servers, often making replication quicker and making it a part of Active Directory management instead of a separate management practice.

- **Standard Primary**   The master copy of the DNS database resides in a standard ASCII text file. Only this primary zone can be directly modified.

- **Standard Secondary**   The zone information is a read-only replica of an existing standard primary zone and helps provide a backup to the primary zone. Zone information is updated on the primary DNS server and then transferred to any secondary servers.

The Name Resolution Process

Resolving a name means determining the IP address that is associated with that name. In DNS, the client that performs name resolution is called a resolver. In Windows, this resolver is a service named the DNS Client service. The resolver operates at the application layer of the TCP/IP model (discussed later in the chapter) and is often built into different programs that may need to resolve host names. For example, when you type an address (an FQDN) into your Web browser, the browser uses DNS to query the name server configured on the local host and resolve the address.

There are two types of queries that a resolver can perform: a forward lookup query, which translates names to IP addresses, and a reverse lookup query, which translates IP addresses to names. Both types of queries are serviced by DNS name servers.

Forward Lookup Queries   The most common type of query is the forward lookup query, where a host or domain name must be resolved to an IP address. In this type of query, a resolver sends a resolution request to its configured name server. If that name server has the information, it passes it back to the client. If it does not, it in turn sends queries to other name servers until it finds the information.

The example shown in Figure 1-8 illustrates this process at work as a resolver on the Internet attempts to resolve the name www.contoso.com.

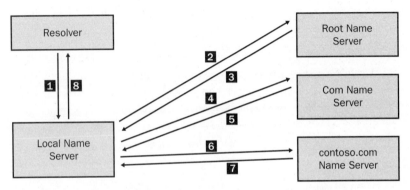

Figure 1-8   Multiple name servers might handle a single query.

1. The resolver sends a query to its local DNS server, asking for resolution of the domain name contoso.com. The name server either returns the information to the resolver or does not. The name server cannot refer the resolver to another name server (though the name server itself can query another resolver). This type of query is a recursive query—the server must eventually either respond with the mapping or a reply that the name/IP was not found.

2. The local name server that receives the request from the resolver checks the zones under its authority. If the requested hostname or domain is in one of its zones, it returns the information to the client. If not, as in this case, the local name server checks its local name cache to see if the name has been recently resolved. If it has not, it sends a query for www.contoso.com to a root name server.

3. The root name server has authority for the root domain and replies to the local server with the IP address of a name server that has authority for the com top-level domain.

4. The local name server sends out another query for www.contoso.com to the IP address supplied by the root name server. These types of queries are called iterative queries because the same query is sent to multiple servers until resolved.

5. The com authoritative server replies with the IP address of a name server that has authority over the contoso.com second-level domain.

6. The local name server sends another query for www.contoso.com to the IP address of the contoso.com name server.

7. The contoso.com name server replies with the IP address for www.contoso.com.

8. The local name server returns the IP address of www.contoso.com to the original resolver.

Reverse Lookup Queries   A reverse lookup query is one in which an IP address is resolved to a host or domain name. Some TCP/IP utilities (such as nslookup, ping, and netstat) use reverse lookups. Reverse lookups can also be useful if you are trying to keep track of network usage, if you are trying to track down a host that is causing issues on the network, or even if you are trying to verify the identity of a host.

Because DNS databases are indexed using names and not IP addresses, searching for a name on the basis of an IP address within a regular DNS database structure would be a slow process. To solve this problem, a special domain was created in the arpa root domain named in-addr.arpa, which stands for Inverse Address. In-addr.arpa uses the IP address as an index to the host's resource record information. When the proper resource record is located, the host name can be extracted.

Nodes in the in-addr.arpa domain are named after the numbers in the dotted decimal representation of an IP address. However, because IP addresses get more specific from left to right and domain names get more specific from right to left, the order of the IP address octets is reversed when building the corresponding name in the in-addr.arpa domain. For example, a host name with the IP address 192.168.201.35 would be a PTR record in the 201.168.192.in-addr.arpa zone file. The entry in that file would take the form 35 IN PTR host_name.

The in-addr-arpa domain is built using a hierarchy just like a standard DNS domain. As the in-addr-arpa domain is built, special resource records called pointer (PTR) records are added to the domain's database to map IP addresses to host names. You'll learn more about resource records in the next section.

Resource Records

Zone files are made up of resource records. A resource record contains a mapping of a hostname or service to an IP address. Table 1-2 shows many of the types of resource records supported by the Windows Server 2003 DNS service.

Table 1-2   DNS Resource Records

Resource Record	Use
A	An address record that maps a host name to an IP. A records use the 32-bit IP version 4 format.
AAAA	Also an address record, AAAA records use the 128-bit format of the next generation of the IP protocol, IPv6.
CNAME	A canonical name record establishes an alias—a synonym for a host name. Using CNAME records, you can have more than one name resolve to a single IP address.
MX	A mail exchange record identifies the mail server for a particular DNS domain.
NS	A name server record identifies a name server for a particular DNS domain.
PTR	A pointer record associates an IP address with a host in a DNS reverse-naming zone.
SOA	A start of authority record is the required first entry for all forward and reverse lookup zones. It specifies the domain for which a DNS server is responsible. It also specifies a variety of parameters that regulate operation of the DNS server.
SRV	The service record allows you to specify what services a server provides and what domain it services. The SRV record is required in order for Active Directory to be used.
WINS	A Windows Internet Name Server record identifies a WINS server that can be consulted to obtain names that are not recorded in the DNS name space.
WINS_R	A reverse WINS record causes Microsoft DNS to use the nbstat command to resolve reverse-lookup (address-to-name) client queries.
WKS	A well-known service record describes services provided by a specific protocol on a specific adapter.

Exam Tip   You should know some of the more important resource records for the exam. These include address (A), canonical name (CNAME), mail exchanger (MX), name server (NS), pointer (PTR), start of authority (SOA), and service (SRV). Remember them by name and acronym and understand their importance.

Using Dynamic DNS

Dynamic DNS, which was introduced to Windows with Microsoft Windows 2000 Server, provides a way for clients to automatically notify a DNS server when their IP address changes and have the server update their resource record. This is particularly useful on networks that use an automatic form of assigning IP addresses like Dynamic Host Configuration Protocol (DHCP) because DHCP clients can inform DNS servers of their IP addresses automatically as soon as they are given the address by a DHCP server. Dynamic DNS can be used only in Active Directory–integrated zones.

How Active Directory Uses DNS

Active Directory and DNS are tightly integrated, even sharing a common namespace. It is essential, therefore, that you understand how each system works and how they work together.

DNS is the locator service used by Active Directory (and by many other Windows components). Active Directory makes its services available to the network by publishing them in DNS. When a domain controller is installed (or when services are added to it), the domain controller uses dynamic updates to register its services as SRV records in DNS. Clients may then locate services through simple DNS queries. The Microsoft DNS Service runs on every Windows Server 2003 domain controller by default.

Lesson Review

The following questions are intended to reinforce key information presented in this lesson. If you are unable to answer a question, review the lesson materials and try the question again. You can find answers to the questions in the "Questions and Answers" section at the end of this chapter.

   1. How does Active Directory use DNS?

   _____

   _____

   2. Which of the following resource record types is used to establish an alias for an existing host name?

      a. An A Record

      b. An ALIAS Record

      c. A CNAME Record

      d. An HINFO Record.

   3. You want to enable Dynamic DNS for a specific zone and configure the server to allow only secure updates. What is required for you to do this ?

      a. The zone must be a root zone.

      b. The zone must be Active Directory—integrated.

      c. The zone must have an SRV record.

      d. You cannot enable DDNS for a specific zone—only for an entire server.

Lesson Summary

- Name resolution services are used to resolve host names to IP addresses, and DNS is the name resolution service of choice in Windows Server 2003. Active Directory is tightly integrated with DNS; domain controllers publish all running services in the DNS database in the form of service (SRV) records. This means that any DNS client can find a service on the network (including Active Directory) using a DNS lookup.

- The DNS namespace for a network mirrors the Active Directory namespace. DNS is divided into domains. Each domain is responsible for the records held in that domain and, thus, for the mapping of host names and services to IP addresses in that domain.

- The DNS namespace is also divided into zones, which are used to designate contiguous portions of the namespace for which a particular server is responsible. A zone encompasses at least one domain and may contain other domains.

Lesson 3: TCP/IP Overview

TCP/IP is an open, standardized suite of networking protocols that define how traffic is carried around on a network. TCP/IP is the standard protocol used on the Internet and is also the protocol of choice in Windows Server 2003. In fact, you cannot run Windows Server 2003 without it. This lesson introduces you to the principles of TCP/IP.

After this lesson, you will be able to

- Identify the role of TCP/IP on a Windows Server 2003 network.
- Explain how IP addresses are formed.
- Describe the use of network IDs, host IDs, and subnets.
- Describe the basic routing process on a TCP/IP network.

Estimated lesson time: 30 minutes

TCP/IP Architecture

The TCP/IP protocol suite includes a number of different protocols and utilities. The protocols in the TCP/IP suite are organized into four logical layers. These four layers, indicated in Figure 1-9, are the application layer, transport layer, Internet layer, and network access layer. The purpose of this layering is to provide a level of abstraction between an application or protocol in one layer and the functioning of the entire network. For example, an application in the application layer needs to know only where to pass information into the transport layer (and how to format that information); it does not need to take into account any specific network configuration beyond that point. Packets of data are passed down the layers on the sending host and back up the layers on the receiving host.

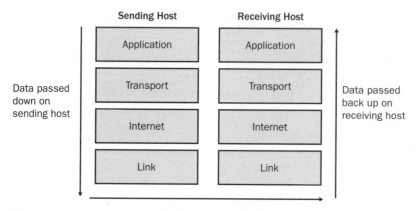

Figure 1-9   There are four logical layers of TCP/IP.

Application Layer

The application layer is at the top of the four-layer model. Most applications and utilities are contained in the application layer and use this layer to gain access to the network functions of TCP/IP. Windows Server 2003 provides two interfaces that allow applications to access the rest of the TCP/IP protocol suite:

- **WinSock**   This is the Microsoft version of the Berkeley Sockets application programming interface (API), which is the standard interface used to access TCP/IP protocols.

- **NetBIOS Helper Service**   Network basic input output system (NetBIOS) is a legacy interface that was originally based on the DOS BIOS but added a number of functions for network access. It is still used for interprocess communications throughout Windows. The NetBIOS Helper Service manages interactions between NetBIOS and sockets.

These two interfaces form two groups of TCP/IP-enabled applications: WinSock applications and NetBIOS applications. Aside from some Windows functions and Microsoft programs, though, most applications use WinSock. A number of familiar TCP/IP applications run in the application layer, including:

- **Hypertext Transfer Protocol (HTTP)**   The protocol used to transfer data between Web servers and browsers

- **File Transfer Protocol (FTP)**   A protocol used for transferring files between computers

- **Simple Mail Transfer Protocol (SMTP)**   A protocol used for sending e-mail between mail servers and from mail clients to mail servers

- **Telnet**   A terminal emulation protocol used to provide remote access to a host

- **Domain Name System (DNS)**   A set of protocols and services that provide name resolution services

Transport Layer

The transport layer controls communication between computers; it passes data up to an application in the application layer or down to the Internet layer for network delivery. The transport layer also specifies a unique identifier for each communicating application in the form of a port number, which is used to keep track of which data packets are associated with which applications.

Data delivery in the transport layer is controlled by two protocols:

- **Transmission Control Protocol (TCP)**   TCP is referred to as a connection-oriented protocol because a connection must be established between two computers before any data is transferred. It is also referred to as a reliable protocol because it checks up on the delivery of data to a remote computer by requiring that an acknowledgment be returned. If the remote computer does not return an acknowledgment within a specified period of time, the source computer retransmits the data. Most applications use TCP to transmit data.

- **User Datagram Protocol (UDP)**   UDP is a connectionless service in that it does not establish a connection before transmitting data. UDP also does not require an acknowledgment of receipt. This provides faster data delivery than TCP but does not offer the capability to retransmit data that is not acknowledged. UDP is often used by applications sending very small amounts of data and by applications that stream media over a network, where retransmittal of data would not be useful.

A port is associated with applications that use either the TCP or UDP protocols; these ports are referred to as TCP ports and UDP ports. A port can have any number between 0 and 65,535. The port numbers from 0 to 1,023 are reserved for common applications. Referred to as the well-known port numbers, these are under the control of the Internet Assigned Numbers Authority (IANA). Ports from 1024 through 49151 are also under the control of IANA and are referred to as Registered Ports; these are used for less well-known applications. Ports between 49152 and 65535 are referred to as dynamic or private ports. You'll learn more about port numbers in Chapter 7.

Internet Layer

The Internet layer is responsible for addressing, packaging, and routing the data that is handed down to it from the transport layer. There are four core protocols in this layer: Internet Protocol (IP), Address Resolution Protocol (ARP), Internet Control Message Protocol (ICMP), and Internet Group Management Protocol (IGMP).

Internet Protocol   IP is a connectionless, and therefore unreliable, protocol that is primarily responsible for addressing packets and routing them between networked computers. Although IP always attempts to deliver a packet, a packet may be lost, corrupted, delivered out of sequence, duplicated, or delayed. IP does not attempt to recover from these types of errors by requesting retransmission of the data. Acknowledging the delivery of packets and recovering lost packets is the responsibility of a higher-layer protocol, such as TCP, or of the application itself.

IP also assigns a Time to Live (TTL) value to each packet, which specifies the maximum length of time that the packet can travel on the network before being discarded. The TTL is measured in seconds, which represent the maximum time a packet can survive on a network. Every instance of IP that processes a packet decrements the TTL by at least one. Any instance of IP that examines a packet with a TTL of zero discards the packet.

Address Resolution Protocol   ARP is responsible for mapping IP addresses to the hardware addresses (or MAC addresses) of the network adapters of computers on the network. When IP readies a packet for transmission to a remote computer, it does so using that computer's IP address. However, the actual network cards (and other network interfaces) on a network transfer data using long hardware addresses that ensure each network interface on a network is uniquely identified.

In the Windows Server 2003 implementation of ARP, ARP translates between IP addresses and hardware addresses and maintains a table of mappings known as the ARP cache. This table is built dynamically. When ARP receives a request to translate an IP address, it checks for the address in its table. If the address is found, ARP returns the address to the requesting software. If the address is not found in the table, ARP broadcasts a packet to the local subnet; this packet contains the IP address for which the hardware address is needed. If a receiving host identifies the IP address as its own, it responds by sending its hardware address back to the requesting host. The response is then stored in the ARP cache.

Internet Control Message Protocol   ICMP provides error reporting and traffic control messaging. With ICMP, computers and routers that use IP communication can report errors and exchange limited control and status information. For example, if IP is unable to deliver a packet to a destination computer, ICMP sends a Destination Unreachable message to the source computer.

Internet Group Messaging Protocol   The Internet Group Membership Protocol (IGMP) is used by hosts to report multicast group membership to adjacent routers. Multicasting allows one host to send content to multiple other hosts simultaneously. Examples would be streaming high-bandwidth media to multiple computers, updating software on a number of computers at once, and some types of distribution lists. Typically, a group of computers becomes part of a multicast group membership so that they can be sent multicast messages.

Network Access Layer

The network access layer is responsible for placing data on the network medium and receiving data off the network medium. This layer contains physical devices such as network cables and network adapters. This layer does not contain the type of software-based protocols that are included in the other three layers, but it does contain such protocols as Ethernet and Asynchronous Transfer Mode (ATM), which define how data is transmitted on the network.

IP Addressing

Every interface on a TCP/IP network is given a unique IP address that identifies it on that network. The IP handles this addressing, defining how the addresses are constructed and how packets are routed using those addresses.

An IP address consists of a set of four numbers, each of which can range from 0 to 255. Each of these numbers is separated from the others by a decimal point, so a typical IP address in decimal form might look something like 192.168.001.102. The reason that each number ranges only up to 255 is that each number is actually based on a binary octet, or an eight-digit binary number. The IP address 192.168.001.102 represented in binary form is 11000000 10101000 00000001 01100110. Computers work with the binary format, but it's much easier for people to work with the decimal representation.

An IP address consists of two distinct portions:

■ The network ID is a portion of the IP address starting from the left that identifies the network segment on which a host is located. Using the example 192.168.1.102, the portion 192.168.1 might be the network ID. When representing a network ID, it is customary to fill in each missing octet with a zero. So, the proper network ID would be 192.168.1.0.

■ The host ID is the portion of the IP address that identifies a particular host on a network segment. The host ID for each host must be unique within the network ID. Continuing the example of the IP address 192.168.1.102 (where 192.168.1.0 is the network ID), the host ID is 102.

Two computers with different network IDs can have the same host ID. However, the combination of the network ID and the host ID must be unique to all computers in communication with each other.

Hosts depend on a second number called a subnet mask to help determine which portion of an IP address is the network ID and which portion is the host ID. The subnet mask defines where the network ID stops and the host ID starts. It is easier to see why this works if you step away from the decimal representation for a moment and look at the numbers in their binary format.

Figure 1-10 depicts a single IP address shown in both decimal and binary format. A subnet mask is also shown in both formats. In binary format, a subnet mask always represents a string of unbroken ones followed by a string of unbroken zeroes. The position of the change from ones to zeroes indicates the division of network ID and host ID in an IP address.

	Decimal	Binary
IP Address:	131.104.16.92	10000011 01101000 00010000 01011100
Subnet Mask:	255.255.0.0	11111111 11111111 00000000 00000000
Network ID:	131.104.0.0	10000011 01101000 00000000 00000000
Host ID:	0.0.16.92	00000000 00000000 00010000 01011100

Figure 1-10 The subnet mask separates the host ID and the network ID.

Classful IP Addressing

IP addresses are organized into classes that help define the size of the network being addressed. This is called classful IP addressing. Five different classes of IP addresses define different size networks, each capable of holding varying numbers of hosts.

Classful IP addressing is based on the structure of the IP address and provides a systematic way to differentiate network IDs from host IDs. As you learned earlier, there are four numerical segments of an IP address ranging from 0 to 255. Here, those segments are represented as w.x.y.z. Based on the value of the first octet (w), IP addresses are categorized into the five address classes listed in Table 1-3.

Table 1-3 IP Address Classes

Class	Network ID	Range of First Octet	Number of Available Network Segments	Number of Available Hosts	Subnet Mask
A	w.0.0.0	1—126	126	16,777,214	255.0.0.0
B	w.x.0.0	128—191	16,384	65,534	255.255.0.0
C	w.x.y.0	192—223	2,097,152	254	255.255.255.0
D	N/A	224—239	N/A	N/A	N/A
E	N/A	240—255	N/A	N/A	N/A

Classes A, B, and C are available for registration by public organizations. Actually, most of these addresses were snapped up long ago by major companies and Internet service providers (ISPs), so the actual assignment of an IP address to your organization will likely come from your chosen ISP. Classes D and E are reserved for special use.

The address class determines the subnet mask used, and therefore determines the division between the network ID and the host ID. For class A, the network ID is the first octet in the IP address (for example the 98 in the address 98.162.102.53 is the network ID). For class B, it is the first two octets; for class C, it is the first three octets. The remaining octets not used by the network ID identify the host ID.

Classless Internet Domain Routing (CIDR)

In the classful method of IP addressing, the number of networks and hosts available for a specific address class is predetermined by the default subnet mask for the class. As a result, an organization that is allocated a network ID has a single, fixed network ID and a specific number of hosts. With the single network ID, the organization can have only one network connecting its allocated number of hosts. If the number of hosts is large, the network will not be able to perform efficiently. To solve this problem, the concept Classless Internet Domain Routing (CIDR) was introduced.

CIDR allows a single classful network ID to be divided into smaller network IDs. The idea is that you take the default subnet mask used for the class to which your IP address range belongs and then borrow some of the bits used for the host ID to use as an extension to the network ID, creating a custom subnet mask.

A custom subnet mask is not restricted by the same rules used in the classful method. Remember that a subnet mask consists of a set of four numbers, similar to an IP address. Consider the default subnet mask for a class B network (255.255.0.0), which in binary format would be:

11111111 11111111 00000000 00000000

This mask specifies that the first 16 bits of an IP address are to be used for the network ID and the second 16 bits are to be used for the host ID. To create a custom subnet mask, you would just extend the mask into the host ID portion. However, you must extend this by adding ones from left to right. Remember that a subnet mask must be an unbroken string of ones followed by an unbroken string of zeroes. For example, a custom subnet mask might look like:

11111111 11111111 11111000 00000000

The value 1111 1000 in decimal format would be 248, making this IP address 255.255.248.0. Table 1-4 shows the possible values for an octet in a custom subnet mask.

Table 1-4   Custom Subnet Mask Values

Binary Value	Decimal Value
10000000	128
11000000	192
11100000	224
11110000	240
11111000	248
11111100	252
11111110	254

In the classful method, each of the four numbers in a subnet mask can be only the maximum value 255 or the minimum value 0. The four numbers are then arranged as contiguous octets of 255 followed by contiguous octets of 0. For example, 255.255.0.0 is a valid subnet mask, whereas 255.0.255.0 is not. The 255 octets identify the network ID, and the 0 octets identify the host ID. For example, the subnet mask 255.255.0.0 identifies the network ID as the first two numbers in the IP address.

When subnetting an existing network ID to create additional subnets, you can use any of the preceding subnet masks with any IP address or network ID. So the IP address 184.12.102.20 could have the subnet mask 255.255.255.0 and network ID 184.12.102.0, as opposed to the default subnet mask 255.255.0.0 with the network ID 184.12.0.0. This allows an organization to subnet an existing class B network ID of 184.12.0.0 into smaller subnets to match the actual configuration of their network.

Exam Tip   If you take some time to examine the binary numbers and the decimal values they represent (shown in Table 1-4), you'll come to understand how they are derived. This understanding will be much more useful to you than memorizing values.

Private Addressing

Every network interface that is connected directly to the Internet must have an IP address registered with the Internet Assigned Numbers Authority (IANA). This prevents IP address conflicts between devices. If you are configuring a private network that is not connected to the Internet or one that exists behind a firewall or proxy server, you can configure devices on your network with private addresses and have only the public address configured on the interface that is visible to the Internet.

Each address class has a range of private addresses available for general use:

- Class A: 10.0.0.0 through 10.255.255.255
- Class B: 172.16.0.0 through 172.31.255.255
- Class C: 192.168.0.0 through 192.168.255.255

You can choose whatever range you like to use for your network and implement custom subnets as you see fit. None of these addresses is ever officially assigned to a publicly accessible Internet host.

IP Routing

Routing is the process of moving information along a path from a source to a destination. On a TCP/IP network, the source and destination are called *hosts* and the information is broken apart into small packets that are transmitted between these hosts. The IP handles the routing of all these packets for the network.

Remember that a protocol such as TCP or UDP hands down a packet of data to the IP protocol for transmission to a remote host. IP must determine where the packet goes. First, it compares the network ID of the local host with the network ID of the destination host identified in the packet. If the two network IDs match, the two hosts are on the same network segment and the packet can be sent directly to the destination host.

If IP determines that the network IDs of the local host and the remote host do not match, that means that the two hosts are on different network segments and the packet cannot be sent directly. Instead, IP must send the packet to a gateway, which is a router connecting one network segment to another. When this gateway receives the packet, its IP protocol goes through the process of comparing network IDs to determine the best place to send the packet. If the destination host is on one of the network segments to which the gateway is directly connected, the gateway can forward the packet straight to the destination host. Otherwise, the gateway forwards the packet on to another gateway, and then perhaps another, until the packet finally reaches its destination. Each time a packet crosses a gateway, that is referred to as a hop. For example, if a packet must cross three routers to reach its destination, that is considered three hops.

Usually, the source host is configured with the IP address of a default gateway, a router to which all packets are sent if the destination host is not found on the same network segment. Routers (and all devices with IP installed, for that matter) are able to consult routing tables that are stored in the router's memory. A routing table holds information on preferred routes for various network IDs. This way, the router can determine the best gateway to which to send a packet based on the network ID of the packet's destination host. There are two ways in which a router can build its routing table:

- **Static** A static router has a routing table that is constructed and updated manually. In other words, someone must actually access the routing table to create routes the router can use.

- **Dynamic** A dynamic router builds and updates its own routing table as it finds appropriate routes. When it finds shorter routes, it favors those over longer routes. Most important, dynamic routers can also share their information with other routers on the network. Almost all the routers in use today are dynamic routers—manual routers are just too much work. Dynamic routers use one of two common routing protocols: Routing Information Protocol (RIP) and Open Shortest Path First (OSPF).

Automatic IP Address Assignment Using DHCP

Dynamic Host Configuration Protocol (DHCP) is an industry standard protocol that lets a server automatically assign IP addresses to clients. This saves the administrative burden of manually assigning IP addresses and other TCP/IP information. Using DHCP is faster and more reliable than manual assignment; it also prevents the introduction of networking errors due to mistyped information.

DHCP is actually a pretty simple mechanism, especially when compared to something like DNS. On the server end, you configure a range of IP addresses that a DHCP server is allowed to assign to clients; this range is called a scope. You also must specify a subnet mask and a default gateway address to be assigned. Optionally, you can include other TCP/IP information, such as DNS and WINS server information. On the client end, you simply tell a client that it should obtain its IP address and other information automatically (the default option for most Windows-based clients).

Whenever TCP/IP loads on a client computer, a message is broadcast to the local IP subnet looking for DHCP servers. Any DHCP server that receives the request and has a valid scope of IP addresses responds with an offer of configuration. When the client receives and accepts an offer of configuration, it configures itself with the IP address and other information provided by the DHCP server. This process is called leasing (the client leases an IP address from the server).

A lease has a time limit, after which the lease expires if it has not been renewed by the client. When the lease is 50 percent through its duration, the client attempts to renew the lease by contacting the leasing server. If successful, the lease is renewed for the full duration. If unsuccessful, the client continues to contact the leasing server until the lease expires. If the lease expires, the IP address is returned to the pool of IP addresses in the server's scope.

DHCP runs as a service on computers running Windows Server 2003. A DHCP server is simply a Windows Server 2003 domain controller or member server that has the DHCP service installed and has been authorized and configured to issue IP addresses to clients.

> **Real World**   **Automatic Private IP Addressing**
>
> Automatic Private IP Addressing (APIPA) is a feature introduced with Windows 2000; it is also included in Windows XP and Windows Server 2003. APIPA allows a computer that is configured to obtain an automatic IP address to assign itself an address from a private range should no DHCP server be available. APIPA assigns addresses in the range 169.254.0.1 through 169.254.255.255—a range reserved by Microsoft for just this purpose.
>
> APIPA is really designed for small networks that don't use a DHCP server. APIPA allows computers running Windows 2000, Windows Server 2003, or Windows XP to plug into a network and recognize one another with little configuration necessary. If your network uses a DHCP server and you see that a client has been assigned an address in the APIPA range, it means the client could not locate a DHCP server.

Lesson Review

The following questions are intended to reinforce key information presented in this lesson. If you are unable to answer a question, review the lesson materials and try the question again. You can find answers to the questions in the "Questions and Answers" section at the end of this chapter.

1. In which of the four layers of the Internet protocol is the routing of packets between source and destination hosts handled?

    a. Application

    b. Transport

    c. Internet

    d. Link

2. Your company has registered the network ID 131.107.0.0, which uses the default subnet mask 255.255.0.0. You would like to create a custom subnet mask that allows you to divide that network into the maximum number of subnets that would allow you to have at least 20 hosts per subnet. What custom subnet mask would you use?

_____

_____

3. Which of the following default subnet masks would be used on a computer with the IP address 157.54.4.201?

   a. 255.0.0.0

   b. 255.255.0.0

   c. 255.255.255.0

   d. 255.255.255.255

Lesson Summary

- TCP/IP protocols are arranged in four logical layers: the application layer, the transport layer, the Internet layer, and the network access layer. Data packets are passed down through the layers on a sending host and back up the layers on a receiving host.

- Each interface on a TCP/IP network is assigned a unique IP address, typically shown as four decimal numbers ranging from 0 to 255. An IP address is divided into a network ID, which determines the subnet on which a host exists, and a host ID, which uniquely identifies the host on that subnet. The separation of network ID and host ID is determined by a subnet mask.

- The primary method of automatically assigning IP addresses to clients on a network is the Dynamic Host Configuration Protocol (DHCP). A DHCP server holds a scope of IP addresses that it can assign, and it is configured with other important information such as subnet mask, default gateway, and DNS servers for the network.

Lesson 4: Remote Access Overview

Remote Access in Windows Server 2003 comes in the form of a service named Routing And Remote Access service This service runs on a Windows Server 2003 system and lets other servers or clients that are not connected via the local network to establish temporary connections over phone lines, Internet connections, and other types of connections. This lesson introduces you to the basics of how Windows Server 2003 provides remote access.

After this lesson, you will be able to

■ Describe how Windows Server 2003 provides remote access through Routing And Remote Access service.

■ Identify the connection methods available for remote access.

■ Describe the remote access protocols.

■ Identify security mechanisms available for remote access.

Estimated lesson time: 20 minutes

What Remote Access Provides

A Windows Server 2003 system running the Routing And Remote Access service is able to accept connections from users that are physically separated from the main network but still need to connect to the main network to access resources. Routing And Remote Access also provides a way to use servers running Windows Server 2003 as routers, letting them connect subnets across a LAN or WAN link.

Once connected, remote access clients use standard tools and applications to access network resources. In fact, Routing And Remote Access really is just another way to transmit standard networking protocols and commands already in use on the network. Instead of being put onto a network cable by a network interface card, the information is formatted (and possibly secured) by Routing And Remote Access and transmitted across whatever type of remote link is configured.

Remote Access Connection Methods

Routing And Remote Access provides two distinct methods of connections for remote users:

■ **Dial-Up Networking**   With dial-up networking, a client makes a temporary, dial-up connection to a physical port on the Routing And Remote Access server. This connection uses the services of a public telecommunications provider such as a public switched telephone network (PSTN), an Integrated Services Digital Network (ISDN), or X.25. A good example of dial-up networking would be if both a client and a server had a standard modem. The client would initiate the dial-up connection using the modem. The connection to the server modem would be made over public phone lines, and the server would authenticate the user and provide the configured access.

- **Virtual Private Networking**   Virtual private networking (VPN) provides a way of making a secured, private connection from the client to the server over a public network such as the Internet. Unlike dial-up networking, in which a connection is made directly between client and server, a VPN connection is logical and tunneled through another type of connection. Typically, a remote user would connect to an Internet service provider (ISP) using a form of dial-up networking (particularly good for users with high-speed connections). The Routing And Remote Access server would also be connected to the Internet (probably via a persistent, or permanent, connection) and would be configured to accept VPN connections. Once the client is connected to the Internet, it then establishes a VPN connection over that dial-up connection to the Routing And Remote Access server.

VPN offers two significant advantages over dial-in access. First, remote users that are not in the same local calling area as the remote access server need not make long-distance calls to connect to the network. Instead, they can make local calls to an ISP. Second, every standard dial-up connection requires that a physical device be present on the Routing And Remote Access server and devoted to that connection, and that a separate phone circuit be available. This places limitations on the number of users that can connect remotely at a single time and also increases the start-up costs and maintenance needed; you must purchase, maintain, and upgrade all the necessary modems and the connection lines they use. Assuming a fairly high-bandwidth Internet connection from the Routing And Remote Access server to the Internet, more remote users are able to connect at the same time using VPN than dial-up connections.

Protocols Used by Routing And Remote Access

There are two general types of protocols that you must be familiar with to work with Routing And Remote Access: remote access (or line) protocols and network transport (or LAN) protocols.

Remote Access Protocols

Remote access protocols govern how information is formatted and transmitted over wide area network (WAN) connections, of which a dial-up connection is one type. Routing And Remote Access supports four remote access protocols:

- **Point-to-Point Protocol (PPP)**   By far the most common remote access protocol in use today. Most dial-in servers, including Routing And Remote Access, support PPP, and it is generally considered to be the best choice for remote access situations. Routing And Remote Access supports PPP for both dial-out and dial-in connections.

- **Serial Line Internet Protocol (SLIP)**   An older protocol developed in UNIX and still in wide use today. Routing And Remote Access supports SLIP in dial-out configurations, but you cannot use a SLIP client to dial in to an Routing And Remote Access server.

- **RAS Protocol**   Used to support the NetBIOS naming convention and is a proprietary protocol, used only between Microsoft-based networks. It is required to support NetBIOS naming and is installed by default when you install the Routing And Remote Access server.

- **NetBIOS Gateway**   Used to provide compatibility with older versions of Routing And Remote Access server that do not support networking protocols such as TCP/IP. The NetBIOS gateway is used to translate data from the NetBIOS Extended User Interface (NetBEUI) protocol to these other protocols.

Exam Tip   Remember the access protocols and what they are used for. PPP is by far the most common; the others are run only under special circumstances. Also remember that PPP allows both dial-in and dial-out access, while SLIP allows only dial-out access (for use in legacy servers).

Remote Access Security

Remote access has always been considered one of the weaker points of networking security. Although it's fairly easy to secure a network from unauthorized physical access, the current popularity of Internet access and remote user access places larger security demands on the modern network. Fortunately, new security technologies and protocols have been developed that ease the problem of remote access security.

Security Through User Authentication

The primary method of securing a remote access connection involves authenticating the user trying to connect. To do this, the user (or the user's client computer) must present some sort of credentials that allow the Routing And Remote Access server to verify that the user is indeed a valid user. Windows Server 2003 supports five different user authentication protocols:

- **Password Authentication Protocol (PAP)**   The most basic form of user authentication. A user's name and password are transmitted over the dial-up connection to the Routing And Remote Access server. This information is transmitted in clear text with no encryption, making it quite vulnerable to snooping. In addition, PAP provides no way for a client and a server to authenticate one another. For the most part, the availability of better authentication protocols is rendering PAP obsolete. In fact, Microsoft recommends that you not use it unless absolutely necessary.

- **Shiva Password Authentication Protocol (SPAP)**   Shiva is a private company (now owned by Intel) that manufactures remote access hardware devices. SPAP is included mainly for compatibility with these devices and really isn't used much on most networks. SPAP offers weak encryption of authentication credentials, but no encryption of data. You should not rely on it when strong encryption is a requirement.

- **Challenge Handshake Authentication Protocol (CHAP)**   This form of authentication is considerably more secure than PAP or SPAP. The server sends the client a challenge and the client uses its credentials to encrypt the challenge. This encrypted information is then sent across the dial-up connection to the server, which decrypts it and attempts to validate the user. If the outcome matches the challenge, the user is authenticated. Since the challenge and response are encrypted, they are considerably less vulnerable to eavesdroppers. CHAP is also commonly referred to as MD5-CHAP because it uses the RSA MD5 hash algorithm for encryption.

- **Microsoft CHAP (MS-CHAP)**   A modified version of CHAP that allows the use of Windows Server 2003 authentication information. There are two versions of MS-CHAP. Version 2 is the most secure and is supported only by Windows 2000, Windows Server 2003, and Windows XP. Version 1 is supported by earlier versions of Windows and other operating systems.

- **Extensible Authentication Protocol (EAP)**   A general protocol for PPP authentication that supports multiple authentication mechanisms. Instead of selecting a single authentication method for a connection, EAP can negotiate an authentication method at connect time. The computer asking for the authentication method is called the authenticator and may require several different pieces of authentication information. This allows the use of almost any authentication method, including secure access tokens or one-time password systems.

Exam Tip   The PAP authentication protocol does not encrypt authentication information. The SPAP protocol provides weak encryption of authentication credentials, but no encryption for data. CHAP, MS-CHAP and EAP provide stronger encryption and should be your choice if encryption is a requirement.

Security Through Connection Control

In addition to being able to authenticate users in a variety of ways, Routing And Remote Access provides a number of methods for securing the actual connection from a client to a server. One such method is the Callback Control Protocol, which allows your Routing And Remote Access servers to negotiate a callback with the other end. For example, a server may be configured to hang up and call a user back at a specified number whenever that user tries to connect. This provides two advantages. The first is that a successful connection can be made only from a particular number—a good way of ensuring that only authorized users can make the connection. The second advantage is that, for users dialing in from another calling area, the company can foot the bill for the long-distance call.

Another way that you can control connections is by configuring a Routing And Remote Access server to accept or reject calls on the basis of Caller ID or Automatic Number Identification (ANI) information. For example, a server could be configured to accept calls only from a certain number.

Security Through Access Control

Routing And Remote Access supports a number of ways to control remote user access to the Routing And Remote Access server. The primary access control method is enabling or disabling the permission to dial in on individual user accounts. In addition to this basic method, Remote Access Policies (RAPs) enable you to extend control over whether users can dial in or not by setting a number of conditions on the access. RAPs are used to configure conditions under which users may connect using a specific remote access connection. These restrictions are based on criteria such as time of day, type of connection, and authentication.

Whereas user accounts define settings for an individual user, remote access policies define settings for a whole group of users. A policy is made up of rules that the system evaluates when it is determining whether a connection is accepted or not. User accounts and policies work together to provide dial-in capability. A policy may be used to define the overall settings for users' connections, but individual settings in a user's account determine whether the user's access is controlled using RAP or not.

Lesson Review

The following questions are intended to reinforce key information presented in this lesson. If you are unable to answer a question, review the lesson materials and try the question again. You can find answers to the questions in the "Questions and Answers" section at the end of this chapter.

1. You want to ensure that all user credentials passed between remote clients and a Routing And Remote Access server are encrypted. Which of the following authentication methods could you use?

   a. PAP

   b. CHAP

   c. SPAP

   d. MS-CHAP

2. Which of the following remote access protocols is the most common used by Routing And Remote Access and allows both dial-in and dial-out access?

    a. PPP

    b. SLIP

    c. RAS

    d. NetBIOS Gateway

3. What are the advantages of using Virtual Private Networking over traditional dial-up remote access?

_____

_____

Lesson Summary

- Windows Server 2003 provides remote access through a service named the Routing And Remote Access service. Clients can access a network by connecting directly to the server or by a Virtual Private Network.

- Routing And Remote Access supports several access protocols, the most important of which is Point-to-Point protocol. Once a connection is made, the remote access protocol dictates the physical aspects of data transfer over the connection.

- Three primary methods for securing remote access are authentication (where the user is authenticated to determine the access he is allowed), connection control (where allowing connections only from certain remote locations is allowed), and access control (where users or groups of users can be given or denied permissions for remote access).

Chapter Summary

- Active Directory is divided into logical structures—which include objects, domains, trees, forests, and organizational units—and physical structures, which include domain controllers and sites.

- In the logical structure, domains are the primary security boundaries of a network. Multiple domains sharing a contiguous namespace are organized into trees. Multiple trees make up a forest. The forest is the outermost boundary of an organization. Organizational Units are used to create administrative boundaries within a domain.

- Domain controllers and sites make up the physical structure. Domain controllers are Windows Server 2003 servers running Active Directory services; each domain controller holds a full replica of the directory partition for that domain. Sites are collections of domain controllers that are connected by fast, reliable connections. Site boundaries are used to control replication traffic.

- Name resolution services are used to resolve host names to IP addresses and DNS is the name resolution service of choice in Windows Server 2003. Active Directory is tightly integrated with DNS; domain controllers publish all running services in the DNS database in the form of service (SRV) records. This means that any DNS client can find a service on the network (including Active Directory) using a DNS lookup.

- The DNS namespace for a network mirrors the Active Directory namespace. DNS is divided into domains. Each domain is authoritative for the records held in that domain and, thus, for the mapping of host names and services to IP addresses in that domain.

- The DNS namespace is also divided into zones, which are used to designate contiguous portions of the namespace for which a particular server is responsible. A zone encompasses at least one domain and may contain other domains.

- TCP/IP protocols are arranged in four logical layers: the application layer, the transport layer, the Internet layer, and the network access layer. Data packets are passed down through the layers on a sending host and back up the layers on a receiving host.

- Each interface on a TCP/IP network is assigned a unique IP address, typically shown as four decimal numbers ranging from 0 to 255. An IP address is divided into a network ID, which determines the subnet on which a host exists, and a host ID, which uniquely identifies the host on that subnet. The separation of network ID and host ID is determined by a subnet mask.

- The primary method of automatically assigning IP addresses to clients on a network is the Dynamic Host Configuration Protocol (DHCP). A DHCP server holds a scope of IP addresses that it can assign, and is configured with other important information such as subnet mask, default gateway, and DNS servers for the network.

- Windows Server 2003 provides remote access through a service named the Routing And Remote Access service. Clients can access a network by connecting directly to the server or by a Virtual Private Network.

- Routing And Remote Access supports several access protocols, the most important of which is Point-to-Point protocol. Once a connection is made, the remote access protocol dictates the physical aspects of data transfer over the connection. A networking protocol, such as TCP/IP, still governs how data is formatted and routed.

- Three primary methods for securing remote access are authentication (where the user is authenticated to determine the access he is allowed), connection control (where allowing connections only from certain remote locations is allowed), and access control (where users or groups of users can be given or denied permissions for remote access).

Exam Highlights

Before taking the exam, review the key points and terms that are presented in this chapter.

Key Points

- The logical components of Active Directory. Understand how domains, trees, forests, and organizational units fit together. Also understand the naming of domains, trees, and forests.

- The physical structure of Active Directory. Know the main function of domain controllers and the extra roles they can assume. Also know how they are grouped into sites and how sites are used to control replication.

- The different trust relationships. Understand how the default two-way transitive trust allows authentication between domains and when other types of trust should be used.

- The basic structure of DNS. Understand how domains relate to one another and how they are named. Also understand what DNS servers are used for and how the DNS database is divided into zones.

- The name resolution process. Understand the basic process for both forward and reverse lookups. Also understand how lookups are used on a Windows Server 2003 network.

- The four layers of the TCP/IP protocol suite and the important protocols found in each.

- How an IP address is structured. Understand both the classful and classless methods for IP addressing. Also understand how the IP protocol uses the IP address and subnet mask to figure out routing.

- The connection methods provided by the Routing And Remote Access service. Understand the difference between dial-up networking and virtual private networking.

- The remote access and networking protocols used by Routing And Remote Access.

- The authentication methods and other security mechanisms used by Routing And Remote Access.

Key Terms

Namespace A namespace is a structure (such as a database) of objects that share a common method of naming, but are uniquely identified within the context of that structure. For example, no two computers can have the same name within a domain.

Object An object is a collection of attributes that define a particular resource. An object class defines the attributes that make up an object.

Root Domain A root domain is a domain at the base of a particular naming structure. The first domain installed on an Active Directory network serves as a root domain for the Active Directory forest *and* the root domain for the first tree in the forest. Additional trees also have a root domain for the tree, which is the first domain installed in the tree.

Operations Master Roles Although most domain controllers are considered equal, certain domain controllers can be chosen to perform operations master roles that are unique to the domain or forest. There are a number of roles that only one domain controller in a forest can hold and some roles that only one domain controller per domain can hold.

Active-Directory Integrated Zone This is a type of DNS zone in which the DNS database is stored as part of the Active Directory database. As such, DNS information is replicated automatically between domain controllers.

Classless Internet Domain Routing (CIDR) CIDR is a method of IP addressing that does not rely on the default subnet masks used in traditional IP address classes A–F. CIDR uses a custom subnet mask to break a network into subnets.

Questions and Answers

Page
1-17

Lesson 1 Review

1. Which of the following represents the outermost boundary for a single schema?

   a. A domain tree

   b. A domain forest

   c. A domain

   d. A domain controller

   The correct answer is b.

2. You are planning to add global catalog servers to your site. What is the recommended placement?

   a. You should place at least one global catalog server in each domain tree.

   b. You should place at least one global catalog server in each domain.

   c. You should place at least one global catalog server in each site.

   d. You should make each domain controller a global catalog server.

   The correct answer is c.

3. What are the advantages of using a cross-link trust?

   Cross-link trusts provide a way to create a direct trust relationship between two domains that may already be linked using a chain of transitive trusts. Cross-link trusts improve performance of queries between the linked domains.

Page
1-28

Lesson 2 Review

1. How does Active Directory use DNS?

   Active Directory uses DNS as a locator service. Domain controllers register all services they provide (including Active Directory) with DNS in the form of SRV records.

2. Which of the following resource record types is used to establish an alias for an existing host name?

   a. An A Record

   b. An ALIAS Record

   c. A CNAME Record

   d. An HINFO Record.

   The correct answer is c.

3. You want to enable Dynamic DNS for a specific zone and configure the server to allow only secure updates. What is required for you to do this ?

   a. The zone must be a root zone.

   b. The zone must be Active Directory—integrated.

   c. The zone must have an SRV record.

   d. You cannot enable DDNS for a specific zone—only for an entire server.

   The correct answer is b.

Page
1-40
Lesson 3 Review

1. In which of the four layers of the Internet protocol is the routing of packets between source and destination hosts handled?

   a. Application

   b. Transport

   c. Internet

   d. Link

   The correct answer is c.

2. Your company has registered the network ID 131.107.0.0, which uses the default subnet mask 255.255.0.0. You would like to create a custom subnet mask that allows you to divide that network into the maximum number of subnets that would allow you to have at least 20 hosts per subnet. What custom subnet mask would you use?

   To start with, you know you will have to borrow some bits from the host ID in the third and fourth octets. Any custom subnet mask with a value greater than 240 in the fourth octet will give you fewer than 20 hosts per subnet. Using 255.255.255.240 as a subnet mask will give you 4095 possible subnets with 31 hosts possible per subnet. It is also common practice to subtract 2 addresses from the possible number of hosts to account for host IDs that contain all zeros or all ones. Even with this margin, you still have 30 possible hosts.

3. Which of the following default subnet masks would be used on a computer with the IP address 157.54.4.201?

   a. 255.0.0.0

   b. 255.255.0.0

   c. 255.255.255.0

   d. 255.255.255.255

   The correct answer is b.

Lesson 4 Review

1. You want to ensure that all user credentials passed between remote clients and an Routing And Remote Access server are encrypted. Which of the following authentication methods could you use?

   a. PAP

   b. CHAP

   c. SPAP

   d. MS-CHAP

   The correct answers are b, c, and d.

2. Which of the following remote access protocols is the most common used by Routing And Remote Access and allows both dial-in and dial-out access?

   a. PPP

   b. SLIP

   c. RAS

   d. NetBIOS Gateway

   The correct answer is a.

3. What are the advantages of using Virtual Private Networking over traditional dial-up remote access?

   The first advantage is that users not in the local calling area need not make long distance calls to connect to the Routing And Remote Access server. Second, using VPN connections dramatically reduces cost by reducing both the hardware needed to provide many simultaneous connections and the need to maintain as many phone circuits. Finally, VPN solutions typically offer higher-speed connections (using broadband Internet connections) at lower prices than conventional dial-up methods.

2 Analyzing an Existing Infrastructure

Exam Objectives in this Chapter:

- Identify network topology and performance levels
    - Identify constraints in the current network infrastructure
    - Interpret current baseline performance requirements for each major subsystem
- Analyze existing network operating system implementation
    - Identify the existing domain model
    - Identify the number and location of domain controllers on the network
    - Identify the configuration details of all servers on the network (server types might include primary domain controllers, backup domain controllers, file servers, print servers, and Web servers)
- Analyze the impact of Active Directory on the existing technical environment
    - Analyze interoperability requirements
    - Analyze the current level of service within an existing technical environment
    - Analyze the current network administration model
    - Analyze network requirements
- Analyze security requirements for the Active Directory directory service
    - Analyze current security policies, standards, and procedures
    - Identify the impact of Active Directory on the current security infrastructure
    - Identify the existing trust relationships
- Analyze the impact of the infrastructure design on the existing technical environment.
    - Analyze hardware and software requirements
    - Analyze interoperability requirements
    - Analyze current level of service within the existing technical environment
    - Analyze network requirements

Why This Chapter Matters

Before delving into the realm of installing Microsoft Windows Server 2003, creating domains, and organizing resources, you must have an in-depth knowledge of how your network is currently configured. A basic understanding of your company, along with an analysis of your current network structure, is vital to the success of your new infrastructure plan.

This chapter is about gathering information; it introduces you to the tasks you need to complete *before* designing your Active Directory directory service and network infrastructure. Before you make a single purchase or recommendation, you must first understand the company itself and then conduct an analysis of the existing network structure and domain model.

Lessons in this Chapter:

Before You Begin

To complete this chapter, make sure you are familiar with the concepts described in Chapter 1, "Introduction to Active Directory and Network Infrastructure."

Lesson 1: Analyzing the Company

The first step in analyzing a company's network infrastructure is to perform an analysis of the company itself. Understanding how a company works and how its information flows lays a critical foundation for the rest of your network design.

After this lesson, you will be able to

- Identify the geographic model of a company.
- Create a geographic map for the company.
- Gather material about the information flow in a company.

Estimated lesson time: 20 minutes

Geographical Considerations

Your first task is to identify the physical locations of the various departments, divisions, or functions in a company. From a networking perspective, one of the biggest ongoing expenses is the connection between physical locations. A wide area network (WAN) link between cities, for example, not only has a lower bandwidth capacity than local area network (LAN) connections, but also is relatively expensive to boot. One of your first design goals, therefore, will be to reduce (or at least control the timing of) network traffic flowing across WAN links. The larger the geographic scope of the network, the more important this goal becomes.

Exam Tip   In versions of Windows prior to Windows 2000, Microsoft recommended creating one domain for each distinct geographic area. This is no longer the case. Keeping to the idea that simpler is better, using one domain for an entire organization is recommended, where possible. Use sites to distinguish geographic boundaries for the purposes of controlling network traffic and use Organizational Units (OUs) to distinguish geographic boundaries for the purpose of administration.

Microsoft defines four basic geographical models: local, regional, national, and international. In addition, there are two other types of offices that may come into play: subsidiary and branch offices.

Local Model

The local geographic model is the simplest and is one in which all resources are connected using fast, permanent links. A local model will usually implement only one site and only one domain. The company will not need to obtain connections between separate locations from outside vendors. In fact, the only link outside the local boundaries will likely be the company's Internet service and any remote-access lines provided to users.

Compared to other models, the local model does not require as much planning. Network traffic, although still important, is not as much of an issue because of the high bandwidth and availability of local connections. The vast majority of networks in the world are local networks.

Regional Model

In the regional model, all locations exist within a single, well-defined geographic area. An example of a regional network is shown in Figure 2-1.

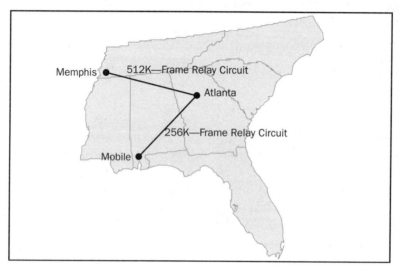

Figure 2-1   A typical regional network

There are a couple of key issues that separate the regional model from its larger, more complex national and international model siblings. Most important, all the connections between locations in the regional model usually are provided by the same vendor. Another important consideration is that networks following the regional model should have relatively simple setup issues. This means that the connections between the locations should be high-speed WAN links with permanent connections.

National Model

The scale of the national model is a step above that of the regional model. Although the name suggests a company that covers an entire country (and that is usually the case), the other main feature that makes a company fit this model is complexity. A company that fits the national model will likely have WAN links of different speeds from different vendors. A slower link (less than 512Kb) between one or more locations would also raise the complexity of your design and could bump a company into a national model. Dial-up connections are more prominently featured and may comprise some of the WAN links instead of just providing remote access to users. Different network topologies such as Asynchronous Transfer Mode (ATM) and Frame Relay may be in use.

In addition to the complexity of connections between locations, companies fitting this model usually consider other factors as well, including:

- Multiple time zones

- Differing laws and regulations

- Larger numbers of users

International Model

As the name suggests, the primary definition of a company that fits the international model is that its networks cross international boundaries, as shown in Figure 2-2. You will find many of the same considerations in the international model as in the national model. There will still be multiple connection vendors, complicated by the fact that connections must now cross international lines. It is essential that you understand the cost of the connections and their reliability. This requires considerably more planning than with the other models.

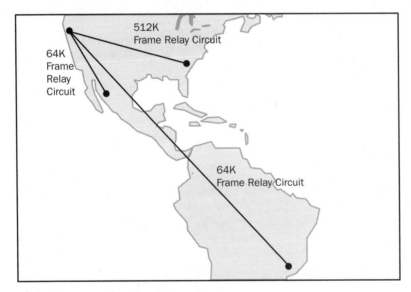

Figure 2-2   An international network

You also must now contend with more serious differences in laws and regulations as well as language differences between locations. You must plan for differences in what content is deemed acceptable, export laws between countries, employee regulations, and even tariffs.

Branch Offices

A branch office is one that is ultimately controlled by your company but maintains a degree of autonomy. Banks, insurance companies, and large chains are examples of companies that traditionally maintain branch offices. A branch office likely will not keep up all the network services that the main office maintains. However, depending on the connection between the branch and the main office, you may find it necessary to replicate some services in the branch office to help stem the flow of data over the connecting network.

Branch offices also do not typically act as links (or hubs) between other offices; each branch office is instead connected directly to a main office, as shown in Figure 2-3. There are exceptions to this, of course. In particularly large, distributed companies such as department stores, you may find that a regional branch connects to a national headquarters. Smaller branch locations, in turn, may connect to the regional branch instead of directly to the headquarters. This helps distribute the authority over the network structure and processes more effectively because each regional branch serves to manage the smaller branch locations.

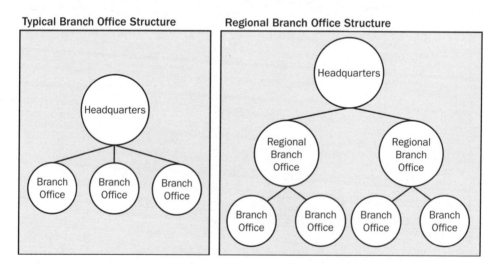

Figure 2-3   A typical branch office structure and a regional branch structure

Branch offices may or may not have information technology (IT) staff or management staff on location and normally do not have users with needs that are as diverse as those of users at a central office. Smaller branch offices rely on the IT staff, networking services, and expert users provided by the central office.

Subsidiary Offices

A subsidiary office is one that is part of the main company, but is not controlled by it. The classic example of this would be a company that acquires another company to market the second company's particular service or bundle the service with its own.

Typically, a subsidiary office maintains its own management and IT staff—after all, it was probably a complete, separate company at one point. This poses a particular challenge for you as a network designer. The subsidiary office likely has its own way of doing things that may not correspond to the main company. There will be administrators who have different methods and may resent having to adapt to new policies. You may find it necessary (whether through functional necessity or managerial mandate) to maintain a separate domain and namespace for the subsidiary office. There may also be different security and network service requirements. Your designs must satisfy both the autonomy of the subsidiary office and the policies set forth by the main company.

Exam Tip   While it is unlikely that you will be shown a company on the exam and asked what kind of model it fits, understanding the basic models will provide you with a way to help identify and recognize the needs of a company.

Recording Your Analysis

In defining the geographic boundaries of your company, you can use a simple map that encompasses the largest geographical area for the company. For example, you could use a map of the western hemisphere for international companies that have locations in North and South America. You might use a map of just the southeast United States for a regional company with locations in Georgia, Alabama, and Tennessee. For particularly complex companies, you may find that you need to create detailed separate maps for each regional location—all tied together by a larger, less detailed map.

Ask yourself the following questions as you go:

- In what cities does the company maintain offices?

- Is an office a major corporate headquarters, a branch office, or a subsidiary office? For subsidiary offices, even small ones, you may have to create separate designs that don't conform to the overall design.

- How many users are at each location?

- How are the locations connected? For now, just note the types of connections (such as a T1 line), the maximum bandwidth the connection provides, and the vendor. Be sure to talk to the network administrators and find out how happy they have been with the connections and vendors, as well as the level of uptime for the connections and what type of redundancy the vendor has in place.

- How is the company charged for bandwidth? Some connections are charged based on the total traffic transmitted across the link during a month. Other connections' charges are based on peak utilization. Be sure to note the pricing structure on your diagrams.

- If the connections cross international boundaries, are there special considerations such as tariffs or export laws?

You will continue to fill in information on these maps and create other design documents as you work through the other lessons in this chapter.

Estimating Current WAN Connection Usage

Once you have created your geographic map or maps and determined the maximum bandwidth of the WAN links between locations, you must next establish the current usage levels on each connection. By comparing the maximum bandwidth with the current usage, you can figure out how much available bandwidth you have to work with.

It is likely that the vendor for each WAN connection can provide you with usage statistics. If not, you will need to use your own tools to gather the information. You should obtain information on how much bandwidth is used at key times during the day to get an idea of regular usage patterns. You should also record the bandwidth usage at key network events—events such as when users log on in the morning (or evening), when backups occur, when replication of directory or other information is scheduled, and so on.

You can record your information on your primary diagram or on a separate diagram for more complex situations. Alongside the maximum bandwidth for the connection, you should note the peak usage, the average usage, and any notes on specific times and causes of high usage.

Information Flow

Information is the lifeblood of the modern company. When designing a network, you must keep in mind that the entire point of what you are doing lies in letting people create, store, disseminate, find, and consume information. You should create a detailed analysis of what kind of information is used, where that information comes from, who creates it, where it is stored, where it is transferred, and who accesses it.

For each department or division of a company, you should talk to key personnel about the kind of information they use. Ask the following questions:

- What sorts of documents do their departments create? What applications do they use?

- Who are those documents for? Are they stored and accessed only by the people who create them? Are they routed to others in the division or in the company? Are they stored and accessed by others? How many others? Are they printed?

- Are documents made public over the Internet or by other means? If so, are the users responsible for publishing the information or is someone else? Who?

- Where are those documents stored? It is important to answer this question both from a user and an IT perspective. A typical user might say "In the My Documents folder" or "on my Z: Drive." A network administrator can tell you whether information is stored on a server or on users' computers and how the location is presented to the user.

- Is information stored in a database? What kind of information and what kind of database? How many users access it? Where is the database located?

The other questions you must ask that are related to information flow are about how people in the company communicate with one another. These are questions such as:

- Is e-mail the primary mechanism for communicating with other employees?

- Is instant messaging used or could it be?

- What is the phone system like? What equipment is used and where is it located? Is it tied into the networking system?

Real World   Talking to People

When you are gathering information, it is tempting to just go out and start talking to people. It's also one of my favorite parts of designing a network because it's the time when I learn the most about a business and the people who work there. However, you should be as prepared as possible. Come up with the questions that need answers first. Decide who can answer those questions for you. Remember that not everyone you talk to will know that much about (or even be interested in) computers. My recommendation is to start with the people in the IT department because they will be most sympathetic to your cause. You must be careful, though, that people don't feel like you are trampling too heavily on their realm. Keep in mind that many of the people you talk to may have had a hand in designing the current network structure.

You also need to interview people in each department. The IT staff can probably help determine who in each department will have the knowledge you're after and who will be interested in helping. Departments often rely on expert users to perform basic administrative services or at the very least coordinate the computing efforts and questions of other users. With a little social networking, you can usually enlist these people to be part of your solution.

Analyze the Current Administration Model

Whereas many of your design goals involve minimizing administrative burden, it's important that you understand how the administration of the IT department is structured. To begin with, there are two basic administrative models: centralized and decentralized.

In the centralized model, a separate IT staff provides administrative services for the network. The IT managers have control over every portion of the network, including the Active Directory structure. There are two main advantages to using a centralized model. First, the administrative structure is less complicated. This means that decisions are easier to make and that you can use fewer OUs when designing an Active Directory structure because there is not as much need for delegating administrative authority. The second advantage is that having a smaller group of people in charge of the network services means a more consistent design and management approach.

The disadvantage of the centralized model is that it doesn't scale very well. When you have a more complex network that is spread out over a larger geographic area, relying on a centralized administration often means slower response times. The decentralized model solves this problem by maintaining some sort of administrative staff at each location. In smaller locations, that staff may even be made up of expert users instead of IT professionals. In some designs, the local administrative staff is given complete control of the resources at their location. As mentioned previously, the real advantage to this model is that when needs or problems arise, there is someone there locally who can handle it. However, this advantage comes with costs. The Active Directory and network structures must be more complex to support the decentralized model. This usually means more OUs or even more domains. Another cost is that maintaining administrative staff at various locations makes it harder to keep the staff up to date, consistent, and well-trained.

When you record details about the administrative model used in a company, include the following information:

- Make a simple organizational flowchart that shows the members of the administrative staff and their relative positions. If the company uses a decentralized model, make a chart for each location.

- Identify the person (or people) who govern the IT budget. Find out when the budget is determined and what aspects will affect your project?

- If any services are outsourced, list the service, the vendor, and the cost.

- Describe how IT decisions are made. Are all decisions made from the top? Is there a certain amount of autonomy granted throughout the chain of command? If so, what are the limits of this autonomy? Basically, what you are after is finding out who makes what decisions in regard to changing and servicing the network.

Future Plans

One of the greatest features in Windows 2003 is its scalability—its ability to allow for growth in size without a corresponding growth in network overhead. That does not mean, however, that you shouldn't be prepared for the future when designing a network. Your plans should allow for changes in a company's focus or planned acquisitions. You should also account for changes in location, including adding extra locations, and changes to the workforce.

Lesson Review

The following questions are intended to reinforce key information presented in this lesson. If you are unable to answer a question, review the lesson materials and try the question again. You can find answers to the questions in the "Questions and Answers" section at the end of this chapter.

1. Aside from network connection issues, what are three complicating factors exhibited by an international company?

   _____

   _____

2. What is the difference between a branch and a subsidiary office?

   _____

   _____

3. You are preparing a geographic map for a company that has three locations within the same state. The link between two of the locations is a dedicated T1 line. The third location links to only one of the first two locations and that link is a 64Kb line. What geographical model would this fall into?

   _____

   _____

Lesson Summary

- The four main geographical company models are local, regional, national, and international. The primary differences between these models (aside from political boundaries) are the complexity of the network and the state of the connections between the locations.

- Two types of offices also play into the geographical considerations: branch offices that are controlled by the company and the subsidiary offices that are owned by the company, but usually have their own staff and networking policies.

- You should gather as much information as possible on how information is created, stored, and transferred within the organization.

Lesson 2: Analyzing the Existing Network Topology

Once you understand the structure of your company, it's time to assess the existing network itself. In this lesson, you learn to gather information on the IP addressing scheme and on how the network is routed, as well as how servers and resources are allocated.

After this lesson, you will be able to

■ Describe the current network environment.

■ Identify and inventory the servers and workstations on the network.

■ Describe performance requirements.

Estimated lesson time: 30 minutes

Network Environment

When creating a geographic map of a company, you identified the major locations and basic information about the network connections between those locations. You will now begin to gather more detailed information about the existing network structure.

Routers and Other Networking Equipment

Start the information gathering by mapping out each geographic location individually. A simple conceptual map will do nicely. Each location should be a single LAN on which all hosts are well connected.

On your map, you need to identify the following:

■ Whether the LAN is separated into subnets.

■ The location of routers—whether they serve to connect subnets on the LAN or connect the LAN to a WAN. Identify the make and model of the routers as well as the type of routing it provides. Also indicate any other services, such as DHCP or DNS that the router provides. Indicate the version of the firmware or software, if applicable. If the router is a Windows-based router, you also need to indicate the other services (if any) that the server provides and the version of Windows it is running.

■ The type of cabling used and where. If the network has been relying on an older standard, it is probably time to upgrade.

■ The location of patch panels and closets. Note what types of components are there and what types of connections they provide.

■ The location of remote access equipment. If your company provides dial-up access to many users, there may be racks of dial-up equipment. You will need to document the vendor, brand, and model of this equipment as well as how it is connected to the network. If it is not controlled by a Windows server, you'll need to decide whether it should be.

In complex environments, you should create a map and set of documents for each LAN. On the geographic map, you should identify how the LANs are connected to one another.

IP Addressing

Once you have described the physical layout of the network, you should focus next on the Internet Protocol (IP) addressing scheme. Your first step should be to find out what IP address or range of addresses the company has leased from its Internet provider. Next, you should determine whether the networking is using that public range of addresses or whether they are using private addressing. You also need to determine whether IP addressing on the network is manual (unlikely on all but the smallest networks) or uses Dynamic Host Configuration Protocol (DHCP) to automatically assign information.

Next, you should document information for each subnet on the network, including:

- The network ID and subnet mask as well as the range of host IDs assigned to hosts on the subnet.

- The default gateway assigned to hosts on the subnet.

- Whether the subnet contains a DHCP server or uses a DHCP relay agent.

- Any optional information the DHCP server is configured to assign, such as DNS server addresses.

- A list of Transmission Control Protocol (TCP) and User Datagram Protocol (UDP) ports used by services on the network, especially if you run custom services or have standard services that vary from using the well-known port numbers.

Servers and Workstations

A huge task in gathering information about a network is putting together data on the computers that make up that network. You should create an inventory of each system and determine when the system is used the most.

Creating an Inventory

Creating inventories of the computers on a network is time consuming and you'll want to take as much advantage of existing information as possible. However, be sure to verify any information you are given as being up to date. If there is not a comprehensive inventory of systems, there are automated solutions available and you can probably get members of the IT staff to assist.

When inventorying a system, you should take the following information into consideration:

- The name of the computer, its current IP configuration, and its location on the network.

- Brand and model of the computer. If the computer is not branded (such as with a custom-built system), you must be even more diligent in listing the brand of components used in building the computer. Make sure you have access to the necessary hardware drivers.

- The brand and model of the motherboard, along with the current basic input/output system (BIOS) revision.

- The processor type and speed.

- The amount and type of memory.

- The size, type, and brand of hard drives and hard drive controllers.

- Brand and type of network adapters. Be sure to specify what types of connections the adapter supports as well as the speed.

- Brands and model numbers of any attached peripherals. Be sure to include the driver or firmware version currently in place.

- Any services running on the system. For servers, this includes services such as DHCP, domain name system (DNS), or Windows Internet Naming Service (WINS). Workstations may also have services running. If the system is a domain controller, you must also gather the information presented in the next lesson.

- Installed software. Be sure to include the name of the software, the version, any updates that have been installed, and the product activation key (if available).

- Shared folders or printers configured on the system. Include the rights and permissions granted to users and groups as well.

- Users that access the system.

> **Note** In addition to the hardware and software requirements necessary to run Windows Server 2003, you must determine the number of domain controllers necessary to support your Active Directory plan and the hardware requirements of each domain controller. You can find a detailed discussion of this in Chapter 5, "Designing a Site Plan."

Identifying Availability

When inventorying a system, especially a server, take the time to note the usage patterns of the system. Talk to the users, if possible, and to the IT staff. The reason for gathering this information is to help determine the best time for taking the system offline and performing upgrades. By and large, you will upgrade and maintain systems after business hours. However, you will find certain systems (such as remote access servers and replication managers) that have peak usage at unusual times. One of the challenges you will face in preparing your design plan is preparing your deployment timing.

Analyzing Performance Requirements

Communication and performance are vital to the network environment. Servers must be able to transfer information to one another and be able to perform tasks in a reasonable amount of time. Users must get adequate responses from network services. As you gather information from administrators and users about the network, you are sure to hear details about network performance. Although you should take this reporting with a grain of salt (after all, what user has ever complained about response being too fast?), you should pay attention nonetheless. When numbers of users all report the same problem, there's likely something going on that could stand improvement.

Address Unresolved Problems

Before you can even begin testing the performance of a network and thinking about whether it meets your requirements, you should make sure that any outstanding problems that could affect performance are addressed. Obviously, this task will involve the IT staff because they are aware of any current issues.

When any reported issues are handled, do your best to make sure that the current network configuration is appropriate and that any recent updates are applied. This means making sure that network hardware, such as a router, is properly configured for its tasks and that firmware is updated to the latest version. For servers, check the event logs for any problems you may be unaware of, apply any necessary updates to the operating system or networking components, and make sure services and networking components are configured properly.

By resolving outstanding issues, verifying configurations, and bringing software up to date, you give the network at least a fighting chance when it's time to gauge its performance.

Testing Current Performance

One of the best ways to gauge performance, or at least perceived performance, on a network is by sitting down with key users and letting them show you. Pay attention to the time it takes to start the computer, to log on to the network, to start applications, and to access network resources.

Check the logs for the major services on the network and see whether things are performing within expectations. Are backups taking longer than expected? How about database access or replication?

Once you have an overall impression of performance on a network, there are a couple of tools that can help you test your servers and network connections and establish some real performance numbers.

- **Performance Console** The Performance console (named Performance Monitor in versions of Windows prior to Windows 2000) tracks resource utilization on a computer. It is useful for establishing a baseline measure of the performance of key system components, including the processor, memory, disk subsystem, and network throughput. The snap-in used in the Performance Console is named System Monitor. Both are referred to within Windows Server 2003 documentation.

- **Network Monitor** Network Monitor is used to view and detect problems on local networks. It works by capturing the frames or packets transferred on the network and giving you tools with which to analyze those frames.

Assessing Requirements

Once you have established the current performance levels of the network, you will need to determine whether they are adequate for your design. First, you'll need to assess whether the servers on the network are capable of running Windows Server 2003 and any services necessary to fill their roles. Second, you'll need to determine if the network itself is capable of handling the traffic required for your implementation.

This assessment is actually one that you will need to revisit often as you prepare your plan, and it will require some give and take. For example, if you determine that your Active Directory design exceeds the capabilities of the current network connection, you will have to decide whether to increase the capacity of the network or rearrange your design.

Lesson Review

The following questions are intended to reinforce key information presented in this lesson. If you are unable to answer a question, review the lesson materials and try the question again. You can find answers to the questions in the "Questions and Answers" section at the end of this chapter.

1. What types of information should you gather when inventorying a server?

   _____

   _____

2. For each subnet on your network, identify the major IP addressing components you will need to record.

   _____

   _____

3. Identify the two major tools used to analyze performance on a Windows network.

_____

_____

Lesson Summary

- Assess the current network environment, including information about the subnets, IP addressing, and networking equipment used in each location.

- Create an inventory of the servers and workstations in each location. Include a description of the hardware, software, and services they use. Also note the usage patterns of the systems so that you can gauge the best time for upgrades.

- When analyzing performance requirements, start by fixing any existing problems and making sure configurations are correct. Get a sense of user experiences and expectations and then test the current performance. Revisit these requirements often as you design your plan.

Lesson 3: Analyzing the Existing Directory Structure

Analyzing a directory structure means identifying the current domain model in use on the network and how resources are allocated among those domains. If Active Directory is already running, you will also identify the current boundaries of the forest and the placement of OUs and domain controllers.

After this lesson, you will be able to

- Describe the current domain model.
- Identify existing trust relationships.
- Describe the current OU structure.
- Identify the placement and roles of domain controllers.

Estimated lesson time: 20 minutes

Analyze an Existing Windows 2000 Infrastructure

If there is an Active Directory structure already in place on the network you are design-ing for, you can be sure that some thought has already been put into its design. As you gather information about the current structure, you should carefully consider why things are done the way they are. If you are satisfied with the basic design, you may need only to tweak the current structure to better meet your design requirements.

Current Domain Model

The first step in documenting the existing domain model is to create a basic diagram like the one shown in Figure 2-4. This diagram should show the existing domains, as well as how they are organized into trees and forests. For more complex structures, you will need to create multiple diagrams—one for each domain tree should suffice.

On the diagram, be sure to include the following information:

- The full name of the domain
- Which domain is the root domain of each tree
- Which domain is the root domain of the forest
- Any shortcut trusts that have been created
- Any forest trusts that link to other forests
- Any one-way trusts linking to Windows NT 4.0 domains

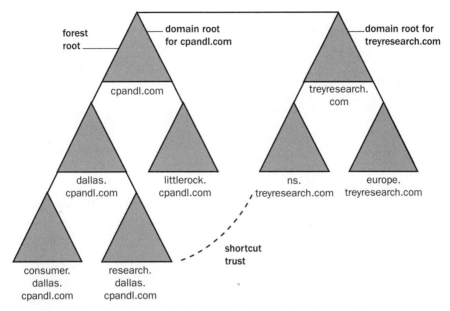

Figure 2-4   Diagramming an existing Windows 2000 domain structure

Current Organizational Unit Structure

Once you have created an overall diagram showing how the domains are related to one another, your next step is to create a diagram for each domain that shows the current OU structure. This should be a relatively simple diagram like the one shown in Figure 2-5.

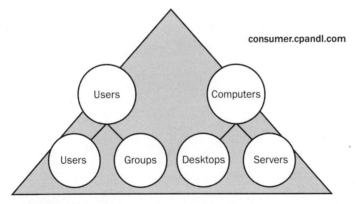

Figure 2-5   Diagramming an organizational unit structure

You also need to gather some information about each OU. This information includes:

■   The objects contained in the OUs (including other OUs).

- How permissions are assigned for administration of the OUs and the objects it contains. This includes the permissions on the unit itself, whether permissions are inherited by objects in the OUs, and any variation in permissions on the objects inside.

- Any Group Policy Objects linked to the OU.

It is up to you whether you build a separate document for each OU that lists this information or whether you include it on some of the documents you have already created. For example, you could create a list of resources contained in the OU or you could go back to the resources document you've already created and list the OU that each resource belongs to.

Real World   Simplify

As you document the current infrastructure, look for ways to simplify it. If there are multiple domains where you could create a single domain with multiple OUs, it may be a good choice to do so. If the existing OU structure is more than a few levels deep and has a complex permissions structure, then the chances are it was not well thought out to begin with or it has grown too complex since its design. Either way, you can likely solve a lot of headaches by reducing the depth of the OU hierarchy and simplifying the permissions placed on the OUs.

You'll be learning more about how to design efficient structures in the coming chapters, but you'll do well to keep an eye out for unnecessary complexities as you gather information on the current implementation.

Current Site and Domain Controller Structure

Your next step is to create another diagram for each domain that shows how the domain is broken down into sites and how domain controllers are positioned in those sites. Even if the domain contains only one site, you should still create a diagram and map out the domain controllers.

You can rely on the documents you created when inventorying your servers and workstations for information on hardware and software. However, you should also list the following information about each domain controller:

- Whether the server performs other domain or forest roles in addition to being a domain controller. These include the operations master roles such as schema master, domain naming master, infrastructure master, and so on. Refer to Chapter 1, "Introduction to Active Directory and Network Infrastructure," for a detailed list of these roles.

- Whether the server is a Global Catalog server.

- Whether the server is a bridgehead server used for replicating Active Directory information to other sites.

- You may also want to list servers that are not domain controllers, but that provide other vital services, such as DNS, DHCP, Web, or mail services. Although you probably already have recorded information about these servers in other design documents (and should refer to those for details), knowledge about server location relative to domain and site structure will be helpful.

Analyze an Existing Windows NT 4.0 Infrastructure

If the organization is currently running a Windows NT 4.0 infrastructure, you'll have a good bit more design work cut out for you than if the organization is already using Windows 2000 and Active Directory. In a Windows NT 4.0 environment, there will be a domain model, but there is no centralized directory service in place. Windows NT 4.0 uses a more complicated system of primary and backup domain controllers and replication is less controllable because Windows NT does not support the use of sites within a domain.

One of your key choices will be whether to upgrade everything in place and retain the existing domain model or whether to modify the existing structure. Remember, in a Windows NT 4.0 environment, domains are the only real administrative boundary available. In Windows 2003, OUs often provide a better administrative boundary than domains. It may be possible, therefore, to reduce the number of domains used on a network (or eliminate multiple domains altogether) if OUs will serve your administrative needs. Because one of your goals is to simplify the administrative overhead (decreasing the cost and increasing the efficiency of administration), the fewer domains you can implement, the better.

> **Exam Tip**   As you work through the case studies presented on the exam, one of the big questions you'll repeatedly find yourself facing is whether to use an OU or a domain to implement a given administrative need.

Keeping the existing Windows NT domain structure intact provides some advantages, including:

- All domain objects upgrade to the Active Directory model.
- Users keep their existing passwords and profiles.
- The implementation takes less time and requires fewer resources.
- System security policies are retained.

However, the obvious disadvantage is that you may end up stuck with a less-than-optimal structure that does not take full advantage of Active Directory capabilities or easily allow for future growth.

When you gather information on the current domain model, you should create a basic conceptual diagram, like the one shown in Figure 2-6, that shows the current domains.

You should identify the following information on the diagram:

■ The domain name

■ The names of servers in the domain

■ The names of domain controllers in the domain

■ The trust relationships between domains

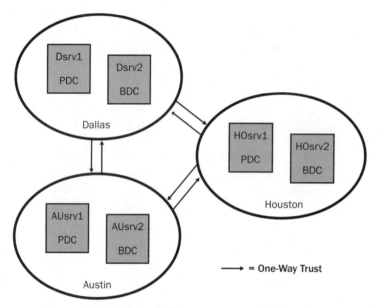

Figure 2-6   Diagramming an existing Windows NT 4.0 domain structure

In addition to the overall domain diagram, you should prepare a separate document for each existing domain. On that document, include the following information:

■ Each server in the domain by name and IP address. Also list the services and roles that each server provides. This includes services such as DNS, DHCP, Internet Information Services (IIS), and Routing And Remote Access. If the server is a file or database server, be sure to list the details. For domain controllers, list whether each is a primary or backup domain controller.

■ The number and names of users in the domain. Although this likely will end up being a large document, it can help identify important design considerations and save you a good bit of hassle during implementation.

■ Resources configured for the domain. This includes shared network resources, printers, and so on.

■ Members of the domain administrators global group. Members of this group represent users who will be able to manage the domain during the process of implementing your design. Include contact details for each member.

Windows 2003 Functional Levels

On a Windows 2003 network, different levels of functionality are attainable within a domain or a forest depending on whether all domain controllers in that domain or forest are running Windows Server 2003. The level at which the domain or forest are running is called the functional level.

Domain Functionality

Domain functionality affects features that will be available within a domain. There are four levels of domain functionality available:

■ **Windows 2000 Mixed**   This is the default functional level. It assumes that domain controllers in the domain may be running Windows NT 4.0, Windows 2000, or Windows 2003. It also offers the least functional feature set.

■ **Windows 2000 Native**   This functional level assumes that domain controllers may be running Windows 2000 or Windows 2003 within the domain. Aside from the Windows Server 2003 functional level, this level offers the most functionality.

■ **Windows Server 2003 Interim**   This functional level assumes that domain controllers will be running both Windows 2003 and Windows NT 4.0. As its name indicates, this level is intended for use during the process of upgrading a network from Windows NT 4.0 to Windows 2003 Server.

■ **Windows Server 2003**   This is the highest functional level for a domain. It assumes all domain controllers in the domain are running Windows Server 2003 and offers the highest feature set.

Forest Functionality

Forest functionality affects features that will be available within a forest. There are three levels of forest functionality available:

■ **Windows 2000**   This is the default functional level for a forest and assumes that domain controllers in the forest may be running Windows NT 4.0, Windows 2000, or Windows 2003.

■ **Windows Server 2003 Interim**   This functional level assumes that domain controllers will be running both Windows 2003 and Windows NT 4.0. This level is intended for use during the process of upgrading a forest from Windows NT 4.0 to Windows 2003 Server.

- **Windows Server 2003**   This is the highest functional level for a forest. It assumes all domain controllers in the forest are running Windows Server 2003.

> **See Also**   For more information about functional levels in Windows 2003, including details on the features supported by each level, see the product documentation or the Microsoft Windows Server 2003 Resource Kit.

Practice: Analyze the Existing Directory Structure

In this practice, you identify the information required to create an Active Directory forest and domain design. If you are unable to answer a question, review the lesson materials and try the question again. You can find answers to the questions in the "Questions and Answers" section at the end of this chapter.

Scenario

Northwind Traders manufactures a line of network appliances designed to help companies improve their data transmission capabilities. Northwind Traders currently uses a Microsoft Windows NT 4.0 master domain model and has a separate resource domain for each geographic location. Each domain is configured with a two-way trust relationship to every other domain.

In recent years, the company has undergone significant growth and expansion and expects substantial growth over the next three years, including growth in market share, revenue, and number of employees. In addition to opening two new offices, the executive management has committed to implementing a new Windows Server 2003 Active Directory design to meet the current and future needs of the company.

The following table shows the geographical locations, the departments residing in each location, and the number of users in each of the locations.

Location	Departments Represented	Number of Users
Paris	Headquarters (HQ) Management staff Finance Sales Marketing Production Research Development Information Technology (IT)	2,000

Location	Departments Represented	Number of Users
Los Angeles	Sales Marketing Finance IT	1,000
Atlanta	Customer Service Customer Support Training	750
Glasgow, Scotland	Research Development Sustained Engineering IT	750
Sydney, Australia	Consulting Production Sales Finance	500

Most of the company's computing services are hosted in its Paris corporate headquarters. The corporate IT department wants to have central control of passwords and security settings. The local IT department in Los Angeles wants to maintain control of its infrastructure without interference from the corporate IT department. The local IT department in Glasgow demands exclusive control over their own environment due to security concerns about their research and development (R&D) data. Corporate management shares security concerns about the R&D data and wants to ensure that it is not compromised.

The following diagram shows the connectivity between the different locations of the company. In addition, Los Angeles and Atlanta have virtual private network (VPN) connections through the Internet to headquarters in Paris.

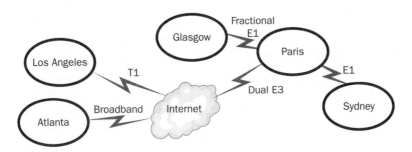

Practice Questions

Based on the scenario, answer the following questions.

1. Sketch a diagram of the current Windows NT domain structure.

2. What requirements does Northwind Traders have for autonomy and isolation?

   _____

   _____

3. What are Northwind Traders' administrative goals?

   _____

   _____

Lesson Review

The following questions are intended to reinforce key information presented in this lesson. If you are unable to answer a question, review the lesson materials and try the question again. You can find answers to the questions in the "Questions and Answers" section at the end of this chapter.

1. You are designing an Active Directory structure for a network that is currently using Windows NT 4.0. There are 12 servers running Windows NT 4.0 and 300 workstations running mixtures of Windows 98, Windows NT 4.0 Workstation, and Windows XP Professional. The entire network is housed in a single building. There are currently three Windows NT 4.0 domains—one for each of the major departments of the company. Each department manages resources in its own domain. What is one method of reducing the complexity of the existing network while still allowing members of each department administrative control over resources in their department?

   _____

   _____

2. You are gathering information about the current domain model of a network running Windows 2000 and Active Directory. You have created a domain map that shows every domain and the trust relationships between those domains. What other documents should you prepare for each domain when assessing the current model?

   _____

   _____

3. List several advantages of keeping an existing Windows NT 4.0 domain model intact when you upgrade to Windows 2003.

_____

_____

Lesson Summary

- When gathering information about a current Windows 2000 infrastructure, you should first create a diagram showing the existing domains and their trust relationships.

- For each Windows 2000 domain, create a diagram of OU structure and a diagram showing site structure and domain controller placement.

- When gathering information about a Windows NT 4.0 infrastructure, create a diagram showing domains and trust relationships. For each domain, gather information on the domain controllers, users, and resources in the domain.

Case Scenario Exercise

Review the following scenario and complete the questions.

Scenario

You have been selected to plan a new infrastructure for Contoso, Ltd., a modem manufacturer with its headquarters in Dallas, Texas. Currently, all servers on its network are running Windows NT Server 4.0. Client computers are running a mix of Windows 98 and Windows 2000 Professional. Contoso has hired you to bring the company network infrastructure up to date. They want all servers to run Windows Server 2003 and want to implement Active Directory. They also want all client computers to run Windows XP Professional.

Background

Contoso has grown over the past decade to become one of the premier high-end modem manufacturers in the country, selling primarily to large companies and Internet Service Providers (ISPs). Two years ago, Contoso acquired a London-based modem manufacturer named Trey Research, which targets a similar market in the European countries.

Geography

In addition to its primary location, Contoso also has two branch offices within the United States—one in Atlanta, Georgia, and one in San Francisco, California. Both branches have fully staffed marketing and sales departments, but do not maintain their own IT staff. Instead, they rely on the IT staff at the Dallas headquarters.

The subsidiary office, a company named Trey Research, is in London, England. The London office maintains full corporate facilities, including its own IT staff and control over its own network infrastructure. The London office also maintains its own namespace.

Network Infrastructure

The Dallas headquarters is connected to the Atlanta branch by means of a 256Kb frame relay circuit and to San Francisco by means of a 128Kb frame relay circuit. Dallas is connected to the London headquarters using a 64Kb frame relay circuit. Both the Dallas and London offices are using a 155 Mbps ATM as a backbone. Clients are connected to the backbone via 10/100 Mbps connections. At the branch offices, clients and servers are all connected via 10/100 Mbps connections.

Currently, each location is configured with its own domain, named after the location. Both branch offices and the subsidiary office are configured to trust the Dallas domain. The Dallas domain is also configured to trust each of the other domains.

Future Plans

There are no current plans to significantly expand the workforce at the current location. However, there is a possibility that the company will be acquiring a small, Montreal-based company that owns a promising, new modem technology. In that case, the Montreal-based company will maintain its own IT staff and namespace. Your plans should allow for that.

IT Management

The IT staff in Dallas is in charge of maintaining the Dallas, Atlanta, and San Francisco locations. A separate IT staff in London manages the network there. However, the senior IT staff in Dallas has the ultimate responsibility for the entire network.

Questions

Given the previous scenario, answer the following questions.

1. Draw a geographic map representing the company. What additional information should you gather regarding the links between locations?

   _____

   _____

2. Assuming that you were to restructure the current domain model when designing the new infrastructure (instead of upgrading everything in place), what additional challenges will you face because of the restructuring?

3. Sketch a diagram for the existing domain model, including trust relationships. For each domain, what other documents should you create?

4. Assuming that London will maintain its own namespace and IT administration, how might you structure your Active Directory design?

Chapter Summary

- The four main geographical company models are local, regional, national, and international. The primary differences between these models (aside from political boundaries) are the complexity of the network and the state of the connections between the locations.

- Two types of offices also play into the geographical considerations: branch offices that are controlled by the company and subsidiary offices that are owned by the company, but usually have their own staff and networking policies.

- You should gather as much information as possible on how information is created, stored, and transferred within the organization.

- Assess the current network environment, including information about the subnets, IP addressing, and networking equipment used in each location.

- Create an inventory of the servers and workstations in each location. Include a description of the hardware, software, and services they use. Also note the usage patterns of the systems so that you can gauge the best time for upgrades.

- When analyzing performance requirements, start by fixing any existing problems and making sure configurations are correct. Get a sense of user experiences and expectations and then test the current performance. Revisit these requirements often as you design your plan.

- When gathering information about a current Windows 2000 infrastructure, you should first create a diagram showing the existing domains and their trust relationships.

- For each Windows 2000 domain, create a diagram of OU structure and a diagram showing site structure and domain controller placement.

- When gathering information about a Windows NT 4.0 infrastructure, create a diagram showing domains and trust relationships. For each domain, gather information on the domain controllers, users, and resources in the domain.

Exam Highlights

Before taking the exam, review the key topics and terms that are presented in this chapter. You need to know this information.

Key Points

- The basic geographic locations and the connections between them govern the physical structure of a network. This includes how IP addressing and routing works, how Active Directory sites are structured, and how network traffic is controlled.

- The administrative and political makeup of a company governs the logical structure of a network. This includes how trees and domains are structured, the trust relationships between domains, and how domains are broken into OUs.

- The key to the functional level of a network is the interoperability requirements between Windows Server 2003 and previous versions of Windows. If all domain controllers run Windows 2003, all features are available. If Windows 2000 domain controllers exist, fewer features are available. If Windows NT 4.0 domain controllers exist, the fewest features are available.

- Your design will impact the network in terms of having to upgrade servers to support the new operating system, upgrade capacity to support increased network traffic, and include down time for the network while the plan is being implemented.

Key Terms

Centralized/Decentralized   A centralized administration model requires fewer OUs and lets you design a simpler structure. A decentralized model usually requires more organization units and sometimes more domains.

WAN Link   A connection between LANs in different locations. WAN links are slower, less reliable, and more expensive than the connections within a LAN. A key goal in designing a network is optimizing the flow of traffic over WAN links.

Functional Level   The feature set available to a domain or forest based on the version of Windows that domain controllers in the domain or forest are running. Older versions mean fewer features.

Questions and Answers

Page
2-11

Lesson 1 Review

1. Aside from network connection issues, what are three complicating factors exhibited by an international company?

   Difference in languages, laws, export regulations, and tariffs are just a few of the issues an international company must contend with.

2. What is the difference between a branch and a subsidiary office?

   The essential difference between a branch and a subsidiary office is that the branch office is controlled by the company, while the subsidiary office (while owned by the company) is more autonomous and may follow its own policies.

3. You are preparing a geographic map for a company that has three locations within the same state. The link between two of the locations is a dedicated T1 line. The third location links to only one of the first two locations and that link is a 64Kb line. What geographical model would this fall into?

   The slow 64Kb link would make network design considerably more complex and would make this company a national model. If all locations connected via high-speed links, this company would likely be a regional model.

Page
2-16

Lesson 2 Review

1. What types of information should you gather when inventorying a server?

   You should first gather information about the server's hardware, including the brand of the computer and the types and capacities of components such as the motherboard, memory, disk subsystem, and peripherals. You should also gather information on the operating system, installed services, and applications.

2. For each subnet on your network, identify the major IP addressing components you will need to record.

   You will need to list the network ID, subnet mask, default gateway, and additional information such as DNS servers. You also must determine whether DHCP is used and how it is configured for the subnet.

3. Identify the two major tools used to analyze performance on a Windows network.

   The Performance console (named Performance Monitor on earlier versions of Windows) is used to track resource utilization on a computer. Network Monitor is used to capture and analyze local network traffic.

Lesson 3 Practice

1. Sketch a diagram of the current Windows NT domain structure.

   The current domain structure follows geographic boundaries, so you should sketch a diagram that shows one resource domain for each city and a single domain containing all user accounts, similar to the one below. You should also include the two-way trust relationships between domains in your diagram.

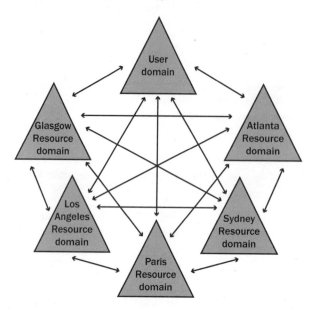

2. What requirements does Northwind Traders have for autonomy and isolation?

   Based on the information in the scenario, Glasgow needs data and service isolation. Los Angeles wants isolation, but probably only needs autonomy.

3. What are Northwind Traders' administrative goals?

   They want centralized control from Paris and some decentralized administration in Los Angeles. Glasgow will maintain its own IT infrastructure.

Lesson 3 Review

1. You are designing an Active Directory structure for a network that is currently using Windows NT 4.0. There are 12 servers running Windows NT 4.0 and 300 workstations running mixtures of Windows 98, Windows NT 4.0 Workstation, and Windows XP Professional. The entire network is housed in a single building. There are currently three Windows NT 4.0 domains—one for each of the major departments of the company. Each department manages resources in its own domain. What is one method of reducing the complexity of the existing network while still allowing members of each department administrative control over resources in their department?

The obvious choice in this situation would be to use a single domain for the company and then create an OU for each department. Even if the entire network was not in one location, you could still create a single domain and use sites to control traffic over a slower WAN connection.

2. You are gathering information about the current domain model of a network running Windows 2000 and Active Directory. You have created a domain map that shows every domain and the trust relationships between those domains. What other documents should you prepare for each domain when assessing the current model?

You should create a document for each domain that shows how the OUs are structured within the domain. You should also gather information about the objects and permissions assigned to each OU. You will also need to create a document for each domain that shows how sites are structured within the domain and the domain controller placement in those sites.

3. List several advantages of keeping an existing Windows NT 4.0 domain model intact when you upgrade to Windows 2003.

There are a number of advantages to this method. All existing domain objects are upgraded to the Active Directory model. Users keep their existing passwords and profiles. The implementation process is faster. System security policies are retained.

Page
2-28

Case Scenario Exercise

1. Draw a geographic map representing the company. What additional information should you gather regarding the links between locations?

The geographic map should represent the Dallas headquarters, both branch locations, and the subsidiary locations. You should indicate on the map the types of connections between each location. In addition to the information presented, you should find out the vendor and cost of each connection. You should also determine the current usage of the WAN links and estimate the available bandwidth.

2. Assuming that you were to restructure the current domain model when designing the new infrastructure (instead of upgrading everything in place), what additional challenges will you face because of the restructuring?

You will have to recreate user profiles and passwords. You will most likely have to redesign system security policies. The implementation will take considerably longer and there will be more downtime for users.

3. Sketch a diagram for the existing domain model, including trust relationships. For each domain, what other documents should you create?

The existing model is a fairly simple one. Each location on the network (the headquarters, both branch offices, and the subsidiary office) is currently in its own domain. Two-way trust relationships are configured between the Dallas domain and every other domain. For each domain, you should also gather information about the servers and services in the domain, the number of users, and members of the domain administrators global group.

4. Assuming that London will maintain its own namespace and IT administration, how might you structure your Active Directory design?

One method that should work pretty well is to create one domain for the headquarters and both branch offices. Because there is a central IT staff in the Dallas headquarters, the OU structure could also be pretty simple. You can use sites to control replication traffic between the locations. Because the London office needs to maintain its own namespace, you will need to create a separate domain tree for that office and give it its own domain. Both the domain trees can be part of the same forest. The domain at the Dallas headquarters should be the forest root domain.

3 Planning an Active Directory Structure

Exam Objectives in this Chapter:

- Design the Active Directory infrastructure to meet business and technical requirements
  - Create the conceptual design of the Active Directory forest structure
  - Create the conceptual design of the Active Directory domain structure
- Design an Active Directory naming strategy
  - Identify Internet domain name registration requirements
  - Specify the use of hierarchical namespace within Active Directory
  - Identify NetBIOS naming requirements

Why This Chapter Matters

Once you have gathered information about a company and network, it is time to turn your attention to designing an Active Directory structure that meets the company's needs. Creating a solid Active Directory design is essential to building a network that meets the current needs of your company and can scale to meet future needs as well. Choices you make during the design phase are often choices you will have a hard time correcting later, so take your time to create a good plan, review it, and revise it as necessary.

Creating this plan involves determining the number of domains you must use and whether you can keep those domains confined to a single-domain tree or forest. You will also decide on a naming strategy for the domains and other elements of Microsoft Active Directory directory service.

Lessons in this Chapter:

Before You Begin

To complete this chapter, make sure you are familiar with the Active Directory concepts described in Chapter 1, "Introduction to Active Directory and Network Infrastructure." You should also have gathered and analyzed any information about the existing Active Directory infrastructure of your company, as discussed in Chapter 2, "Analyzing an Existing Infrastructure."

Lesson 1: Designing a Forest and Domain Model

The first step in designing an Active Directory structure is to identify the overall forest and domain model the network should use. This includes figuring out whether you can use one domain or need to create multiple domains. You'll also decide whether you must create multiple domain trees or even multiple forests.

After this lesson, you will be able to

■ Create the conceptual design of the Active Directory forest structure.

■ Distinguish the various forest and domain models and their purposes.

■ Decide on a forest and domain model for a given situation.

Estimated lesson time: 40 minutes

Using a Single Domain

The simplest Active Directory model is a single domain, as shown in Figure 3-1. The vast majority of networks in the world are able to use a single domain, so although it may not seem quite as sophisticated as the other models, you should give using a single domain serious consideration in most situations. In fact, a useful exercise in planning an Active Directory structure is to *always* start out assuming that you'll use a single domain and then challenge yourself to keep it that way. This is a good method for distinguishing the impulse to create a more complicated structure from the actual need to do so.

contoso.com

Figure 3-1   A typical single-domain model

In the single-domain model, all objects are located within the same security boundaries, so you won't have to worry about planning trust relationships with other domains or implementing cross-domain authentication and permissions. It is also much easier to support a strong, centralized IT staff when using a single domain.

When using a single-domain model, user and group planning is simpler, as is the implementation of group policy. In fact, almost all management functions are simpler—and simpler means less planning, less administration, less troubleshooting, and a lower total cost in the end.

Active Directory domains are scalable and can grow much larger than Windows NT domains, which removes a significant obstacle that prevented the use of single-domain networks in structures based on Windows NT, in which the Security Accounts Manager (SAM) could support only up to 40,000 objects in a domain. By contrast, an Active Directory domain can hold more than one million objects. The scalability of the Active Directory domain is further achieved through the use of two elements: organizational units (OUs) and sites.

When using a single-domain model, you rely on OUs to delegate administrative permissions over objects in the domain. Organizational units represent the smallest unit of administrative control in Active Directory. This differs from Windows NT domains (where the domain was the smallest administrative unit), so the need to define domains just for delegation of administrative tasks is eliminated. OUs are essentially containers into which you can place the objects of a domain. You can then assign administrative permissions to the OU. You can even nest OUs (create OUs inside other OUs) for further control.

Typically, the structure of OUs follows an organization's business or functional structure. For example, you might create an organizational unit for each major geographic location, so that local administrators can control resources in those locations—all while still functioning within a single domain. Figure 3-2 shows a single domain broken into organizational units for this purpose. You will learn more about planning organizational units in Chapter 4, "Designing an Organizational Unit Structure."

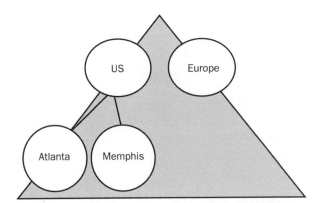

Figure 3-2   Using organizational units to divide administrative tasks by geographic location

Whereas organizational units are used to break up a domain logically to delegate administrative authority, sites are used to break up a domain physically to control replication traffic between domain controllers that are separated by wide area network (WAN) links. A site is a group of domain controllers that exist on one or more Internet Protocol (IP) subnets and are connected by a fast, reliable network connection. Fast means connections of at least 1 Mbps. In other words, a site usually follows a local area network's (LAN) boundaries. If different LANs on the network are connected by a

WAN, you'll likely create one site for each LAN. You'll learn more about planning sites and domain controller placement in Chapter 5, "Designing a Site Plan."

> ### Real World   Simple Structures
>
> Throughout this section (and throughout most of the book), you'll notice one idea repeated often: Keep your design as simple as you can get away with. Every additional element you add to your design complicates the deployment and administration of the network that much more, and this complication compounds as you add more complex elements. For example, just deciding to use two domains instead of a single domain increases overhead. Add another domain tree and you're forced to deal with not only additional domains, but a new naming structure as well. Add another forest and, well, you get the idea.
>
> It is a natural human impulse to want to organize complex situations by dividing and categorizing. You're likely to find yourself thinking, "Well, there are two departments and I could create two domains just to make things neat and tidy." Resist this impulse. Remember that the two most important reasons for using multiple domains from the pre-Active Directory days are gone. First, Active Directory domains do not have a real limit on the number of users or resources they can hold. Second, the use of sites to control replication over lower-speed WAN links means that domains no longer have to be used for that purpose. It is entirely possible to use a single domain on complex networks that span multiple geographic locations.
>
> If you need a more complicated structure because of the political, technical, or administrative climate of a company, try your best to let that complexity settle to the bottom of the Active Directory structure. Using more organizational units is better than using more domains. Using more domains is better than using more trees. Using more trees is better than using more forests. Add complexity at higher levels only when there is a technical necessity to do so.

Using Multiple Domains

Whereas the single-domain model offers the strong advantage of simplicity, there are times when you need to use multiple domains. When you need to use multiple domains, it is best to try to plan domains so that they are all in the same domain tree. Since all domains in a tree share a contiguous namespace, the administrative overhead is significantly less than using multiple trees.

When defining multiple domains, it is best to define the domain boundaries according to company boundaries that are least likely to change. For example, creating domains according to geographical boundaries is usually a safer bet than creating domains according to different departments because departments are more likely to change than are geographic locations. Figure 3-3 shows multiple domains organized according to geography. Although you can define domain boundaries based on any criteria (Figure 3-4 shows multiple domains organized according to department), you'll often find that using OUs or even groups to create those boundaries is a better choice.

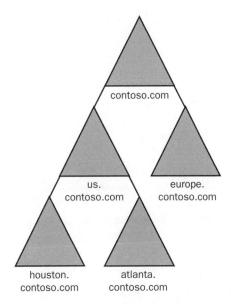

Figure 3-3   Multiple domains organized by geography

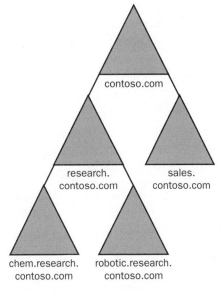

Figure 3-4   Multiple domains organized by function

There are a number of reasons that you might need to define multiple domains. These reasons include the following:

- You need to implement different domain-level security policies. Certain policies can only be controlled at the domain level. For example, one department may enforce tighter password policies or account lockout policies than another department.

- You need to provide decentralized administration. This is particularly true of companies that maintain a presence in different geographic locations. Each location may have its own information technology (IT) staff that needs to manage resources in that location. Each domain's owners can create, remove, back up, and restore domain controllers, and may even be responsible for determining the structure and policies of their own location.

- You need to optimize replication traffic across WAN links more than you can by dividing a domain into multiple sites. For a domain to function, there must be replication between the domain controllers in that domain. Even if you partition a domain into multiple sites to control replication traffic between controllers, you may have WAN links that are just too slow or unreliable to properly handle the replication traffic. In such a case, you may want to create a different domain for that location.

- You need to provide a different namespace for different locations, departments, or functions. Even though domains in the same tree form a contiguous namespace, there may be a need to distinguish between two structures in the namespace. For example, you may find that supporting two slightly different namespaces such as hr.contoso.com and sales.contoso.com is more efficient than using a single namespace like contoso.com.

- You need to retain an existing Windows NT domain architecture. If you need to maintain the Windows NT domains that already exist on a network, you'll have no choice but to use multiple Active Directory domains.

- You want to put the schema master in a different domain than the domains that contain users or other resources. Although you can restrict unauthorized access to the schema using normal means, the schema is an awfully important resource in an Active Directory network. To provide higher security, you can place the computer that fills the schema master role in its own domain.

Exam Tip   Deciding whether to use multiple domains or to use organizational units to delegate administration is an art and one you'll have to practice for the exam. In general, keep in mind that the best course is usually to push for complexity at the lower levels. Use multiple organizational units unless you must meet one of the specific requirements for using multiple domains listed in this section.

Whereas there are many advantages to using multiple domains, and there are times you won't be able to avoid it, you should keep in mind that using multiple domains also has some drawbacks. The costs involved in implementing multiple domains include the following:

- Each domain requires one domain controller, and organizations that require fault tolerance or load balancing require at least two domain controllers for each domain. Thus, there is added expense, increased initial deployment time, and increased administrative burden in the form of extra domain controllers for each additional domain you create.

- Group policy and access control are applied at the domain level. Each additional domain you create means having to apply those security measures on the new domain. Although it is not too difficult to support group policies or delegate administration across many domains, there is additional planning and management required.

- Two-way transitive trust relationships are created automatically between parent and child domains when the child domain is created. This means that authentication happens automatically. However, you may need to set up shortcut trusts between domains that are distant in the domain hierarchy but between which authentication needs to occur regularly. Also, although trusts are configured automatically, access to resources between domains is not. You'll have to plan and implement interdomain resource access manually using security groups. See Chapter 4 for more on using groups.

- By default, only members of the Enterprise Admins group are given administrative rights across domains. You'll have to add additional administrative rights manually. Each time a domain is added, a Domain Admins global group is also added. Monitoring the membership of this group requires additional administration.

- If a user from one domain logs on in a second domain, the domain controller for the second domain must be able to contact the domain controller in the user's home domain. In the event the domain controllers cannot communicate, the user is likely to experience a loss of service. You'll have to configure more trust links to solve this problem, which increases the necessary setup and maintenance.

Real World   Choosing a Forest Root Domain

A forest root domain is the first domain you create in an Active Directory forest; it provides the foundation for the forest structure. Every other domain you create in the forest, even in different domain trees, derives its distinguished name and default domain name system (DNS) name from the forest root domain name.

When planning the forest root domain, you have two choices. You can either use an existing domain or create a dedicated domain. Using an existing domain means that the forest root domain also contains other resources such as users and groups. If you're using a single-domain model, this is your only choice. If you are using multiple domains, you can also create a domain that is dedicated to being the forest root domain and does not hold other resources. The primary advantage to this is that the domain administrators in the forest root can more easily regulate membership in the Enterprise Admins and Schema Admins universal groups. Another advantage is that, because the dedicated root domain doesn't represent a particular location or function, it is better isolated from changes to a company's structure. Yet another advantage is that the forest root domain will be smaller (because it does not house other resources), so you can more easily replicate it across the enterprise to provide fault tolerance.

Although Windows Server 2003 provides tools that let you safely rename domains (even the root domain), it's not a particularly simple process and it's much better to get it right during the planning phase. You should also be aware that, whereas you can rename the forest domain, you cannot change *which* domain is the forest root.

Using Multiple Trees Within a Forest

A domain tree is a hierarchical arrangement of domains that share a contiguous namespace. The first domain you create in a tree becomes the tree root domain and any domain you add to the tree becomes a child of that root. Determining whether a forest needs multiple trees is actually not too complicated a process. There is really one overriding reason why you would want to use multiple domain trees, and that is if you need to support multiple DNS namespaces in a forest. As such, using multiple trees also represents a good way to merge separate forests to take advantage of a common schema and global catalog, yet maintain separate namespaces. Figure 3-5 shows two separate namespaces in two separate trees.

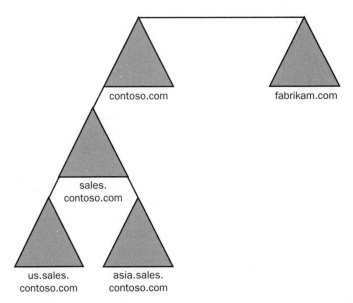

Figure 3-5   Using two trees to facilitate separate namespaces

Exam Tip   Although you may come up with other reasons to use multiple trees in a forest in real life, there is only one good reason to make use of multiple trees on the exam: You require more than one DNS namespace.

Although the decision to use multiple trees is based on the necessity for distinct namespace (and therefore a decision that pretty much makes itself), there are some disadvantages to using multiple trees that you should be aware of. These disadvantages include the following:

■ Because each tree requires a separate DNS name, the IT staff is responsible for maintaining more DNS names than are needed for a single-domain model.

■ More trees mean more domains because each tree must have at least one domain. Therefore, all the issues concerning the use of multiple domains apply.

■ Non-Microsoft lightweight directory access protocol (LDAP) clients may not be able to perform a global catalog search and instead may need to perform a separate LDAP search within each tree. This decreases the perceived response time for the client.

With these disadvantages in mind, it is worthwhile to consider whether it is a viable alternative to consolidate the namespace and use a single tree with different domains instead of using multiple trees. Although some loss of namespace distinction occurs, the benefits might outweigh this loss. Figure 3-6 shows the same environment from Figure 3-5 reorganized into a single tree.

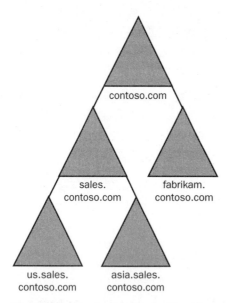

Figure 3-6 Separate namespaces reorganized under a single tree

Using Multiple Forests

A forest is a group of one or more domain trees that do not form a contiguous namespace but share a common schema, directory configuration, global catalog, and automatic two-way transitive trust relationships between domains. There is always at least one forest on a network, and it is created when the first domain controller on a network is installed. The first domain created becomes the forest root domain.

Forests represent the ultimate security boundaries. No administrative control or user access is possible between forests unless the permission is explicitly configured. This configuration happens using a type of trust new to Windows Server 2003 named the forest trust, which is used for managing the security relationship between two forests. This new feature simplifies cross-forest security administration by allowing all domains in one forest to trust all domains in another forest through the use of transitive trust relationships. However, the forest trust is not transitive at the forest level. In other words, if one forest trusts a second, and the second forest trusts a third, the first forest does not automatically trust the third forest. You should also be aware that the use of forest trusts requires that both forests be raised to Windows 2003 functional level, which means all domain controllers in both forests must be running Windows Server 2003.

By and large, you should strive to avoid using multiple forests if at all possible. Nonetheless, there are a few situations for which you might need to implement multiple forests. These situations include:

- Linking two existing separate organizations. Whether because of merger or acquisition, you might find that two completely separate forests need to be linked together to share resources. This link might be a temporary situation while one forest is migrated into another, or it might be a more permanent situation in which both companies need to remain relatively autonomous.

- Creating an autonomous unit. Because forests represent the ultimate security boundary, you can use a separate forest to create a network where the administration must be largely independent of the primary forest. In this situation, the IT staff of the separate forest can maintain and modify the schema without consequence to other forests—useful if a group needs to install or test directory-enabled applications (or otherwise modify the directory structure) without depending on the central IT staff or if you want to deploy a pilot Active Directory rollout. In an autonomous forest, authority still resides with the central IT staff, but the administrators of the autonomous forest are granted a degree of flexibility.

- Creating an isolated unit. An isolated forest differs from an autonomous forest mainly in the level of control by administrators outside the forest. An isolated forest is assured that no administrator outside the forest can interfere with the management of the isolated forest. This is useful in situations where high security or meeting legal requirements are necessary.

Before planning to implement multiple forests, you must understand that much of the functionality that is available within the scope of a single forest is not available between forests. Maintaining multiple forests also requires significantly more administration than maintaining a single forest.

The disadvantages of a multiforest design include the following:

- Users require more training in how to find resources. Searching for resources within the bounds of a single forest is relatively simple from the user perspective, thanks to the global catalog. Using more than one forest means using more than one global catalog and users are forced to specify which forest they want to search when looking for resources.

- Users logging on to computers in forests outside their own must use the default user principal name when logging on. This requires extra training for those users.

- Additional IT staff must often be employed to monitor and manage a separate forest, which requires the cost of training more IT professionals and the cost of their time invested in these activities.

- Administrators need to keep up with multiple schemas.

- There are separate configuration containers for each forest. Topology changes need to be replicated to other forests.

- Any replication of information between forests must be manually configured.

- Administrators have to configure DNS name resolution across forest boundaries to provide domain controller and resource location functionality.

- Administrators have to configure the access control lists of resources to allow access to appropriate groups from different forests as well as create new groups to accommodate forest roles across forests.

Exam Tip   When you are thinking about the information provided in an exam question and trying to determine whether or not multiple forests are necessary, the chances are they are not. Using multiple forests is strongly discouraged except when autonomy or isolation is necessary. Normally, it is much better to create multiple domain trees within a single forest. However, because forest links are new to Windows Server 2003, you will likely encounter some questions that feature their use.

Practice: Creating a Forest and Domain Model

In this practice, you will create a forest and domain design for Northwind Traders. If you are unable to answer a question, review the lesson materials and try the question again. You can find answers to the questions in the "Questions and Answers" section at the end of this chapter.

Scenario

Northwind Traders manufactures a line of network appliances designed to help companies improve their data transmission capabilities. Northwind Traders currently uses a Microsoft Windows NT 4.0 master domain model. In recent years, the company has undergone significant growth and expansion and expects substantial growth during the next three years, including growth in market share, revenue, and number of employees. In addition to opening two new offices, the executive management has committed to implementing a new Windows Server 2003 Active Directory design to meet the current and future needs of the company.

The following table shows the geographical locations, the departments residing in each location, and the number of users in each of the locations.

Location	Departments Represented	Number of Users
Paris	Headquarters (HQ) Management staff Finance Sales Marketing Production Research Development Information Technology (IT)	2,000

Location	Departments Represented	Number of Users
Los Angeles	Sales Marketing Finance IT	1,000
Atlanta	Customer Service Customer Support Training	750
Glasgow, Scotland	Research Development Sustained Engineering IT	750
Sydney, Australia	Consulting Production Sales Finance	500

Most of the company's computing services are hosted in its Paris corporate headquarters. The corporate IT department wants to have central control of passwords and security settings. The local IT department in Los Angeles wants to maintain control of its infrastructure without interference from the corporate IT department. The local IT department in Glasgow demands exclusive control over their own environment due to security concerns about their research and development (R&D) data. Corporate management shares security concerns about the R&D data and wants to ensure that it is not compromised.

The following diagram shows the connectivity between the different locations of the company. In addition, Los Angeles and Atlanta have virtual private network (VPN) connections through the Internet to headquarters in Paris.

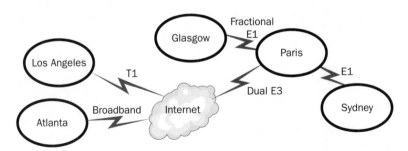

Practice Questions

Based on the scenario, answer the following questions.

1. What forest model would you propose? How many forests would you use? Why?

   _____

   _____

2. Draw a diagram of your proposed domain design for Northwind Traders.

Lesson Review

The following questions are intended to reinforce key information presented in this lesson. If you are unable to answer a question, review the lesson materials and try the question again. You can find answers to the questions in the "Questions and Answers" section at the end of this chapter.

1. You are designing the forest model for a company and are considering whether to use a single domain or multiple domains. What are some reasons you might need to use multiple domains?

   _____

   _____

2. Why might you designate a dedicated domain as the forest root domain for a company?

   _____

   _____

3. What is the primary reason for using multiple domain trees on a network? What are the disadvantages?

   _____

   _____

4. What are the reasons you might need to implement multiple forests?

   _____

   _____

Lesson Summary

- Use a single domain whenever possible because it is by far the simplest structure to plan, deploy, and maintain.

- Use multiple domains when you need to implement different security policies, provide decentralized administration, optimize replication traffic, or retain an existing domain structure.

- Use multiple domain trees when you need to support multiple DNS namespaces.

- Use multiple forests when you need to provide support for multiple distinct companies or when you need to provide autonomy or isolation to a unit within a company.

Lesson 2: Defining a Naming Strategy

Once you have decided how to create the structure of your forest and domains, turn your attention to the naming of the elements in that structure. This lesson looks at the use of the Lightweight Directory Access Protocol (LDAP), at the various names used in Active Directory, and at how to create a naming strategy for your network.

After this lesson, you will be able to

- Explain the naming conventions used in Active Directory.
- Identify Internet domain name registration requirements.
- Identify NetBIOS naming requirements.
- Create a naming structure for an Active Directory environment.

Estimated lesson time: 20 minutes

Active Directory Naming and LDAP

The LDAP is a standardized protocol used by clients to look up information in a directory. An LDAP-aware directory service (such as Active Directory) indexes all the attributes of all the objects stored in the directory and publishes them. LDAP-aware clients can query the server in a wide variety of ways.

Every object in Active Directory is an instance of a class defined in the Active Directory schema. Each class has attributes that ensure unique identification of every object in the directory. To accomplish this, Active Directory relies on a naming convention that lets objects be stored logically and accessed by clients by a standardized method. Both users and applications are affected by the naming conventions that a directory uses. To locate a network resource, you'll need to know its name or one of its properties. Active Directory supports several types of names for the different formats that can access Active Directory.

These names include:

- Relative Distinguished Names
- Distinguished Names
- User Principal Names
- Canonical Names

Relative Distinguished Names

The relative distinguished name (RDN) of an object identifies an object uniquely, but only within its parent container. Thus the name uniquely identifies the object *relative* to the other objects within the same container. In the example

CN=wjglenn,CN=Users,DC=contoso,DC=com,

the relative distinguished name of the object is CN=wjglenn. The relative distinguished name of the parent organizational unit is Users. For most objects, the relative distinguished name of an object is the same as that object's Common Name attribute.

Active Directory creates the relative distinguished name automatically, based on information provided when the object is created. Active Directory does not allow two objects with the same relative distinguished name to exist in the same parent container.

The notations used in the relative distinguished name (and in the distinguished name discussed in the next section) use special notations called LDAP attribute tags to identify each part of the name. The three attribute tags used include:

- **DC**   The Domain Component (DC) tag identifies part of the DNS name of the domain, such as COM or ORG.

- **OU**   The Organizational Unit (OU) tag identifies an organizational unit container.

- **CN**   The Common Name (CN) tag identifies the common name configured for an Active Directory object.

Distinguished Names

Each object in the directory has a distinguished name (DN) that is globally unique and identifies not only the object itself, but also where the object resides in the overall object hierarchy. You can think of the distinguished name as the relative distinguished name of an object concatenated with the relative distinguished names of all parent containers that make up the path to the object.

An example of a typical distinguished name would be:

CN=wjglenn,CN=Users,DC=contoso,DC=com.

This distinguished name would indicate that the user object wjglenn is in the Users container, which in turn is located in the contoso.com domain. If the wjglenn object is moved to another container, its DN will change to reflect its new position in the hierarchy. Distinguished names are guaranteed to be unique in the forest, similar to the way that a fully qualified domain name uniquely identifies an object's placement in a DNS hierarchy. You cannot have two objects with the same distinguished name.

Canonical Names

An object's canonical name is used in much the same way as the distinguished name—it just uses a different syntax. The same distinguished name presented in the preceding section would have the canonical name:

contoso.com/Users/wjglenn.

As you can see, there are two primary differences in the syntax of distinguished names and canonical names. The first difference is that the canonical name presents the root of the path first and works downward toward the object name. The second difference is that the canonical name does not use the LDAP attribute tags (e.g., CN and DC).

User Principal Names

The user principal name that is generated for each object is in the form user-name@domain_name. Users can log on with their user principal name, and an administrator can define suffixes for user principal names if desired. User principal names should be unique, but Active Directory does not enforce this requirement. It's best, however, to formulate a naming convention that avoids duplicate user principal names.

Security Identifiers

As you know by now, Active Directory follows the multimaster replication model, in which every replica of the Active Directory partition held on every domain controller is considered an equal master. Updates can be made to objects on any domain controller, and those updates are then replicated to other domain controllers.

The multimaster model works well for most operations, but not for all. Certain operations need to be handled by only one domain controller in each domain, or even in each forest. To perform these special operations, you can designate certain domain controllers as operations masters. You can find an overview of all the operations master roles in Chapter 1. For the purposes of creating a naming strategy, though, there are two operations master roles you need to give special consideration: the domain naming master and the relative ID master. Both of these servers should be available when new security principals are being created and named.

The Domain Naming Master   Only one domain in each forest can assume the role of domain naming master. The domain naming master handles adding and removing domains in a forest; it also generates the unique security identifier (SID) for each domain in the forest. This is the only domain controller from which you can create or delete a domain and you must be a member of the Enterprise Admins group to do so.

By default, the domain naming master is installed on the first domain controller in the forest, and if that domain has only one domain controller, that domain controller holds all the per-forest and per-domain operations master roles (operations masters are also known as flexible single master operations or FSMO).

The Relative ID Master   The relative identifier (RID) master allocates sequences of RIDs to each of the domain controllers in its domain. Whereas the schema master and domain naming master perform forestwide functions, one RID master is assigned per domain. Because each domain controller can create objects in Active Directory, the RID master allocates to each domain controller a pool of 500 RIDs from which to draw when creating the object. When a domain controller has used more than 400 RIDs, the RID master gives it another batch of 500 RIDs.

Creating the Naming Strategy

Creating a naming strategy requires that you think about the naming requirements both from an Active Directory and a DNS standpoint. Clients use DNS to resolve the IP address of servers providing important Active Directory network services, so it follows that Active Directory and DNS are inextricably linked.

> **Note**   You'll find lots of good advice on creating a DNS strategy in Chapter 6, "Designing a DNS Structure," so this chapter won't focus on DNS except to touch on how it affects your Active Directory naming strategy.

In DNS, names are arranged hierarchically and build as you move from parent domains to child domains. For example, a domain named contoso.com might have a child domain named sales.contoso.com. That domain, in turn, might have a child named europe.sales.contoso.com. Each domain is named according to the full path of domain names that identifies it in the DNS hierarchy all the way up to the root domain (identified by a period).

Active Directory follows the DNS naming convention. When you create the first Active Directory domain, it becomes the root domain for the forest and the root domain for the first domain tree in that forest. That root domain begins the namespace. Each domain you add under that root gets its name from its parent domain and the hierarchy it fits into.

All Active Directory domain names are identified by a DNS name as well as by another name called a Network Basic Input/Output System (NetBIOS) name, a legacy naming system used on earlier Windows systems and still supported in Windows Server 2003. Unlike the hierarchical DNS naming structure, NetBIOS uses a flat namespace; each resource on the network (domains, computers, and so on) has a single name that can be resolved to an IP address. When you install Windows and name a computer, it is a NetBIOS name you are supplying. Windows automatically generates a NetBIOS name for each service running on a computer by appending the computer name with an extra character. Domains are also given a NetBIOS name.

With the advent of DNS as the primary naming system for Active Directory, NetBIOS names have taken on a secondary importance. However, NetBIOS names are still supported and used. DNS simply uses the computer name as the relative distinguished name and appends the DNS domain hierarchy to create the fully qualified domain name.

The following is an example of NetBIOS and DNS names that are given to the same domain:

- **NetBIOS name**   SALES

- **Fully Qualified Domain Name (FQDN)**   sales.contoso.com

Generally, the NetBIOS name is the same as the first naming component in the DNS name. However, a NetBIOS name can be only 16 characters in length, and the last character is reserved to specify the type of NetBIOS service. Each name in the DNS naming convention can have up to 64 characters, which means DNS names longer than 15 characters cannot be used as NetBIOS names without being truncated.

During installation, you can configure each name to meet your needs. This means that you can specify a NetBIOS and DNS name that are different for a single domain. However, keep in mind that a good design should preclude this option just because having more than one name for a single entity is bound to be confusing. If you are creating a new Active Directory design, create DNS names that fit the NetBIOS naming conventions (i.e., limit DNS names to 15 characters). If you are creating a design for an existing network in which DNS names are used that don't comply with NetBIOS naming conventions, though, you do have the option to use different names. The problem with this approach is mainly a possibility of introducing confusion for the managers and users of the network. If you are forced to use different names, you should at least make sure that the names are similar enough to avoid confusion.

Supporting Registered DNS Names

Since Active Directory and DNS namespaces are linked and you are almost certain to be connecting most networks to the Internet, you need to take into account how your naming strategy fits into the Internet namespace and works with the company's registered DNS name.

You have several options at your disposal, including:

- Use the registered DNS name of the company as the name of the Active Directory root domain. This is the most common configuration and the one recommended most often by Microsoft. It is also the easiest option to plan and implement. The only real drawback to this method is that it requires that your DNS system be able to use service (SRV) records, which may be an issue if you are running DNS servers on platforms other than Windows 2003 servers.

> **Exam Tip**   Because using the registered DNS name as the name of the Active Directory root domain is the choice recommended by Microsoft, you should start any related exam questions by assuming that this is the choice you will make and then look for requirements that might change your mind. Usually, these requirements are security needs that are met by using a subdomain of the registered name as the root domain.

- Use a subdomain of the registered DNS name as the root domain for Active Directory. For example, a company might have the registered name fabrikam.com. You could use a subdomain of that (e.g., internal.fabrikam.com) as the root domain for the forest. You could then use another DNS zone to hold resource records for public hosts. This method provides an additional level of security because Active Directory data is separated from public resources.

- Use a different internal and external name. This option is really only a possibility if you do not plan to connect a network to the Internet and use a registered DNS name. Given that domain name registration is a simple process, you are almost always better off using a registered name, even if you do not host any publicly available resources.

Choosing Domain Names

Although it is possible to change domain names after deployment, it can be difficult. It's better just to get things right from the start. When you are deciding on domain names to use, keep the following guidelines in mind:

- Use only Internet standard characters, including: a–z, 0–9, and hyphen (-). Although the Windows Server 2003 implementation of DNS supports other characters, using standard characters ensures interoperability with other DNS implementations.

- Use short domain names that are easily identifiable and that conform to NetBIOS naming requirements.

- Use only registered domain names as the base for your root. Even if you don't use the registered DNS domain as the forest root name, it will help prevent confusion. For example, a company might have the registered domain contoso.com. Even if you don't use contoso.com as the root domain name for your forest, you should still use a name that is derived from that name (e.g., sales.contoso.com).

- Do not use the same domain name twice. Even though it is possible to use the same domain name on networks that do not communicate (e.g., you could create a domain named microsoft.com on a private network not connected to the Internet), it is not a good practice. It always causes confusion at some point.

- For added security, create separate external and internal namespaces to help prevent unauthorized access to private resources. Base the internal name on the external name (e.g., contoso.com and local.contoso.com) rather than creating separate names.

Naming Security Principals

Security principal objects are Active Directory objects that are assigned security identifiers so that they can be used to log on to the network and be granted access to domain resources. An administrator needs to provide names for security principal objects (user accounts, computer accounts, and groups) that are unique within a domain. Thus, you need to design a naming strategy that allows for this.

When an administrator adds a new user account to the directory, the administrator must provide the following information:

- A name the user must use to log on to the network

- The name of the domain that contains the user account

- Other attributes such as first name, last name, telephone number, and so on

Ideally, you should create a naming strategy that provides a method for creating the names in a consistent manner. The names of security principal objects can contain all Unicode characters *except* certain special LDAP characters that include: a leading space, a trailing space, and any of the following characters: # , + " \ < >.

In addition to these character exclusions, security principal names must conform to the following guidelines:

- User account names can be a maximum of 20 characters.

- Computer account names can be a maximum of 15 characters.

- Group account names can be a maximum of 63 characters.

In addition, security principal names cannot consist only of periods, spaces, or the at (@) sign. Any leading periods or spaces typed into a user name are dropped.

It is possible to use the same security principal name in different domains. For example, you might have a user named wjglenn in the hr.contoso.com domain and in the sales.contoso.com domain. This does not present a problem because each object's distinguished name, relative distinguished name, and canonical name are generated automatically by Active Directory and still uniquely identify each object globally.

Lesson Review

The following questions are intended to reinforce key information presented in this lesson. If you are unable to answer a question, review the lesson materials and try the question again. You can find answers to the questions in the "Questions and Answers" section at the end of this chapter.

1. Describe the components of distinguished names, relative distinguished names, and canonical names, and explain how they are generated.

   _____

   _____

2. What is the difference between DNS and NetBIOS domain names?

   _____

   _____

3. You are deciding how to create a namespace for a company that has the registered DNS name proseware.com. The company is connected to the Internet and hosts several services that are available to the Internet. What two options do you have for building the namespace with regard to the registered DNS name?

   _____

   _____

4. You are planning a network in which there are two domains that hold user accounts. You notice that each domain has a user named Keith Harris. You do not want to violate the naming convention that you have set up for the organization, which would result in both users being given the principal name kharris. Based on this situation, which of the following statements is true?

   a. You can do this with no manual intervention.

   b. You can do this, but you will have to manually change the relative distinguished name of the user object.

   c. You can do this, but you will have to manually change the distinguished name and canonical name of the user object.

   d. Active Directory does not allow two users with the same name to be created in the same forest.

Lesson Summary

- Active Directory supports several types of names: distinguished names, relative distinguished names, canonical names, and user principal names.

- Two operations master roles you need to take into consideration when implementing a naming scheme are: the domain naming master, which handles adding and removing domains; and the relative ID master, which allocates sequences of RIDs to each of the domain controllers in its domain.

- The DNS namespace is hierarchical. The NetBIOS namespace is flat. Names for both are created for each object in Active Directory. NetBIOS names (such as computer and domain names) can only be 15 characters, while DNS names can be up to 64. You should plan for short (15 characters or fewer) names that fit both requirements.

- You have three options for handling registered DNS names. The first is to use the registered DNS name of the company as the name of the Active Directory root domain. The second is to use a subdomain of the registered DNS name as the root domain for Active Directory. The third is to use a different internal and external name, although this option is not recommended.

Case Scenario Exercise

Review the following scenario and complete the questions.

Scenario

You have been selected to plan a new Active Directory structure for Fourth Coffee, a supplier of coffee for restaurants in the southeast United States. Currently, all servers on its network are running Windows NT Server 4.0. Client computers are running a mix of Windows 98 and Windows NT Professional 4.0. Fourth Coffee has hired you to bring the company network infrastructure up to date. They want all servers to run Windows Server 2003 and want to implement Active Directory. They want all client computers to run Windows XP Professional. They would also like to simplify the network infrastructure as much as possible.

Background

Fourth Coffee has grown over the past several years to become one of the leading suppliers of fine coffees to major restaurant and hotel chains. Last year, Fourth Coffee acquired a Jamaican-based coffee grower that it plans to incorporate into its network structure.

Geography

Fourth Coffee's corporate headquarters is in Nashville, Tennessee. In addition to its primary location, Fourth Coffee also has branch offices in Houston, Texas, and Rome, Georgia. Both branches have fully staffed marketing and sales departments, but do not maintain their own IT staff. Instead, they rely on the IT staff at the Nashville headquarters.

The newly acquired coffee grower and exporter, a company named Northwind Traders, is located in Kingston, Jamaica. The Jamaica office maintains full corporate facilities, including its own IT staff. Although the local IT staff manages its own facilities, the network infrastructure comes under the direction of the IT staff in the Nashville headquarters. The Kingston office has its own namespace, northwindtraders.com, and must keep that namespace in your new infrastructure design.

Network Infrastructure

The Nashville headquarters is connected to the Houston branch by means of a 512Kb frame relay link. Nashville is also connected to Rome by means of a 512Kb frame relay link. Nashville is connected to the Kingston headquarters using a 64Kb demand-dial line. At all locations, clients and servers communicate via 10/100 Mbps connections.

Currently, each location is configured with its own Windows NT domain, named after the location. This decision was made primarily to control replication traffic across the WAN links between the headquarters and branch offices. All domains are configured with two-way trust relationships. You do not need to retain any existing domains.

Future Plans

There are no current plans to expand the workforce or for new acquisitions. However, management would like to eventually discontinue the use of the name Northwind Traders and the northwindtraders.com domain name and bring everything under the Fourth Coffee brand. For now, however, the northwindtraders.com namespace must be included in your design.

IT Management

The IT staff in Nashville sets structure and policy requirements for the entire network. They are also responsible for directly managing the Houston and Rome branch offices. A separate IT staff in Kingston manages the network there. However, the senior IT staff in Nashville has ultimate responsibility for the entire network.

Questions

Given the previous scenario, answer the following questions.

1. Draw a geographic map representing the company and identify the forest and domain model you might choose based on the fact that the company wants to simplify the infrastructure as much as possible.

_____

_____

2. List the advantages of using a single domain for the Nashville, Rome, and Houston offices versus creating multiple domains. What would be the advantages of using multiple domains instead?

_____

_____

3. Instead of using a single domain to hold the Nashville, Rome, and Houston offices, you have decided to use a domain for each. You do not want the Rome and Houston offices to appear subsidiary to the Nashville office, but you must use the registered DNS name fourthcoffee.com. Create a domain hierarchy for those offices. What would you choose as your forest root domain?

_____

_____

4. Do the names that you have chosen for the domains in the Active Directory structure meet the requirements for DNS names? For NetBIOS names? If they do not meet one of the requirements, what would be the disadvantage?

_____

_____

Chapter Summary

- Use a single domain whenever possible because it is by far the simplest structure to plan, deploy, and maintain.

- Use multiple domains when you need to implement different security policies, provide decentralized administration, optimize replication traffic, or retain an existing domain structure.

- Use multiple domain trees when you need to support multiple DNS namespaces.

- Use multiple forests when you need to provide support for multiple distinct companies, or when you need to provide autonomy or isolation to a unit within a company.

- Active Directory supports several types of names: distinguished names, relative distinguished names, canonical names, and user principal names.

- Two operations master roles you need to take into consideration when implementing a naming scheme are: the domain naming master, which handles adding and removing domains; and the relative ID master, which allocates sequences of RIDs to each of the domain controllers in its domain.

- The DNS namespace is hierarchical. The NetBIOS namespace is flat. Names for both are created for each object in Active Directory. NetBIOS names (such as computer and domain names) can be only 15 characters, but DNS names can be up to 64. You should plan for short (15 characters or fewer) names that fit both requirements.

- You have three options for handling registered DNS names. The first is to use the registered DNS name of the company as the name of the Active Directory root domain. The second is to use a subdomain of the registered DNS name as the root domain for Active Directory. The third is to use a different internal and external name, although this option is not recommended.

Exam Highlights

Before taking the exam, review the key topics and terms that are presented in this chapter. You need to know this information.

Key Points

- When faced with creating additional domains or additional organizational units, it's best to use additional organizational units unless requirements dictate the use of additional domains.

- Use multiple domain trees only when you need to support more than one DNS namespace in a forest.

- Using multiple forests is strongly discouraged, except under extreme requirements. It is almost always better to create multiple trees in the same forest.

- Using the registered DNS name as the name of the Active Directory root domain is the method favored by Microsoft and likely to be the best choice on exam questions, unless requirements dictate otherwise.

Key Terms

NetBIOS   A flat namespace used as the primary name resolution method in previous versions of Windows. The reliance on DNS by Active Directory has pushed NetBIOS to background importance, but it is still supported and used.

Autonomous/Isolated   An autonomous domain is one that still relies on structure from the central IT staff and domain structure, but needs a certain degree of freedom to modify the Active Directory structure and schema. An isolated domain is one that is autonomous *and* does not rely on or allow access by the rest of the network.

Forest Root Domain   A forest root domain is the first domain you create in an Active Directory forest; it provides the foundation for the forest structure. Every other domain you create in the forest, even in different domain trees, derives its distinguished name and default DNS name from the forest root domain name.

Questions and Answers

Page
3-14

Lesson 1 Practice

1. What forest model would you propose? How many forests would you use? Why?

One solution is to create two forests for Northwind Traders. There are other possible solutions. This solution uses a separate forest for Research and Development because of their data and service isolation needs. The rest of the organization does not require service isolation. Therefore, a single forest will serve the needs of the rest of the organization.

2. Draw a diagram of your proposed domain design for Northwind Traders.

One possible solution is to use a regional domain model and dedicated forest root domains. For the Northwind Traders corporate forest (CORP), five domains are required—one empty root domain and four regional domains. For the R&D forest, only one domain is required.

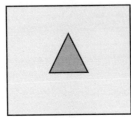
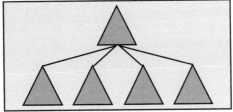

R&D Forest   NWtraders Forest

Page
3-14

Lesson 1 Review

1. You are designing the forest model for a company and are considering whether to use a single domain or multiple domains. What are reasons you might need to use multiple domains?

The reasons for using multiple domains are: to implement different domain-level security policies (password or account policies, for example), to provide decentralized administration with greater local administrative control, to optimize replication traffic over WAN links to a greater degree than sites allow, to distinguish between locations or departments in the namespace, to retain an existing Windows NT 4.0 domain structure, or to put the computer serving as schema master in a different domain than those hosting resources.

2. Why might you designate a dedicated domain as the forest root domain for a company?

The reasons for using a dedicated forest root domain are that the domain administrators in the forest root can regulate membership in the Enterprise Admins and Schema Admins universal groups more easily; that it is better isolated from changes to a company's structure; and that the forest root domain is smaller (because it does not house other resources), so you can more easily replicate it across the enterprise to provide fault tolerance.

3. What is the primary reason for using multiple domain trees on a network? What are the disadvantages?

Pretty much, the only reason to use multiple trees in a forest is when you need to support multiple DNS namespaces. There are two primary disadvantages, which include having to maintain extra DNS resources and having to support more domains.

4. What are the reasons you might need to implement multiple forests?

Forests represent the ultimate security boundaries. No administrative control or user access is possible between forests unless the permission is explicitly configured. For this reason, you can use multiple forests to: support multiple, separate companies; provide administrative autonomy; and create an isolated unit.

Page
3-23

Lesson 2 Review

1. Describe the components of distinguished names, relative distinguished names, and canonical names, and explain how they are generated.

Distinguished names identify an object globally; they contain the common name of the object, the common name of the object's parent containers, and the domain information. Relative distinguished names identify an object within a parent container; they contain only the common name of the object itself. Canonical names work like distinguished names (in that they identify an object globally), but have a different syntax. All three names are generated automatically by Active Directory based on the common name of the object and its parent containers.

2. What is the difference between DNS and NetBIOS domain names?

The DNS namespace is a hierarchy, whereas the NetBIOS namespace is flat. NetBIOS names support the legacy naming resolution in Windows. DNS names can be up to 64 characters, but NetBIOS names can only be 15 characters.

3. You are deciding how to create a namespace for a company that has the registered DNS name proseware.com. The company is connected to the Internet and hosts several services that are available to the Internet. What two options do you have for building the namespace with regard to the registered DNS name?

Your first option is to use the registered DNS name proseware.com as the root domain name for the Active Directory structure. Your second option is to use a subdomain of proseware.com (such as sales.proseware.com) as the root domain name.

4. You are planning a network in which there are two domains that hold user accounts. You notice that each domain has a user named Keith Harris. You do not want to violate the naming convention that you have set up for the organization, which would result in both users being given the principal name kharris. Based on this situation, which of the following statements is true?

    a. You can do this with no manual intervention.

    b. You can do this, but you will have to manually change the relative distinguished name of the user object.

    c. You can do this, but you will have to manually change the distinguished name and canonical name of the user object.

    d. Active Directory does not allow two users with the same name to be created in the same forest.

The correct answer is a.

Page 3-26

Case Scenario Exercise

1. Draw a geographic map representing the company and identify the forest and domain model you might choose based on the fact that the company wants to simplify the infrastructure as much as possible.

The geographic map should represent the Nashville headquarters, both branch locations, and the Kingston location. You should indicate on the map the types of connections between each location. The simplest structure to create would consist of two domain trees, each with one domain. A single domain in one tree named fourthcoffee.com could hold resources for the Nashville headquarters and the Rome and Houston branch offices. You could use sites to control replication traffic between locations. You must create a separate domain tree for the Kingston company, primarily because the northwindtraders namespace must be preserved.

2. List the advantages of using a single domain for the Nashville, Rome, and Houston offices versus creating multiple domains. What would be the advantages of using multiple domains instead?

A single domain would be simpler to create and manage, and would also offer the benefit of a more centralized administration. You could create sites to control replication traffic across WAN links and create organizational units to divide administrative tasks if you need to do that. The advantages of using multiple domains in this situation are that you could gain even more control over replication traffic, and that you could implement separate security requirements for each domain, if necessary.

3. Instead of using a single domain to hold the Nashville, Rome, and Houston offices, you have decided to use a domain for each. You do not want the Rome and Houston offices to appear subsidiary to the Nashville office, but you must use the registered DNS name fourthcoffee.com. Create a domain hierarchy for those offices. What would you choose as your forest root domain?

The best course here is to name the forest root domain using the registered DNS name fourth-coffee.com. Then, make each of the three locations a child domain of that root domain, as shown in Figure 3-7.

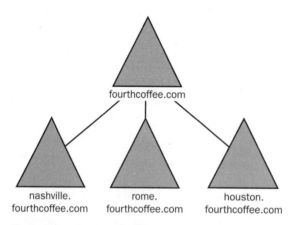

Figure 3-7   The fourthcoffee.com domain hierarchy

4. Do the names that you have chosen for the domains in the Active Directory structure meet the requirements for DNS names? For NetBIOS names? If they do not meet one of the requirements, what would be the disadvantage?

The name fourthcoffee meets both the DNS and NetBIOS naming requirements, which are 64 characters and 15 characters respectively. The name northwindtraders (which comes in at 16 characters) does not meet NetBIOS naming requirements. You could use different DNS and NetBIOS names and, in this case, the ramifications might not be too great. Normally, the biggest problem with configuring different names lies in introducing confusion for administrators and users. However, in this case, you could alleviate that concern to some degree by simply cutting off a character of the name and making the NetBIOS name northwindtrader.

4 Designing an Administrative Security Structure

Exam Objectives in this Chapter:

- Design the Active Directory infrastructure to meet business and technical requirements
    - ❑ Create the conceptual design of the organizational unit (OU) structure
- Design an OU structure
    - ❑ Identify the Group Policy requirements for the OU structure
    - ❑ Design an OU structure for the purpose of delegating authority
- Design a user and computer account strategy
    - ❑ Specify account policy requirements
    - ❑ Specify account requirements for users, computers, administrators, and services
- Design a security group strategy
    - ❑ Define the scope of a security group to meet requirements
    - ❑ Define resource access requirements
    - ❑ Define administrative access requirements
    - ❑ Define user roles
- Design a user and computer authentication strategy
    - ❑ Identify common authentication requirements
    - ❑ Select authentication mechanisms
    - ❑ Optimize authentication by using shortcut trust relationships
- Design a strategy for Group Policy implementation.
    - ❑ Design the administration of Group Policy Objects (GPOs)
    - ❑ Design the deployment strategy of GPOs
    - ❑ Create a strategy for configuring the user environment with Group Policy
    - ❑ Create a strategy for configuring the computer environment with Group Policy

Why This Chapter Matters

In the previous chapter, you learned how to design the Active Directory structure for an organization. This design involved determining the number of domains you must use and whether you can keep those domains confined to a single domain tree or forest. Once that phase of your design is finished, it is time to turn your attention to planning the administrative security structure of each domain. You'll use information you gathered about the company and the information technology (IT) staff to determine how best to delegate administrative authority within domains.

The first step in designing an administrative security structure is planning the use of organizational units (OUs) within each domain. The next step in designing this structure is creating strategy for implementing user accounts, computer accounts, and groups. Following this, you'll design an effective implementation of Group Policy.

Lessons in this Chapter:

Before You Begin

To complete this chapter, make sure you are familiar with the Active Directory service concepts described in Chapter 1, "Introduction to Active Directory and Network Infrastructure." You should also have gathered and analyzed any information about the existing Active Directory infrastructure of your company, as discussed in Chapter 2, "Analyzing an Existing Infrastructure." Although creating the actual design of your Active Directory structure (covered in Chapter 3, "Planning an Active Directory Structure") is required before designing your administrative security structure, it is not necessary that you read Chapter 3 before you learn the concepts presented in this chapter.

Lesson 1: Designing an Organizational Unit Structure

The first step in designing an administrative security structure is to create a plan for using organizational units within each domain in the environment. This includes determining the best way to delegate administrative control over the resources in each domain. You must also determine how Group Policy requirements affect that design.

After this lesson, you will be able to

■ Explain the reasons for using organizational units.

■ Determine methods for using organizational units to delegate administrative control.

■ Understand how inheritance affects your organizational unit plan.

■ Explain how Group Policy requirements affect your design.

Estimated lesson time: 40 minutes

Understanding Organizational Units

As you remember from Chapter 1, the organizational unit (OU) serves as a container into which you can place the resources and accounts of a domain. You can then assign administrative permissions to the OU and let the objects inside inherit those permissions.

OUs can contain any of the following objects:

■ Users

■ Computers

■ Groups

■ Printers

■ Applications

■ Security policies

■ Shared folders

■ Other OUs

Organizational units are primarily an administrative tool. They do not show up in the DNS naming structure for an organization, so end users are not burdened with having to navigate the OU structure. This means that the OU structure you design is primarily to make things easier for the administrators of the network. Specifically, you use OUs to organize the accounts and resources in a domain so that you can both ease the management of those objects and make the objects easier to find.

Often, designers create an OU structure that is based on departmental division or geographic locations because it is an obvious dividing point to use, but this is sometimes not necessary and can even be counterproductive. You should not create an OU structure just for the sake of having structure. Instead, you should use OUs to accomplish a specific purpose. These specific purposes include the following:

- Delegating administrative control of objects
- Limiting the visibility of objects
- Controlling the application of Group Policy

Of these three reasons for creating OUs, the first—delegating administrative control—should be the driving influence of your OU structure design. You should always start by creating an OU structure that delegates control effectively and then further refine it by creating OUs that control Group Policy and hide objects. The next few sections look at each of these reasons for creating OUs in detail.

> **Note** Although you should not create separate OUs based on geographic locations just because it's an obvious dividing point for structure, there are times when it is an appropriate decision. When the network is dispersed over a wide area and connected by slower wide area network (WAN) links, you can make it easier to design site boundaries (the subject of Chapter 5, "Designing a Site Plan") by creating a separate OU for each location and then creating nested OUs that delegate administrative control.

Using OUs to Delegate Administrative Control

It's tempting just to create an OU structure that is based on geographic locations or on the organizational chart of your IT department. However, using such political boundaries to create an OU structure does not really achieve a design that enhances the administration of Active Directory objects—and easing the administrative burden should be the goal behind your OU design.

Remember that you are not creating an OU structure to make things easier for users or simply to be more organized. You are creating an OU structure to make it easier for administrators to manage the objects placed in those OUs and to make it easier to assign the appropriate permissions to those administrators. Thus, you should create an OU hierarchy that follows the administrative and security needs of the business. Keep the design as simple as possible and use OU names that mean something to the people who will use them—the administrators.

There are two basic OU designs you can use to delegate administration: an object-based design or a task-based design. These designs are covered in the following sections.

Using an Object-Based Design

In an object-based OU structure, shown in Figure 4-1, delegation of control is assigned according to the type of object that is stored in the OUs. You might choose to group OUs around the following types of objects:

- Users
- Computers
- Sites
- Domains
- Organizational units

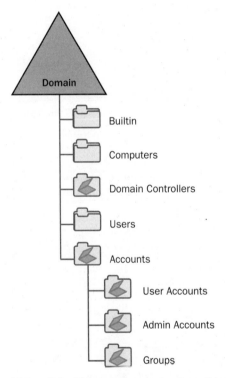

Figure 4-1   This is an example of an object-based OU structure.

Delegate the administration of objects within the OU to a specific individual or group by using the following general steps:

1. Place the individual or group that needs administrative rights into a security group (see Lesson 2 for more on using security groups).

2. Place the set of objects to be controlled into an OU.

3. Delegate the administrative tasks for the OU to the group you configured in step 1.

Using a Task-Based Control Design

In a task-based design, delegation of control is assigned based on the administrative tasks that need to be accomplished instead of being based on the objects that need administration. Such tasks include:

- Creating, deleting, and modifying user accounts
- Resetting passwords
- Defining group policy
- Controlling group membership and permissions

Planning the OU Structure

Active Directory directory service lets you control the delegation of administrative tasks to a precise level. For example, you could assign one group full control of all objects in an OU. You could then give another group the rights only to create, delete, and manage a certain type of object in the OU. You could then give another group the right to control a certain attribute of a certain type of object (such as the ability to reset passwords for user accounts). You can also make these permissions inheritable so that they apply not only to a single OU, but also to any lower-level OUs that are created. This granularity of control allows a great degree of flexibility.

If you choose an object-based OU structure, this means you can place all the objects of a certain type into the same container. You can then assign a fairly complex set of administrative permissions on the OU that control what each administrator can do. You can then create lower-level OUs that control Group Policy application or perform some other task, yet still have the same permissions structure inherited by the lower-level OUs. An example of a structure like this one is shown in Figure 4-2.

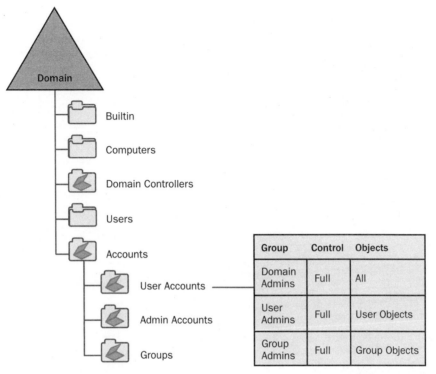

Figure 4-2   You can create complex permissions for a relatively simple OU structure.

A well-designed OU structure allows administrators to delegate authority effectively. You should give careful consideration to the top-level OUs in a structure. Top-level OUs should always be based on a relatively static aspect of the organization to prevent the need to change the top-level OUs during a reorganization of the company. For example, the following types of top-level organization are based on static aspects that are less likely to change:

- **Physical locations**   Often, different physical locations (especially those over a wide area such as different countries) have different IT staffs and, therefore, different administrative needs. Creating a separate top-level OU for each location is really an application of a task-based design; it's just that the different administrative tasks are based on location, as shown in Figure 4-3.

- **Types of administrative tasks**   Basing the top-level structure on administrative tasks ensures a relatively static structure. No matter how your company might reorganize itself, the basic types of administrative tasks are unlikely to change much.

- **Types of objects**   As with a task-based structure, basing your top-level OUs on types of objects ensures a plan that is resistant to change.

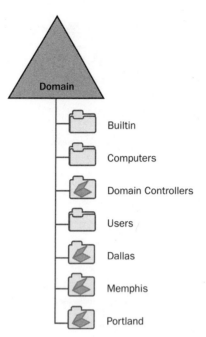

Domain

Builtin

Computers

Domain Controllers

Users

Dallas

Memphis

Portland

Figure 4-3 Administrative tasks are based on location in this top-level OU design.

Each of these options represents a better top-level OU structure than, for example, basing OUs on divisions of the company, which are more likely to change.

When planning the top-level OU structure in a multidomain environment, consider creating a top-level design that is consistent across every domain on the network. Using an object-based or task-based design (described in the next sections) is particularly effective in this situation. Creating a top-level OU structure that is consistent across domains keeps administration and support consistent throughout the network.

Lower-level OUs (those created inside the top-level OUs) should represent more detailed levels of administrative authority within your organization or should be used for other purposes such as Group Policy application. Remember that by default, lower-level OUs inherit the permissions of their parent OUs. When you are constructing your plan, you also need to plan where you want inheritance to happen and where you don't.

When designing lower-level OUs, it's easy to get carried away. Remember that your main goal is to design a structure that simplifies the administration of accounts and resources as much as possible. To this end, keep your design as simple as possible. If you create a nested OU structure that is too deep, you not only create a more confusing structure, but also may reduce performance. An OU may have multiple levels of Group Policy being applied to it—from the domain, site, and any parent OUs. The more policies that need to be applied, the longer the response time and the slower the perceived performance.

> **Exam Tip**   Initially, you should create an OU structure that effectively enables delegation of administration, whether you create an object-based or a task-based design. Once you have completed this initial OU design, you should then create additional OU structures to control the application of Group Policy to users and computers and to limit the visibility of objects.

Using OUs to Limit Object Visibility

Some organizations require that certain objects be hidden from certain administrators or other users. Even when you deny permission to modify an object's attributes, users who have access to the container that holds the object can still see that it exists. You can hide objects from view by putting them into an OU and then limiting the users who are given the List Contents permission for that OU. This effectively makes the objects placed in that container invisible to users who do not have the List Contents permission. An example of this type of design is shown in Figure 4-4.

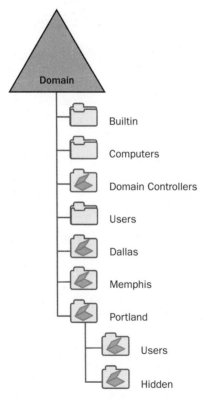

Figure 4-4   It's possible to use OUs to hide objects.

Although the need to limit object visibility is a secondary concern to creating a good administrative structure, you may find that political, legal, or security considerations force you to hide objects. The best way to do this is to concentrate first on creating a good OU structure based on controlling administrative authority. Place the objects where they need to be in that OU structure. After you have done this, create new OUs that are used to hide objects inside the new structure.

Using OUs to Control Group Policy

You are going to learn more about planning Group Policy in Lesson 3, later in this chapter. In this section, however, you'll get an introduction to the third good reason for using OUs—controlling the application of Group Policy.

Group Policy provides a way to apply uniform configuration settings to any number of objects all at once. You can use Group Policy to define user settings such as password restrictions or computer settings. Using Group Policy involves creating an object named a Group Policy Object (GPO) that holds the configurations you want to apply. Once you have created the GPO, you can link it to a domain, site, or OU.

If you apply a GPO at the site or domain level, it affects more objects than if you apply a GPO at an organizational unit level. However, you also have less control over each individual object. Although you can filter the objects that receive a GPO, filtering can result in unnecessary complications and should be relied on only occasionally instead of as a normal practice.

It is much better to create a Group Policy plan that applies GPOs efficiently from the outset, and linking GPOs to OUs provides a way to effect such a plan. Creating GPOs for OUs gives you much better control over the application of Group Policy, because it eliminates the need to filter Group Policy settings.

However, you'll need to plan carefully. Creating GPOs for OUs means that there are more GPOs to manage. Conflicts between GPOs can occur because organizational units can be nested and Group Policy is inherited from parent OUs; therefore, an object may have a number of GPOs applied to it based on its position in the OU hierarchy.

Once you have created an OU structure based on the delegation of administrative control in a domain, you can create additional OUs inside that structure that control the application of group policy. For example, if you used an object-based top-level OU structure and created an OU that contains user accounts, you could divide that OU into several lower-level OUs for users who have different Group Policy requirements.

When you are designing an OU structure to control the application of Group Policy, there are a few guidelines you should keep in mind:

- Plan an OU structure that allows the fewest GPOs possible. The more GPOs you have associated with any object, the longer it takes for users to log on to the network.

- Create top-level OUs based on objects or tasks and create lower-level OUs to control Group Policy.

- Create additional organizational units to avoid the need to use filters to exempt a group of users in an organizational unit from a GPO.

Default Containers and OUs

A number of default OUs and containers are created during the installation of Active Directory. These default OUs and containers include the following:

- **Domain container**   The Domain container serves as the root container for the Active Directory hierarchy. Administrative permissions applied to this container can affect child containers and objects across the domain. Do not delegate control of this container; it must be controlled by the service administrators.

- **Built-in container**   The Built-in container holds the default service administrator accounts.

- **Users container**   The Users container is the default location for storing new user accounts and groups created in the domain. Again, you should not change the default permissions on this container. If you need to delegate control over users, create new OUs and move the user objects into them. Also, you cannot link GPOs to the default Users container. To apply Group Policy to users, you must also create OUs and move the users there.

- **Computers container**   The Computers container is the default location for storing new computer accounts created in the domain. As with the Users container, you should create new OUs to assign permissions or GPOs to computers.

- **Domain Controllers OU**   The Domain Controllers OU is the default location for storing the computer accounts of domain controllers. This OU has a default set of policies applied to it. To ensure that these policies are applied uniformly to all domain controllers, it is recommended that you do not move the computer objects of the domain controllers out of this OU. By default, the service administrators control this OU. Do not delegate control of this OU to individuals other than the service administrators.

The default containers are controlled by service administrators, and it is recommended that you let control stay in the service administrators' hands. If you need to delegate control over objects in the directory, you should create new OUs and then move the objects into these OUs. Delegate control over these OUs to the appropriate administrators. This makes it possible to delegate control over objects in the directory without changing the default control given to the service administrators.

Planning for Inheritance

Each OU inherits the permissions of its parent OU by default. In the same way, objects in an OU inherit permissions from the OU (and from each parent of that OU). Inheritance provides an efficient way to grant or delegate permissions to objects. The advantage of inheritance is that an administrator can manage permissions of all objects in an OU by setting permissions on the OU itself instead of having to configure all of the child objects individually. Actually, administrators can assign permissions to an object itself, to an object and all of its child objects, to only the child objects, or to specific types of child objects (such as computers or users).

When you create an OU design, you should take full advantage of inheritance. Organize the OUs logically to create a simple structure in which inheritance does most of the work for you.

There are also times when inheritance gets in the way of what you need to accomplish with your OU design. You may need the specific permissions on an object to override the permissions the object inherits from a parent. You can block inheritance of the permissions that apply to a parent OU so that they do not apply to the child OU.

Standard Models for OU Structure

Creating an OU structure can be a difficult task. Fortunately, there are a number of standard models on which you can base your design. Each model describes the categories of OUs and the relationships the OUs share with one another.

You can base an OU design on the following five OU models:

- Location-based
- Organization-based
- Function-based
- Hybrid of location, then organization
- Hybrid of organization, then location

See Also   The OU models described in this section should cover most situations and are those you are likely to see on the exam. However, these models certainly do not represent the only way to design an OU structure. Consult the *Microsoft Windows Server 2003 Deployment Kit*, part of the *Microsoft Resource Kit* collection (Microsoft Press, 2003), or check out the various articles on Active Directory deployment available at *http://www.microsoft.com/technet*.

Location-Based

In the location-based OU model, shown in Figure 4-5, network administration is distributed among a number of geographic areas. This model is useful if each location has its own administrative requirements that differ from other locations.

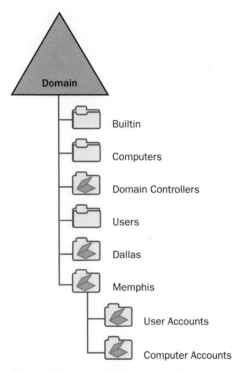

Figure 4-5   The location-based OU model distributes network administration geographically.

The location-based model provides a number of advantages, including the following:

- OUs are resistant to changes. Companies may reorganize their resources or departments, but geographic locations tend to remain more static.

- A centralized administrative staff can easily implement domain-wide policies.

- It is easier to figure out where resources are located.

- It is easy to create new OUs if a merger or expansion takes place.

There are also certain disadvantages to the location-based model, including the following:

- Because you are creating a structure based on geography, this suggests you will need network administrators at each location.

- The design does not follow business or administrative structure.

> **Note**   Assigning Group Policy Objects to sites (which are typically based on location) can provide many of the same benefits as the location-based OU model, without the disadvantages. You'll learn more about designing sites in Chapter 5.

Organization-Based

In the organization-based OU model, shown in Figure 4-6, network administration is divided into departments or business units so that each has its own administrator. This model is useful if the company has a strong division structure.

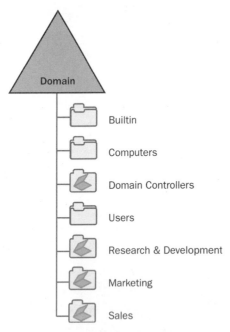

Figure 4-6   The organization-based OU model divides network administration according to departments or business units.

The organization-based model provides a number of advantages, including the following:

- This structure helps maintain a certain level of autonomy for each department or business unit.

- It accommodates mergers and expansions.

- This structure is friendly to administrators because the structure can be understood by anyone in the company.

There is also a major disadvantage to the organization-based model. This structure is vulnerable to reorganization. A change in department may require a change in top-level OU structure.

Function-Based

In the function-based OU model, shown in Figure 4-7, the administrative staff is decentralized but bases its administrative model on business functions within the organization. This is an ideal choice for small organizations that have job functions that span several departments.

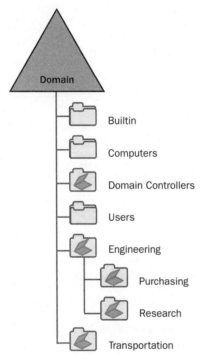

Figure 4-7   The function-based OU model bases its administrative model on business functions.

The function-based model provides the significant advantage of being relatively immune to reorganizations.

However, there is also a significant disadvantage to the function-based model. You will likely have to create additional levels of OUs to delegate administrative control of user accounts, computers, printers, and network shares.

Hybrid of Location, then Organization

In this model, shown in Figure 4-8, you create top-level OUs that represent the geographic locations of the company and then create lower-level OUs by organization.

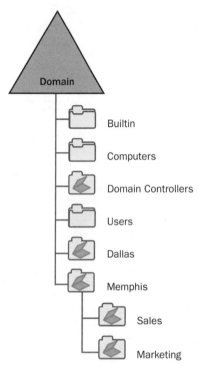

Figure 4-8   This hybrid OU model is based first on location, then organization.

The hybrid of location, then organization model provides two advantages, as follows:

■ It allows for additional departmental and divisional growth.

■ It allows for distinct security boundaries.

There are also certain disadvantages to this hybrid model, including the following:

■ You would likely have to redesign the structure if the administrative staff becomes reorganized.

■ This model requires cooperation among administrators if they are in the same location but different departments.

Hybrid of Organization, then Location

In this model, shown in Figure 4-9, you create top-level OUs that represent the organization of the company, and then create lower-level OUs by location.

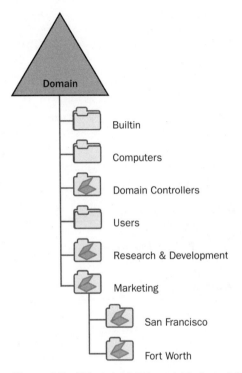

Figure 4-9   This hybrid OU model is based first on organization, then location.

This hybrid model provides the single big advantage of allowing for strong security between departments or divisions while still letting you delegate administrative control based on location.

However, the disadvantage of this model is that it is vulnerable to reorganization—just like the organization-based model.

Practice: Designing an Organizational Unit Structure

In this practice, you design an organizational unit structure for Northwind Traders. If you are unable to answer a question, review the lesson materials and try the question again. You can find answers to the questions in the "Questions and Answers" section at the end of this chapter.

Scenario

Northwind Traders manufactures a line of network appliances designed to help companies improve their data transmission capabilities. Northwind Traders currently uses a Microsoft Windows NT 4.0 master domain model. In recent years, the company has undergone significant growth and expansion and expects substantial growth over the next three years, including growth in market share, revenue, and number of employees. In addition to opening two new offices, the executive management has committed to implementing a new Windows Server 2003 Active Directory design to meet the current and future needs of the company.

The following table shows the geographical locations, the departments residing in each location, and the number of users in each of the locations.

Location	Departments Represented	Number of Users
Paris, France	Headquarters (HQ) Management staff Finance Sales Marketing Production Research Development Information Technology (IT)	2,000
Los Angeles	Sales Marketing Finance IT	1,000
Atlanta	Customer Service Customer Support Training	750
Glasgow, Scotland	Research Development Sustained Engineering IT	750
Sydney, Australia	Consulting Production Sales Finance	500

To remain compatible with the previous domain design, employees in specific organizations have user accounts in remote domains. The following table shows the user account membership information.

Users	Have User Accounts In (domain)
All personnel in Sales and Marketing	NAwest domain
All personnel in Production	AsiaPacific domain
All personnel in Research and Development	Glasgow domain
All personnel in Finance	Corp domain

Northwind Traders has already decided on its forest and domain design, as shown in the following diagram.

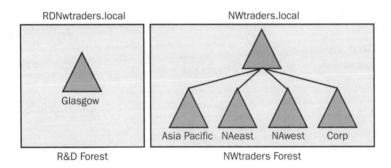

Practice Questions

Based on the newly approved forest and domain design, create the organizational unit structure for Northwind Traders. Use the table to complete your design.

Domain	Organizational Units
nwtraders.local	
Corp.nwtraders.local	
NAwest.nwtraders.local	
NAeast.nwtraders.local	
Glasgow.RDNwtraders.local	
AsiaPacific.nwtraders.local	

Lesson Review

The following questions are intended to reinforce key information presented in this lesson. If you are unable to answer a question, review the lesson materials and try the question again. You can find answers to the questions in the "Questions and Answers" section at the end of this chapter.

1. What are the three specific purposes for which you would create an OU? Of those three, which should be the driving influence of your overall OU design?

   _____

   _____

2. Describe the difference between an object-based and a task-based OU structure.

   _____

   _____

3. You are preparing your directory plan. One of the requirements is that you be able to delegate control of user objects by assigning Group Policy. What must you do?

   _____

   _____

4. What are the advantages of using a location-based OU model? What are the disadvantages?

   _____

   _____

Lesson Summary

- Create an OU structure that makes it easier to delegate control to administrators and that makes it easier to find resources and accounts. You can create either an object-based or a task-based administrative structure.

- Specific reasons for creating an OU are to delegate control of administration, limit the visibility of objects, and control the application of Group Policy. Start by focusing on the delegation of administration and then fill out the structure according to your other needs.

- Base your top-level OUs on a relatively static aspect of the business such as geography, administrative tasks, or objects, and then use lower-level OUs to represent more detailed levels of administrative authority.

- Take advantage of inheritance in your designs to facilitate the flow of permissions throughout the structure. Block inheritance where you need object permissions to override the permissions that would be inherited from the parent.

Lesson 2: Planning an Account Strategy

Once you have designed your OU structure, the next step in creating your administrative plan is to create an account strategy. This lesson covers how to plan user accounts, computer accounts, and groups.

After this lesson, you will be able to

- Describe the types of accounts available in Active Directory.
- Create a strategy for implementing user accounts.
- Create a strategy for implementing groups.

Estimated lesson time: 25 minutes

Types of Accounts

An account in Active Directory is a list of attributes that defines a security principal, such as a user or group of users. You can create five types of accounts in Active Directory. They are described below; this chapter is primarily concerned with computer, user, and group accounts.

- **Computer**   Whenever a computer running Microsoft Windows NT, Windows 2000, Windows XP, or Windows Server 2003 joins a domain, a computer account is created for it. Computer accounts provide a way to authenticate a computer's access to the network and to resources in the domain.

- **User**   A user account is a collection of attributes about a person. The user object is stored in Active Directory and enables single sign-on to the network. A user has to enter credentials (name and password) only once and is given appropriate permissions throughout the network.

- **Group**   A group is a collection of users, computers, or other groups to which you can assign permissions. By assigning permissions to groups and then placing members in those groups, you save the effort of having to assign permissions to each member individually.

- **InetOrgPerson**   An InetOrgPerson account works much the same as a user account, except that InetOrgPerson accounts are compatible with other Lightweight Directory Access Protocol (LDAP)–based directory services. This allows compatibility between Active Directory and other systems.

- **Contact**   A contact is an object that is stored in Active Directory but does not have permissions associated with it. This means it cannot be used to log on to the network or to access resources. Contacts are often associated with users outside the network to which a mail system can send messages.

Planning Computer Accounts

Computer accounts allow computers within a domain to take advantage of many of the same security features, such as authentication, that are designed for user accounts. Computer accounts allow member computers to be authenticated in a manner that is transparent to users, and they allow you to add application servers as member servers within trusted domains and to demand authentication from the users and other services that access these resource servers.

Because you can place computer accounts in OUs and assign Group Policy to them, you can control the security and authentication measures taken for different types of computers. For example, computers that are located within a public kiosk will have different security requirements than workstations located in a private, controlled environment.

New computer accounts are created any time a computer joins the domain. Another part of your account strategy, therefore, is to define the users who have the right to add computers to the domain and, thus, create computer accounts in the process.

You'll also need to plan a convention for naming computers. A good convention should make each computer readily identifiable by owner, location, type of computer, or any combination of the three. For example, naming a server that is based in Dallas DAL-SVR1 identifies the location and type of computer. Naming a server that belongs to Barry Potter BPOTTER1 identifies the primary user of the computer.

Planning User Accounts

User accounts provide a way to identify the users who log on to a network, control what resources those users can access, and provide all kinds of information about the users. Administrators are just users with greater power over resources that relate to network management. Groups are used to efficiently organize collections of users that share common security or access requirements.

User accounts provide users with the ability to log on to the domain or a local computer and access resources. User account objects contain information about users and associate certain privileges and restrictions with the user. Every object in the Active Directory is associated with an Access Control List (ACL), which is basically a list of the permissions assigned to users and groups for accessing the object.

Types of User Accounts

Windows Server 2003 provides two main types of user accounts, including:

- **Local user accounts**   Local user accounts are created within a particular computer's security database and govern access to resources on that computer. Local user accounts are intended to control access on stand-alone computers or computers in a work group. When you first install a server, local accounts are used and managed using the Computer Management console, under the node named Local Users and Groups. When you promote a server to become a domain controller, the Computer Management tool denies access to that node and the Active Directory Users and Computers tool is used instead (user accounts on domain controllers are stored in the Active Directory).

- **Domain user accounts**   Domain user accounts are created within the Active Directory and allow users to log on to a domain and access resources anywhere on the network. You create a domain user account using the Active Directory Users and Computers tool. User accounts are replicated to all domain controllers in a domain, so any domain controller can authenticate a user once replication of the account has occurred.

Built-In User Accounts

Windows automatically creates a number of default user accounts called built-in user accounts. Both locally and within a domain there are two key accounts created: Administrator and Guest.

The Administrator account is the most powerful user account because it is automatically made a member of the Administrators group. This allows the ultimate level of control over an individual computer and grants almost all user rights to a user. The domain-level Administrator account has ultimate control over the entire domain; it belongs to the Domain Admins group by default (and in the root domain of a forest, it belongs to the Enterprise Admins and Schema Admins groups as well). The Administrator account cannot be deleted, but you can (and for security purposes, should) rename the account. You should also ensure that this account does not have a blank password, and you should not distribute the password to others.

The Guest account is the other basic built-in user account, and it is used to provide a single set of permissions to any users who must log on to the network occasionally but who do not have regular user accounts. The Guest account is given this ability by being included automatically in the local Guest group. In domain environments, the Guest account is also a member of the Domain Guests group. The Guest account is disabled by default and is really meant to be used only on low-security networks. You cannot delete the Guest account, but you can disable and/or rename it.

Naming User Accounts

Planning a solid naming convention for user accounts lets you standardize the way users are identified in a domain. Using a consistent convention also helps users and administrators recognize and remember user names.

There are a number of considerations to take into account when planning a naming strategy for users. These considerations include:

- Every user must have a logon name that is unique within the domain. In addition, the user's full name must be unique within the OU where the account is stored.

- User logon names can contain more than 20 characters, but for compatibility with pre–Windows 2000 operating systems, user logon names should be limited to 20 characters. User logon names are not case-sensitive and pre–Windows 2000 logon names cannot contain the following characters: "/ \ [ ] : ; | = , + * ? < >

- Whatever convention you decide on must allow for some flexibility to accommodate users with identical logon names. If you decide on a convention, for example, that uses a user's first initial and last name, you may need to add a middle initial or even a second character from the first name if two names result in the same logon name.

- Compatibility with other applications must be considered. Some applications, such as e-mail systems, may have other characters that are not allowed in a user name, or they may have different length requirements.

There are many different conventions you could use to create names, and every administrator and designer has his or her favorite. However, a good naming convention should always provide names that are easy to remember and that provide enough detail to distinguish people with similar names.

Planning a Password Policy

Passwords are one of the most important aspects of network security, and therefore a policy for determining passwords for users should be given due consideration. Windows Server 2003 provides stronger built-in defaults for passwords than do previous versions. For example, Windows Server 2003 includes a new feature that checks the complexity of the password for the Administrator account. If the password is blank or does not meet complexity requirements, Windows warns you about the dangers of not using a strong password. If you leave the password blank, you cannot access the account over the network.

Creating a strong password policy ensures as much as possible that users follow the password guidelines required by a company. There are a number of considerations you should take into account when planning a password policy, including the following:

- You should implement a policy setting to remember at least the last 24 passwords used. This prevents users from switching between just a few passwords when their password expires.

- Users should be required to change their passwords at regular intervals. Microsoft suggests allowing passwords for no longer than 42 days, which also happens to be the default setting in Windows Server 2003. This prevents a person who finds out a password from being able to access the network after the password's expiration date. You should require administrators to change their passwords more often than regular users.

- Users should also have to retain a password for a certain number of days, to prevent them from quickly changing passwords until they get back to one they like. Microsoft's recommendation is to keep passwords for at least one day.

- Passwords should be at least seven characters. Longer passwords are harder to crack than shorter passwords.

- Passwords should be complex. They should use upper- and lowercase alphanumeric and non-alphanumeric characters.

Creating an Authentication Strategy

It is also important that domain controllers be able to verify the identity of a user or computer so that appropriate access can be granted to system and network resources. This verification process is called authentication, and it occurs whenever a user logs on to the network.

When creating an authentication strategy, you should take the following measures into account:

- Create an account-lockout policy. Account-lockout policies disable a user account after a specified number of failed attempts to log on. This prevents so-called dictionary attacks in which an automated routine tests password after password. Create an account-lockout policy that allows users to attempt logon several times though, to prevent valid users who have problems typing or remembering complex passwords from being locked out. Users should be allowed at least five attempts to correctly type their passwords. You should also set the duration of time that an account is locked out and the interval that must elapse after a failed logon attempt before the lockout counter is reset.

- Consider assigning logon hours to ensure that employees use computers only during business hours. This policy should apply to both interactive logon (when a user is at the workstation) and network logons. Logon hours are particularly useful in environments where computers are more accessible and where multiple work shifts are used. Enforcing logon hours may also be required for some government security certifications.

- Create a ticket expiration policy. When a user logs on, a ticket is assigned that the client computer uses to authenticate itself when accessing network resources. The lifetime of a ticket should be long enough that it is convenient for users, but short enough to prevent attackers from being able to access and break into the stored credentials. Ticket lifetime is set to 10 hours in the Default Domain GPO and this should be fine on most networks. Decreasing the lifetime increases security, but also increases network traffic due to additional ticket granting.

- Have administrators log on as regular users on their desktop systems. Administrators should log on with a regular user account and use the Run As command to perform administrative tasks. When logging on to domain controllers or other servers, administrators should log on as an administrator. You should also limit the users who are made part of the Administrators group. Instead, use OUs to delegate administrative authority to administrators' user accounts.

- Rename and disable the built-in Administrator account and the built-in Guest account. Because they are well-known accounts, they are often targets for attackers.

Planning Groups

Groups simplify the assignment of permissions by organizing users. It is much easier, for example, to assign permissions to one group and then to include users in that group than it is to assign and manage permissions for many users individually. Changing a particular permission for all of those users becomes a single step when those users are members of a group.

As with user accounts, there are both local and domain-level groups. Local groups are stored in a local computer's security database and are intended to control resource access on that computer. Domain groups are stored in Active Directory and let you gather users and control resource access in a domain and on domain controllers. This chapter focuses on domain groups.

Group Types

When you create a group in Windows Server 2003, you must specify the type of group you want to create and the scope the group will assume.

Windows includes two group types:

■ **Security groups**   Security groups are used to group domain users into a single administrative unit. Security groups can be assigned permissions and can also be used as e-mail distribution lists. Users placed into a group inherit the permissions assigned to the group for as long as they remain members of that group. Windows itself uses only security groups.

■ **Distribution groups**   These are used for nonsecurity purposes by applications other than Windows. One of the primary uses is within an e-mail server as a mailing list. You cannot assign permissions to a distribution group.

Group Scopes

Group scopes determine where in the Active Directory forest a group is accessible and what objects can be placed into the group. Windows Server 2003 includes three group scopes: global, domain local, and universal.

■ **Global groups**   are used to gather users that have similar permissions requirements. Global groups have the following characteristics:

   ❏ Global groups can contain user and computer accounts only from the domain in which the global group is created.

   ❏ When the domain functional level is set to Windows 2000 native or Windows Server 2003 (i.e., the domain contains only Windows 2000 or 2003 servers), global groups can also contain other global groups from the local domain.

   ❏ Global groups can be assigned permissions or be added to local groups in any domain in a forest.

■ **Domain local groups**   exist on domain controllers and are used to control access to resources located on domain controllers in the local domain (for member servers and workstations, you use local groups on those systems instead). Domain local groups share the following characteristics:

   ❏ Domain local groups can contain users and global groups from any domain in a forest no matter what functional level is enabled.

   ❏ When the domain functional level is set to Windows 2000 native or Windows Server 2003, domain local groups can also contain other domain local groups and universal groups.

■ **Universal groups**   are normally used to assign permissions to related resources in multiple domains. Universal groups share the following characteristics:

   ❏ Universal groups are available only when the forest functional level is set to Windows 2000 native or Windows Server 2003.

❑ Universal groups exist outside the boundaries of any particular domain and are managed by Global Catalog servers.

❑ Universal groups are used to assign permissions to related resources in multiple domains.

❑ Universal groups can contain users, global groups, and other universal groups from any domain in a forest.

❑ You can grant permissions for a universal group to any resource in any domain.

Table 4-1 summarizes the items that groups of different scopes can contain in mixed and native mode domains.

Table 4-1   Group Scopes and Functionalities

Scope	Items Group Can Contain in Windows 2000 Native or Windows Server 2003 Functional Level	Items Group Can Contain in Lower Functional Levels
Global (G)	User accounts and global groups from the local domain	Users and computers from the same domain
Domain local (DL)	User accounts, universal groups, and global groups from any domain; domain local groups from the same domain	Users and global groups from any domain
Universal (U)	User accounts, universal groups, and global groups from any domain	Designer cannot create universal groups in lower functional levels

Group Nesting

Active Directory allows you to nest groups (i.e., place groups inside other groups), and doing so is an effective way of organizing users. For example, suppose you had junior-level administrators in four different geographic locations, as shown in Figure 4-10. You could create a separate group for each location (named something like Dallas Junior Admins). Then, you could create a single group named Junior Admins and make each of the location-based groups a member of the main group. This approach would allow you to set permissions on a single group and have those permissions flow down to the members, yet still be able to subdivide the junior administrators by location.

When nesting groups, you need to keep one caveat in mind: Try to minimize the level of nesting—in fact, try your best to keep it to one level of nesting. The deeper the nesting, the more complicated it is to keep track of the permissions structure.

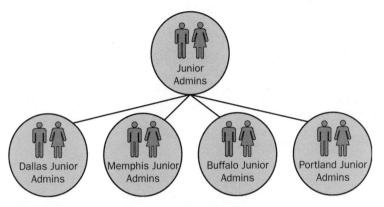

Figure 4-10   This shows an example of nesting groups.

Naming Groups

Just as with user accounts, you will need to establish a convention for naming groups. A consistent naming convention helps users and administrators identify and remember groups more easily and makes the job of tracking group membership easier as well.

You should take the following considerations into account when establishing a group naming convention:

- Each group in a domain must have a name that is unique to that domain.

- Group names can contain up to 64 characters.

- There are certain characters you cannot use in pre–Windows 2000 group names. Invalid characters in group names include: " / \ [ ] : ; | = , + * ? < >

- Group names are not case-sensitive, but Windows does preserve the case of the characters you enter.

Putting Users and Groups Together

Now that you understand the available group types and group scopes, and how user accounts are planned, it's time to look at how users and groups fit together in your account strategy.

There are a number of recommended guidelines for using groups, including the following:

- Avoid assigning permissions to user accounts. Assigning permissions to groups provides a more flexible and easy-to-manage permissions structure. This is possible with a carefully designed group structure.

- Create domain local groups that represent the domain controller resources you want to control access to and how those resources will be used. Assign the appropriate permissions on the resource to the group. If resources are on a member server or workstation, you will use local groups instead of domain local groups.

- Create global groups that help organize users. For example, you might create a group named Executives.

- Place global groups inside domain local groups.

- Do not place users into universal groups—only into global groups. This helps cut down on replication of objects to the Global Catalog. Instead, universal groups should be used to hold global groups with common requirements.

Of course, no one can force you to follow these recommendations, but doing so is in your best interests in the real world and you'll be expected to understand these practices on the exam. The following sequence succinctly describes the recommended strategy for using security groups:

1. Place user accounts into global groups.

2. Place global groups into universal groups.

3. Place universal groups into domain local groups.

4. Assign permissions to the domain local groups.

Exam Tip You can remember Microsoft's guidelines for using groups with one simple acronym: AGUDLP. Accounts (A) go into global groups (G), which go into universal groups (U), which go into domain local groups (DL), which are assigned permissions (P). You can remember the acronym with the phrase All Good Users Do Love Permissions.

Practice: Planning an Account Strategy

In this practice, you explore the requirements involved in planning an account strategy. Thinking of the company you work for now (or have worked for in the past), describe the requirements in place for an account strategy. Use the following questions to guide your thoughts; the answers will vary depending on your experience.

1. What are the naming conventions in your organization?

   _____

   _____

2. What password requirements do you have in your organization?

   _____

   _____

3. What group strategies do you use on your network?

   _____

   _____

Lesson Review

The following questions are intended to reinforce key information presented in this lesson. If you are unable to answer a question, review the lesson materials and try the question again. You can find answers to the questions in the "Questions and Answers" section at the end of this chapter.

1. What are the five types of accounts you can create in Active Directory for Windows Server 2003?

   _____

   _____

2. You are creating a password policy. What are the recommended requirements you should impose for passwords?

   _____

   _____

3. What is the recommended strategy for placing users into security groups?

   _____

   _____

Lesson Summary

- Active Directory in Windows Server 2003 provides five types of accounts: user, computer, group, contact, and InetOrgPerson.

- Computer accounts allow member computers to be authenticated in a manner that is transparent to users. You should create a plan for naming computer accounts and define who has the right to add computer accounts to Active Directory.

- User accounts identify a user and authenticate users for access to network resources. Your user account strategy should include a solid naming convention, a password policy, and an authentication policy.

- Groups simplify the assignment of permissions by organizing users. The scope of a group determines where in Active Directory a group is accessible and what objects can become members. Group scopes include global groups, universal groups, and domain local groups.

- When placing users into groups, remember user accounts go into global groups; global groups go into universal groups; universal groups go into domain local groups; and permissions are assigned to domain local groups.

Lesson 3: Designing a Group Policy Implementation

Group Policy provides a powerful and efficient means to configure settings for many users and computers at once. Group Policy is also used to distribute and update software in an organization. This lesson presents an overview of Group Policy in Windows Server 2003 and examines strategies for building a solid Group Policy structure.

After this lesson, you will be able to

- Explain how Group Policy works and what it is used for.
- Describe how Group Policy Objects are combined.
- Decide on a strategy for implementing Group Policy in an organization.

Estimated lesson time: 40 minutes

Understanding Group Policy

A group policy is a collection of user and computer configuration settings that you can link to computers, sites, domains, and OUs in Active Directory. Such a collection of group policy settings is called a Group Policy object (GPO).

Any computer running Windows 2000, Windows XP, or Windows Server 2003 (whether it is part of Active Directory or not) contains one local GPO with policies that are applied to that computer. If the computer is a part of Active Directory, then any number of additional nonlocal GPOs may also apply to that computer.

There are two basic types of Group Policy settings available:

- **Computer Configuration settings**   Used to set group policies that apply to specific computers, regardless of who logs on to them
- **User Configuration settings**   Used to set group policies that apply to specific users, regardless of which computer they log on to

No matter which type of setting you are configuring (computer or user), there are three categories of settings available: Software Settings, Windows Settings, and Administrative Templates.

Software Settings

The Software Settings node contains settings you can also use to deploy software to client computers using Group Policy. This requires that the client computers be running Windows 2000 Professional, Windows 2000 Server, Windows XP Professional, Windows XP 64-Bit Edition, or Windows Server 2003, and that they are members of the domain. You can specify which users or computers will get the software, you can specify upgrades when necessary, and you can even remove the software.

Two components work together to provide this function:

- **Windows Installer service**   This is a service that uses Windows Installer packages (described next) as instruction sets to deploy and update software.

- **Windows Installer Packages**   These are self-executing script files that contain all the instructions necessary for the Windows Installer service to carry out installation, updating, or repair of software. Windows Installer Package files have the file extension msi.

Once the Windows Installer service installs an application, it tracks the state of the application. It can be used to reinstall an application, to repair missing or corrupted files, and to remove the application when it is no longer needed.

There are two ways to deploy software using Group Policy: publishing and assigning. When an application is assigned to a user, a shortcut becomes available to the user and appears on the user's Start menu or desktop. This appearance is called advertising the application to the user. When the user starts the shortcut (or opens a file associated with the program), the installation routine is started. When an application is assigned to a computer, the application is installed the first time the computer starts up following the assignment.

When you publish an application, you make it available for users to install when they want to. Applications can be published only to users; you cannot publish an application to a computer. The application becomes available in the Add/Remove Programs Control Panel tool and will also be installed on demand if a user opens a file associated with the program.

Windows Settings

The Windows Settings category lets you change a number of configurations related to the Windows environment. These settings include the following:

- **Scripts**   When setting up a computer configuration, you can identify scripts that should run at startup or shutdown of a computer. When setting up a user configuration, you can identify scripts that run when the user logs on or off. Scripts can be written in any ActiveX scripting language, including VBScript, JScript, Perl, MD-DOS batch files, and others.

- **Security Settings**   There are a host of security settings for both computer and user configurations.

- **Internet Explorer Maintenance**   This setting is available only for users. It lets you manage and customize Internet Explorer on client computers.

- **Remote Installation Services**   RIS is a service that lets you set up new client computers remotely and automatically. This setting is also available only for user configurations. It controls the behavior of remote operating-system installations.

- **Folder Redirection**   Also available only for user configurations, this setting lets you redirect special Windows folders (such as My Documents, Start Menu, and Application Data) from their default location in a user's profile to an alternate network location. This lets you centrally manage folders for users.

Administrative Templates

The Administrative Templates category (available for computer and user configurations) contains all registry-based Group Policy settings. Table 4-2 lists the Administrative Templates settings available for both user and computer configurations.

Table 4-2   Administrative Template Settings

Node	Computer Configuration	User Configuration	Description
Control Panel	n/a	X	Determines Control Panel tools available to a user
Desktop	n/a	X	Controls appearance of a user's desktop
Network	X	X	Controls settings for Offline Files and Network and Dial-Up Connections
Printers	X	n/a	Controls printer settings
Start Menu and Taskbar	n/a	X	Controls configuration settings for a user's Start menu and taskbar
System	X	X	Controls logon/logoff (for user), startup/shutdown (for computers), and group policies themselves
Windows Components	X	X	Controls built-in components of Windows such as Windows Explorer, Internet Explorer, and Windows Installer

Resolving GPOs from Multiple Sources

Because GPOs can come from different sources to apply to a single user or computer, there must be a way of determining how those GPOs are combined. GPOs are processed in the following order:

1. **Local GPO**   The local GPO on the computer is processed and all settings specified in that GPO are applied.

2. **Site GPOs**   GPOs linked to the site in which the computer resides are processed. Settings made at this level override any conflicting settings made at the preceding level. If multiple GPOs are linked to a site, the site administrator can control the order in which those GPOs are processed.

3. **Domain GPOs**   GPOs linked to the domain in which the computer resides are processed and any settings are applied. Settings made at the domain level override conflicting settings applied at the local or site level. Again, the administrator can control the processing order when multiple GPOs are linked to the domain.

4. **OU GPOs**   GPOs linked to any OUs that contain the user or computer object are processed. Settings made at the OU level override conflicting settings applied at the domain, local, or site level. It is possible for a single object to be in multiple OUs. In this case, GPOs linked to the highest level OU in the Active Directory hierarchy are processed first, followed by the next highest level OU, and so on. If multiple GPOs are linked to a single OU, the administrator again gets to control the order in which they are processed.

> **Exam Tip**   An easy way to remember the order in which GPOs are processed is that first the local GPO is processed and then Active Directory GPOs are processed. Active Directory GPOs are processed starting with the farthest structure from the user (the site), then the next closest structure to the user (the domain), and finally the closest structure (the OU).

Working with Group Policy Inheritance

By default, child containers inherit Group Policy from their parent containers. However, you can override inherited settings by placing different settings directly on the child object. Within a GPO, you can also specify that a particular setting is enabled, disabled, or not configured. Settings that are not configured for the parent container are not inherited at all by the child container. Settings that are enabled or disabled are inherited as such.

If GPOs are configured for both a parent and a child, settings in the GPOs are combined if the settings are compatible. For example, a setting on the parent OU that calls for a certain password length and a setting on the child OU that calls for a certain account lockout policy would both be used. When settings are incompatible, the default is for settings linked to the child container to override settings linked to the parent container.

> **Tip**   The General tab of a GPO's Properties dialog box has options to disable unused computer and user configuration settings in the GPO. Most policies use only a fraction of the available settings. Since all settings in all policies must be processed, requiring a computer to process unconfigured settings requires unnecessary system resources. By disabling the unused settings, you can ease the load on client computers having to process the policy.

Of course, inheritance as just described is only the default. There are also two other mechanisms you can use to control the inheritance of Group Policy, including:

- **No Override**   When you link a GPO to a container, you can configure a No Override option that prevents settings in the GPO from being overridden by settings in GPOs linked to child containers. This provides a way to force child containers to conform to a particular policy.

- **Block Inheritance**   You can configure the Block Inheritance option on a container to prevent the container from inheriting GPO settings from its parent containers. However, if a parent container has the No Override option set, the child container cannot block inheritance from this parent.

These two options create powerful exceptions to the inheritance rule, but you should resort to using them only in rare circumstances. It is much better to create a solid Group Policy design using OUs that places Group Policy where it needs to be instead of creating a system of exceptions that can be difficult to keep track of.

> **Exam Tip**   In questions that deal with Group Policy, keep the rules of inheritance in mind. Also remember how Group Policy is combined: First, the local GPO is applied, then the domain, site, and OU GPOs. Finally, remember that GPOs cannot be linked directly to users, groups, or to Built-in containers. GPOs can be linked only to a site, domain, or OU.

Filtering GPOs with Permissions

One potential problem with group policy can arise when you want to, for example, link a GPO to an OU that has 500 users and 20 groups and you don't want to have the settings applied to all of those people.

To prevent a policy from applying to either a user or a group, you can change permission settings for those users. Two permissions are needed for a policy to apply: the Read permission on the policy (because logically, if you cannot read a policy, then you cannot apply it) and the Apply Group Policy permission (which speaks for itself). The way to prevent a user or group from having a policy applied is to change permissions so that you deny the ability to read or apply the policy in question.

Planning a GPO Structure

Group Policy is implemented by first creating GPOs and then linking them to sites, domains, and OUs. Although some GPOs may need to be applied at the domain or site level, the majority of GPOs should be applied at the OU level.

Linking GPOs to a Domain

GPOs linked to a domain apply to all users and computers in the domain. This is a powerful policy, so you should keep GPOs at this level to a minimum. The typical use for GPOs at the domain level is to implement corporate standards. For example, a company might have a standard requirement that all users and computers use the same password and authentication policy company-wide. This would be a perfect application of a domain-based GPO.

Linking GPOs to a Site

Very few GPOs are linked to sites, mostly because it is more efficient to link GPOs to geographically-based OUs. However, there are circumstances in which linking a GPO to a site is an appropriate choice. If you have requirements for settings that are common to all computers in a particular physical location and that location is defined by a site, then linking a GPO to that site might make sense. For example, computers in a particular branch office might need a particular network configuration applied for Internet connectivity. A site-based GPO would be ideal for that situation.

Linking GPOs to OUs

For the most part, it's better to link GPOs to a well-thought-out OU structure than to sites or domains. OUs provide the most flexibility because you can, at least in part, design the structure to facilitate Group Policy. Also, OUs offer more administrative flexibility. You can move users and computers between OUs easily and also rearrange or rename the OUs themselves.

> ### Real World   Redirecting New User and Computer Accounts
>
> By default, new user and computer accounts are created in the Users and Computers containers, respectively. You cannot link a GPO to either of these built-in containers. Even though the built-in containers inherit GPOs linked to the domain, you may have a situation that requires user accounts and computer accounts to be stored in an OU to which you can link a GPO.
>
> Windows Server 2003 includes two new tools that let you redirect the target location for new user and computer accounts. You can use redirusr.exe to redirect user accounts and redircomp.exe to redirect computer accounts. Once you choose the OU for redirection, new user and computer accounts are created directly in the new target OU, where the appropriate GPOs are linked. For example, you could create an OU named New Users, link an appropriate GPO to the OU, and then redirect the creation of new-users accounts to the New Users OU. Any new users created would immediately be affected by the settings in the GPO. Administrators could then move the new user accounts to a more appropriate location later.
>
> You can find both of these tools in the %windir%\system32 folder on any computer running Windows Server 2003. You can learn more about using these tools in Knowledge Base article 324949, "Redirecting the Users and Computers Containers in Windows Server 2003 Domains," in the Microsoft Knowledge Base at *http://support.microsoft.com.*

Planning the Deployment of GPOs

An important aspect of planning Group Policy for a company is creating a plan for the management of Group Policy following the initial deployment. Part of this management plan will be determining who manages Group Policy within an organization. Another part is making sure that the client computers on the network can accept settings imposed by a GPO.

Administration of Group Policy

Most likely, the creation and management tasks involved with GPOs will need to be delegated to different administrators in an organization. Based on your organization's administrative model, you need to determine which aspects of configuration management can best be handled at the site, domain, and OU levels. You also need to determine how responsibilities at each site, domain, and OU level might be further subdivided among the available administrators or administrative groups at each level.

When deciding whether to delegate authority at the site, domain, or OU level, you should be aware of the following points:

■ Authority delegated at the domain level affects all objects in the domain if the permission is set to inherit to all child containers.

■ Authority delegated at the OU level can affect either that OU only, or that OU and its child OUs.

■ Managing permissions is easier and more efficient if you assign control at the highest OU level possible.

■ Authority delegated at the site level is likely to span domains and can influence objects in domains other than the domain where the GPO is located.

To manage GPOs, administrators must have the following permissions:

■ Editing GPOs linked to sites requires Enterprise Administrative permissions.

■ Editing GPOs linked to domains requires Domain Administrative permissions.

■ Editing GPOs linked to OUs requires permissions for the OU.

Client Requirements for Supporting Group Policy

For client computers to accept Group Policy settings, they must be members of Active Directory. Support for Group Policy for key operating systems includes the following:

■ Windows 95/98/Me do not support Group Policy.

■ Windows NT 4.0 and earlier versions do not support Group Policy.

■ Windows 2000 Professional and Server support many of the Group Policy settings available in Windows Server 2003, but not all. Unsupported settings are ignored.

■ Windows XP Professional, Windows XP 64-bit Edition, and Windows Server 2003 fully support Group Policy.

See Also   You can find out more about the specific support Windows 2000 Professional has for Group Policy settings in Windows Server 2003 in the *Microsoft Windows Server 2003 Deployment Kit* (Microsoft Press, 2003).

Practice: Designing a Group Policy Implementation

In this practice, you modify the organizational unit structure that supports Northwind Traders' Group Policy requirements. If you are unable to answer a question, review the lesson materials and try the question again. You can find answers to the questions in the "Questions and Answers" section at the end of this chapter.

Scenario

Northwind Traders is progressing with its Active Directory design project. The company has already decided on an organizational unit structure, as shown in the following table.

Domains	Organizational Units
Nwtraders.local	None
Corp.nwtraders.local	HQ Management Finance IT
NAwest.nwtraders.local	Sales Marketing IT
NAeast.nwtraders.local	Customer Service Customer Support Training
Glasgow.RDNwtraders.local	Research Development Sustained Engineering IT
AsiaPacific.nwtraders.local	Consulting Production

The following table shows the geographical locations, the departments in each location, and the specific Group Policy requirements for each location.

Location	Departments Represented	Group Policy Requirements
Paris	HQ Management staff Finance Sales Marketing Production Research Development Information Technology (IT)	Due to the confidential nature of their work, all executives require that their laptop computers have specific security settings. However, they do not want these security settings to be applied to their desktop computers. All servers in the Finance department must use IPSec for all communications.

Location	Departments Represented	Group Policy Requirements
Los Angeles	Sales Marketing Finance IT	All personnel in the Sales department must have a customer tracking application installed on their computers. All laptop computers in this location must have a password-protected screen saver configured on them.
Atlanta	Customer Service Customer Support Training	All personnel in the Customer Support department who work in the call center have specific applications that must be installed on their computers.
Glasgow, Scotland	Research Development Sustained Engineering IT	All computers, even new computers that have just joined the domain, require an IPSec policy to be applied. All computers in the Research department require specific security settings.
Sydney, Australia	Consulting Production Sales Finance	All computers in the Production department are used by multiple people on different shifts. These computers require specific desktop and user interface settings for users who log on to these computers.

Practice Questions

Based on the scenario, modify the OU structure to support Northwind Traders' Group Policy requirements by answering the following questions.

1. Which additional OUs must be created to support Group Policy?

_____

_____

2. Who will be responsible for managing Group Policy in each domain?

_____

_____

Lesson Review

The following questions are intended to reinforce key information presented in this lesson. If you are unable to answer a question, review the lesson materials and try the question again. You can find answers to the questions in the "Questions and Answers" section at the end of this chapter.

1. To what objects can you apply settings using Group Policy? What types of settings can you enforce using Group Policy?

   _____

   _____

2. In what order are GPOs resolved when they come from multiple sources? What happens when multiple GPOs are linked to a single container in Active Directory?

   _____

   _____

3. You are preparing a plan for a GPO that will be linked to an OU that contains user and group accounts. You want the GPO to apply settings to all accounts in the OU except for two group accounts. What could you do?

   _____

   _____

Lesson Summary

- Group Policy lets you apply settings to many user and computer objects at once. You can use Group Policy to deploy and update software to client computers, configure and enforce Windows settings, and distribute registry settings using Administrative Templates.

- When planning Group Policy, you need to determine what settings need to be deployed to clients and the best way to go about that. You can link GPOs to domains, sites, and OUs. GPOs linked to domains and sites should be kept to a minimum. Most GPOs should be linked to a well-planned OU structure.

- You should plan your OU structure to take full advantage of GPO inheritance. Remember not to plan too deep because every GPO that must be applied to a client uses more system resources. Remember also that you can block the inheritance of a GPO linked to a parent or set a No Override option that prevents child objects from blocking or overriding GPOs inherited from a parent. You can also prevent GPOs from affecting certain objects by filtering with permissions.

Case Scenario Exercise

You have been selected to plan an administrative structure for Humongous Insurance, a national provider of health insurance. All servers on its network have recently been upgraded to Windows Server 2003 Enterprise Edition. Client computers are running a mix of Windows NT Professional 4.0, Windows 2000 Professional, and Windows XP Professional. Humongous Insurance has hired you to design an OU, account, and Group Policy structure.

Background

Humongous has grown over the past several years to become one of the leading suppliers of health insurance to major corporations and government institutions across the United States.

Geography

Humongous Insurance's corporate headquarters is in Los Angeles, California. In addition to its primary location, Humongous Insurance also has major corporate offices in Buffalo, New York, and in Dallas, Texas. There are also hundreds of branch offices in cities throughout all fifty states. All three main corporate offices have a fully staffed IT department that is responsible for maintaining its own network structure. The corporate headquarters in Los Angeles maintains the executive IT staff, which is ultimately responsible for all decisions and directives concerning the network. The IT staff in Los Angeles also provides support for branch offices.

Network Infrastructure

The Buffalo, Dallas, and Los Angeles offices are connected to one another via 1 Mbps frame relay links. Branch offices are connected by a variety of links of different speeds and types.

The network is configured as a single domain named humongousinsurance.com. The Buffalo, Dallas, and Los Angeles locations are each configured as their own site, as are each of the branch offices. This decision was made primarily to control replication traffic across the WAN links.

IT Management

The IT staff in Los Angeles sets structure and policy requirements for the entire network. They are also responsible for directly managing the branch offices. A separate IT staff in Buffalo and one in Dallas manages the networks there. However, the senior IT staff in Los Angeles has the ultimate responsibility for the entire network.

Requirements

The IT staff in Los Angeles has set a number of standards that must be followed by all locations. Computer account names for servers must describe the location of the computer and its function. Computer account names for workstations must describe the user of the computer and the location. Password policies are strict. Passwords must be changed once each month and passwords cannot be reused within 12 months. When the wrong credentials are entered more than five times, the user account is disabled until the user contacts an administrator.

The IT staff also wants to use Group Policy to deploy standardized installations of software across the network to certain computers. The staff does not want the users to have to make too many decisions about the installation. Ideally, they would like the installation to be started automatically without requiring the users' input.

Questions

Given the previous scenario, answer the following questions.

1. Sketch out an OU design for the company using the location-based model. What would be the advantages and disadvantages of using the location-based model?

2. Based on the company's corporate requirements, what password policy settings would you enforce? What authentication policy settings would you use?

3. What computer-account naming strategy would you use for servers on the network? For user workstations?

4. Based on the scenario, what method would you use to deploy software using Group Policy?

Chapter Summary

- Create an OU structure that makes it easier to delegate control to administrators and that makes it easier to find resources and accounts. You can create either an object-based or a task-based administrative structure.

- Specific reasons for creating an OU are to delegate control of administration, limit the visibility of objects, and control the application of Group Policy. Start by focusing on the delegation of administration and then fill out the structure according to your other needs.

- You should base your top-level OUs on a relatively static aspect of the business such as geography, administrative tasks, or objects, and then use lower-level OUs to represent more detailed levels of administrative authority.

- Take advantage of inheritance in your designs to facilitate the flow of permissions throughout the structure. Block inheritance where you need object permissions to override the permissions that would be inherited from the parent.

- Active Directory in Windows Server 2003 provides five types of accounts: user, computer, group, contact, and InetOrgPerson.

- Computer accounts allow member computers to be authenticated in a manner that is transparent to users. You should create a plan for naming computer accounts and define who has the right to add computer accounts to Active Directory.

- User accounts identify a user and authenticate users for access to network resources. Your user-account strategy should include a solid naming convention, a password policy, and an authentication policy.

- Groups simplify the assignment of permissions by organizing users. The scope of a group determines where in Active Directory a group is accessible and what objects can become members. Group scopes include global groups, universal groups, and domain local groups.

- When placing users into groups, remember that user accounts go into global groups; global groups go into universal groups; universal groups go into domain local groups; and permissions are assigned to domain local groups.

- Group Policy lets you apply settings to many user and computer objects at once. You can use Group Policy to deploy and update software to client computers, configure and enforce Windows settings, and distribute registry settings using Administrative Templates.

- When planning Group Policy, you need to determine what settings need to be deployed to clients and the best way to go about deploying them. You can link GPOs to domains, sites, and OUs. GPOs linked to domains and sites should be kept to a minimum. Most GPOs should be linked to a well-planned OU structure.

- You should plan your OU structure to take full advantage of GPO inheritance. Remember not to plan too deep because every GPO that must be applied to a client uses more system resources. Remember also that you can block the inheritance of a GPO linked to a parent or set a No Override option that prevents child objects from blocking or overriding GPOs inherited from a parent. You can also prevent GPOs from affecting certain objects by filtering with permissions.

Exam Highlights

Before taking the exam, review the key topics and terms that are presented in this chapter. You need to know this information.

Key Points

- You should start by creating an OU structure that delegates administrative control effectively. Once you have created this structure, you can create lower-level OUs to control Group Policy or hide objects.

- When placing users into groups, remember the acronym AGUDLP. User accounts go into global groups, which go into universal groups, which go into domain local groups, which have permissions applied to them.

- GPOs are processed first locally, then in Active Directory starting with the farthest point from the user. The order of GPO processing is: local, then site, then domain, then OU.

- Finally, remember that GPOs cannot be linked directly to users, groups, or to Built-in containers. GPOs can be linked only to a site, domain, or OU.

Key Terms

OU Model   You can use any of the five standard organizational unit models described in this chapter: location-based; organization-based; function-based; hybrid of location, then organization; and hybrid of organization, then location.

Account   Windows Server 2003 provides five types of accounts that you can create: user accounts, which allow people to log on to the network; computer accounts, which allow authentication of computers in Active Directory; groups, which let you organize users and other groups for assigning permissions; contacts, which reference people outside the network; and the InetOrgPerson object, which works like a user account and is compatible with other LDAP-based directory services.

Group Policy   You can use Group Policy to deploy software and Windows settings to client computers. Create a collection of settings, referred to as a Group Policy object, and then link the GPO to a domain, site, or OU.

Questions and Answers

Page
4-19

Lesson 1 Practice

Based on the newly approved forest and domain design, create the organizational unit structure for Northwind Traders. Use the table to complete your design.

Domain	Organizational units
nwtraders.local	None
Corp.nwtraders.local	HQ Management Finance IT
NAwest.nwtraders.local	Sales Marketing IT
NAeast.nwtraders.local	Customer Service Customer Support Training
Glasgow.RDNwtraders.local	Research Development Sustained Engineering IT
AsiaPacific.nwtraders.local	Consulting Production

Page
4-20

Lesson 1 Review

1. What are the three specific purposes for which you would create an OU? Of those three, which should be the driving influence of your overall OU design?

The three purposes for using OUs are to delegate administrative control of objects, to limit the visibility of objects, and to control the application of group policy. Of these, you should let the delegation of administrative control be the driving design influence.

2. Describe the difference between an object-based and a task-based OU structure.

In an object-based OU structure, delegation of control is assigned according to the type of object that will be stored in the OUs. In a task-based OU structure, delegation of control is assigned based on the administrative tasks that need to be accomplished rather than on the objects that need administration.

3. You are preparing your directory plan. One of the requirements is that you be able to delegate control of user objects by assigning Group Policy. What must you do?

Because the built-in Users container is not an OU, you cannot link a GPO to it. You will need to create a new OU, place users inside it, and then link a GPO to that OU.

4. What are the advantages of using a location-based OU model? What are the disadvantages?

The advantages include greater resistance to company reorganization; easier implementation of domain-wide policies by a central administrative staff; greater ease locating resources; and ease in creating new OUs for new locations. The disadvantages include potential difficulty restricting administrative rights; the possible need for administrators at each location; and a design that may not follow any business or administrative structure.

Page
4-31

Lesson 2 Review

1. What are the five types of accounts you can create in Active Directory for Windows Server 2003?

The five types of accounts you can create are computer, user, group, contact, and InetOrgPerson.

2. You are creating a password policy. What are the recommended requirements you should impose for passwords?

At least the last 24 passwords used should be remembered. Users should also be required to change their passwords at regular intervals. The default (and Microsoft's recommendation) is 42 days. Users should also have to retain passwords for at least one day to prevent them from rapidly switching back to their favored passwords. Passwords should be at least seven characters and should be complex (a mix of alphanumeric and non-alphanumeric characters and a mix of upper and lower case).

3. What is the recommended strategy for placing users into security groups?

Place user accounts into global groups. Place global groups into universal groups. Place universal groups into domain local groups. Assign permissions to the domain local groups.

Page
4-41

Lesson 3 Practice

1. Which additional OUs must be created to support Group Policy?

Creating OUs is only one possible way to filter the application of Group Policy. You can use other methods, such as security groups, to accomplish the same goal.

Create a new OU in the HQ Management OU named Laptops. This OU will contain all the computer accounts for the executives' laptop computers.

Create a new OU named LaptopComputers in the NAwest domain to simplify the application of Group Policy settings to all laptop computers in this location.

Create a new OU named CallCenter in the CustomerSupport OU. This OU will contain all the computer accounts for the computers in the call center and will enable you to easily apply specific group policy settings to these computers.

Create a new OU in the Glasgow domain named ComputerAccounts, and use the redircmp.exe command to cause all newly created computer accounts to be redirected to the new OU.

2. Who will be responsible for managing Group Policy in each domain?

The IT group in Paris will manage all Group Policy settings in Atlanta, Paris, and Sydney. The local IT staff will manage Group Policy settings in all other locations.

Page
4-42

Lesson 3 Review

1. To what objects can you apply settings using Group Policy? What types of settings can you enforce using Group Policy?

Group Policy lets you apply settings to users and computers in Active Directory. You can use Group Policy to deploy and update software, configure Windows settings, and distribute registry settings via Administrative Templates.

2. In what order are GPOs resolved when they come from multiple sources? What happens when multiple GPOs are linked to a single container in Active Directory?

GPOs on the local computer are always resolved first. After this, Active Directory GPOs are resolved. First, GPOs linked to the site are resolved, followed by GPOs linked to the domain, and, finally, GPOs linked to OUs. If settings are compatible, they are combined. Otherwise, each subsequent GPO overrides settings made by the previously applied GPO. If multiple GPOs are configured for a single container, the administrator can determine the order in which they should be applied.

3. You are preparing a plan for a GPO that will be linked to an OU that contains user and group accounts. You want the GPO to apply settings to all accounts in the OU except for two group accounts. What could you do?

You have a couple of options. You could create a new child OU in the existing OU and then move the two group accounts into it. You would then need to override the settings made by the GPO or block the inheritance of that GPO from the parent container. Your other option is to leave the two groups where they are and filter out the GPO by removing the permissions for those two groups from reading or applying the GPO.

Page
4-44

Case Scenario Exercise

1. Sketch out an OU design for the company using the location-based model. What would be the advantages and disadvantages of using the location-based model?

A location-based design would have an OU for each of the major corporate locations and probably just one OU that encompassed all of the branch offices together. The location-based model provides several advantages, including being resistant to corporate restructuring, letting a centralized staff implement domain-wide policies, and making it easier to find resources based on their location. The disadvantages include the possible need for network administrators at each location and a design that doesn't really follow administrative procedures.

2. Based on the company's corporate requirements, what password policy settings would you enforce? What authentication policy settings would you use?

To meet requirements, you should implement password policy settings that include the following: Maximum Password Age policy set to 30 days and Enforce Password History policy set to 12 passwords. Password security is further supported by the default settings that require password complexity and a minimum password age of 1 day. Authentication requirements could be met by creating an account lockout policy that disables accounts after five failed password attempts. You could strengthen authentication requirements further by implementing logon hours and creating a ticket expiration policy.

3. What computer-account naming strategy would you use for servers on the network? For user workstations?

Servers should be identified by location and function. Ideally, the server name should indicate that the computer is a server. Using the letters SRV is a popular way to achieve this. The location could be identified by the first three letters of the city name (another solution would be to use three-letter airport codes). How you identify the function is pretty much up to you, but you should be consistent throughout the network. Using a computer name such as SRV-DAL-EXCH could indicate a server in Dallas that runs Exchange Server, for example.

4. Based on the scenario, what method would you use to deploy software using Group Policy?

You should use Group Policy to assign the applications to computers. When an application is assigned to a computer, the application is installed the first time the computer starts up following the assignment.

5 Designing a Site Plan

Exam Objectives in this Chapter:

- Design the Active Directory infrastructure to meet business and technical requirements.
  - ❑ Design the Active Directory replication strategy.
- Design an Active Directory directory service site topology.
  - ❑ Design sites.
  - ❑ Identify site links.
- Design an Active Directory implementation plan.
  - ❑ Design the placement of domain controllers and global catalog servers.
  - ❑ Plan the placement of flexible operations master roles.
  - ❑ Select the domain controller creation process.
- Design migration paths to Active Directory.
  - ❑ Define whether the migration will include an in-place upgrade, domain restructuring, or migration to a new Active Directory environment.

Why This Chapter Matters

In Chapter 3, "Planning an Active Directory Structure," and Chapter 4, "Designing an Administrative Security Structure," you learned to design the logical side of an Active Directory (AD) infrastructure. This included the forest and domain structure as well as an administrative structure of organizational units, users, and groups. In this chapter, you learn to use sites to define the physical structure of a network. One of the primary tasks of any network designer is controlling the traffic that occurs between remote locations over WAN links, and sites are the main tool you will use to achieve that control.

In this chapter, you learn to determine the placement of sites and specify how those sites are linked. You also learn to create designs that optimize the intrasite and intersite replication process. You learn how to determine the placement of domain controllers and how to plan other roles your servers may play. Finally, you learn how to plan a migration path from previous versions of Windows.

Lessons in this Chapter:

Before You Begin

To complete this chapter, make sure you are familiar with the Active Directory concepts described in Chapter 1, "Introduction to Active Directory and Network Infrastructure." You should also have gathered and analyzed any information about the existing Active Directory infrastructure of your company, as discussed in Chapter 2, "Analyzing an Existing Infrastructure." In particular, you use the geographic and network topology information you gathered about a company to design a site topology.

Lesson 1: Designing a Site Topology

The first step in designing a site plan is to decide on the site topology—the placement of the sites themselves and how those sites are linked. This lesson looks at how sites are used, then describes the factors you must take into account when designing a site topology.

After this lesson, you will be able to

- Explain how sites are used to control network traffic across wide area network (WAN) links.
- Specify site boundaries based on the physical network structure.
- Identify how sites are linked.

Estimated lesson time: 20 minutes

Why Sites Are Used

As you remember from Chapter 1, a site is a group of domain controllers existing on one or more Internet Protocol (IP) subnets that are connected by a fast, reliable network connection. Because sites are based on IP subnets, they typically follow the topology of a network and, therefore, the geographic boundaries of a company as well, as shown in Figure 5-1. Sites are connected to other sites using WAN links.

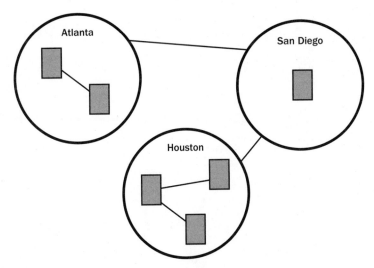

Figure 5-1   A simple site topology is based on geography.

Sites in Active Directory provide a way to abstract the logical organization of the directory structure (the forest, domain, and organizational unit [OU] structure) from the physical layout of the network. Sites take the responsibility for representing the physical layout within Active Directory. Because sites are independent of the domain structure, a single domain can include multiple sites or a single site can include multiple domains, as shown in Figure 5-2.

A single site for each domain   A single domain spanning two sites   A single site spanning two domains

Figure 5-2   Sites and domains are independent.

Sites are not part of the Active Directory namespace. When a user browses the logical namespace, computers and users are grouped into domains and OUs without reference to sites. However, site names are used in the Domain Name System (DNS) records, so sites must be given valid DNS names.

Unless you configure your own sites in Active Directory, all domain controllers are automatically made a part of a single site—a default site named "Default-First-Site-Name" that is created when you create the first domain. Sites contain only two types of objects. The first type is the domain controllers contained in the site. The second type of object is the site links configured to connect the site to other sites.

Generally speaking, sites are used to control traffic over WAN links. More specifically, sites are used to control the following:

- Workstation logon traffic
- Replication traffic
- Distributed File System (DFS)
- File Replication Service (FRS)

Controlling Workstation Logon Traffic

When a user logs on to the network, Microsoft Windows 2000 and Microsoft Windows XP computers search for domain controllers in the same site as the workstation. During logon, domain controllers use a client's IP address to determine which site the client is actually from and send the site information back to the client. The domain controller also sends information to the client about the closest domain controller. This information is cached for future use to increase logon efficiency.

Using a domain controller in the same site prevents authentication traffic from crossing WAN links unnecessarily. If there is no domain controller at a client's location, the client authenticates itself using a domain controller in a site that has the lowest cost connection relative to other sites. Service (SRV) records are created in DNS and provide each site with a preferred domain controller for authentication.

Controlling Replication Traffic

Active Directory uses a replication model called multimaster replication, in which all replicas of the Active Directory database are considered equal masters. Changes made to the Active Directory database on any domain controller are automatically replicated to all other domain controllers in the domain.

Within the boundaries of a site, domain controllers replicate changes as they happen. When a change is made on one domain controller, it notifies its replication partners (the other domain controllers in the site); the partners then request the changes and replication occurs almost immediately. Replication between domain controllers in the same site is transmitted in an uncompressed format. Because a high bandwidth connection is assumed, using an uncompressed format ensures that the replication happens as quickly as possible, even though it generates more network traffic.

Replication between sites happens a bit differently. When replication occurs between sites, a single domain controller for each domain in each site collects and stores the directory changes, compresses them, and then transmits them at a scheduled time to a domain controller in another site. Between sites, replication is optimized for efficiency rather than for speed. You'll learn more about the replication process in Lesson 3.

Controlling a Distributed File System (DFS) Topology

Distributed File System (DFS) is a server component that provides a unified naming convention for folders and files stored on different servers on a network. DFS lets you create a single logical hierarchy for folders and files that is consistent on a network, regardless of where on the network those items are actually stored.

Files represented in the DFS might be stored in multiple locations on the network, so it makes sense that Active Directory should be able to direct users to the closest physical location of the data they need. To this end, DFS uses site information to direct a client to the server that is hosting the requested data within the site. If DFS does not find a copy of the data within the same site as the client, DFS uses the site information in Active Directory to determine which file server that has DFS shared data is closest to the client.

See Also   For more information on using DFS in Windows Server 2003, check out the document "Simplifying Infrastructure Complexity with Windows Distributed File System," available at *http://www.microsoft.com/windowsserver2003/techinfo/overview/dfs.mspx.*

Controlling the File Replication Service (FRS)

Every domain controller has a built-in collection of folders named SYSVOL (for System Volume). The SYSVOL folders provide a default Active Directory location for files that must be replicated throughout a domain. You can use SYSVOL to replicate Group Policy Objects, startup and shutdown scripts, and logon and logoff scripts. A Windows Server 2003 service named File Replication Service (FRS) is responsible for replicating files in the SYSVOL folders between domain controllers. FRS uses site boundaries to govern the replication of items in the SYSVOL folders.

See Also   For more information on the FRS in Windows Server 2003, read the white paper, "Technical Overview of Windows Server 2003 File Services," available at *http://www.microsoft.com/windowsserver2003/techinfo/overview/file.mspx.*

Choosing Site Boundaries

To design an effective site topology, you must first have gathered information about the physical network structure; this was the subject of Chapter 2. In particular, you need the following information:

- The geographic locations in which the company maintains offices

- The layout and speed of the local area networks (LANs) in each location

- The Transmission Control Protocol/Internet Protocol (TCP/IP) subnets in each location

- The total and available bandwidth of WAN connections between each location

In addition to having information about the physical structure of the network, you must also have a logical Active Directory design in place. This includes a forest and domain plan, and an administrative hierarchy. You should also have information on the DNS structure for Active Directory.

Once you have all this information, you're ready to figure out where you will locate your site boundaries. For the most part, sites will follow geographic boundaries because each distinct location will be part of the same high-speed LAN. However, this is not always the case. If an entire network is connected with fast, reliable links, you can consider the network a single site.

In general, though, you should use the following guidelines when creating a site design:

- Create a site for each LAN or set of LANs that is connected by a high-speed back-bone. Typically, but not always, these LANs coincide with the geographic locations of a company. Keep in mind, however, that even though two distant sites are connected by a high-speed link, the latency between the two locations is often a good reason to create separate sites anyway.

- Create a site for each geographic location at which you plan to put a domain controller. Lesson 2 covers the placement of domain controllers in more detail.

- Create a site for each location that contains a server running a site-aware application. If a location has servers that host shares in a DFS hierarchy, for example, you could create a site to control client access to those DFS shares.

Exam Tip   There is debate in the real world over what constitutes a fast connection, and you'll see documentation that ranges from 512 Kbps to 3 Mbps as the recommended speed for intrasite communications. However, for the purposes of designing sites on the exam, a fast connection is one that is at least 10 Mbps. In other words, a site usually follows a LAN's boundaries. If different LANs on the network are connected by a WAN, your best bet is to create a site for each LAN.

Sometimes it will not make sense to create a site for a geographic location, even if there is relatively low bandwidth between that location and the rest of the network. This especially holds true for smaller locations that do not have many users, do not have any domain controllers, and do not have any servers hosting site-aware services. In cases like this, it is often better to add the IP subnet for the location to another site on the network, even if there is limited bandwidth. The traffic generated by authentication requests from such a small site is relatively minor. Creating a new site comes with its own overhead in the form of increased network traffic (because domain controllers must track sites and refer users) and increased management. You must weigh the benefits of creating sites to control traffic with the overhead created by the sites themselves.

When you create a site plan, you should start by making a simple diagram that represents all the sites on the network, as shown in Figure 5-3. Include the total and available bandwidth for the connections between sites. For each site, you should then include the following information:

- **The name of the site**   This should be the actual name for the site object that will be created in Active Directory. If the site is not named after the location, you should also include the location on your diagram.

■ **The subnets that are included in the site** You should list the IP address range of the subnet, the name that will be assigned to the subnet object in Active Directory, and the subnet mask.

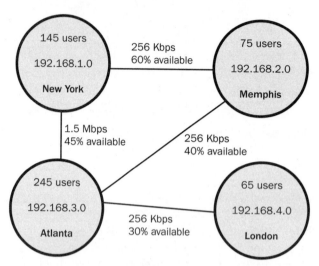

Figure 5-3 A typical site diagram includes available bandwidth between locations.

The Site Topology Owner

When designing a site plan, you should also give consideration to the people who will manage the site structure after its deployment. The site topology owner is the name given to the administrator (or administrators) that oversee the site topology. The owner is responsible for making any necessary changes to the site as the physical network grows and changes. The site topology owner's responsibilities include:

■ Making changes to the site topology based on changes to the physical network topology.

■ Tracking subnetting information for the network. This includes IP addresses, subnet masks, and the locations of the subnets.

■ Monitoring network connectivity and setting the costs for links between sites.

Lesson Review

The following questions are intended to reinforce key information presented in this lesson. If you are unable to answer a question, review the lesson materials and try the question again. You can find answers to the questions in the "Questions and Answers" section at the end of this chapter.

1. You are designing a site plan for a company that has full corporate offices in Atlanta, Chicago, and Los Angeles. Each location is connected to the other two locations via a 512 Kbps connection. How many sites should you define?

   _____

   _____

2. For what functions are sites used to control network traffic?

   _____

   _____

3. What are the basic guidelines you should use when determining whether to create a site?

   _____

   _____

Lesson Summary

- Sites are used to control network traffic generated by workstation logon, Active Directory replication, Distributed File System (DFS), and File Replication Service (FRS).

- When preparing to design a site structure, you need to know the geographic locations of your company, the layout and speed of the LANs in each location, the TCP/IP subnets in each location, and the bandwidth between locations.

- You should create a site for each LAN (or set of LANs on a high-speed backbone), each location with a domain controller, and each location that hosts a site-aware service.

Lesson 2: Planning Domain Controllers

Once you have defined the site boundaries for a network, the next step in creating a site plan is to determine the number and placement of domain controllers in those sites. You must also determine whether each domain controller meets the hardware requirements for running Windows Server 2003 and for meeting the demands placed on it. This lesson covers how to assess the need for domain controllers in a site, whether domain controllers should play any additional roles, and how to determine the capacity required by each domain controller.

After this lesson, you will be able to

- Determine the placement of domain controllers within sites.
- Determine the placement of forest root domain controllers.
- Create a plan for global catalog servers.
- Specify operations masters roles for servers.
- Identify capacity requirements for domain controllers.

Estimated lesson time: 30 minutes

Planning Domain Controller Placement

Domain controllers are responsible for authenticating user logons, maintaining security policy for a domain, and maintaining and replicating the Active Directory database throughout a domain. An important part of designing a site plan is creating a plan for placing domain controllers. Specifically, you need to determine the following when planning domain controller placement:

- Whether a location needs a domain controller
- The number of domain controllers required in a site
- The placement of forest root domain controllers

Determining Whether a Location Needs a Domain Controller

The first step in creating a plan for the domain controllers on a network is figuring out where domain controllers should go. There is often a tendency to use too few domain controllers, with the assumption that the fewer domain controllers a domain has, the less management they require. There is also a tendency to place too many domain controllers, assuming that every distinct location on a network should have at least one. The assumptions behind both tendencies can be accurate, but are not always.

You should use the following guidelines to help determine whether you should place a controller in a site:

- If the site contains a large number of users, placing a domain controller in the site ensures that the authentication of user logons does not generate network traffic that must cross a WAN link to get to a remote domain controller.

- If users must be able to log on to the domain even when a WAN link is down, you should place a domain controller in the local site. If the WAN link is unavailable and no local domain controllers are available to process logon requests, users log on by using cached credentials, and they cannot access resources on any computers other than the one to which they are logged on.

- If there are site-aware applications in the site that users from the domain need to access, you should place a domain controller in the site. The servers that host the site-aware applications can then authenticate users using the local domain controller instead of generating authentication traffic that must cross a WAN link.

- If the site is a hub site (one that serves to connect other, smaller sites to one another), and the smaller sites do not have their own domain controllers, placing a domain controller in the hub site ensures better logon response.

As you can see, most of the decisions to place domain controllers in sites require that you strike a balance between the additional overhead of having extra domain controllers and the savings in authentication traffic that must cross WAN links. When you place a domain controller for any of the previous reasons, you should be aware of the following concerns:

- Domain controllers must be maintained. You should place domain controllers only in locations that have administrators qualified to manage the domain controllers. If there is no local administrator, you must set up access so that the Information Technology (IT) staff can manage the domain controller remotely.

- Domain controllers must be secured. Place domain controllers only in sites where you can ensure the physical security of the domain controller.

Determining the Number of Domain Controllers Required

Once you determine where domain controllers should be placed, your next challenge is determining how many domain controllers a site needs to fulfill the needs for each domain in the site.

The number of users from a domain that are located in a site is the primary factor in determining the number of domain controllers the site needs for that domain. To determine the basic number of domain controllers required for each domain in a site, consider the following:

- If a site contains fewer than 1,000 users in a particular domain, only one domain controller for the domain is required in the site.

- If a site contains between 1,000 and 10,000 users in a particular domain, you should place at least two domain controllers for the domain in the site.

- For each 5,000 additional users a site contains for a domain, you should place an additional domain controller for the domain in the site. For example, if a site contains 20,000 users from a domain, you should place four domain controllers for that domain in the site.

You also must consider the overhead that intersite replication causes when figuring out the number of domain controllers you need in a site. The basic rule of thumb is that for every 15 replication connections to a site, you should add an extra domain controller to handle the load.

Real World   Domain Controller Redundancy

Even if you can support the requirements of a site with only one domain controller, you must place at least two domain controllers in a site to provide a level of fault tolerance if one domain controller fails. Also, a second domain controller can help balance the load even when it is not technically required. In general, you can provide a decent level of fault tolerance by placing one domain controller more than the minimum number you determine will handle the load. Having an extra domain controller available prevents the remaining domain controllers from becoming overloaded if one fails.

Placing Forest Root Domain Controllers

The first domain created in a new forest is called the forest root domain, and it holds a special place among domains in the forest. The forest root domain provides the foundation for the forest structure and namespace. Also, the forest-level administrative groups Enterprise Admins and Schema Admins are located in the forest root domain.

Trust relationships between domains are transitive and all authentication between different regional domains flows either through the forest root domain (and is thus the responsibility of the forest root domain controller) or through specially configured shortcut trusts directly between the regional domains. If there are multiple domains in the same site, but the forest root domain is in a different site, you can create a shortcut trust or you can add a forest root domain controller to the local site to ensure that user authentication between the domains in the local site can occur even when a WAN link is down.

Planning Operations Masters Servers

Running contrary to the model that multimaster replication provides, there are tasks that can be performed only on a particular domain controller. These domain controllers fill what are known as operations masters roles. Operations masters are domain controllers that are assigned to complete certain tasks for a domain or forest; an operations master's duties are always specific to the domain or forest, and no other computer is allowed to complete these tasks. The tasks are separated into manageable areas, and because one server is responsible for one task, no other computer can take on that role.

Forest-Wide Operations Masters Roles

There are two forest-wide operations masters roles in Windows Server 2003. These roles are:

- **Schema Master**   The first domain controller in the forest holds the role of the Schema Master and is responsible for maintaining and distributing the schema to the rest of the forest. It maintains a list of all the possible classes of attributes that define the objects found in AD. If the schema needs to be updated or changed, as in the case of installing an application that must make modifications to the classes or attributes within the schema, it must be updated on the Schema Master (that is, the domain controller [DC] serving as the Schema Master must be available), and the update must be performed by a member of the Schema Admins group. If the DC serving as the Schema Master is unavailable and you must make the changes to the schema, then you can move this role to another available DC.

- **Domain Naming Master**   The domain controller for the forest records the additions and deletions of domains to the forest; this operations master is important in maintaining the integrity of the domain. The Domain Naming Master is queried when new domains are added to the forest. Keep in mind that if the Domain Naming Master is not available, then new domains cannot be added; however, this role can be moved to another system if necessary. Another important point to remember about the Domain Naming Master (in a multiple domain environment) is that it must also be a global catalog server. This is because it queries the global catalog to verify that the creation of any additions to the forest is unique.

These two roles are automatically assigned to the first domain controller in the forest. In a single-domain forest (or in a multiple-domain forest where all domain controllers in the forest root domain host the global catalog), you should leave both the forest-wide operations masters roles on the first domain controller that is created in the forest root domain.

In a multiple-domain forest where the global catalog is not hosted on all domain controllers, you should move all of the forest-level operations masters roles to a domain controller in the forest root domain that is not designated as a global catalog server.

Domain-Wide Operations Masters Roles

There are three domain-wide operations masters roles in Windows Server 2003. These roles include:

- **Primary Domain Controller (PDC) Emulator**   The PDC Emulator is responsible for emulating a Windows NT 4 PDC for clients that have not migrated to Windows Server 2003. One of the PDC emulator's primary responsibilities is to log on legacy clients. The PDC emulator is also consulted if a client fails to log on.

- **Relative Identifier (RID) Master**   The RID Master is responsible for assigning blocks of RIDs to all domain controllers in a domain. A Security Identifier (SID) is a unique identifier for each object in a domain. SIDs are made up of two parts. The first part is common to all objects in the domain; a unique identifier (the RID) is then suffixed to create the unique SID for each object in a domain. Together, the RID and the suffix uniquely identify the object and specify where it was created.

- **Infrastructure Master**   This server records changes made concerning objects in a domain. All changes are reported to the Infrastructure Master first, and then they are replicated out to the other domain controllers. The Infrastructure Master deals with groups and group memberships for all domain objects. It is also an Infrastructure Master's role to update other domains with changes that have been made to objects. You should not assign the Infrastructure Master role to a domain controller that hosts the global catalog unless all domain controllers in the domain also host the global catalog. This is because the Infrastructure Master will not work properly if it contains any references to objects that are not part of the domain. If the Infrastructure Master is also a global catalog server, then the global catalog will have objects that the Infrastructure Master doesn't hold and it will interfere with the job of the Infrastructure Master.

All three domain-wide roles are automatically assigned to the first domain controller in the domain. Whenever possible, you should place all three domain-level roles on a single server in the domain. In fact, because the first domain controller installed assumes all three roles, it is best to just leave them that way. This greatly simplifies administration. Just remember that you'll either have to make sure that server does not host the global catalog or, if it does host the global catalog, that all other domain controllers in the domain host the global catalog as well.

Remember that users throughout the domain need regular access to the server (or servers) that fill these roles. If there are multiple sites in the domain, you should put the operations masters in the site that holds the largest number of users. If several sites hold large numbers of users, you need to make sure the operations masters are in a site that is relatively accessible to them all.

Planning Global Catalog Servers

A global catalog server is a domain controller that maintains a subset of Active Directory object attributes that are most commonly searched for by users or client computers, such as a user's logon name. Global catalog servers provide two important functions. They allow users to log on to the network, and they allow users to locate Active Directory objects anywhere in a forest without referring to specific domain controllers that store the objects.

The Active Directory is composed of three partitions:

- **Schema Partition**   This partition stores the definitions of all objects that can be created in a forest along with their attributes. There is only one schema partition for a forest. A copy is replicated to all domain controllers in the forest.

- **Configuration Partition**   This partition defines the Active Directory domain, site, and server object structure. There is only one configuration partition for a forest. A copy is replicated to all domain controllers in the forest.

- **Domain Partition**   This partition identifies and defines objects specific to a domain. Each domain has its own domain partition and a copy of it is replicated to all domain controllers in a domain.

Like all domain controllers, a global catalog server stores full, writable replicas of the schema and configuration directory partitions and a full, writable replica of the domain directory partition for the domain that it is hosting. In addition, a global catalog server stores the global catalog, which contains a subset of information in the domain partition and is replicated among domain controllers in the domain.

When a user attempts to log on or to access a network resource from anywhere in the forest, the global catalog is consulted for the resolution to the request. Without the global catalog, that request for access would have to be fielded by each domain controller in the forest until a resolution could be found. If your network uses a single domain, this function of the global catalog isn't really necessary because all domain controllers in the domain would have information on all users and objects on the network. With multiple domains, however, this function of the global catalog is essential.

The other function that the global catalog provides, which is useful whether you have one or many domains, is to assist in the authentication process when a user logs on to the network. When a user logs on using a user principal name (e.g., user@domain.com), that name is checked against the global catalog before the user is resolved. This provides the ability for users to log on from computers in domains other than where their user accounts are located. It also allows users to continue logging on to the network when a domain controller is unavailable, possibly due to a WAN link being down.

Note   Windows Server 2003 also includes a new feature named universal group membership caching. When this feature is enabled for a site, domain controllers in that site cache universal group membership information for users when they log on. The domain controllers also update this cache by contacting global catalog servers at set intervals. When the universal group membership caching feature is enabled, the domain controllers can authenticate users without referring to the global catalog. This feature is useful in small sites where placing a global catalog server would cause undue replication traffic.

The first domain controller installed in a forest becomes the global catalog server by default. Unlike operations masters roles, however, you can assign multiple domain controllers to serve as global catalog servers. Placing an appropriate number of global catalog servers in each location ensures a reasonable response for users when they log on to the network from a remote domain.

Exam Tip   In a single domain forest, make all domain controllers global catalog servers, because no extra space or replication traffic is generated. In multiple-domain forests, you can create as many global catalog servers as you want to achieve load balancing and redundancy of services. Microsoft recommends placing at least one global catalog server in each site.

Although you can make any domain controller a global catalog server, you should be careful when deciding which servers should fill the role. To start with, you cannot make the same domain controller an infrastructure master and a global catalog server. Also, you should note that being a global catalog server uses a significant amount of resources on the domain controller. For this reason, you would probably not want to make a global catalog server out of a domain controller that was fulfilling other demanding roles.

When placing global catalog servers in sites, use the following guidelines:

- If a site has more than 100 users, place a global catalog server in the site to help reduce authentication traffic over the WAN links. For smaller sites, use the universal group membership caching feature instead.

- If a site has multiple domain controllers, use multiple global catalog servers. The general rule of thumb is that you should place a number of global catalog servers equal to half the number of domain controllers in the site.

- Place global catalog servers in sites if particular applications in the site need to routinely search for information in the Active Directory. Being able to query a local global catalog server improves performance and reduces traffic over WAN links.

Planning Domain Controller Capacity

A domain controller's capacity refers to the number of users in a site that the domain controller can support. Understanding the demands that will be placed on each domain controller and planning the hardware requirements to handle those demands will help prevent a lot of frustration for administrators when they later find domain controllers becoming unresponsive under their load.

The primary factor in gauging the capacity requirements of a domain controller is the number of users that must be authenticated in the domain. Once you have estimated hardware requirements based on the number of users, you should then adapt those requirements to cover additional roles and services the domain controller will run.

Determining Processor Requirements

The number of processors a domain controller requires depends primarily on the number of users who will be logged on in the domain. To determine the processor requirements based on the number of users in a domain, consider the following.

- If there are fewer than 500 users, a domain controller running Windows Server 2003 requires a single processor with a speed of 850 MHz or better.

- If there are between 500 and 1,500 users, a domain controller running Windows Server 2003 requires two processors with a speed of 850 MHz or better.

- If there are more than 1,500 users, a domain controller running Windows Server 2003 should have four processors with a speed of 850 MHz or better.

> **Real World**   **Processing Power**
>
> While you should remember the requirements listed in the section, "Determining Processor Requirements," for the exam, there are other ways to approach processor requirements. As the number of users rise, domain controllers need more processing power. Instead of adding more processors, you can add more processing power. For example, a single 1.6 GHz processor could replace a dual 850 MHz setup; a 3 GHz processor could support as many users as a quad 850 MHz setup.
>
> Although multi-processor systems offer the advantage of being able to service more requests simultaneously, this benefit often does not outweigh the costs of using multiple processors. Systems that use multiple processors normally cost more than systems that use a single, more powerful processor. Also, some software is licensed based on the number of processors in a system.

Determining Disk Space Requirements

As with processor requirements, the amount of disk space required by a domain controller is mostly based on the number of users in the domain. To determine the disk requirements for a domain controller, consider the following:

- The drive that contains the Active Directory database (NTDS.dit) requires at least 400 MB of storage for every 1,000 users. This covers the space needed for the DNS partition.

- The drive that contains the Active Directory transaction log files requires at least 500 MB of disk space.

- The drive that holds the SYSVOL shared folder also requires at least 500 MB of disk space.

- The drive that holds the Windows Server 2003 operating system files needs around 2 GB of disk space.

Once you have figured out the minimum disk space requirements for your domain controllers, you must then provide extra disk space on the domain controllers that will host a global catalog. If a forest contains only one domain, designating a domain controller as a global catalog server does not increase the database size. However, if a forest contains more than one domain, each additional domain adds approximately 50 percent of its own database size to the global catalog.

Determining Memory Requirements

Once again, users are the primary determinant for the amount of memory a domain controller requires. To determine the memory requirements for a domain controller, consider the following:

- If there are fewer than 500 users, the domain controller requires 512 MB of memory.

- If there are between 500 and 1,000 users, the domain controller requires 1 GB of memory.

- If there are more than 1,000 users, the domain controller requires 2 GB of memory.

Tip   Microsoft offers a utility called the Active Directory Sizer Tool, which lets you estimate the hardware required for deploying Active Directory based on the number of users, domain information, and site topology of your network. You can find the tool at *http://www.microsoft.com/windows2000/downloads/tools/sizer/default.asp*. Even though the tool is designed for Windows 2000, it is still a useful tool for estimating hardware requirements for Windows Server 2003.

Practice: Planning Domain Controllers

In this practice, you design the placement of domain controllers and global catalog servers for Northwind Traders. If you are unable to answer a question, review the lesson materials and try the question again. You can find answers to the questions in the "Questions and Answers" section at the end of this chapter.

Scenario

Northwind Traders manufactures a line of network appliances designed to help companies improve their data transmission capabilities. Northwind Traders currently uses a Microsoft Windows NT 4.0 master domain model. In recent years, the company has undergone significant growth and expansion. The company expects substantial growth during the next three years, including growth in market share, revenue, and number of employees. In addition to opening two new offices, the executive management has committed to implementing a new Windows Server 2003 Active Directory design to meet the current and future needs of the company.

The geographic layout of the Northwind network is shown below. The IT staff at the corporate headquarters in Paris anticipate performing a good deal of searches on the information that will be contained within the Active Directory database. They have made this claim based on the amount of time spent searching the current master domain model for various resources and account information. In addition, there are quite a few representatives from regional offices who roam the Paris headquarters. They will need to log on easily in Paris and any other locations that they visit.

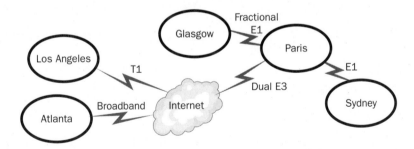

The Sydney office plans to roll out a number of server-based, site-aware Microsoft Distributed Component Object Model (DCOM) applications that will require quick response time.

Practice Questions

Based on the scenario, answer the following questions.

1. How many domain controllers would you place in each site? Why? Use the table below to complete your design.

Domain	Number of Domain Controllers in Each Site				
	Paris	**Glasgow**	**Sydney**	**Atlanta**	**Los Angeles**
Nwtraders.local					
AsiaPacific.nwtraders.local					
NAeast.nwtraders.local					
NAwest.nwtraders.local					
Corp.nwtraders.local					
RDNwtraders.local					
Glasgow.RDNwtraders.local					

2. In which sites will you place global catalog servers? In which sites will you enable universal group membership caching? Use the following table to complete your design.

Site	Number of Global Catalog Servers for Nwtraders.local Forest	Number of Global Catalog Servers for RDNwtraders.local Forest	Enable Universal Group Membership Caching for Site (Yes/No)
Paris			
Glasgow			
Sydney			
Atlanta			
Los Angeles			

Lesson Review

The following questions are intended to reinforce key information presented in this lesson. If you are unable to answer a question, review the lesson materials and try the question again. You can find answers to the questions in the "Questions and Answers" section at the end of this chapter.

1. What are the reasons for placing domain controllers into a site? What are reasons you might not be able to place a domain controller into a site?

   _____

   _____

2. You are determining the number of domain controllers to place in a site. There are 15,000 users in the site, and there are eight replication connections to the site. How many domain controllers should you place?

   _____

   _____

3. What are the recommendations for placing global catalog servers?

   _____

   _____

Lesson Summary

- The primary reason for placing a domain controller in a site is to cut down on WAN traffic between sites. This traffic comes in the form of users contacting domain controllers for authentication, site-aware applications using domain controllers for searches, and replication.

- If a site has fewer than 1,000 users, one domain controller is sufficient. If there are between 1,000 and 10,000 users, two domain controllers are recommended. Add an additional domain controller for every 5,000 users above 10,000. Even in sites with less than 1,000 users, though, you should consider using a second domain controller for the purposes of fault tolerance.

- When possible, you should make a single domain controller responsible for filling all the operations masters roles of a forest or domain. Just remember the rule that the Infrastructure Master should not host the global catalog unless all other domain controllers in the domain also host the global catalog.

- Global catalog servers maintain a subset of Active Directory object attributes that are most commonly searched for by users or client computers. They allow users to log on to the network and they allow users to locate AD objects anywhere in a forest without referring to specific domain controllers that store the objects.

- The hardware requirements for a domain controller are largely dependent on the number of users that must be authenticated within the domain. Once you establish requirements that meet these needs, you must also take into account whether the domain controller will host the global catalog or assume other roles.

Lesson 3: Planning a Replication Strategy

Active Directory replication is a vital process and deserves proper planning. A well-planned replication process ensures a responsive directory, a reduction in network traffic across WAN links, and a reduction in administrative overhead. This lesson examines the replication process and examines methods for building a solid replication strategy.

After this lesson, you will be able to

- Explain how Active Directory replication occurs within and between sites.
- Explain the use of site links, site-link bridges, and bridgehead servers.
- Define a replication strategy for a company.

Estimated lesson time: 25 minutes

The Replication Process

As you know, Windows Server 2003 uses a multimaster replication model where all domain controllers store a master copy of the Active Directory database. When you create, delete, or move an object or make changes to an object's attributes on any particular domain controller, those changes are replicated to other domain controllers.

Intrasite versus Intersite Replication

Because Active Directory can hold thousands, or even millions, of objects, replicating changes to those objects can easily consume network bandwidth and the system resources of domain controllers. Replication is handled differently between domain controllers in the same site (intrasite replication) and between domain controllers in different sites (intersite replication).

Intrasite replication sends replication traffic in an uncompressed format. This is because of the assumption that all domain controllers within the site are connected by high-bandwidth links. Not only is the traffic uncompressed, but also replication occurs according to a change notification mechanism. This basically means that if changes are made in the domain, those changes are quickly replicated to the other domain controllers.

Intersite replication sends all data compressed. This shows an appreciation for the fact that the traffic will probably be going across slower WAN links (as opposed to the LAN connectivity intrasite replication assumes), but it increases the load on the server side because compression/decompression is added to the processing requirements. In addition, the replication can be scheduled for times that are more appropriate to your organization. For example, you may decide to allow replication only during slower times of the day. Of course, this delay in replication (based on the schedule) causes a delay in replicating changes between servers in different sites.

See Also   For details on how the change notification system works and to learn more about the basic mechanics of replication, check out the *Directory Services Guide* of the *Microsoft Windows Server 2003 Server Resource Kit* (Microsoft Press, 2003).

You create additional sites when you need to control how replication traffic occurs over slower WAN links. For example, suppose you have a number of domain controllers on your main LAN and a few domain controllers on a LAN at a branch location. Those two LANs are connected to one another with a relatively slow WAN link. You would want replication traffic to occur as needed between the domain controllers on each LAN, but you would not want replication to occur as needed over the WAN link. To address this situation, you would set up two sites—one site that contained all the domain controllers on the main LAN and one site that contained all the domain controllers on the remote LAN.

Replication Transports

All communication within a network requires some transport to carry the information. The same is true of Active Directory replication traffic. The two transports that are used to replicate data are Remote Procedure Call (RPC) and Simple Mail Transfer Protocol (SMTP).

RPCs are for sending replication messages within a site and between sites. RPC is the default protocol for all Active Directory replication because it is an industry standard and is compatible with most network types.

SMTP can be used for replication between sites that are not connected with permanent connections (which are required for RPCs). One caveat regarding SMTP is that it doesn't replicate domain partition information to DCs in the domain. Because SMTP is used only for replication between sites, this is not a problem for replication of domain partition information within the domain (because this will automatically use RPC). This shows that SMTP is useful only for replication of the schema and the global catalog.

How Replication Happens

Each domain controller in a site is represented by a server object. Each server object has a child object named NTDS Settings that represents the replicating domain controller in the site. Each NTDS Settings object has a connection object that stores the attributes for a replication connection from one domain controller to another. The connection object represents a communication channel for replicating information from one domain controller to another. There must be a connection object at both ends for replication to occur.

A service named the Knowledge Consistency Checker (KCC) automatically creates the web of connection objects necessary for domain controllers to replicate to one another. However, you can also create connection objects manually if necessary.

The KCC creates different replication topologies (which basically means where the connection objects are located and how they are configured) for intrasite and intersite replication. The KCC also adjusts the topologies it creates whenever domain controllers are added, removed, or moved between sites.

See Also For more information on the topologies created by the KCC, refer to the *Directory Services Guide* of the *Windows Server 2003 Resource Kit* (Microsoft Press, 2003).

Site Links

A site link is an Active Directory object that represents the physical connectivity between two or more sites. For replication to occur between sites, you must establish a link between the sites. There are two components to this link: the actual physical connection between the sites (usually a WAN link) and a site link object. The site link object determines the protocol used for transferring replication traffic (IP or SMTP) and governs when replication is scheduled to occur.

All sites contained within the site link are considered to be connected by means of the same network type. You must manually link sites to other sites using site links so that domain controllers in one site can replicate directory changes from domain controllers in another site. You can use a single site-link object to control more than a single pair of sites. For example, if your network consists of four sites that all use the same protocol, are connected with the same type and speed WAN link, and should follow the same schedule, you can configure a single site-link object to connect all the sites. Also, if there is more than one WAN connection between two sites, you need to create only one site link because you cannot assign a site link to a specific connection.

If the network is more complicated than this, where connections of different types and speeds are used, you'll need to create separate site links to handle the different types of connections. When possible, though, group the WAN links of the same speed by creating a single WAN link for them.

Site-Link Transitivity and Site-Link Bridges

By default, site links are transitive, as shown in Figure 5-4. This means that if sites A and B are linked, and sites B and C are linked, then sites A and C are linked through a transitive connection. Although you can disable site-link transitivity for a transport, it is not recommended except in special circumstances. These circumstances include:

■ To achieve complete control over replication patterns

- To keep a particular replication path from being used
- If your network is not fully routed, or firewalls block two sites from directly replicating

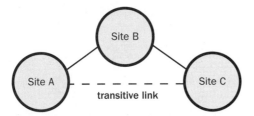

Figure 5-4   Site links are transitive by default.

If you disable site link transitivity for a transport, all site links for that transport are affected and become nontransitive. You must then create site-link bridges (covered in the next section) to provide transitive connections.

Site-link bridges are logical connections that use site links as their underlying transport. When site-link transitivity is enabled, these logical site link bridges are automatically created between all sites. When site-link transitivity is disabled, you must create the site link bridges yourself. Figure 5-5 shows a simple set of four sites that are connected via site links in a round-robin fashion. If site-link transitivity is disabled for these sites, you need to create site link bridges manually to ensure that all the sites can replicate. Basically, you'll have to use site-link bridges to ensure that all sites have a replication path to all other sites whenever site-link transitivity is disabled. Think of it this way. When site-link transitivity is enabled, all site links are bridged so that all sites can replicate to one another. When transitivity is disabled, you must create the bridges yourself, because the only sites linked are those with an actual site link configured between them. A site-link bridge forwards replication traffic between connected sites across multiple site links.

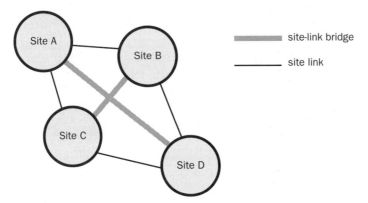

Figure 5-5   Site-link bridges are used when site-link transitivity is disabled.

> **Exam Tip**   You should use the default configuration (where site-link transitivity is enabled) anytime it is possible. The two reasons you'll see on the exam for disabling transitivity and using site-link bridges are when you want total control over replication paths (due to WAN link limitations of firewall configurations) and when your network is not fully routed.

Assigning Site-Link Costs

All site links are assigned a cost that is used in determining the routing preference they are given relative to other site links. By default, all site links are assigned a value of 100. Making a site link more expensive than another site link causes the replication process (and the process of other applications and services such as the Domain Controller Locator) to favor the less expensive site link when both paths would reach the final destination.

Costs along site links are cumulative. For example, consider the diagram shown in Figure 5-6. If a domain controller in Site A needs to replicate information to a domain controller in Site D, it is going to use the path that travels through Site B because the cumulative cost (600) is less than the cumulative cost of the other available path (1000).

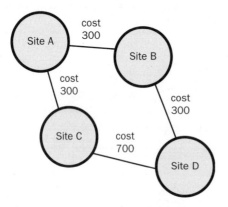

Figure 5-6   Site-link costs are cumulative.

It is recommended that you configure site-link costs consistently across a network based on the available bandwidth of the connection. Table 5-1 shows recommended costs to assign for various levels of available bandwidth.

Table 5-1   Recommended Site-Link Costs by Available Bandwidth

Available Bandwidth (Kbps)	Site-Link Cost
9.6	1042
19.2	798
38.4	644

Table 5-1   Recommended Site-Link Costs by Available Bandwidth (Continued)

Available Bandwidth (Kbps)	Site-Link Cost
56	586
64	567
128	486
256	425
512	378
1024	340
2048	309
4096	283

Scheduling Site-Link Availability

By default, site links are made available all the time, which means that replication can occur as needed. However, you can change the times that site links are available if you need to exert tighter control over replication. For example, you could schedule a site link to be available only during off hours so that replication didn't compete with other WAN usage. Keep in mind, though, that although blocking replication during certain times gives priority to other WAN traffic, it also increases the latency of replication—the time it takes for all the domain controllers in a domain to arrive at the same state.

When replication between two sites traverses multiple site links, the replication of the domain will not complete until each site link, in sequence, has had the opportunity to replicate.

In addition to the scheduled times during which the site link is available, the other scheduling concept you need to be aware of is the replication interval. This value indicates how often replication over a site link should occur. The default replication interval is 180 minutes, meaning that replication between site links occurs roughly every three hours, assuming the site link schedule allows it. As with setting a schedule, setting a replication interval is something of an art. Setting longer intervals reduces the amount of traffic over the WAN, but also increases replication latency.

Creating Site Links

When you install Active Directory, a default site-link object is created for IP and is named DEFAULTIPSITELINK. This default site-link object is associated with the default site. No default site-link object is created for the SMTP protocol.

When you create additional site links, keep the following in mind:

■ Make sure that all sites can connect to one another.

■ When you add a site to a link, make sure you know whether the site is already a member of another link and remove it if necessary. Otherwise, the KCC will build a topology based on both memberships.

■ Use a consistent naming scheme for site links that identifies their purpose.

■ Use RPC over IP as the transport protocol for all site links unless your network is not fully routed and you are forced to use SMTP.

Bridgehead Servers

Once you have created site links, the KCC automatically designates one or more domain controllers for each domain in the site as bridgehead servers. Replication happens through these bridgehead servers instead of happening directly between all domain controllers, as shown in Figure 5-7. Remember that within a site, domain controllers (including the bridgehead servers for other sites) replicate as needed. During the times that site links are scheduled to be available, bridgehead servers will then initiate replication with bridgehead servers in other sites according to the replication interval.

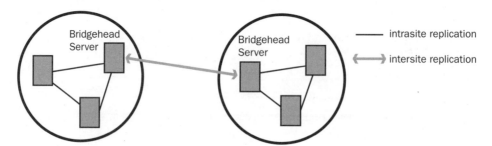

Figure 5-7   Bridgehead servers are responsible for transmitting replication information between sites.

The replication connections created by the KCC are randomly distributed between all possible bridgehead servers in a site to share the replication workload. Normally, the KCC only performs this distribution when new connection objects are created. However, the Windows Server 2003 Resource Kit offers a tool named Active Directory Load Balancing (ADLB) that you can use to redistribute the roles of bridgehead servers at other times (such as when new domain controllers are added).

Practice: Creating a Site Design and Replication Strategy

In this practice, you create a site design for Northwind Traders. If you are unable to answer a question, review the lesson materials and try the question again. You can find answers to the questions in the "Questions and Answers" section at the end of this chapter.

Scenario

Northwind Traders manufactures a line of network appliances designed to help companies improve their data transmission capabilities. Northwind Traders currently uses a Microsoft Windows NT 4.0 master domain model. In recent years, the company has undergone significant growth and expansion. The company expects substantial growth during the next three years, including growth in market share, revenue, and number of employees. In addition to opening two new offices, the executive management has committed to implementing a new Windows Server 2003 Active Directory design to meet the current and future needs of the company.

The following table shows the geographical locations, the departments residing in each location, and the number of users in each of the locations.

Location	Departments Represented	Number of Users
Paris, France	Headquarters (HQ) Management staff Finance Sales Marketing Production Research Development Information Technology (IT)	2,000
Los Angeles, CA, United States	Sales Marketing Finance IT	1,000
Atlanta, GA, United States	Customer Service Customer Support Training	750
Glasgow, Scotland	Research Development Sustained Engineering IT	750

Location	Departments Represented	Number of Users
Sydney, Australia	Consulting Production Sales Finance	500

Most of the company's computing services are hosted in the corporate HQ in Paris. The corporate IT department wants to have central control of passwords and security settings. The local IT department at the Los Angeles office wants to maintain control of its infrastructure without the interference from the corporate IT department. The local IT department at the Glasgow office demands that they have exclusive control over their own environment due to security concerns of their research and development data. Corporate management shares the security concern over the R&D data and wants to ensure that this data is not compromised.

The following illustration shows the connectivity between the different locations of the company. In addition, Los Angeles and Atlanta have virtual private network (VPN) connections through the Internet to the headquarters in Paris. The table following the network diagram summarizes the rest of the connectivity information about Northwind Traders.

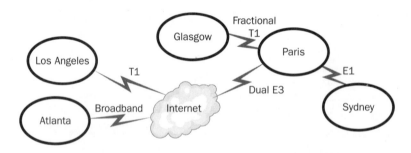

Link	Type	Speed	Available Bandwidth
Paris – Internet	Dual, redundant E3	34.368 Mbps	10 Mbps
Paris – Glasgow	Fractional E1	768 Kbps	128 Kbps
Paris – Sydney	E1	2.048 Mbps	32 Kbps
Atlanta – Internet	Broadband	1.5 Mbps	384 Kbps
LA – Internet	T1	1.544 Mbps	56 Kbps

Practice Questions

Based on the scenario, answer the following questions.

1. Draw a site map for Northwind Traders, including all site links that you will create. Indicate the cost that you will assign to each site link. In addition, specify the schedule information for site links that will not use the default schedule.

   _____

   _____

2. Will you disable bridging of all site links? If so, will you create any site-link bridges?

   _____

   _____

Lesson Review

The following questions are intended to reinforce key information presented in this lesson. If you are unable to answer a question, review the lesson materials and try the question again. You can find answers to the questions in the "Questions and Answers" section at the end of this chapter.

1. What characteristics of WAN links would indicate that they should share a common site link?

   _____

   _____

2. Describe the differences between intrasite and intersite replication.

   _____

   _____

3. Describe the reasons you might want to disable site-link transitivity.

   _____

   _____

Lesson Summary

- Intrasite replication is optimized for speed. Domain controllers replicate changes when they occur in uncompressed format. Intersite replication is optimized to preserve bandwidth. Replication occurs through bridgehead servers, the data is compressed, and you can schedule the availability of site links and the interval at which replication occurs.

- A service named the Knowledge Consistency Checker (KCC) automatically creates and adjusts the topology of replication-connection objects necessary for domain controllers to replicate to one another.

- A site link is an Active Directory object that represents the physical connectivity between two or more sites. For replication to occur between sites, you must establish a link between the sites. All sites contained within the site link are considered to be connected by means of the same network type. All site links are assigned a cost that is used in determining the routing preference they are given relative to other site links. By default, all site links are assigned a cost of 100.

- By default, site links are transitive. You can disable transitivity, but you must then create site-link bridges to ensure a complete replication path throughout the domain.

Lesson 4: Designing a Migration Path

If you are designing an Active Directory structure for a network that is already running Microsoft Windows NT 4 or Windows 2000, you are going to have to give some thought to how you are going to implement Windows Server 2003 and your new network design. If you followed the recommendations from Chapter 2, you already have a good idea of the existing network infrastructure along with a good set of diagrams. This lesson presents an overview of migration concerns from both Windows NT 4 and Windows 2000 to Windows Server 2003.

After this lesson, you will be able to

- Identify important concerns about migrating from Windows NT 4 domains.
- Identify important concerns about migrating from Windows 2000 domains.

Estimated lesson time: 10 minutes

Migrating from Windows NT 4 Domains

There are many differences between Windows NT 4 and Windows Server 2003. From a domain-design perspective, one of the biggest differences is simply that Windows NT 4 did not use sites. Windows NT 4 domains were used both to form replication boundaries and to form logical security boundaries. This means that the creation of domains on a Windows NT 4 network followed different logic. Often, multiple domains were created to help control replication traffic where a single domain and multiple sites would work in Windows Server 2003. Also, multiple Windows NT 4 domains may have been created to build an administrative structure where a single domain and multiple organizational units would suffice in Windows Server 2003.

With these differences in mind, there are two methods you can use to migrate from a Windows NT 4 domain structure to a Windows Server 2003 domain structure: a domain restructuring or an in-place domain upgrade.

A domain restructuring offers more long-term benefits than an in-place upgrade. Most multiple-domain Windows NT 4 structures can be restructured into a single (or at least fewer) Windows Server 2003 domain. Also, a well-considered structure of sites and organizational units almost always makes for a more efficient network.

An in-place domain upgrade does offer a few shorter-term benefits, though, and may be worth considering. In particular, an in-place domain upgrade is useful in the following circumstances:

- The current domain structure translates well to Windows Server 2003.
- You are limited in the amount of design and deployment time you are given.

- You want to minimize changes to the current administrative structure or flow of information on the network.

- You want to minimize the effect that users and administrators experience during the migration.

Migrating from Windows 2000 Domains

If you are upgrading from a Windows 2000 domain structure, your job is considerably easier than if you are upgrading from Windows NT 4. Most of the Active Directory implementation you find in Windows Server 2003 was also present in Windows 2000, which means that a designer has already put a good bit of thought into the forest and domain structure, the administrative structure, the placement of sites and domain controllers, and the replication topology.

The solution that is both the least expensive and the least design-intensive is to upgrade the domain controllers in place and use the current domain structure. Upgrading domains in place also minimizes the impact of the upgrade on users and network availability. You have the choice of upgrading some or all of your domain controllers from Windows 2000, but keep in mind that some functions that are new to Windows Server 2003 will not be available unless all domain controllers in a domain or forest are running Windows Server 2003. This functionality is referred to as the functional level of the forest or domain. For a refresher on functional levels, see Chapter 1.

To prepare a Windows 2000 forest for upgrade to Windows Server 2003, or for the introduction of a new Windows Server 2003–based domain controller, you must first run the Active Directory Preparation tool (Adprep.exe), which you can find in the \i386 folder on the Windows Server 2003 CD. This tool prepares the forest and domains by extending the schema with new modifications, resetting permissions on built-in containers and objects in the Active Directory, and updating administrative tools.

See Also   This section provides only a high-level look at the concepts of migration. For more information on upgrading and restructuring, refer to the *Microsoft Windows Server 2003 Deployment Kit* (Microsoft Press, 2003).

Lesson Review

The following questions are intended to reinforce key information presented in this lesson. If you are unable to answer a question, review the lesson materials and try the question again. You can find answers to the questions in the "Questions and Answers" section at the end of this chapter.

1. From the perspective of designing a domain structure, what are the primary differences between Windows NT 4 and Windows Server 2003?

   _____

   _____

2. In what circumstances should you consider an in-place domain upgrade instead of a domain restructuring when migrating from Windows NT 4 to Windows Server 2003?

   _____

   _____

3. Can you upgrade some of the domain controllers in a Windows 2000 domain to Windows Server 2003?

   _____

   _____

Lesson Summary

- From a design perspective, the biggest differences between Windows NT 4 and Windows Server 2003 domains are the introduction of sites to abstract the physical network structure from the logical domain structure and the introduction of organizational units to subdivide domains into administrative boundaries.

- When migrating from Windows NT 4 to Windows Server 2003, you should consider an in-place domain upgrade instead of restructuring in the following circumstances: the current domain structure translates well, you want to minimize user impact, you want to minimize changes to administrative structure or information flow, or you have a limited amount of time or money.

- If you are upgrading from Windows 2000 to Windows Server 2003, the easiest and most cost-effective migration path is to perform an in-place domain upgrade.

Case Scenario Exercise

Review the following scenario and complete the questions.

Scenario

You have been selected to create a site plan for Contoso, Ltd., a modem manufacturer with its headquarters in Dallas, Texas. Currently, all servers on its network are running Windows NT Server 4.0. Client computers are running a mix of Windows 98 and Windows 2000 Professional. Contoso has hired you to bring the company network infrastructure up-to-date. They want all servers to run Windows Server 2003 and want to implement Active Directory. They also want all client computers to run Windows XP Professional.

Background

Contoso has grown over the past decade to become one of the premier high-end modem manufacturers in the country, selling primarily to large companies and Internet service providers. Two years ago, Contoso acquired a London-based modem manufacturer named Trey Research, which targets a similar market in the European countries.

Geography

The Dallas headquarters has 1,900 users and a fully-staffed IT department. In addition to its primary location, Contoso also has two branch offices within the United States—one in Memphis, Tennessee, and one in San Diego, California. The San Diego branch has 185 users and maintains its own IT staff. The Memphis branch has 35 users and does not maintain an IT staff. Instead, they rely on the IT staff at the Dallas headquarters. The Memphis office is located in a small building with an open workspace and, because there is no IT staff, they are unable to provide maintenance or physical security for servers.

Trey Research, the subsidiary office, is in London, England. The London office has 215 users and maintains full corporate facilities, including its own IT staff and control over its own network infrastructure. The London office also maintains its own namespace.

Network Infrastructure

The Dallas headquarters is connected to the Memphis branch by means of a 512 Kbps connection. Dallas is connected to San Diego by means of a 512 Kbps connection. Dallas is connected to the London headquarters using a 256 Kbps connection. The Dallas and London offices are using a 155 MB ATM as a backbone to connect the network segments within each LAN. Clients are connected to the backbone via 10/100 Mbps connections. At both branch offices, clients and servers are all connected via 10/100

Mbps connections. The Dallas network consists of fourteen subnets, the San Diego network consists of three subnets, and the Memphis office is on a single subnet.

Currently, each location is configured with its own domain, named after the location. It has already been decided that one domain named contoso.com will be created and it will cover the Dallas, San Diego, and Memphis locations. A second domain in a separate tree named treyresearch.com will be created for the London-based company.

Future Plans

There are no current plans to significantly expand the workforce at the current locations. However, there is a possibility that the company will be acquiring a small, Montreal-based company that owns a promising, new modem technology. In that case, the Montreal-based company will maintain its own IT staff and namespace. Your plans should allow for that.

IT Management

The IT staff in Dallas is in charge of maintaining the Dallas, and Memphis locations. The London and San Diego locations have their own IT staff. However, the senior IT staff in Dallas has the ultimate responsibility for the entire network.

Questions

Given the previous scenario, answer the following questions.

1. How many sites would you plan on using? Sketch out a diagram of these sites.

_____

_____

2. What is the minimum number of domain controllers you should use in each site?

_____

_____

3. How many site links should you create for this network?

_____

_____

4. Where should you place global catalog servers on the network?

_____

_____

Chapter Summary

■ Sites are used to control network traffic generated by workstation logons, Active Directory replication, Distributed File System (DFS), and File Replication Service (FRS).

■ When preparing to design a site structure, you need to know the geographic locations of your company, the layout and speed of the LANs in each location, the TCP/IP subnets in each location, and the bandwidth between locations.

■ You should create a site for each LAN (or set of LANs connected by a high speed backbone), each location that has a domain controller, and each location that hosts a site-aware service.

■ The primary reason for placing a domain controller in a site is to cut down on WAN traffic between sites. This traffic comes in the form of users contacting domain controllers for authentication, site-aware applications using domain controllers for searches, and replication.

■ If a site has fewer than 1,000 users, one domain controller is sufficient. If there are between 1,000 and 10,000 users, two domain controllers are recommended. Add an additional domain controller for every 5,000 users above 10,000. Even in sites with fewer than 1,000 users, though, you should consider using a second domain controller for the purposes of fault tolerance.

■ When possible, you should make a single domain controller responsible for filling all the operations masters roles of a forest or domain. Just remember the rule that the Infrastructure Master should not host the global catalog unless all other domain controllers in the domain also host the global catalog.

■ Global catalog servers maintain a subset of Active Directory object attributes that are most commonly searched for by users or client computers. They allow users to log on to the network and they allow users to locate AD objects anywhere in a forest without referring to specific domain controllers that store the objects.

■ The hardware requirements for a domain controller are largely dependent on the number of users that must be authenticated within the domain. Once you establish requirements that meet these needs, you must also take into account whether the domain controller will host the global catalog or assume other roles.

■ Intrasite replication is optimized for speed. Domain controllers replicate changes, when they occur, in uncompressed format. Intersite replication is optimized to preserve bandwidth. Replication occurs through bridgehead servers, the data is compressed, and you can schedule the availability of site links and the interval at which replication occurs.

- A service named the Knowledge Consistency Checker (KCC) automatically creates and adjusts the topology of replication-connection objects necessary for domain controllers to replicate to one another.

- A site link is an Active Directory object that represents the physical connectivity between two or more sites. For replication to occur between sites, you must establish a link between the sites. All sites contained within the site link are considered to be connected by means of the same network type. All site links are assigned a cost that is used in determining the routing preference they are given relative to other site links. By default, all site links are assigned a value of 100.

- By default, site links are transitive. You can disable transitivity, but you must then manually create site-link bridges to ensure a complete replication path throughout the domain.

- From a design perspective, the biggest differences between Windows NT 4 and Windows Server 2003 domains are the introduction of sites to abstract the physical network structure from the logical domain structure and the introduction of organizational units to subdivide domains into administrative boundaries.

- When migrating from Windows NT 4 to Windows Server 2003, you should consider an in-place domain upgrade instead of restructuring if the current domain structure translates well, if you want to minimize user impact, if you want to minimize changes to administrative structure or information flow, or if you have a limited amount of time or money.

- If you are upgrading from Windows 2000 to Windows Server 2003, the easiest and most cost-effective migration path is to perform an in-place domain upgrade.

Exam Highlights

Before taking the exam, review the key topics and terms that are presented in this chapter. You need to know this information.

Key Points

- Sites are used to control traffic over WAN links generated by workstation logon traffic, replication traffic, Distributed File System (DFS), and File Replication Service (FRS). Create a site for each LAN or set of LANs that is connected by a high-speed backbone (10 Mbps or higher). Create a site for each geographic location where you plan to put a domain controller. Create a site for each location that contains a server running a site-aware application.

- Place domain controllers in locations with a large number of users if users must be able to log on when a WAN link is down, or if the location holds a site-aware application.

- Use one domain controller in sites with fewer than 1,000 users, two domain controllers for between 1,000 and 10,000 users, and an additional domain controller for every 5,000 users above 10,000.

- In a single domain forest, make all domain controllers global catalog servers because no extra space or replication traffic is generated. In multiple-domain forests, you can create as many global catalog servers as you want to achieve load balancing and redundancy of services. Microsoft recommends placing at least one global catalog server in each site.

- Intrasite replication is optimized for speed. Domain controllers replicate changes, when they occur, in uncompressed format. Intersite replication is optimized to preserve bandwidth. Replication occurs through bridgehead servers, the data is compressed, and you can schedule the availability of site links and the interval at which replication occurs.

Key Terms

Knowledge Consistency Checker   The Knowledge Consistency Checker is a Windows service that creates and manages the replication topology of a domain using replication-connection objects.

Site-Link Transitivity   By default, site links are transitive. The connection provided by a site link is accessible even between sites that are not directly linked. You can disable site-link transitivity, but you must then create site-link bridges between sites that are not directly linked.

Operations Masters   Certain roles in a domain and in a forest can be held only by one domain controller. There are three domain-wide operations masters roles: Primary Domain Controller (PDC) Emulator, Relative Identifier (RID) Master, and Infrastructure Master. There are two forest-wide operations masters roles: Schema Master and Domain Naming Master.

Questions and Answers

Page
5-9

Lesson 1 Review

1. You are designing a site plan for a company that has full corporate offices in Atlanta, Chicago, and Los Angeles. Each location is connected to the other two locations via a 512 Kbps connection. How many sites should you define?

You should define three sites, one for each location. To be part of the same site, a 10 Mbps or better connection should connect subnets.

2. For what functions are sites used to control network traffic?

Sites are used to control network traffic generated by workstation logon, Active Directory replication, DFS, and FRS.

3. What are the basic guidelines you should use when determining whether to create a site?

You should create a site for each LAN or set of LANs connected by a high-speed backbone. You should create a site for each location at which you plan to place a domain controller. You should also create a site for each location running a server that hosts a site-aware application or where there is high latency caused by geographic distance or the type of WAN link (e.g., a satellite link).

Page
5-20

Lesson 2 Practice

1. How many domain controllers would you place in each site? Why? Use the table below to complete your design.

Domain	Number of Domain Controllers in Each Site				
	Paris	Glasgow	Sydney	Atlanta	Los Angeles
Nwtraders.local	2	0	1	1	1
AsiaPacific.nwtraders.local	1	0	2	0	0
NAeast.nwtraders.local	1	0	0	2	0
NAwest.nwtraders.local	1	0	0	0	2
Corp.nwtraders.local	3	1	1	2	1
RDNwtraders.local	1	2	0	0	0
Glasgow.RDNwtraders.local	1	2	0	0	0

This is just one possible answer.

Paris will host one domain controller for every other domain to enable easy logon for users from other locations when they are in Paris. It will also host three domain controllers for the corp.nwtraders.local domain, two for local authentication, and a third one for managing replication to remote offices. For redundancy purposes, it will also host two domain controllers for the forest root domain (nwtraders.local).

Glasgow will host two domain controllers for the RDNwtraders.local forest root domain and two for the Glasgow.RDNwtraders.local domain. Two domain controllers for each domain are required to support fault tolerance for Active Directory. Glasgow will also host one domain controller for the corp.nwtraders.local domain so that traveling users from headquarters can log on Each of the remaining sites will host two domain controllers for the local regional domain for fault tolerance, one domain controller for the forest root domain, and one domain controller for the corp.nwtraders.local domain to enable traveling users from headquarters to log on without using the WAN link.

2. In which sites will you place global catalog servers? In which sites will you enable universal group membership caching? Use the following table to complete your design.

Site	Number of Global Catalog Servers for Nwtraders.local Forest	Number of Global Catalog Servers for RDNwtraders.local Forest	Enable Universal Group Membership Caching for Site (Yes/No)
Paris	2	1	No
Glasgow	1	1	No
Sydney	1	0	No
Atlanta	1	0	No
Los Angeles	1	0	No

To support local logon, each site except for Paris will host one copy of the global catalog for nwtraders.local forest. Paris will have two copies of the global catalog to support both the large number of users in the location and the volume of Active Directory searches that are performed by the local IT staff.

Lesson 2 Review

1. What are the reasons for placing domain controllers into a site? What are reasons you might not be able to place a domain controller into a site?

If the site contains many users, a local domain controller cuts down on authentication traffic to other sites. If the WAN link between sites goes down, having a local domain controller ensures continued authentication. If there are site-aware applications in a site, having a local domain controller cuts down on WAN traffic.

You should not place a domain controller in a site if no one in that location can manage the domain controller (and you cannot set up remote access) or if you cannot guarantee the physical security of the domain controller.

2. You are determining the number of domain controllers to place in a site. There are 15,000 users in the site, and there are eight replication connections to the site. How many domain controllers should you place?

You should place at least three domain controllers in the site. For between 1,000 and 10,000 users, two domain controllers are recommended. You should add another domain controller for every 5,000 users above 10,000.

3. What are the recommendations for placing global catalog servers?

You should place at least one global catalog server in each site. In a single domain forest, you should make all domain controllers global catalog servers, because no extra space or replication traffic is generated. In multiple domain forests, you can create as many global catalog servers as you want to achieve load balancing and redundancy of services.

Page
5-31

Lesson 3 Practice

1. Draw a site map for Northwind Traders, including all site links that you will create. Indicate the cost that you will assign to each site link. In addition, specify the schedule information for site links that will not use the default schedule.

Create one site link for each WAN link or VPN connection. Set schedules on connections with less than 64 Kbps available bandwidth to ensure that these connections are not available for replication between 8 A.M. and 5 P.M. local time in each location connected by the site link. The local times are converted to Greenwich Mean Time (GMT) for standardization. The site-link costs are calculated by using the formula provided in the chapter.

2. Will you disable bridging of all site links? If so, will you create any site-link bridges?

Answers may vary. However, one possible answer is to disable bridging of all site links due to the regional domain model and the limited availability of bandwidth on the WAN links. No need to create any site-link bridges.

Page
5-31

Lesson 3 Review

1. What characteristics of WAN links would indicate that they should share a common site link?

WAN links of the same speed and type should be grouped under the same site link, unless you need to use multiple schedules.

2. Describe the differences between intrasite and intersite replication.

Intrasite replication is optimized for high-performance networks. It happens on a change-notification basis and sends data uncompressed. Intersite replication is optimized to preserve bandwidth. It occurs only over designated bridgehead servers, the data is compressed, and it relies on the scheduled availability of site links and the specified replication interval.

3. Describe the reasons you might want to disable site-link transitivity.

If you disable site-link transitivity, you must manually configure site-link bridges to define the replication path between many sites. For this reason, it's recommended that you leave transitivity enabled. Reasons you might want to disable transitivity include if your network is not fully routed or if you need total control over the replication paths on the network.

Page
5-35

Lesson 4 Review

1. From the perspective of designing a domain structure, what are the primary differences between Windows NT 4 and Windows Server 2003?

   The primary differences are the introduction of sites to abstract the physical network structure from the logical domain structure and the introduction of organizational units to subdivide domains into administrative boundaries.

2. In what circumstances should you consider an in-place domain upgrade instead of a domain restructuring when migrating from Windows NT 4 to Windows Server 2003?

   You should consider an in-place domain upgrade instead of restructuring in the following circumstances: the current domain structure translates well, you want to minimize user impact, you want to minimize changes to administrative structure or information flow, or you have a limited amount of time or money to effect the migration.

3. Can you upgrade some of the domain controllers in a Windows 2000 domain to Windows Server 2003?

   Yes, it is possible to have a mixed domain. The state of domain controllers in a domain or forest is referred to as a functional level. If all domain controllers in a forest or domain are running Windows Server 2003, the forest or domain is said to be of a Windows Server 2003–functional level and all features provided by Windows Server 2003 are available.

Page
5-37

Case Scenario Exercise

1. How many sites would you plan on using? Sketch out a diagram of these sites.

   You are probably going to want to use three sites for this network: a combined site for the Dallas and Memphis locations, a site for the San Diego location, and a site for the London location. The reasons for not creating a separate site for Memphis are that there are few enough users that WAN traffic from workstation logons will not be significant, there is no IT staff in the Memphis office to maintain a domain controller, and there is not adequate physical security to place a domain controller.

2. What is the minimum number of domain controllers you should use in each site?

   The minimum number of domain controllers for a site is one. However, the number of users in the Dallas site calls for a second domain controller to handle authentication requests. In addition, it is recommended that you create two domain controllers per site for the purpose of fault tolerance.

3. How many site links should you create for this network?

   You will need to create two site links, one for the Dallas/Memphis site to connect to the San Diego site and one for the Dallas-to-London connection.

4. Where should you place global catalog servers on the network?

   If possible, you should let all domain controllers act as global catalog servers because you will have domain controllers in each major location. The authentication traffic generated by the 35 users in the Memphis site will not be significant, and you cannot place a domain controller there anyway. If you choose not to make all domain controllers global catalog servers, you should make sure there is a global catalog server in each site.

6 Designing a DNS Structure

Exam Objectives in this Chapter:

- Design the network services infrastructure to meet business and technical requirements
  - ❏ Create the conceptual design of the DNS infrastructure
- Analyze DNS for Active Directory directory service implementation
  - ❏ Analyze the current DNS infrastructure
  - ❏ Analyze the current namespace
- Design a DNS name resolution strategy
  - ❏ Create the namespace design
  - ❏ Identify DNS interoperability with Active Directory, WINS, and DHCP
  - ❏ Specify zone requirements
  - ❏ Specify DNS security
  - ❏ Design a DNS strategy for interoperability with UNIX Berkeley Internet Name Domain (BIND) to support Active Directory
- Design a DNS service implementation
  - ❏ Design a strategy for DNS zone storage
  - ❏ Specify the use of DNS server options
  - ❏ Identify the registration requirements of specific DNS records
- Design DNS service placement

Why This Chapter Matters

Before attempting to design a Domain Name System (DNS) structure for a company, a clear understanding of the company's infrastructure should be diagramed with detailed information on the location of servers, routers and switches, domain controllers, application servers, users, groups, organizational units, and so on, as discussed in Chapter 2, "Analyzing an Existing Infrastructure." Without this information, it would be nearly impossible to design a DNS structure because it is based on the physical topology of the company's network.

This chapter is about designing your network services infrastructure so that DNS will work with your other network services such as Windows Internet Name Service

(WINS), Dynamic Host Configuration Protocol (DHCP) and Active Directory directory services. Unless you are designing a network from the ground up, most organizations will have a DNS infrastructure in place. In fact, in many occurrences, this DNS service may be UNIX based, and require you to integrate a BIND DNS version with Active Directory, so it is very important that you are able to identify the DNS implementation type when analyzing the current DNS system. You will begin your journey by analyzing an existing DNS implementation and then examining the strategy to design and implement DNS where there is no current DNS infrastructure in place.

Lessons in this Chapter:

Before You Begin

To complete this chapter, make sure you are familiar with the concepts described in Chapter 1, "Introduction to Active Directory and Network Infrastructure." You should also make sure that you understand how to gather information about the existing network, as described in Chapter 2.

Lesson 1: Analyzing the Existing DNS Implementation

Unless you are tasked with building a network infrastructure from the ground up, most network administrators have to understand and work with DNS infrastructures that are already in place. This lesson includes an overview of the DNS components and discusses some of the terminology you will need to understand before you can design and implement a DNS strategy for your company.

The first step in analyzing a company's network infrastructure is to perform an analysis of the company itself. As discussed in Chapter 2, understanding how a company works and how its information flows lays a critical foundation for the rest of your network design. In this lesson, you learn to gather information regarding the DNS infrastructure that is in place.

After this lesson, you will be able to

- Identify the various components of a DNS infrastructure.
- Describe the various DNS server types and their functions in an existing infrastructure.
- Identify the current namespace.

Estimated lesson time: 20 minutes

DNS Overview

Most human beings do not like working with numbers or having to memorize Internet Protocol (IP) addresses to connect to a resource on the network. It's a lot easier to memorize www.microsoft.com as an address than 172.16.45.67. When a Fully Qualified Domain Name (FQDN) such as www.microsoft.com is entered by a user on a network, there must be a method or component that takes that name and resolves it to an IP number. DNS does exactly that. As you saw in Chapter 1, this name resolution process can be quite involved. In this section, you will look at the various components that make it all happen.

Components of DNS

Because you have already gathered all of the information pertaining to the physical locations of the various departments and divisions of your company, and have created network diagrams of the present infrastructure, you are almost ready to analyze the DNS structure of the company. The diagrams you have created illustrate where all servers, routers, switches, and so on are located. This information, combined with the locations and total amount of hosts, subnets, and routers, will help you to understand how the present DNS infrastructure is configured.

The ability to recognize the components of a DNS infrastructure begins with knowing and understanding how DNS functions. DNS is a database. Like any database, it keeps track of records or, more specifically, resource records. Table 6-1 shows some of the more popular resource record types a DNS server may store in a zone.

Table 6-1   DNS Resource Records

Record Type	Description
SOA (Start of Authority)	Contained in the beginning of every zone
NS (Name Server)	Indicates that the server is authoritative for the zone
A (host)	Maps the FQDN (Fully Qualified Domain Name) to an IP address
PTR (Pointer Record)	Maps an IP address to an FQDN
CNAME (Canonical name)	Creates an alias name for an FQDN
MX (Mail Exchange)	Specifies a mail exchange server that processes or forwards mail for a particular DNS domain
SRV (Service)	Specifies the location of the servers that perform a specific service, such as mail servers, domain controllers, Web servers, etc.

DNS Zones

A zone is defined as a contiguous portion of a DNS tree that is administered as a separate entity by a DNS server. It can store information about one or more domains. A zone contains resource records associated with a particular domain. For example, Contoso's DNS namespace for the domain contoso.com may have originally been configured as a single zone, but as the domain grows and many subdomains are added—such as ftp.contoso.com, www.contoso.com, marketing.contoso.com, and so on—you can assign different zones to each subdomain.

Windows Server 2003 allows you to choose between several different zone types (as shown in Figure 6-1).

- **Primary zone**   Contains a local copy of the DNS zone where resource records are created and updated.

- **Secondary zone**   A read-only copy of a DNS zone. It can be updated only through replication from a primary zone, and is used for redundancy and load balancing.

- **Active Directory integrated zone**   A primary zone stored in Active Directory.

- **Stub zone**   A copy of a zone that contains only the resource records needed to identify authoritative DNS servers, thereby simplifying DNS administration and improving name resolution.

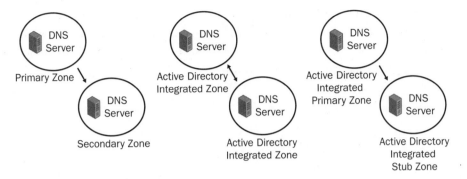

Figure 6-1   You can choose between several different zone types.

Configuring zones will be covered later in the chapter. For now, you want to be able to recognize how the current DNS infrastructure is configured for documentation purposes only.

Zone Transfers

Having only one DNS server on a network holding all of the resource records would not be prudent. There must be a method to replicate this important data to other DNS servers.

Zone transfers may occur three different ways in Windows Server 2003:

- **Incremental Zone Transfer (IXFR)**   In an incremental zone transfer (IXFR), servers keep track of, and transfer only, changes that are made to resource records in a particular zone, the advantage being that less traffic is sent over the network.

- **Full Zone Transfer (AXFR)**   In this type of zone transfer, a response to a DNS query will transfer the entire zone to the secondary DNS server. This type of zone transfer across a slow wide area network (WAN) link can be problematic, so it is important to document which type of zone transfer is occurring on the network.

- **Fast zone transfer**   Fast zone transfer allows more than one resource record to be transferred in a message as it replicates from one DNS server to another. This is the default zone transfer methodology for Windows Server 2003.

Later, you will design your DNS infrastructure based on the topology of your network. For now, you should be able to look at the current system and determine how it is configured.

Server Roles

Each of your DNS servers can perform different functions on your network. Now that you have a network diagram of the location of these servers, you can update the server information by noting the role of each server on your diagram. This is covered in more detail in Lesson 4.

- **Primary Name Server**   A primary name server is the DNS server that contains the local zone database file. This file can be updated and is usually replicated to a secondary DNS server, through the zone transfer process, to provide fault tolerance.

- **Secondary Name Server**   A secondary name server is not required on a network, but is highly recommended. It provides both fault tolerance and load balancing features because it holds a copy of the zone file maintained by the primary DNS server.

- **Caching-Only Server**   A caching-only server, as its name implies, caches the answers to queries and returns the results. This saves time and reduces network traffic because calls to multiple DNS servers are not required.

> **Exam Tip**   It is very important that an understanding of the components be mastered before taking the exam. Before a design of a DNS infrastructure can be considered, you should know the various DNS server types: primary, secondary, and caching-only.

Identifying Current Namespace

Determining the current namespace for an organization is quite simple. Since you have already gathered information on the Active Directory namespace design, you are able to answer the following question: Is the company using the same namespace design for both the public and the private network? For example, if the company's public name is sales.contoso.com, is the internal Active Directory namespace also contoso.com? Examples of the two DNS namespace designs are shown in Figures 6-2 and 6-3. You will have a chance to look at the design ramifications of this later, in Lesson 2. For now, you are only concerned with identifying and analyzing the current DNS namespace.

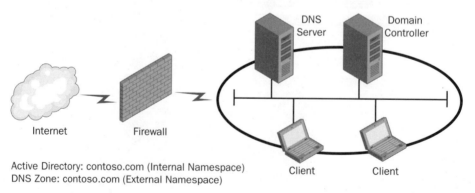

Active Directory: contoso.com (Internal Namespace)
DNS Zone: contoso.com (External Namespace)

Figure 6-2   This diagram shows the DNS design with same namespace.

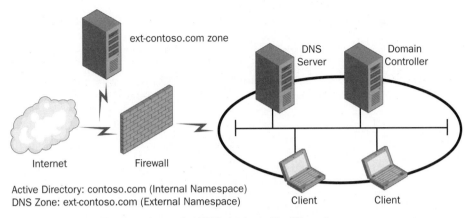

Figure 6-3   This diagram shows the DNS design with different namespace

> **Exam Tip**   It is important to see the relationship of the Active Directory namespace hierarchy as it relates to the DNS namespace. In many cases these will be one and the same, but you can also have two totally different namespace designs. This will be addressed in Lesson 2.

Documenting Your Findings

As you examine the DNS infrastructure in place, you should ask yourself the following questions:

- Is Active Directory directory service in place?

- What are the locations of the DNS servers?

- Which zone type or types are implemented? There are several different ways a network can be configured to use DNS. Your concern at this time is to understand how the current DNS infrastructure supports replication or fault tolerance of the resource records.

- How many users are at each location? Once again, this was done in your beginning analysis. You can see how important it is to document everything you do, so you are not repeating steps when different areas need to be covered.

You can now use the diagrams and maps you created earlier when doing your initial analysis. This diagram should show the existing DNS servers, as well as how they are organized into trees and forests. You can copy these diagrams and simply add the DNS server and zone information to them.

At this stage, you should now have the answers to the following questions:

- Is the company using the same Active Directory (internal) namespace as the DNS (external) namespace?

- Which zone type is the company using: Active Directory integrated or standard primary and secondary zones?

- Which methods of zone transfers or replication are implemented: AXFR, IXFR or fast zone transfer?

- How many DNS servers are spread throughout the organization, and what is the server role (primary, secondary, or caching-only) of each server?

- What type of DNS security, if any, is implemented?

You will continue to fill in additional information on these maps and diagrams as you work through the other lessons in this chapter.

Real World   Converting BIND DNS Administrators

In many organizations, an Information Technology (IT) professional is designated as the DNS guru, or the person who manages the DNS infrastructure. In attempting to analyze the current DNS infrastructure in a company, you must be very careful not to come across as someone who wishes only to change or modify the current DNS infrastructure. If the present DNS system is BIND DNS, and you want to implement Microsoft Windows Server 2003 DNS, be careful of your approach. DNS administrators usually have a personal attachment to the DNS type they are currently running.

Trying to get an administrator to drop BIND DNS, and switch to a different DNS implementation, is easier said than done. You may want to approach this analysis portion of the project as an information-gathering phase to determine how Microsoft's Active Directory can be integrated with the current BIND DNS infrastructure, rather than a "let's dump this and replace it" attitude. Lesson 2 will show you how Active Directory can work with BIND DNS.

Lesson Review

The following questions reinforce key information presented in this lesson. If you are unable to answer a question, review the lesson materials and try the question again. You can find answers to the questions in the "Questions and Answers" section at the end of this chapter.

1. What are the three zone transfer methods that may be used to replicate zone file data?

_____

_____

2. What is one advantage of using Active Directory integrated zones as a zone type for a larger organization?

_____

_____

3. In analyzing the current network infrastructure of your company, you note that there are several DNS servers spread out throughout the organization. One of the servers is taking a long time to update its records. What could be some of the reasons for this time delay?

_____

_____

Lesson Summary

- The first step in analyzing your current DNS infrastructure is creating diagrams and maps of the system. In most cases, the diagrams and maps should have already been created when analyzing the Active Directory infrastructure.

- Identifying the components of your current DNS infrastructure begins by understanding how DNS functions. Basically, DNS is a database that stores resource records that must be maintained on DNS servers. This information must also be replicated to other DNS servers for fault tolerance and load balancing.

- Replication of zones files is done through a method called zone transfers. There are three zone transfer methods used by Windows Server 2003 DNS: IXFR, AXFR, and fast zone transfer.

Lesson 2: Designing a DNS Name Resolution Strategy

Now that you understand the components needed in a DNS infrastructure and are aware of your company's network topology, it's time to look at the design strategy you would use that would incorporate the Active Directory namespace, UNIX BIND DNS servers, and other networking services, such as DHCP and WINS. In this lesson, you learn how to integrate these components and look at DNS security features that help you mitigate potential threats to your DNS infrastructure.

After this lesson, you will be able to

- Create the namespace design.
- Identify DNS interoperability with Active Directory, WINS, and DHCP.
- Specify zone requirements.
- Describe DNS security.
- Design a DNS strategy for interoperability with UNIX BIND to support Active Directory.

Estimated lesson time: 40 minutes

Creating the Namespace Design

In Chapter 2, you looked at how to create a conceptual map of your Active Directory namespace. In this section, you will examine DNS namespace planning. Much of the data gathered in your Active Directory analysis can be used for this area. When designing the DNS namespace, it is important that the Active Directory namespace be considered and that the Internet namespace not conflict with your company's internal namespace.

DNS Namespace Design

In designing a DNS namespace for your organization, you should first design the Active Directory environment and then support that design with a DNS structure. A good starting ground to designing your DNS namespace is to ask yourself the following questions:

- What name has your organization registered for use on the Internet? For example, contoso.com could be the DNS namespace used by your domain.

- Will your DNS servers function on your company's private (internal) network or on the Internet?

- Will DNS support your organization's implementation of Active Directory?

- Is there a naming convention your company will follow when selecting domain names for computers?

Choosing a Name

It is recommended that you choose and register a unique DNS domain name for your organization. This name will be a second-level domain within one of the top-level domains used on the Internet. Table 6-2 shows some of the top-level domains you may be able to choose from.

Table 6-2   Top-Level Domains

Name	Description
com	Delegated to commercial organizations such as Microsoft Corporation
edu	Delegated to educational organizations such as Harvard Law School
gov	Delegated to governmental organizations such as the White House in Washington, D.C.
mil	Delegated to military operations such as the Defense Data Network (DDN)
net	Delegated to networking organizations such as the National Science Foundation (NSF)
org	Delegated to noncommercial organizations such as the Center for Networked Information Discovery and Retrieval (CNIDR)

For example, a second-level domain could be contoso.com. Once you decide on your parent domain name, you can create subdomains based on the location or organizational name within the company. For example, namerica.contoso.com could be a subdomain name at your organization. Another subdomain could be added, such as sales.namerica.contoso.com.

DNS Namespace Design with Active Directory

Before you can implement a DNS namespace properly, the Active Directory structure must be available. Because you have already finished designing your Active Directory structure, you are now ready to support it with the proper DNS structure.

Active Directory domains are named with DNS names. The names you choose to use for your Active Directory domains should start with the DNS domain suffix your organization reserved for use on the Internet, such as contoso.com. This can be combined with geographical locations or divisional names in your organization form created earlier.

Your map should have already identified the following:

- Whether the local area network (LAN) is separated into subnets. This information can be used when deciding on the zones you may wish to create and the zone transfer method you will select, and it may help you to decide whether a subdomain should be created.

- The location of routers, and all services that they provide, as well as firewalls and proxy servers. This will assist you in securing DNS resources. Later, you will see how a router or firewall can filter traffic on particular ports to increase security.

- Next, you should review the document information for each subnet on the network you created. If you recall, this document described the network identity (ID), subnet mask, and ranges of hosts on the subnet, DHCP, and DNS configurations. This can be used to determine the amount of users on the network or in a particular location, and will help in your DNS server placement.

Interoperability with Active Directory, DHCP, and WINS

When designing your DNS name resolution strategy, you should plan to integrate other networking services to optimize performance. In this section, you look at how Active Directory integration can improve network performance and lessen administrative overhead. You also see how DHCP not only automatically configures your client workstations with IP configuration information, but also communicates with DNS Server service to perform dynamic updates. Last, you will examine WINS and how DNS can be optimized to forward queries to a WINS server to resolve Network Basic Input/Output system (NetBIOS) names and services. Let's begin with Active Directory integration.

Active Directory Integration

As you learned in Chapter 1, Active Directory is the tool used to manage, organize, and locate resources on your network. DNS Server service is integrated into the design and implementation of Active Directory, making them a perfect match.

Installing Active Directory

When you add the Domain Controller role to a server and there is no authoritative DNS server for the domain, you are prompted to install DNS Server. This is necessary because a DNS server is required to locate the domain controller you have just installed with Active Directory, as well as other domain controllers in the Active Directory domain. You are also prompted to install DNS if your current DNS infrastructure does not support DNS dynamic updates.

As you saw in the previous lesson, one advantage of integrating DNS with Active Directory is the ability to replicate zones without having to store the text files on a DNS primary server. Let's look in more detail at the benefits of using Active Directory integration:

- Any domain controller running the DNS Server service can be designated as the primary source for a zone and can update a zone. In other words, there is not one primary DNS server, as in the standard primary zone methodology, which can be a single point of failure for a network. For example, if the primary DNS server goes down, no client updates to the database can be made because the secondary

DNS servers are updated through replication (zone transfers) only. In the Active Directory integrated model, a master copy of the zone is maintained by Active Directory and replicated to all domain controllers.

- Using Active Directory can improve security (covered later in this section) because Access Control Lists (ACLs) can be used to secure DNS objects stored in the Active Directory database. For example, you can use an ACL to restrict which client computers can perform dynamic updates, just as you use an ACL to restrict access to printers or folders in your network.

- Zones are replicated and synchronized automatically to new domain controllers that are added to your network. No additional administrative work needs to be done.

- Database replication is more efficient for your network because you will not have to maintain two separate replication topologies—one for replicating the data exchanged between domain controllers, and the other for replicating zone databases between DNS servers. You can now manage both of these replication strategies in a single administrative task.

- Directory replication is faster than standard DNS replication because only changes to directory-stored zones are replicated, versus standard zone file transfers that can use up large amounts of limited bandwidth.

As you can see, the benefits of implementing this strategy are well worth the minimal initial effort. Let's now look at DHCP as it integrates with DNS.

DHCP (Dynamic Host Control Protocol)

In the old days, the network administrator had to manually create A (host) records and PTR records for new users that joined a domain. It was not unheard of to make a typo while entering the information, so it was both time consuming and error prone.

When you install Windows Server 2003 DHCP service, you can enable the DHCP server to perform updates on behalf of DHCP clients to any DNS server that supports dynamic updates. In other words, DHCP can register the A (host) records and PTR records for all DHCP-enabled clients. DHCP clients can provide their FQDN to the DHCP server, as well as instructions on how it would like the server to process DNS dynamic updates. You can configure a DHCP Server on Windows Server 2003 in one of the following ways:

- Have the server update both DNS A and PTR records if requested by the client.

- Have the server update both DNS A and PTR records regardless of whether the client requests it or not.

- Have the server never register and update client information in DNS.

- Always register and update client information in DNS regardless of whether the client requested to perform its own updates.

- Never register and update client information in DNS.

By default, DHCP servers running Windows Server 2003 and Windows 2000 use the first option, and register and update client information with the authoritative DNS server of the zone in which the DHCP server is located. DHCP can also be configured to instruct DNS Server to discard client A and PTR records when the client lease is deleted.

DHCP integration enhances performance and can save time for administrators. Let's now look at the interoperability with WINS.

WINS (Windows Internet Name Service)

In some instances, legacy NetBIOS names cannot be resolved by querying the DNS server, but can be resolved using WINS. DNS provides name resolution for the DNS domain namespace, and WINS provides name resolution for the NetBIOS namespace. To make it possible for DNS to search the NetBIOS namespace when a name cannot be resolved within the DNS namespace, Windows Server 2003 defines two resource records to identify WINS servers:

- WINS resource record
- WINS reverse lookup (WINS-R) resource record

WINS Resource Record

The WINS resource record instructs the DNS service to use WINS to look up and forward queries for host names not found in the zone database. For example, if client A queries its preferred DNS server for client B.sales.contoso.com, the following steps would occur (illustrated in Figure 6-4):

1. The preferred DNS server would first check to see if the IP address was in its cache.

2. The DNS server would query other DNS servers on behalf of the client until the authoritative DNS server for the zone, sales.contoso.com, was located.

3. The DNS server in Step 3 in Figure 6-4 would look in its zone file for a matching resource record.

4. If no resource record is found and the zone is enabled to use WINS lookup, the server separates the host portion of the FQDN (client B) and sends a NetBIOS name request to the WINS server using this host name.

5. If the WINS server can resolve the name, the IP address of client B is returned to the DNS server.

6. The DNS server creates an A record using the IP address resolved through the WINS server and returns the record to the preferred DNS server that was queried by client A.

7. The preferred DNS server passes the answer back to the requesting client.

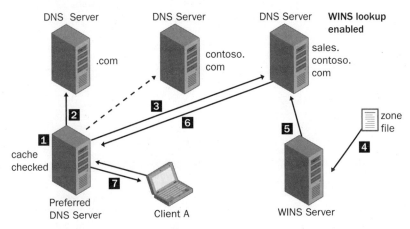

Figure 6-4   This shows the integration of WINS with DNS.

WINS Reverse Lookup Record

The WINS-R record is added to your reverse lookup zones when WINS-R lookup is enabled. If you recall, a reverse lookup zone resolves a host name to an IP address number. A WINS database is not indexed by IP addresses, so it is not possible to send an IP address to a WINS server and receive the host name associated with that node. Instead, the DNS server sends a node adapter status request to the IP address designated in the DNS reverse query. The DNS server receives a node status response, which includes the NetBIOS name of the node. It then appends the DNS domain name to this NetBIOS name and forwards the result to the client.

Zone Requirements

In Lesson 1, you briefly examined the various zone types available in Windows Server 2003. Here, the zone types will be addressed in more detail so that you can determine which zone type is best suited for your organization.

Standard Primary Zone

This zone type is usually implemented when there are UNIX or older DNS systems in place, and usually consists of a primary and at least one secondary DNS server. Replication of this data occurs between this primary DNS server and the secondary DNS server through a process called *zone transfers*. The primary DNS server is the only server that can be updated; the secondary DNS server is read-only, so changes can only occur to it through replication.

Replication, or zone transfers, between primary and secondary DNS servers may occur:

- When the refresh interval expires for the zone.
- When the master server notifies the secondary DNS server of changes.
- When the DNS Server service is started on a secondary DNS server in the zone.
- When the secondary server initiates a transfer from its master server.

Active Directory Integrated Zone

This zone type is usually implemented when an Active Directory infrastructure is in place and no legacy DNS infrastructure exists. DNS zones can be stored in the domain or application partitions of Active Directory. Partitions are data structures used by Active Directory to separate data for replication purposes. This will be covered in Lesson 3.

Let's look at some of the available zone replication scopes that are possible when selecting this zone type:

- Replicate zone data to all DNS servers running on domain controllers in the Active Directory forest.
- Replicate zone data to all DNS servers running on domain controllers in the Active Directory domain. This is the default configuration.
- Replicate zone data to all domain controllers in the Active Directory domain.
- Replicate zone data based on the specified application directory partition.

One of the major advantages of this zone type, as compared to the standard primary zone type, is that a master copy of the zone file is stored in the Active Directory database and replicated to all domain controllers. In other words, there is not just one copy of the file, which is a single point of failure, but multiple copies stored on domain controllers. Also, each of these copies can be updated, whereas only the primary DNS zone file is updateable in a standard primary zone.

If your network will use Active Directory, it is recommended that the Active Directory integrated zone type be used for the following reasons:

- Improved security through secure dynamic updates and the use of discretionary access control list (DACL)
- Directory-integrated zones are automatically stored on each domain controller
- Directory replication is faster than standard DNS replication methods

DNS Security

In designing your name resolution strategy, you must also consider the methods you will use to reduce the risk of attacks to your DNS infrastructure.

Because your DNS servers may be exposed to the Internet, security should be one of your major concerns. Windows Server 2003 DNS has additional security features to help protect your DNS infrastructure against attackers. In this section, you will look at some of the potential attacks that can be made against your DNS infrastructure and how you can protect against such attacks.

As you read this section, it is critical that you understand, as a security professional or a network administrator, that any system is vulnerable to attack. If a system is connected to the Internet, that vulnerability is greatly increased. Hence, adhering to the guidelines in this section does not guarantee your network will be safe from intruders. Rather, these guidelines will make it more difficult for the attacker to penetrate your network, and hopefully will steer the intruder to systems that have little or no security implemented. The only surefire way of protecting your network from outside intruders is to unplug the network cable from your servers and place them in a cipher-locked room!

Potential Security Threats

There are many books written on the subject of network security, so this section is just the tip of the iceberg. See "Checklist: Securing your DNS infrastructure" in Windows Server 2003 Help and Support Center for more details, as well as the following URL: *http://www.microsoft.com/technet/security/prodtech/windows/win2003/*.

Let's begin by looking at the ways an attacker may threaten your DNS infrastructure:

- Footprinting is the process by which information about your network, or business, is obtained through nonintrusive methods. The attacker may use tools or programs such as the "whois" command, nslookup, and axfr (a program offered free on the Internet, which transfers zone file information from any domain that is not properly secured and creates a compressed file of the data that can be read offline at the attacker's leisure). The zone data obtained can be used to determine your company's DNS domain names, computer names, and IP addresses.

- Denial-of-service (DoS) attacks are made to prevent legitimate users from accessing resources on a network. The most infamous DoS attack was the "ping of death." By sending a ping packet that was too large for a server to properly handle, the server became unavailable to all users. A DNS DoS floods the server with recursive queries; this, in turn, overworks the server's CPU until its limit is reached and the DNS server cannot function.

■ Redirection is used by an attacker to redirect queries made to a legitimate DNS server to a DNS server controlled by the attacker. This is usually accomplished by the attacker polluting the DNS cache of the DNS server with erroneous DNS data, such as a resource record that points to the attacker's server. Once this man-in-the-middle attack is accomplished, the attacker can have clients send network requests, which may include passwords, to his or her server.

As you can see, if left alone, DNS can be quite vulnerable. After all, it was designed as an open protocol with very limited or no security in mind.

Securing Your DNS Infrastructure

Let's look at some guidelines you can follow to help secure your DNS infrastructure.

■ Eliminate direct communication between clients and DNS servers on the Internet. You can use a private DNS namespace for your company's internal DNS servers, and host the external DNS namespace on external DNS servers. If an internal host needs to query an external name, the internal DNS server can forward the request to an external DNS server.

■ To prevent external computers from accessing your internal DNS namespace, configure your firewall to allow User Datagram Protocol (UDP) and Transmission Control Protocol (TCP) port 53 communication only between your internal and external DNS servers.

■ To further prevent an attacker from initiating a DNS denial-of-service attack, limit the IP addresses your DNS Server service listens on to only IP addresses used by your DNS clients. You should also disable recursion for the DNS Server service on DNS servers that are not configured to perform recursive queries.

■ To prevent an attacker from polluting your DNS cache, be sure the default "Secure cache against pollution" option is selected. If you change this default setting, you risk an attacker adding erroneous resource records to your zone file.

■ Use the DACL on DNS servers running on domain controllers to control permissions for the DNS Server service. This DACL is part of the DNS object's security descriptor, which grants or denies specific users and groups permission to access the object.

■ To prevent footprinting through DNS zone transfers, restrict zone transfers to occur only between DNS servers that are listed in the name server (NS) resource records of the zone. This is the default, but if you want added security, you can specify that zone transfers only occur between specific IP addresses.

■ For increased file system security, always use the NTFS file system instead of File Allocation Table (FAT) or FAT32 for DNS servers running the Windows Server 2003 operating system.

- If your DNS infrastructure is using the Active Directory integrated zone type, be sure to allow only secure dynamic updates.

Now that you see all of the options you have to protect your DNS server from an attack, there is still the issue of replication (zone transfer) data being intercepted or captured as it traverses a public network.

Any time data is transmitted across the Internet, there is the danger that someone with a protocol analyzer, also known as *sniffer software*, may capture the packets and look at their contents. Let's end this security section with a brief discussion of securing replication data.

Securing Replication Data

You have seen how important it is that DNS zone information be replicated to a secondary DNS server for both fault tolerance and load balancing. But what can happen when this data is sent over a WAN where the Internet is used as the backbone? Your data can be intercepted by someone using a protocol analyzer, which can capture packets and look at the contents in them. There are several options you can use to prevent this from occurring, or at least to reduce the possibility.

- Encryption using Internet Protocol Security (IPSec)
- Encryption using a Virtual Private Network (VPN)
- Encryption using Active Directory

Zone replication traffic can be encrypted using IPSec or VPN tunneling encryption. Whichever one of these you choose, select the strongest level of encryption, such as 3DES (pronounced triple-des). Realize, once again, that any data that is encrypted can be decrypted. The question, however, is how long will it take? Also, regardless of how strong the encryption, there are other variables that could make it easy to crack, such as the fixed encryption key, which in many instances is advertised over the Internet by unscrupulous individuals. Once again, do not assume encryption ensures guaranteed protection from unauthorized users.

If you choose to use Active Directory integrated zones, security is a built-in function. Active Directory can be configured to allow only registered Active Directory integrated zone DNS servers to replicate to each other. You can configure all replication traffic that is sent between DNS servers to be encrypted.

Interoperability with UNIX Berkeley Internet Name Domain (BIND)

As you saw in Lesson 1, not all organizations use Microsoft DNS Server for name resolution. In this section, you will examine what needs to be done to integrate your Windows Server 2003 Active Directory services with a BIND DNS implementation. If the organization wants to continue to use BIND DNS servers, you can have your newer Microsoft DNS servers work with the older BIND versions or even with Windows NT DNS implementations. Windows 2003 treats these versions as traditional DNS servers, which support:

- Standard primary zones.

- Standard secondary zones.

- Delegated domains.

Microsoft-Tested BIND Versions

The Microsoft Windows Server 2003 DNS development team has tested Windows Server 2003 DNS Server and Client services with the following BIND DNS server implementations:

- BIND 4.9.7

- BIND 8.1

- BIND 8.2

- BIND 9.1.0

When a user attempts to log on to a Windows Server 2003 network, DNS is required to locate a domain controller and any other network resources the client needs to access. In fact, when you install Windows Server 2003 on the first server in your organization and add the Domain Controller role, you can choose to have the wizard install the DNS Server role and add new zones based on the DNS name you specified in the wizard. In many organizations, a BIND version of DNS is already running. This BIND version, unfortunately, might not support the DNS requirements for deployment of Active Directory. You can correct these problems by doing the following:

- Upgrade all BIND DNS servers to version 8.1.2 or later to meet DNS requirements for Active Directory support.

- Verify that the BIND DNS implementation you are using supports the service location (SRV) resource record. Remember that the SRV record specifies the location of services. For example, _http._tcp.contoso.com IN SRV 0 0 80 could be an SRV record that pointed all users to a Web server named webserver.contoso.com.

- Verify that the BIND DNS implementation you are using supports dynamic updates, as described in Request For Comments (RFC) 2136. This is not a requirement, but it is highly recommended. If this feature is not supported, additional manual administration of SRV records will be needed for DNS configuration support of Active Directory to work properly.

Zone Transfer Issue with BIND

Transferring zones between Windows Server 2003 DNS servers is not a problem. By default, the DNS Server service will use the fast zone transfer method, which uses a compression algorithm to improve performance. This method allows multiple resource records to be sent in one message, increasing the speed of the zone transfer.

Windows Server 2003 DNS servers can also be configured to transfer a zone using an uncompressed transfer format to enable zone transfers that do not support the fast transfer method, such as BIND servers running versions prior to 4.9.4. Also, BIND servers do not recognize WINS or WINS-R records, so if you are replicating zone data to this type of server, you must select the Do Not Replicate This Record check box.

Practice: Designing a DNS Namespace for Forests and Domains

In this practice, you will design a DNS namespace for Northwind Traders. If you are unable to answer a question, review the lesson materials and try the question again. You can find answers to the questions in the "Questions and Answers" section at the end of this chapter.

Scenario

Northwind Traders manufactures a line of network appliances designed to help companies improve their data transmission capabilities. Northwind Traders currently uses a Microsoft Windows NT 4.0 master domain model. In recent years, the company has undergone significant growth and expansion. The company expects substantial growth over the next three years, including growth in market share, revenue, and number of employees. In addition to opening two new offices, executive management has committed to implementing a new Windows Server 2003 Active Directory design to meet the current and future needs of the company.

The following table shows the geographical locations, the departments residing in each location, and the number of users in each of the locations.

Location	Departments Represented	Number of Users
Paris	Headquarters (HQ) Management staff Finance Sales Marketing Production Research Development Information Technology (IT)	2,000

Location	Departments Represented	Number of Users
Los Angeles	Sales Marketing Finance IT	1,000
Atlanta	Customer Service Customer Support Training	750
Glasgow, Scotland	Research Development Sustained Engineering IT	750
Sydney, Australia	Consulting Production Sales Finance	500

Most of the company's computing services are hosted in the corporate headquarters in Paris. The corporate IT department wants to have central control of passwords and security settings. The local IT department in Los Angeles wants to maintain control of its infrastructure without the interference from the corporate IT department. The local IT department in Glasgow demands that it have exclusive control over its own environment due to security concerns regarding research and development (R&D) data. Corporate management shares the security concerns about the R&D data and wants to ensure that it is not compromised.

The following diagram shows the connectivity between the different locations of the company. In addition, Los Angeles and Atlanta have virtual private network (VPN) connections through the Internet to the Paris headquarters.

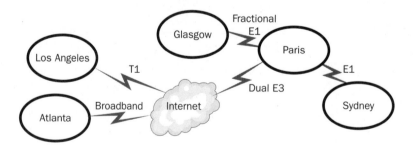

Northwind Traders has decided to adopt the forest and domain design shown below. Corporate IT management has determined that it wants to use Active Directory domain names that are not resolvable on the Internet.

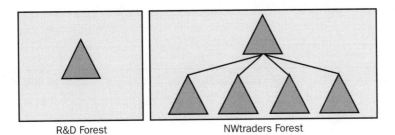

R&D Forest   NWtraders Forest

Practice Question

Based on the scenario, answer the following question.

1. Using the forest and domain diagram presented in the scenario, identify the naming strategy would you use for Northwind Traders. Explain your strategy.

_____

_____

Lesson Review

The following questions reinforce key information presented in this lesson. If you are unable to answer a question, review the lesson materials and try the question again. You can find answers to the questions in the "Questions and Answers" section at the end of this chapter.

1. Your organization has over 350 users that are running Windows 98 and Windows NT Workstation operating systems. Users are constantly relocating to different locations throughout the company, requiring you to update host records in DNS. In designing your network strategy, which feature of DNS would lessen the administrative work of creating and updating these records?

_____

_____

2. Your manager is concerned that DNS replication data traversing the network is vulnerable to attack. He read an article in a computer journal that discussed how a protocol analyzer could be introduced to the company's network, and that the replication data from a zone transfer could be captured. What could you tell the manager to assure him or her that the data was not vulnerable?

    _____

    _____

3. What is the recommended BIND version for Active Directory support?

    _____

    _____

Lesson Summary

- Designing a DNS namespace begins with understanding your current Active Directory environment. First, consider designing the Active Directory structure and then support that design with a DNS structure.

- It is critical that diagrams, maps, and well-written documentation be part of the design process.

- One of the most important aspects of your DNS design is securing the DNS components to reduce the risk of threats to your infrastructure. Footprinting, denial-of-service attacks, and polluting the DNS cache are some examples of the possible threats to your DNS infrastructure.

Lesson 3: Designing a DNS Implementation

Now comes the time when you decide whether or not a server should be a caching-only server or a primary DNS server, or which resource records will need to be created. The design should take into account the replication or zone transfer methodology, while keeping a close watch on your company's bandwidth limitations. In this lesson, you design a DNS zone storage strategy and configure the various server options. You also look once again at the resource records available to you in DNS.

After this lesson, you will be able to

- Design a strategy for DNS zone storage.
- Identify the use of DNS server options.

Estimated lesson time: 15 minutes

When designing a DNS implementation, you should already have a good understanding of your network topology, location of users, servers, routers, and so on. Figure 6-5 illustrates a high-level network diagram. This can later be modified to include more specific information such as zone types, DNS server placement, and so on.

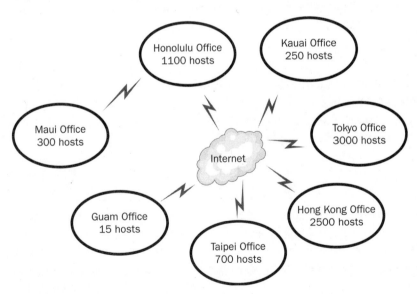

Figure 6-5   This is an example of a high-level network diagram.

In this lesson, you are now prepared to make decisions in the following areas:

- Which zone types will be part of your design, for instance, Active Directory integrated, standard primary, or other types?

- Where will the DNS servers be placed on your network? This is covered in greater detail in Lesson 4.

- Will your design need to consider integration with UNIX BIND DNS, or older versions of DNS?

- Will your design incorporate integration with other networking services such as DHCP and WINS?

- Will your DNS namespace design integrate with your Active Directory namespace?

Zone Storage

In Lesson 1, you briefly looked at the various methods by which zones could be stored in your DNS infrastructure. If you install Active Directory on a server, you can store your zone files two different ways:

- A text-based file stored in the systemroot\System32\DNS folder on each DNS server computer. For example, if you created a zone file for a domain named marketing.contoso.com, the zone file would be called marketing.contoso.com.dns. Note that the extension of zone files is "dns."

- In the Active Directory tree under the domain or application directory partition (discussion follows). The benefits of using Active Directory integrated zones were covered in Lesson 2.

Application Directory Partitions

As you learned in Lesson 2, DNS zones can be stored in the Active Directory database. You can also store a zone in an application directory partition. An application directory partition gives you the ability to store data in Active Directory that you want to replicate only to specific domain controllers.

Stub Zones

A stub zone is a copy of a zone that contains only the resource records needed to identify an authoritative DNS server. An authoritative DNS server is a server that hosts resource records for a particular DNS zone. For example, an authoritative DNS server for the zone training.contoso.com would contain resource records for that zone. Rather than a DNS server having to query the Internet to locate an authoritative DNS server, the DNS server can simply refer to the list of name servers (NS resource records) in the stub zone.

Distributing a list of authoritative DNS servers for a zone can be implemented by using stub zones. Unlike secondary zones, which primarily are used for redundancy and load-balancing reasons, stub zones are used to improve name resolution performance.

Reverse Lookup Zone Design

For security reasons, sometimes it is necessary that a node identify itself to a server with its host name, but only the IP address is known. In these cases, a reverse lookup must be initiated. Designing a reverse lookup zone is similar to a forward lookup zone, the only difference being that now you need to consider the replication of reverse lookup zone files across the domain. The same zone types may be implemented for reverse lookup zones as with forward lookup zones:

- Active Directory integrated zones

- Traditional primary zones

- Traditional secondary zones

DNS Server Options

When designing your DNS infrastructure, you must decide which servers will host primary and secondary copies of zones. If Active Directory will be used, you also must determine which servers will be domain controllers or member servers for your domain.

The decisions you make here will, of course, determine the hardware requirements needed. That is, additional memory may be needed if the role of the server will be both a primary DNS server and a domain controller. This is covered in more detail in Lesson 4.

Configuration of the DNS Server

After deciding on the role of the server, you will need to configure it. Before configuring the computer, you should:

- Determine if Active Directory will be deployed. If it is, the Active Directory Installation Wizard can install and configure DNS.

- Verify that the operating system is configured correctly, and that TCP/IP is also configured.

- Verify that the server has enough disk space and memory to handle the zone it will host.

Placement of the server is covered in more detail in Lesson 4. It is recommended that each remote site have at least one DNS server.

Lesson Review

The following questions are intended to reinforce key information presented in this lesson. If you are unable to answer a question, review the lesson materials and try the question again. You can find answers to the questions in the "Questions and Answers" section at the end of this chapter.

1. You are the network administrator of a Windows Server 2003 network that houses a legacy computer program running on a UNIX computer. The computer program requires that all workstations connecting to it be authenticated by verification of the workstation's host name. Users call and complain that they are no longer able to access the program and that they are receiving permission errors. What could be the possible cause of this problem?

   _____

   _____

2. You are preparing to install a server on your network with the Windows Server 2003 operating system. This will be the first server on your network, and you plan to add the Domain Controller role after installing the operating system. What steps will you need to take to install DNS on this computer?

   _____

   _____

3. You have recently installed Active Directory and have created a zone domain named sales.contoso.com. List the two ways you can store this zone file.

   _____

   _____

Lesson Summary

- A zone file can be stored two different ways. It can be a text-based file stored in the systemroot\System32\DNS folder on each DNS server computer or stored in the Active Directory in the case of an Active Directory–integrated zone.

- An application directory partition gives you the ability to store application-specific data in Active Directory that you want to replicate only to specific domain controllers.

- Designing a reverse lookup zone is similar to a forward lookup zone. You must still consider replication of the zone for fault tolerance and load balancing.

Lesson 4: Designing a DNS Service Placement Strategy

Because you have already recorded information about all of your network's servers in your design documents, this knowledge, combined with information pertaining to the DNS zone types, WAN and LAN topologies, and the amount of users on your network, means you are now ready to design a DNS service placement strategy. In this lesson, you will examine server placement for optimal performance.

After this lesson, you will be able to

■ Design a DNS service placement.

Estimated lesson time: 25 minutes

Designing DNS Service Placement

Deploying DNS servers on your network requires careful analysis of all the information gathered to this point. That is, you should now have diagrams and maps of all your network resources and should have a good idea of bandwidth issues and your servers' hardware capacities. For example, your high-level network diagram can now be modified to show how many DNS servers are in each location. See Figure 6-6.

This section covers some of the questions you should ask that will lead you in the right direction in choosing the correct amount of servers and their placement on the network.

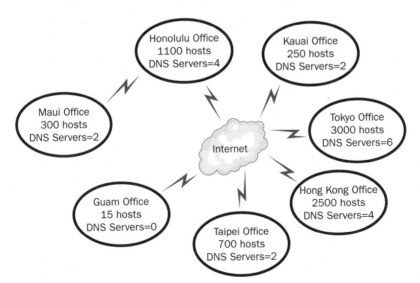

Figure 6-6   This high-level diagram shows server placement.

Server Placement

In deciding how many DNS servers you will deploy for your network, and where you should place them, you will need to answer the following questions:

■ How many zones will the DNS server host? The more zones, the more random access memory (RAM) each server should have.

■ How large are the zones? (You can base this answer on how many resource records are in the zone or the size of the zone file). This also will influence your decision on the server's memory or the server that will be selected to handle the particular zone.

■ How many DNS queries from clients do you expect the DNS server service to receive? Obviously, if a DNS server is bombarded constantly with queries from clients, performance will suffer. Consider using multiple DNS servers to load balance these requests.

■ Which servers will host primary and secondary copies of zones? The answer to this question will assist you in assessing the effect of zone transfer traffic propagating across your network. If this type of traffic is a big issue, you may consider using caching-only DNS servers in remote areas where WAN links are slow. Caching-only servers are discussed later in this section.

■ If you are using Active Directory, will the DNS server be a domain controller or a member server? DNS servers that are also domain controllers will perform both DNS functions and domain controller functions. This could influence the hardware requirements for the server.

■ Will your network use DNS servers running only Windows Server 2003, or will you have a mixture of DNS servers from other operating systems? If other DNS implementations are present, be sure to review any issues associated with each type of configuration.

■ If a DNS server unexpectedly goes down, will users have an alternate DNS server to contact for name resolution? This is critical because many companies rely on DNS not only to resolve internal names, but also to access resources across the Internet. DNS was designed to have at least two servers for each zone. Primary and secondary servers provide fault tolerance, as does creating Active Directory integrated zones.

■ If a DNS server is located in a remote subnet and the DNS server's router fails, is there an alternate DNS server available for name resolution? If the subnet has many users that rely on DNS for name resolution, you might consider installing a DNS server on the local subnet.

For example, if a location has only three users, it may not be cost effective to purchase a DNS server. You will want users to issue queries to a DNS server closest to their location. Sending name resolution traffic, as well as zone transfer traffic, over a slow WAN link will make the link even slower. One solution to such a problem is caching-only DNS servers, discussed later in this section.

Monitoring DNS Performance

Microsoft has also done some testing to help you determine if your DNS servers are performing optimally. Over a course of 4 days, they monitored a DNS server that was configured as follows:

- Intel Pentium III 733 MHz single-processor
- 256 RAM
- 4 GB Hard drive

You should determine a baseline for your company, but the study conducted by Microsoft is a good benchmark to help you determine if your DNS server's performance has degraded over a period of time. You can monitor such events as:

- The total amount of queries received by the DNS server.
- The average number of queries received each second.
- The total number of responses sent by the DNS server.
- The average number of responses sent by the DNS server each second.

The DNS server that Microsoft monitored performed 9,500 queries per second and 1,300 dynamic updates per second with processor utilization at 75 percent. You can also use DNS performance counters to measure and monitor the other areas in which a DNS server functions. For example, you can monitor the AXFR Request Sent performance counter to see if an excessive amount of full zone transfer requests is being made by a secondary server. Your baseline would determine if the zone transfer requests were indeed excessive or just normal occurrences.

Caching-Only Servers

To increase name resolution speed and eliminate zone transfer traffic, you may want to use a caching-only server. A caching-only server, as shown in Figure 6-7, does not host a zone. Rather, its only purpose is to cache queries so that future requests for the same resource record are done instantly because the results of the previous query are already in cache. In other words, the caching-only server will not have to forward repeated queries to another server. This speeds up the name-resolution process while reducing network traffic.

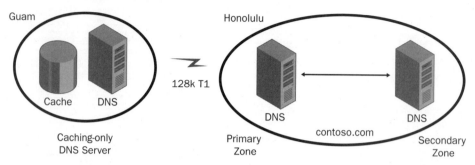

Figure 6-7   A caching-only server does not host a zone.

> **Real World   More memory!**
>
> If you've heard it once, you've heard it a thousand times: More memory improves performance. That especially holds true for DNS servers. In fact, adding more RAM to your DNS server produces the most noticeable improvement in performance. When the DNS Server service starts, it loads all of its configured zones into memory. Approximately 4 megabytes (MB) of RAM is used by DNS, even if there are no zones present. Each addition of a zone or a resource record consumes additional memory. Each resource record uses approximately 100 bytes of memory.

Load Balancing

It is always better to have as many servers as possible when you are designing your DNS infrastructure. If 1000 users are all trying to connect to one DNS server so they can resolve an FQDN, it goes without saying that the process will be slow. Load balancing is accomplished by providing clients with varied ordered addresses of multiple DNS servers. Load balancing improves scalability, allowing your DNS servers to handle many more simultaneous requests than would otherwise be possible. As shown in Figure 6-8, configuring clients to first query a DNS server on their local subnet adds the benefit of improved responsiveness.

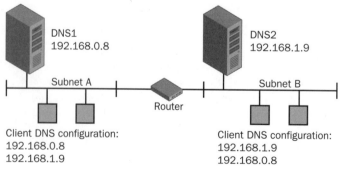

Figure 6-8   This diagram gives an example of load balancing.

Remote Locations

The worst nightmare for a network administrator is to have users complaining that the system is too slow. If your remote users have to go over a high-latency or overloaded WAN link to access your DNS server, you may consider using caching-only servers.

> **Exam Tip** As you work through the case studies presented on the exam, be particularly aware of topology diagrams that depict slow WAN links between various locations.
>
> Avoid topologies that require replication across a slow link. Instead, choose topologies that use caching-only servers in remote locations connected to the central network using a slow link.

As you can see, one of the most important aspects of designing your DNS infrastructure is having the correct amount of DNS servers on your network, and placing them in the areas that optimize performance and offer fault tolerance, load balancing, and enhanced security measures.

Practice: Designing a DNS Infrastructure

In this practice, you will evaluate a design for a DNS infrastructure for Northwind Traders. If you are unable to answer a question, review the lesson materials and try the question again. You can find answers to the questions in the "Questions and Answers" section at the end of this chapter.

Scenario

Northwind Traders manufactures a line of network appliances designed to help companies improve their data transmission capabilities. Northwind Traders currently uses a Microsoft Windows NT 4.0 master domain model. In recent years, the company has undergone significant growth and expansion. The company expects substantial growth over the next three years, including growth in market share, revenue, and number of employees. In addition to opening two new offices, executive management has committed to implementing a new Windows Server 2003 Active Directory design to meet the current and future needs of the company.

The following illustration shows the connectivity between the different locations of the company. In addition, Los Angeles and Atlanta have virtual private network (VPN) connections through the Internet to the Paris headquarters.

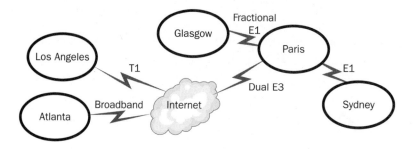

Practice Questions

Based on the scenario, answer the following questions.

1. You would like to minimize the administrative overhead of DNS zones on the network. How would you do this?

_____

_____

2. You are also concerned about the security of automated DNS updates from clients on the network. How can you continue to ensure minimal DNS administration while ensuring a secure DNS environment for automatic updates?

_____

_____

Lesson Review

The following questions are intended to reinforce key information presented in this lesson. If you are unable to answer a question, review the lesson materials and try the question again. You can find answers to the questions in the "Questions and Answers" section at the end of this chapter.

1. You are designing a DNS infrastructure and need to decide where DNS servers should be located. You have already created diagrams, maps, and documentation of the network topology and infrastructure. Why are these elements critical in your decision-making process regarding server placement?

_____

_____

2. A remote office has a secondary DNS server on their local network and is experiencing an excessive amount of zone transfer data across their low-bandwidth WAN connection. This traffic is slowing down your network and users are complaining that email and Web access is extremely slow. What can you do to lessen the amount of zone transfer data traversing your slow WAN link?

_____

_____

3. List several reasons why having multiple DNS servers on your network is recommended.

_____

_____

Lesson Summary

- Information that is obtained to create your network documentation is critical when designing DNS service placement. An overview of the network topology and available bandwidth are important elements that greatly influence your design.

- Multiple DNS servers provide enhanced performance through load balancing, and the use of caching-only servers on remote networks will reduce zone transfer traffic use on limited bandwidth.

- When configuring a server to be a DNS server, you should be aware if any other services will run on the server. For example, a DNS server that will also be a domain controller will require more memory to optimize its performance. Remember that the size of the zone file and the amount of resource records influence the amount of server memory needed.

Case Scenario Exercise

Review the following scenario and complete the questions.

Scenario

You have been selected to plan a new DNS infrastructure for MTS Consulting, Inc., a hotel management consulting firm with its headquarters in Honolulu, Hawaii. They recently hired a computer consultant to upgrade all of their servers to Windows Server 2003 and implemented Active Directory. Client computers are running a mix of Windows 98 and Windows 2000 Professional. MTS has hired you to design a DNS infrastructure that will integrate with their Active Directory infrastructure. All client computers will run Windows XP Professional.

Background

MTS has grown over the past two years to become one of the foremost hotel management consulting firms in the Pacific Rim area. Last month they opened offices in Japan, Taiwan, Hong Kong, and a small office in Guam. MTS manages over 300 hotels in the Pacific Rim. MTS is responsible for total management of all hotel operations such as reservations (which can also be made from online customers), linens, dining services, electrical functions, plumbing, plant security, payroll, and so on. Computer programs are three-tier systems, which rely on Web browsers and Internet connectivity to function.

Geography

In addition to its Honolulu location, MTS also has two branch offices, one in Maui and another in Kauai. Both branches manage all Hawaii hotel operations and have fully staffed IT personnel.

Network Infrastructure

The Honolulu office is connected to the Maui and Kauai offices by means of a 256 Kb fractional T1 line and a backup Integrated Services Digital Network (ISDN) circuit. The Guam office is connected to Honolulu by means of a 128 Kb fractional T1 line. Offices in Japan, Taiwan, and Hong Kong use the Internet to connect to all offices throughout the Pacific Rim. These offices rely on the Internet service providers (ISPs) that service these areas. Clients in all offices throughout the Pacific Rim are connected via 10/100 Mbps connections. See Figure 6-9 for a partial network diagram.

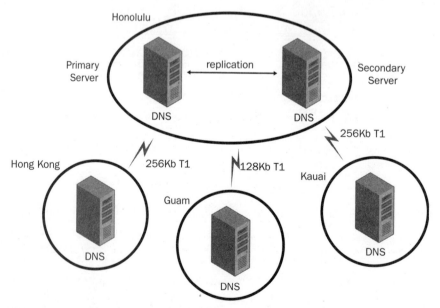

Figure 6-9   This diagram shows a partial network.

Future Plans

There are no current plans to significantly expand the workforce at the current locations. However, there is a possibility that the company will be expanding its operations to Beijing, China, within the next couple of years.

IT Management

The IT staff in Honolulu is in charge of maintaining the Honolulu, Maui, Kauai, and Guam locations. A separate IT staff is located in Tokyo, Taipei, and Hong Kong. However, the senior IT staff in Honolulu has the responsibility for designing and maintaining the DNS infrastructure.

Questions

Given the previous scenario, answer the following questions. You can find the answers in the "Questions and Answers" section at the end of this chapter.

1. What additional information should you gather to assist you in the placement of the DNS servers?

   _____

   _____

2. Assuming that you will use zone transfers to replicate DNS zone files from the Honolulu office to the Tokyo office, what are some of the concerns you should have with the current network topology? What steps can you take to mitigate, or possibly eliminate, some of the risks associated with the present network infrastructure?

   _____

   _____

3. Users in the Guam office are complaining that it takes too long to access resources on the Internet, even though a DNS server is in their office. You discover that the bulk of network traffic from Guam to Honolulu is zone transfer data, and that this is using up too much of their limited bandwidth. What steps can you take to help the Guam office with this problem?

   _____

   _____

4. You have just been contracted to assist MTS in setting up an office in China. The manager there says they already have UNIX BIND DNS operating there. His DNS administrator insists that his experience with this implementation warrants the company not switching. It is critical that DNS integrate with Active Directory. What, if any, are your concerns?

_____

_____

Chapter Summary

- The first step in analyzing your current DNS infrastructure is creating diagrams and maps of the system. In most cases, the diagrams and maps should have already been created when analyzing the Active Directory infrastructure.

- Identifying the components of your current DNS infrastructure begins by understanding how DNS functions. Basically, DNS is a database that stores resource records that must be maintained on DNS servers. This information must also be replicated to other DNS servers for fault tolerance and load balancing.

- Replication of zones files is done through a method called zone transfers. There are three zone transfer methods used by Windows Server 2003 DNS: IXFR, AXFR, and fast zone transfer.

- Designing a DNS namespace begins with understanding your current Active Directory environment. First, consider designing the Active Directory structure and then support that design with a DNS structure.

- One of the most important aspects of your DNS design is securing the DNS components to reduce the risk of threats to your infrastructure. Footprinting, denial-of-service attacks, and polluting the DNS cache are some examples of the possible threats to your DNS infrastructure.

- Zone files can be stored two different ways. They can be text-based files stored in the systemroot\System32\DNS folder on each DNS server computer, or stored in Active Directory under the domain or application directory partition.

- An application directory partition gives you the ability to store application-specific data that you want to replicate only to specific domain controllers in Active Directory.

- Designing a reverse lookup zone is similar to a forward lookup zone. You must still consider replication of the zone for fault tolerance and load balancing.

- Information that is obtained to create your network documentation is critical when designing DNS service placement. An overview of the network topology and available bandwidth are important elements that greatly influence your design.

■ Multiple DNS servers provide enhanced scalability through load balancing, and the use of caching-only servers on remote networks will reduce zone transfer traffic.

■ When configuring a server to be a DNS server, you should be aware if any other services will run on the server. For example, a DNS server that will also be a domain controller will require more memory to optimize its performance. Remember that the size of the zone file and the amount of resource records influence the amount of server memory needed.

Exam Highlights

Before taking the exam, review the key topics and terms presented in this chapter. You need to know this information.

Key Points

■ In analyzing a current DNS infrastructure, documentation, diagrams, and maps are the most important elements. This lays a critical foundation for the rest of your network design.

■ Designing a DNS namespace begins with understanding your current Active Directory environment. Consider designing the Active Directory structure and then supporting that design with a DNS structure.

■ Securing your DNS infrastructure begins with an understanding of the potential risks. Footprinting, denial-of-service attacks, and polluting the DNS cache are some examples of the possible threats to your DNS infrastructure.

■ In designing your DNS name resolution strategy, integration of other networking services, such as DHCP and WINS, should be considered to optimize performance.

Key Terms

Zone   A zone is a contiguous portion of a DNS tree that is administered as a separate entity by a DNS server.

Zone transfer   A process in which DNS data is replicated from one DNS server to another. There are three types of zone transfers in Windows Server 2003: IFXR, AXFR, and fast zone transfer.

Caching-only server   A DNS server that caches the answers to queries and returns the results. This saves time and reduces network traffic because calls to multiple DNS servers are not required.

BIND (Berkley Internet Name Domain)   An implementation of DNS available for most UNIX systems. Microsoft requires version 8.1.2 or later to meet DNS requirements for Active Directory support.

Questions and Answers

Page
6-9

Lesson 1 Review

1. What are the three zone transfer methods that may be used to replicate zone file data?

   The three zone transfer methods are: IXFR, AXFR, and fast zone transfer. Fast zone transfer is the default zone transfer method in Windows Server 2003.

2. What is one advantage of using Active Directory integrated zones as a zone type for a larger organization?

   The biggest advantage is the avoidance of zone transfers. Replication can occur through Active Directory replication.

3. In analyzing the current network infrastructure of your company, you note that there are several DNS servers spread out throughout the organization. One of the servers is taking a long time to update its records. What could be some of the reasons for this time delay?

   It is important to understand more than just the placement of servers in an organization if you are to fully understand and improve your troubleshooting skills. Your analysis of the current network should have also revealed the WAN link speeds between subnets, which can have a significant effect on zone transfers. If only a slow link is available, you may want to consider alternative ways to update resource records.

Page
6-23

Lesson 2 Practice

1. Using the forest and domain diagram presented in the scenario, identify the naming strategy would you use for Northwind Traders. Explain your strategy.

   Different answers are possible, but a good naming strategy is illustrated in the following diagram. Since the domain names are not to be resolvable from the Internet, the .local namespace is used.

RDNwtraders.local

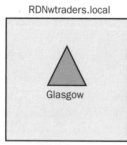

Glasgow

R&D Forest

NWtraders.local

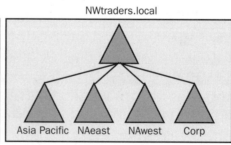

Asia Pacific   NAeast   NAwest   Corp

NWtraders Forest

Lesson 2 Review

1. Your organization has over 350 users that are running Windows 98 and Windows NT Workstation operating systems. Users are constantly relocating to different locations throughout the company, requiring you to update host records in DNS. In designing your network strategy, which feature of DNS would lessen the administrative work of creating and updating these records?

   You can configure the DHCP server to perform updates on behalf of DHCP clients. DHCP will register the A (host) records and PTR records for all DHCP-enabled clients, saving the administrator from manually entering the information into DNS.

2. Your manager is concerned that DNS replication data traversing the network is vulnerable to attack. He read an article in a computer journal that discussed how a protocol analyzer could be introduced to the company's network and that the replication data from a zone transfer could be captured. What could you tell the manager to assure him or her that the data was not vulnerable?

   You could inform the manager that zone transfers can be restricted based on IP addresses and that the replication data between the DNS servers could also be encrypted.

3. What is the recommended BIND version for Active Directory support?

   BIND DNS servers should be running versions 8.1.2 or later.

Lesson 3 Review

1. You are the network administrator of a Windows Server 2003 network that houses a legacy computer program running on a UNIX computer. The computer program requires that all workstations connecting to it be authenticated by verification of the workstation's host name. Users call and complain that they are no longer able to access the program and that they are receiving permission errors. What could be the possible cause of this problem?

   Because the UNIX program is verifying the workstation by using its host name, a reverse lookup zone is needed on this network. Reverse lookup zones resolve an IP address to a host name, whereas a forward lookup zone resolves host names to IP addresses. It is apparent from the information given in this question that users at one time were able to access the program. Hence, it appears that the DNS server that contained the reverse lookup zone is unavailable. In any event, the administrator needs to verify that a reverse lookup zone is available for the users and he or she should examine the possibility of creating a secondary zone for fault tolerance.

2. You are preparing to install a server on your network with the Windows Server 2003 operating system. This will be the first server on your network, and you plan to add the Domain Controller role after installing the operating system. What steps will you need to take to install DNS on this computer?

   Because there are no DNS servers on the network and you are running the Active Directory Installation Wizard, you will be prompted to install DNS, and it will automatically configure DNS on the server based on the TCP/IP configuration of the server.

3. You have recently installed Active Directory and have created a zone domain named sales.contoso.com. List the two ways you can store this zone file.

If the zone is not Active Directory integrated, the zone file is stored in a text-based file. If the zone is Active Directory integrated, the zone is stored in the Active Directory tree under the domain or application directory partition.

Page 6-34

Lesson 4 Practice

1. You would like to minimize the administrative overhead of DNS zones on the network. How would you do this?

First, you should recommend that only servers running Windows Server 2003 or Windows 2000 Server be used as DNS servers. You should also recommend that all DNS servers use Active Directory integrated zones.

2. You are also concerned about the security of automated DNS updates from clients on the network. How can you continue to ensure minimal DNS administration while ensuring a secure DNS environment for automatic updates?

You should specify that only secure dynamic updates are allowed on all servers.

Page 6-34

Lesson 4 Review

1. You are designing a DNS infrastructure and need to decide where DNS servers should be located. You have already created diagrams, maps, and documentation of the network topology and infrastructure. Why are these elements critical in your decision-making process regarding server placement?

Your documentation will indicate the available bandwidth between your company's locations and also give details regarding information such as the total number of servers, the location of routers, the total number of users on a subnet, and other factors that would be pertinent in deciding where a DNS server should be placed, as well as the hardware requirements for the particular server.

2. A remote office has a secondary DNS server on their local network and is experiencing an excessive amount of zone transfer data across their low-bandwidth WAN connection. This traffic is slowing down your network, and users are complaining that email and Web access is extremely slow. What can you do to lessen the amount of zone transfer data traversing your slow WAN link?

You should consider designating a caching-only server on the remote network. Since caching-only servers do not host zones, this will reduce the amount of traffic sent over the WAN link.

3. List several reasons why having multiple DNS servers on your network is recommended.

There are a number of advantages to having multiple DNS servers on your network. One reason is that in the event of a DNS server crash, users have an alternate DNS server to access. Another reason why multiple DNS servers on your network is recommended is load balancing. Load balancing enables DNS services to scale beyond the capacity of a single DNS server.

Case Scenario Exercise

1. What additional information should you gather to assist you in the placement of the DNS servers?

There is no indication of how many users are located in the various offices throughout the Pacific Rim or of the number of requests that will be made to the DNS server by these users. This information is critical because the placement of DNS servers, as well as the quantity of servers, depends on this information. You would also need to know the available bandwidth and latency between the different locations.

2. Assuming that you will use zone transfers to replicate DNS zone files from the Honolulu office to the Tokyo office, what are some of the concerns you should have with the current network topology? What steps can you take to mitigate, or possibly eliminate, some of the risks associated with the present network infrastructure?

With the current network infrastructure, zone transfers from Tokyo to Honolulu will be over the Internet. These zone transfers are susceptible to many threats such as footprinting and denial-of-service attacks. Also, it is very possible that the zone data could be captured with a protocol analyzer and viewed by an intruder. Some of the possible solutions you may implement to mitigate these threats are: create a VPN between Tokyo and Honolulu, which would encrypt all zone transfers; use Active Directory integrated zones; and restrict zone transfers to only authorized DNS servers.

3. Users in the Guam office are complaining that it takes too long to access resources on the Internet, even though a DNS server is in their office. You discover that the bulk of network traffic from Guam to Honolulu is zone transfer data, and that this is using up too much of their limited bandwidth. What steps can you take to help the Guam office with this problem?

Because zone transfer data seems to be the culprit in this question, the quickest and easiest solution to the problem would be to make the DNS server a caching-only server. Users will see an increase in speed when attempting to connect to Web sites because queries will be cached on the server, reducing the need for recursive queries. Also, since caching-only servers do not host zone files, the bandwidth connecting the two locations will no longer be used for zone transfer data. This will free up the limited bandwidth space for other needed traffic.

4. You have just been contracted to assist MTS in setting up an office in China. The manager there says they already have UNIX BIND DNS operating there. His DNS administrator insists that his experience with this implementation warrants the company not switching. It is critical that DNS integrate with Active Directory. What, if any, are your concerns?

You would first want to make sure that the BIND version used in the Beijing office was version 8.1.2 or later, to meet the DNS requirements for Active Directory support. It is not mandatory for the BIND version to support dynamic updates of resource records, but it is mandatory that the BIND version support the SRV resource record. SRV records are used to locate services running on the Active Directory network.

7 Designing a WINS Structure

Exam Objectives in this Chapter:

- Design the network services infrastructure to meet business and technical requirements

    - Create the conceptual design of the WINS infrastructure

- Design a NetBIOS name resolution strategy

    - Design a WINS replication strategy

Why This Chapter Matters

Like Domain Name System (DNS), your Windows Internet Networking System (WINS) infrastructure is based on both the physical and logical topology of the company's network. Before attempting to design a WINS infrastructure for a company, the company's existing physical topology should be diagramed with detailed information on the location of servers, routers and switches, domain controllers, application servers, users, groups, organizational units, and so on. All of this was covered in Chapter 2, "Analyzing an Existing Infrastructure."

This chapter is about designing a conceptual WINS infrastructure. The good news is that all of your hard work of gathering information to design the DNS infrastructure (the subject of Chapter 6) can be used here—no reinventing the wheel. You will begin your journey with an overview of WINS and how it works. From there, you will design a WINS infrastructure and then examine how WINS servers can replicate to other WINS servers, much like a DNS server replicates to other DNS servers.

Lessons in this Chapter:

Before You Begin

To complete this chapter, make sure you are familiar with the concepts described in Chapter 1, "Introduction to Active Directory and Network Infrastructure."

Lesson 1: Understanding WINS

Windows Internet Networking System (WINS) is a distributed database that stores network Basic Input/Output System (NetBIOS) names and services. The NetBIOS names are mapped to Internet Protocol (IP) addresses and, like DNS, WINS makes it possible for you to access resources on your network using easy, friendly names instead of hard-to-remember IP addresses. This lesson includes an overview of the WINS components and discusses some of the terminology you will need to understand before you can design and implement a WINS strategy for your company.

After this lesson, you will be able to

- Identify the various components of a WINS infrastructure.
- Describe NetBIOS name resolution and why it is still needed in a Windows Server 2003 environment.
- Describe two reasons WINS should be considered in your network design.

Estimated lesson time: 40 minutes

WINS Overview

Many administrators thought WINS would not be included with Windows Server 2003 and were a little surprised to see that not only it is included, but also that it has been improved. As long as there are computers running versions of Windows older than Windows 2000, there will be a need for WINS. The good news for those of you who have worked with WINS in Windows 2000 is that the interface has not changed with the 2003 version. There are a couple of new features in this newer version that make your job as a network administrator easier.

What's New in Windows Server 2003

- Advanced WINS database filtering and search capability help you locate records without having to look at all record types. For example, you can now look for only records that are mapped to a specific IP address or record owner. WINS databases can grow to be quite large and unwieldy, so this feature can save you a lot of time.

- Similar to DNS, you can now restrict or block name records from specific replication partners and only accept name records from the WINS servers you want. For example, you can define a list that controls which servers will update a specific WINS server during pull replication. Push and pull replication is covered in Lesson 3.

NetBIOS Name Resolution Overview

In the early eighties, Sytek Corporation developed NetBIOS for IBM to enable their applications to communicate over a network. After twenty years, many applications are still using NetBIOS.

Previous versions of Windows used NetBIOS names to identify resources that were on a network. A NetBIOS name is a 16-byte address used to identify a network resource, just as a host name identifies resources on a TCP/IP network. The first 15 characters of the NetBIOS name are specified by the administrator, and the 16th character, a hexadecimal number, is reserved to indicate the resource type. Most people refer to the name they give their workstation as the computer name. This, in fact, is the NetBIOS name, which can be used by other workstations to access it. See Table 7-1 and Table 7-2 for examples of NetBIOS names used by various Microsoft components.

Table 7-1 Microsoft Component NetBIOS Unique Names

Unique names	Description
computer_name[00h]	WINS client registration of computer name done by Workstation service
computer_name[03h]	Registered by the Messenger service of the WINS client
computer_name[20h]	Registered by the Server service on the WINS client
username[03h]	The username registered by the Messenger service, which allows the user to receive "net send" commands

Table 7-2 Microsoft Component NetBIOS Group Names

Group names	Description
domain_name[1Ch]	Registered by the Domain Controllers within the domain
__MSBROWSE__[01h]	Registered by the Master Browser for each subnet
domain_name[1Eh]	Used by browsers to elect a Master Browser

To access a share called Payroll on a computer with a NetBIOS name of HR_Director, you would type **hr_director\payroll** at the Run command prompt. Your workstation would broadcast the name hr_director[20h] on the local area network (LAN) segment so it could get the IP address of the target workstation. See Figure 7-1.

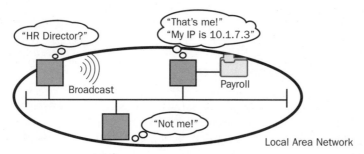

Figure 7-1   Broadcasting a NetBIOS name

As you can see from Figure 7-1, all workstations that receive the name resolution broadcast message are asked if they own the NetBIOS name hr_director[20h]. The workstation configured with the computer name of hr_director will then respond to the workstation requesting it.

The problem with this scenario is that broadcast traffic was needed to perform the Net-BIOS name resolution. Broadcast traffic, sometimes a necessary evil in networks, must be sent to every port on a network, and as a result can slow down your network. Network administrators try to reduce broadcast traffic as much as possible. WINS is one of the ways to do this. Creating an Lmhosts file is one remedy covered in this section. Adding routers to a network segment is another, and will be covered in more detail in Chapter 8, "Designing a Network and Routing Infrastructure." Which method a client uses to execute name resolution is determined by a node type. See Table 7-3 for the node types available for NetBIOS name resolution.

Table 7-3   NetBIOS Node Types

Name resolution mode	Description
B-node	Uses broadcast messages to register NetBIOS names or resolve NetBIOS names to IP addresses
P-node	Uses unicast to directly communicate with a NetBIOS name server (WINS) to register or resolve NetBIOS names
M-node	Uses broadcast (B-node) first when attempting to register or resolve a Net-BIOS name, and then queries a WINS server (P-node) if unsuccessful with the broadcast. The "M" stands for "mixed" because it uses a mix of B-node and P-node.
H-node	Uses hybrid (h-mode), a combination of P-node and then B-node. In other words, it first communicates with the WINS server to resolve the NetBIOS name and if unsuccessful, attempts a broadcast message.

By default, Windows Server 2003 computers use b-node unless WINS is configured; then h-node is the default node type. For a quick way to see which node type is used by a client, type ipconfig /all at the command prompt of the client's workstation. See

Figure 7-2. Since the node type in the output is hybrid (h-node), you can surmise that a WINS server is configured on this network. Node types can also be configured automatically on client computers using Dynamic Host Control Protocol (DHCP), which is covered in Chapter 8.

Figure 7-2   Node type displayed in Ipconfig /All screen

For now, you should understand that routers are used to reduce broadcast traffic and, by default, do not let broadcast traffic go through them. For example, in Figure 7-3, notice that a router divides Segment 1 and Segment 2. If Segment 2 had a workstation named Computer 2-1 on it and Computer 1-1 tried to access it using the Universal Naming Convention (UNC) name \\Computer2-1, there would be a problem. Why? Because Router A would not let this broadcast frame, which is requesting a NetBIOS-name-to-IP address resolution, go through it. Only workstations on Segment 1 would hear the "shout," or broadcast, for Computer 2-1. Because there is no Computer 2-1 on the local segment, Computer 1-1 would not receive a message. After a timeout period, Computer 1-1 would assume that the system was not available.

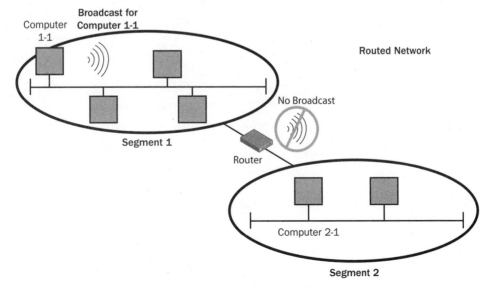

Figure 7-3   NetBIOS name resolution in a routed network

One solution you can use to solve the problem of remote NetBIOS name resolution is to use an Lmhosts file. The Lmhosts file is located in the directory %system-Root%\System32\Drivers\Etc, and can be edited to include the NetBIOS names you wish to resolve. It is a text-based file that contains NetBIOS-to-IP address mapping. The following code is an excerpt of an Lmhosts file with the entry of Computer 2-1 and its IP address.

```
192.168.8.2computer2-1 #PRE
```

```
192.168.8.3computer2-2
```

Finally, the most efficient way to resolve NetBIOS names across a routed network, and at the same time reduce broadcast traffic over your local network, is WINS.

Let's look at how the same scenario would occur if a WINS server were configured on this LAN, and if the workstations in question were WINS clients. You will learn more about WINS servers and clients later in this lesson. For now, this overview shows you why you want to use WINS. Note in Figure 7-4 that instead of broadcast traffic going over the LAN, the workstation simply connects to the WINS server and asks it to resolve the NetBIOS name to an IP address. The WINS server checks its database for an entry and returns the IP address—no broadcast traffic and no need to create a text file with multiple records in it!

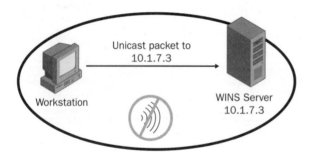

Figure 7-4   NetBIOS name resolution using WINS

That's WINS in a nutshell. As you can see, there are several reasons WINS should be considered in your network design:

- To reduce broadcast traffic on a local segment
- To enable NetBIOS name resolution across a routed network
- To centralize administration of NetBIOS resources

Let's look into NetBIOS name resolution in more detail.

NetBIOS Name Resolution Processes

As you have just seen, there are three ways a NetBIOS name resolution process may occur:

- Broadcast traffic
- Lmhosts files
- WINS

Broadcasting is ineffective when interacting across routers, and it can also create too much traffic on a local network segment. Lmhosts files can be cumbersome, and because they are static files, they must be manually updated using a text editor each time a new workstation is added to a segment. This process is prone to typos or incorrect name-to-IP-address mappings being entered by the creator of the file. WINS, on the other hand, is dynamically updated by client computers on startup, creates no broadcast traffic, and works across routers. Now let's look at the components of WINS.

WINS Components

For WINS to function on a network, a minimum of two components are needed:

- A WINS server
- A WINS client

WINS Server

The WINS server is the component that enables clients to register their NetBIOS names and IP addresses dynamically so that they do not have to be entered manually by the administrator. The WINS server also responds to queries from clients asking for a NetBIOS name to be resolved to an IP address. If there is an entry for the record queried in the WINS database, the IP address is returned to the requestor. See Table 7-4 for the functions of a WINS server.

Table 7-4   WINS Server Functions

Function	Description
Name Registration	At startup, a WINS client registers its NetBIOS name and IP address to the WINS server it is configured to use. This information is stored in the WINS database.
Name Renewal	The WINS client must renew its NetBIOS name or the name can be issued to another client requesting that same name.
Name Release	When a WINS client will no longer need to use the NetBIOS name (e.g., the computer is properly shutdown), the client sends a message to the WINS server to release it.
Name Query and Name Resolution	The WINS server can search its database for names that have been registered by WINS clients.

Just as DNS needs to replicate the information stored in a database to another DNS server, if fault tolerance is required, WINS should be configured with a minimum of two servers:

- A primary WINS server that performs all name registration, name renewal, name release, and name query and resolution functions.

- A secondary WINS server that performs all of the same functions but is usually used when the primary server is unavailable and the WINS client is configured with both primary and secondary WINS servers. If the primary WINS server is unable to resolve a name for a client that also has a secondary WINS server configured in its list of WINS servers, the secondary WINS server database will be examined. Windows XP and Windows 2000 clients can be configured to list as many as 12 of these secondary WINS servers.

Real World   Problems with Duplicate Names

In large organizations using NetBIOS names, it is very important to have a naming strategy as opposed to random creation of NetBIOS names by multiple help-desk personnel. In many cases where there is not a naming convention standard, problems arise when one individual arbitrarily creates a computer name for a workstation and another individual creates the same name for a different workstation. If the other workstation is not turned on and the requestor attempts to create a computer name that is the same as one that is currently in the WINS database, WINS will attempt to contact the other workstation using its IP address. If no reply is given, it attempts to contact the workstation several times and then it issues the computer name to the new workstation. Duplicate NetBIOS names can create as much havoc as duplicate IP addresses.

WINS Clients

For a client to register its NetBIOS names with a WINS server, it must be configured as a WINS client or, using the correct terminology, be WINS-enabled. WINS-enabled clients not only register their names to the WINS server, they also:

- Renew their names
- Release their names
- Obtain mappings from the WINS database

The following platforms may be configured as WINS clients.

- Windows Server 2003 Family, including 64-bit versions of Datacenter and Enterprise Editions

- Windows XP Professional, Home Edition, and 64-bit editions

- Windows Millennium Edition

- Windows 2000 Family

- Windows NT Server

- Windows NT Workstation

- Windows 95, 98

- Windows for Workgroups

- Microsoft LAN Manager

- MS-DOS clients

- OS/2 clients

- Linux and UNIX clients using SAMBA software

Note that Linux and UNIX clients can also be WINS-enabled clients. You will see later that client workstations that are not WINS-enabled may still be able to participate in the WINS processes, such as name registration and name resolution, using WINS proxies.

WINS clients use unicast packets instead of broadcast packets to communicate with WINS servers. You can now select up to 12 WINS servers for redundancy when configuring a client. This should not be done, however, unless completely necessary because it can slow down your network performance. For example, if a NetBIOS name could not be resolved on the primary WINS server, it would continue examining each WINS server database. This could be a waste of time.

WINS Proxies

Sometimes your network may have client workstations that use NetBIOS but are not WINS-enabled. In Figure 7-5, Subnet A has a non-WINS client that will use broadcast packets to resolve a NetBIOS name. Note that the subnet does not contain a WINS server and that a router separates Subnet A from Subnet B. Note also that Subnet A contains a WINS-enabled client that is configured as a WINS proxy. A WINS proxy is a WINS-enabled computer that is configured to register, release, and query NetBIOS names for clients that are non-WINS-enabled.

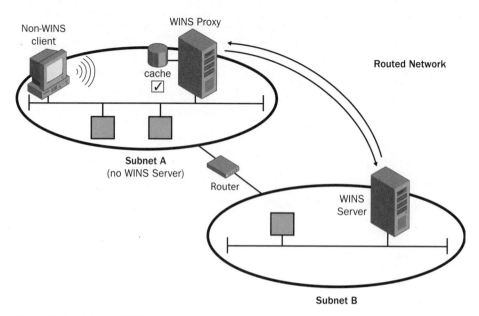

Figure 7-5   Using a WINS proxy

On most networks a WINS proxy is not necessary because most computers are WINS-enabled. In Figure 7-5, if a client computer, which is not WINS-enabled, attempted to resolve a NetBIOS name, the following would occur:

1. The non-WINS client would send a name query broadcast that would be intercepted by the WINS proxy.

2. The WINS proxy would check its cache for an entry of the NetBIOS name and associated IP address mapping.

3. If the NetBIOS name is in cache, the WINS proxy would send the IP address to the non-WINS client.

4. If the NetBIOS name is not in cache, the WINS proxy would send the query to the WINS server it is configured to use for names resolution.

5. If a WINS server is not available on the local segment, the WINS proxy can query a WINS server across a router because this is not broadcast traffic, but unicast traffic, to a specific IP address.

If a network segment has non-WINS clients on it, you must configure at least one of the WINS-enabled client workstations to be a WINS proxy.

> **Real World**   **Enabling Routers to Accept Broadcast Traffic**
>
> It is possible for routers to permit broadcast packets to pass through. However, routers by their very nature are used to reduce the size of broadcast domains. For that reason, network administrators may choose to restrict routers from allowing NetBIOS broadcast packets to pass through them. For example, if a subnet has grown and is experiencing many collisions and excessive broadcast traffic, one solution is to split the subnet into two smaller subnets and to place a router between both of them. By doing this, you have taken one large broadcast domain and made it into two smaller broadcast domains, thereby reducing broadcast traffic. Think twice before considering such a venture, or even discussing it with the routing professional at your organization, unless you are prepared for a prolonged conversation.

WINS Database

The WINS database uses the Extensible Storage Engine (ESE) to operate. This is the same engine used by Active Directory directory service, Microsoft Exchange, and many other Windows components. ESE is built on JET (Joint Engine Technology). Most database programs such as Microsoft SQL Server, Oracle, and Sybase allow transactions to first be written to a log file before being written to the database file. This improves performance because input/output (IO) to a file can be done quickly; subsequent transactions can be written to the area of the database where the data should be stored. ESE also separates log files and transactions to optimize performance.

For example, if a WINS-enabled client is booted, the client will register its name and IP number to the WINS server. The WINS server will write this transaction to a log file immediately. Later, when the processor is idle, transactions will be permanently written directly to the database. There are a couple of advantages to this methodology:

- Improved performance
- Fault tolerance

The improved performance has already been demonstrated, but how is fault tolerance gained in this example? Because all transactions are written to a log file first, a hard-disk crash of the database file could easily be restored from a backup tape combined with the log files you have stored on a different drive or tape. This would allow you to bring the server back to the point of failure. That is, transactions could be restored right up to the point when the crash occurred if you restored your WINS database backup and the current log files.

Now that you have had a lesson in how most databases work, let's look at the WINS database.

WINS Database Files

WINS uses the JET database format to store data in five different file types:

- **Log Files** As you learned earlier, transactions are stored in log files. These files begin with the letter "J" followed by a decimal number if the log file is a new transaction, for instance, J10.log. If a log file becomes full, it is renamed with a hexadecimal number appended to the previous name, such as J100000F.log. Then, a new log file with the original filename is created.

  Log files can grow quickly. As you learned in your earlier brief database lesson, writing to log files increases speed and efficiency of data storage as well as providing for recovery in case of a failure or crash. Log files should not be deleted until a backup of the WINS database has occurred.

  After all, once the database has been backed up, there is no reason to keep a copy of the log files because the transactions have already been posted to the database and backed up to tape or another media. If, however, the database crashes and there is no backup of the log files, losing the database would mean losing the files to recover. If you do not have a software or hardware redundant array of independent disks (RAID) system in place, you would be able to return the system only to the point of your last backup. All transactions that occurred between that backup and the crash would be lost.

- **Checkpoint files** Checkpoint files are used during a recovery process. These files indicate the location of the information that was successfully written from the transaction log files to the database file.

- **Wins.mdb** The WINS server database file contains two tables: the IP address-to-owner ID mapping table and the name-to-IP address mapping table.

- **Winstmp.mdb** This is a temporary file created by the WINS server service to aid in index maintenance.

- **Res#.log** Reserved log files are used if your server runs out of disk space and cannot create additional transaction log files. The server places outstanding transactions into these reserved log files, and the WINS service shuts down and logs an event to Event Viewer.

Database Size

As more and more records are added to your database, the size of the database can grow considerably. When records are deleted, which is covered in Lesson 3, not all of the space is automatically reclaimed by the server. This means that the size of the database can be larger than the space that is actually in use by active records. To fix this problem, you can compact the WINS database, which recovers this unused space. Windows Server 2003 supports two ways of compacting the WINS database:

- **Dynamic** Dynamic database compaction happens automatically as a background process. When the database is idle, dynamic database compaction takes place. Your WINS server does not need to be shut down during this time.

- **Manual** Manual compaction requires that the WINS server be stopped and taken offline. It is more efficient than dynamic compaction and should be done monthly on large networks, less frequently on smaller networks.

Lesson Review

The following questions reinforce key information presented in this lesson. If you are unable to answer a question, review the lesson materials and try the question again. You can find answers to the questions in the "Questions and Answers" section at the end of this chapter.

1. What are the four node types available for NetBIOS name resolution?

2. A B-node client computer, which is not WINS-enabled, needs to access a resource on your network by using a NetBIOS name. There is no WINS server available on the client's network segment, but a WINS server is available across a router on a different subnet. What possible solutions are available to allow the client to access network resources using the NetBIOS names?

3. WINS database utilizes five different file types for operation. List the five file types and a brief description of their function.

Lesson Summary

- Windows Internet Networking System (WINS) is a distributed database that stores NetBIOS names and services. The NetBIOS names are mapped to IP addresses and, like DNS, WINS makes it possible for you to access resources on your network using easy, friendly names instead of hard-to-remember IP addresses.

- NetBIOS name resolution is still necessary in networks that have older Windows operating systems running such as Windows NT, Windows 95/98, and so on. There are three ways NetBIOS name resolution can occur on a Windows Server 2003 network: Broadcasts, Lmhosts files, and WINS.

- To improve WINS database performance, transactions are written to transaction log files first and then later written to the WINS database. This also aids in data recovery in case of a database crash.

- A WINS proxy is a WINS-enabled computer that is configured to register, release, and query NetBIOS names for clients that are non-WINS-enabled. On network segments that do not have a WINS server available, B-node client workstations, which are not WINS-enabled, will contact the WINS proxy through broadcasts, which in turn will contact the WINS server across the router on behalf of the non-WINS-enabled client.

Lesson 2: Designing a WINS Infrastructure

Once you understand the structure of your company, it's time to design a WINS infrastructure for NetBIOS name resolution. Your design must take into account non-WINS clients as well as WINS clients and must consider where WINS proxy agents should be placed on your network, as well as the quantity and placement of WINS servers.

As you recall from Lesson 1, you may determine that WINS is not needed on your network. Remember, if all of your workstations and servers are running Windows 2000 and later operating systems, NetBIOS name resolution is not needed. Also, WINS is not needed on a local area network (LAN) because the workstations can be configured as B-nodes and perform NetBIOS name resolution using broadcasts. On smaller networks, this additional traffic will not be a problem.

This chapter assumes you have client workstations that are running earlier Windows operating systems, so WINS will be needed. In this lesson, you will learn to use the information you obtained earlier to design your Active Directory and DNS infrastructure to now design a WINS infrastructure.

After this lesson, you will be able to

- Create the conceptual design of a WINS infrastructure.
- Determine the placement and amount of WINS servers required.
- Design a WINS strategy for a non-routed and a routed network.

Estimated lesson time: 25 minutes

Creating the Conceptual Design

After creating your network diagrams and maps as discussed in Chapter 2 and Chapter 6, "Designing a DNS Structure," you should already know the following information:

- Whether the LAN is separated into subnets. This is important because a determination will need to be made on which subnet a WINS server should be placed.

- The location of routers—whether they connect subnets on the LAN or connect the LAN to a wide area network (WAN). Later in this section, you will learn how routers can add a dimension of complexity to broadcast traffic.

- Location of all servers and workstations.

- The processor type and speed of servers. This information will come into play when you need to decide which server may be configured as a WINS server.

- The amount and type of memory. There are certain memory requirements for a WINS server to perform optimally.

- Any services running on the system. You may want to know if other services such as DNS or Dynamic Host Configuration Protocol (DHCP) are also running on your WINS server.

- Total amount of users that access the system and their locations.

In creating a conceptual design, you want to have an overview of the present topology and then base your NetBIOS name-resolution strategy on the most efficient method to implement. Where are the routers placed on your network? This is important because WINS does generate traffic that can be a problem where slow links are involved. That is, should you use broadcasting, Lmhosts files, or WINS in your strategy? Here are some questions you may want to ask to help with your design.

- How many WINS servers do I need?

- What effect will WINS communication traffic have on any of my slower WAN links?

- What level of fault tolerance do I need, if any?

- What replication strategy will I use? (This is covered in more detail in Lesson 3.)

Designing a NetBIOS Name Resolution Strategy

Once you have a good handle on your topology, you can now look at the best way to handle NetBIOS name resolution. You have already looked at how broadcasts can be used to resolve NetBIOS names and how Lmhosts files can be configured on client computers. This second lesson will look into how WINS can be configured to enhance performance.

How Many WINS Servers?

Great news here. On a small network, a single WINS server can service up to 10,000 clients for NetBIOS name resolution! You may still want to add a secondary WINS server for fault tolerance reasons. After all, if your single WINS server crashes, there is no other method of NetBIOS name resolution in place; your users may only be able to access network resources using NetBIOS broadcast requests. This means all routed requests will not function unless Lmhosts files were configured for each workstation.

On larger enterprise networks, you may need more than one WINS server. The recommendations for these types of networks are one WINS server and a backup server for every 10,000 computers on the network. This is based on WINS servers running on computers that have a minimum of the following:

- 350 MHz processor or above

- 128 megabytes (MB) of random access memory (RAM)

- Integrated Device Electronics (IDE) disk drive

For this type of performance, no other services except WINS should be running on the server. To improve performance of a WINS server, you can:

- Install multiple processors. Windows Server 2003 WINS supports multiple CPUs, and performance can increase by almost 25 percent if two CPUs, instead of one, are installed in a WINS server.

- Increase the WINS server's RAM.

- Install high-performance hard disks. It is recommended that you use a disk drive that is dedicated to the WINS database and separate from the system.

- Install a high-bandwidth network card.

Designing a WINS Server Placement Strategy

Your goal, when designing a WINS strategy for your network infrastructure, is to have the WINS service available to client workstations when they need it. Availability is at risk when there is only one WINS server configured to support a large number of users. If that server should fail, all of the users will now need to resolve NetBIOS names using one of the other methods covered earlier: Lmhosts files or broadcasts. In situations in which a slow link exists between two subnets, it is highly recommended that a WINS server be placed in both subnets to maximize performance of client name-resolution requests.

Just as much thought had to go into deciding where to place your DNS servers, you can see that placing your WINS servers in the right location can also influence performance. For example, a remote site that has several thousand users may warrant placing a WINS server there to avoid the prospect of sending the traffic generated from name registrations over a 128Kb frame relay connection. Once again, your network topology diagrams are critical in making such decisions.

Performance Over Slow Links

Even though WINS servers are used to reduce traffic, specifically broadcast traffic, there is still network traffic generated by clients when the client:

- Registers a NetBIOS name

- Renews a NetBIOS name

- Releases a NetBIOS name

- Requests a NetBIOS name resolution

In Lesson 1, you learned that on startup, a WINS-enabled workstation would automatically register its NetBIOS name and IP address with a designated WINS server. On larger networks this creates the biggest traffic load. The WINS-enabled client also registers its user name, domain name and, depending on the operating system version, any services it may be running. Windows XP clients that are WINS-enabled usually register more NetBIOS names than other WINS-enabled clients. Windows XP clients can register names for the Server service, the Replicator service, Messenger service, the Computer Browser service, and additional services. Figure 7-6 illustrates the WINS database entries for a WINS-enabled client workstation running Windows XP.

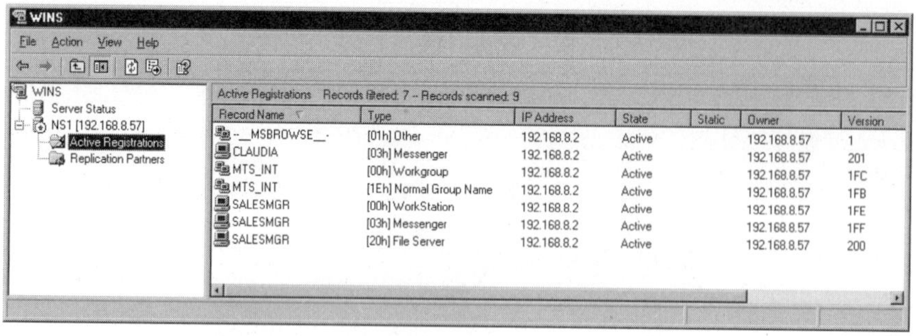

Figure 7-6   WINS database entries from XP client registration

Each time one of the client machines shuts down at the end of the day, it releases these names, also creating additional traffic. As you can see, designing your WINS infrastructure over a routed network poses additional problems and is more complex. If a WINS server is across a router, and if thousands of workstations were started up each morning and shut down each night, you can see the possibility of a lot of traffic being generated over the WAN link.

In the next lesson, you will look at the additional traffic created by replication occurring between multiple WINS servers. In any event, you should be aware of how your network topology affects your NetBIOS name-resolution strategy.

Fault Tolerance

When designing your WINS infrastructure, you should consider the possibility of something going wrong—because it usually does. Having only one WINS server on a routed network, regardless of how small the network is, can create problems if a WINS server unexpectedly crashes due to hardware failure or is inadvertently shut down for maintenance by a junior network administrator who is not aware that the server is running WINS. By placing secondary WINS servers throughout your network infrastructure, you reduce the effects of one server being unavailable for your clients. If cost is a factor preventing you from implementing this, Lmhosts files configured with #PRE-tag entries for critical servers are a good way of ensuring that clients can access network resources in the event of a downed router or WINS server.

Real World   Label Your Servers

In large and small organizations alike, it is not uncommon to see five or six servers side by side in a cipher-locked server room with no labels on them. The labels, wherever they are, should include such information as computer name, IP configuration, hardware specs, operating system (OS) information, and one of the most important pieces of information of all—a list of the services running on the server. Why is this information so important? Suppose one of these servers has a hardware failure. Is it important for you to know that the server in question is a primary WINS server, or that it is your only DNS server on the network? Of course it is. In fact, this information is vital in helping you to decide on the direction you will take in rectifying the problem.

For security reasons, you may want to have this documentation in a book that is not in close proximity to the servers. This is added protection in case an intruder is able to get in front of your servers. Most likely, if this is the case, it's too late to worry about securing this information. If an intruder is already in your house looking through your belongings in your bedroom safe, it's a little late to worry about whether or not you left your personal phone book out for his perusal. Servers should all be locked in secure areas, first and foremost.

Exam Tip   Be careful to not lose focus of why WINS is implemented on networks; the primary reason is to reduce broadcast traffic.

Non-Routed Networks

On a small LAN with one WINS server, you will not see as much of a problem with a WINS server crashing as you would in a routed network. Users on the LAN would be able to access all network resources located on the LAN using broadcast requests. However, they may see a noticeable degradation in performance on low-bandwidth networks.

Routed Networks

On a routed network, where users on a remote segment rely on the WINS server across the router to perform NetBIOS name resolution, a WINS server that is made unavailable could prevent users from doing their jobs. For example, all applications that relied on NetBIOS name resolution would not function. Access to servers and printers may not be possible for all remote users. Another possible problem could arise if the router connecting to the subnet containing the WINS server failed. In designing your WINS infrastructure, all of these scenarios must be considered.

In situations in which WINS is a required method of NetBIOS name resolution, and a router separates the subnet from accessing the WINS server, your only solution might be to include a WINS server for each subnet.

In Figure 7-7, note that Atlanta has two subnets: Subnet A and Subnet B. A router connects each subnet over a high-speed line. Because the WINS servers are replicated with one another in this scenario, if one of them should be made unavailable, each client would have the other WINS server configured as the secondary WINS server. Also note that the clients in Florida would be able to access any NetBIOS resources in Atlanta because replication is taking place between each of their WINS servers. This could be through a slow WAN line such as a 128Kb frame relay connection.

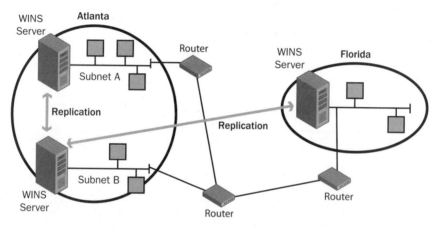

Figure 7-7   Replicating WINS data on a routed network

If the router in Florida were made unavailable, clients in Florida would not be able to access any resources in Atlanta if they were using NetBIOS names or IP addresses because this router is the only link that connects Florida to Atlanta. However, the WINS server in Florida would handle all NetBIOS name resolutions for the Florida subnet. If the WINS server in Florida failed, and the router was still functioning, WINS-enabled clients in Florida would not be able to access resources across the router using NetBIOS names unless the clients were configured with the Atlanta WINS server as their secondary WINS server.

In designing your NetBIOS name resolution strategy, it is critical that you recognize any areas that are potential failure points. You should ask yourself questions such as: "If that particular router goes down, will my entire network not function?" "Should I place a secondary WINS server in that subnet in case my primary WINS server fails?"

Lesson Review

The following questions are intended to reinforce key information presented in this lesson. If you are unable to answer a question, review the lesson materials and try the question again. You can find answers to the questions in the "Questions and Answers" section at the end of this chapter.

1. When deciding which computers (servers) to configure as WINS servers, what are some of the criteria you should use?

   _____

   _____

2. WINS servers in a routed network are sometimes a requirement. Describe why a WINS server or servers may still be required on local non-routed networks.

   _____

   _____

3. Identify the network traffic that is generated by a WINS-enabled client.

   _____

   _____

Lesson Summary

- Before a conceptual NetBIOS name-resolution design can be created, a thorough understanding of the present network topology and documentation (network maps, inventory of all servers and workstations, etc.) must be available.

- Even though WINS servers are used to reduce traffic, specifically broadcast traffic, network traffic is still generated by WINS-enabled clients as well as replication data between WINS servers (replication data is discussed later in Lesson 3).

- Selecting the server that will run the WINS service should be based on CPU speed, memory, hard disk type, and network adapter card. Computers with two CPUs and high-performance disk drives should be selected when scalability is required. Placement of these servers should also be carefully analyzed. Fault tolerance and availability of the WINS service can be obtained through the use of multiple servers and replication.

- Special consideration should be given when designing a WINS infrastructure over a routed network because broadcast packets will not usually pass through a router. Also, the possibility of a router failing should be part of the analysis and may determine if additional WINS servers should be placed on various subnets.

Lesson 3: Designing a WINS Replication Strategy

In designing your WINS infrastructure you must take into account the process of replicating your WINS database from one WINS server to another WINS server located on a different subnet. This is very important; you want users from a subnet to be able to access resources located on a different subnet using NetBIOS-friendly names. This lesson will show you how a WINS server can be selected as a push or pull partner, which enables this replication to take place.

After this lesson, you will be able to

- Design a strategy for WINS replication.
- Describe the standard deletion and tombstone deletion processes.
- Identify push and pull partners.

Estimated lesson time: 25 minutes

Creating a Replication Strategy

Once you have documented your WINS infrastructure and have determined the placement of all of your WINS servers, routers, subnets, users, and so on, it's time to create a replication strategy to improve performance and to add fault tolerance to your enterprise network. On smaller networks where only one or two WINS servers are needed, a replication strategy is simple and effortless to create. On larger enterprise networks, a lot of thought must be put into designing and implementing a replication strategy.

Replication Example

Let's begin by looking at a very basic example of two subnets, each containing one WINS server that supports a couple of hundred users. See Figure 7-8.

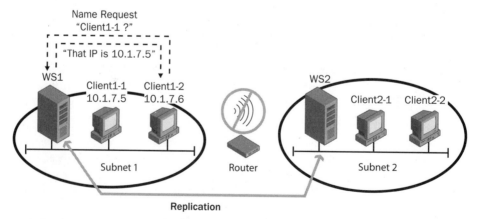

Figure 7-8   Basic replication design for two subnets

In the diagram, Subnet 1 contains a single WINS server named WS1 that services all client computers on that subnet. When Client1-1 starts up, it registers all of the NetBIOS information you learned earlier to the WINS database. All of the WINS-enabled client computers in this subnet are configured to use WS1 as their primary WINS server. When Client1-2 initiates a connection to \\client1-1, a name-resolution request is made to the WINS server. The database is checked, and the IP address is returned.

Subnet 2 also has a WINS server, named WS2, which services all WINS-enabled workstations on Subnet 2. When Client2-1 starts up, it too registers its NetBIOS information to the WINS server, as do all WINS-enabled workstations in Subnet 2. But what would happen if Client1-1 tried to access Client2-1 using NetBIOS name resolution? The router in the diagram indicates that broadcast traffic would not pass through it, so NetBIOS name resolution would have to occur in one of the two other ways you learned: Lmhosts files or WINS. Let's assume that there are no Lmhosts files configured for any of the clients. When Client1-1 queries the WINS database on the WS1 server, there will not be an entry for Client2-1, or for any other clients in Subnet 2 for that matter, in the WINS database because Subnet 2 clients register all NetBIOS information to only the WINS database on the WS2 server.

For both of these WINS servers to be able to resolve NetBIOS names for either subnet, there must be a method of transferring, or replicating, the database information from one WINS server to another. This replication process is done by configuring the WINS servers as one of the following:

- Push partner
- Pull partner
- Push/Pull partner

Push Partners

A push partner sends messages to all of its pull partners that changes have taken place in its database. For example, three workstations have registered their NetBIOS names to their configured WINS server database and now want to notify their pull partner of these changes. You can configure a push partner to notify their pull partners when one of the following occurs:

- The WIN server starts.
- An IP address change occurs for one of its NetBIOS name-to-address mapping changes.
- A certain threshold has been reached such as a particular amount of changes to the WINS database.

Pull Partners

A pull partner requests an update of its WINS database from another WINS server configured as a push partner. You can configure a pull partner to notify their pull partners when one of the following occurs:

- The WINS server starts.

- A time interval has elapsed.

Pull partners should be configured over slow links connecting WINS servers. You can choose to have a pull occur when little traffic is going over the link, such as late at night.

Push/Pull Partners

This is the default configuration of a WINS server. A push of an updated WINS database will occur as discussed previously, and the WINS server is also configured to pull WINS database information from another WINS server at a designated time. This type of configuration is recommended in most cases.

Exam Tip Remember that push partners are used over high-speed links, whereas pull partners are usually configured over slower WAN links.

After configuring both WINS servers as Push/Pull partners, both servers, after replication, will contain NetBIOS records from both subnets. Now, any WINS-enabled client on either subnet can access resources on a different subnet using the NetBIOS name of that resource.

Deleting and Tombstoning Records

As your WINS database grows and replicates its records to other WINS servers, some records become obsolete and need to be deleted from the database. Deleting records from a WINS database is a very simple process; all you need to do is select the records and press the delete key. However, there are two methods of deleting records from a WINS database:

- **Simple Deletion** A simple deletion deletes records from your local WINS server. If these records have been replicated to other WINS servers, the records will remain in the databases of those WINS servers. These records can subsequently reappear on your local WINS server after replication has occurred, which could defeat your intended purpose.

- **Tombstoned Deletion** Tombstoning is the marking of records released from active use by the local WINS server. Hence, users attempting a name-resolution query from that local server will receive an error because the records are marked for deletion; however, the records will remain present in the WINS database for replication purposes until a specified time period has elapsed. At that time, the records will be automatically removed from all WINS servers.

Securing Your WINS Infrastructure

Any time replication information from one server will traverse a network to reach another server, you risk the possibility of interception of that data. Just as DNS zone transfers are susceptible to this type of attack, so is WINS replication data.

Because WINS servers may be exposed to the Internet just like DNS servers are, security should be of concern. Replication traffic between WINS servers across a public network such as the Internet can be intercepted. NetBIOS names and IP addresses of your servers and workstations can be made available to unauthorized personnel. As with DNS, there are a couple of options you can use to protect your WINS replication data:

- Encryption using Internet Protocol Security (IPSec)

- Encryption using a Virtual Private Network (VPN)

As a network administrator, it is very important that your design always includes security measures to protect the information and network resources of your company. All WINS servers should be secured by cipher-locked doors, and access should be restricted to authorized personnel using Active Directory directory services.

Practice: Designing a WINS Replication Strategy

In this practice, you will design a WINS replication strategy for Northwind Traders. If you are unable to answer a question, review the lesson materials and try the question again. You can find answers to the questions in the "Questions and Answers" section at the end of this chapter.

Scenario

Northwind Traders has decided to include WINS as part of its Windows Server 2003 Active Directory design. Northwind Traders' current network infrastructure is illustrated in the diagram below. The IT management team wants to see a proposal for an effective WINS replication scheme that will ensure the smooth implementation of WINS. Specifically, the proposed WINS design must address the issue of fault tolerance.

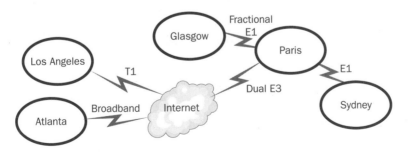

Practice Question

Based on the scenario, answer the following question.

1. Sketch a diagram of the solution you would propose as a WINS replication strategy for Northwind Traders. What are the benefits of this strategy?

_____

_____

Lesson Review

The following questions are intended to reinforce key information presented in this lesson. If you are unable to answer a question, review the lesson materials and try the question again. You can find answers to the questions in the "Questions and Answers" section at the end of this chapter.

1. You are designing a WINS replication strategy for two subnets. What questions should be asked when making a determination of whether or not a WINS server should be a push or a pull partner?

_____

_____

2. List the three ways a push partner notifies its pull partner to update its WINS database.

_____

_____

3. You are the administrator of a large enterprise network and receive a phone call from a junior network administrator working at one of your branch offices. The administrator is responsible for several WINS servers and says that he deleted over 25 obsolete records from his database, but that they keep reappearing the next day. How would you explain this occurrence to the administrator? What steps can the administrator take to ensure that the records are permanently removed from all WINS servers?

_____

_____

Lesson Summary

- In designing your WINS infrastructure, you must take into account the process of replicating your WINS database from one WINS server to another WINS server located on a different subnet. This will ensure that users from either subnet can resolve NetBIOS names.

- WINS servers can be configured as push, pull, and push/pull partners. In designing a replication strategy, bandwidth is one of your most important concerns. For example, you should configure a WINS server as a pull partner if a slow link is used to replicate data. This replication can be set to occur every 12 hours or so. On a LAN, where high-speed bandwidth is available, WINS servers can replicate traffic to each other every 15 minutes without creating a traffic problem.

- As your WINS database grows and replicates its records to other WINS servers, some records become obsolete and need to be deleted from the database. There are two methods used to delete these records: simple deletion and tombstoned deletion.

Case Scenario Exercise

You have been selected to plan a NetBIOS name-resolution strategy for Contoso, Ltd., a modem manufacturer with its headquarters in Dallas, Texas. There is a mixed-server environment of Windows NT 4.0, Windows 2000 Server, and Windows Server 2003. Client computers are running a mix of Windows 98, Windows 2000 Professional, Windows XP, and several workstations running the Linux operating system. Contoso has hired you to design a NetBIOS name-resolution plan that would improve performance and include a fault-tolerance strategy. Many of the company's computer programs rely on NetBIOS over TCP/IP functionality, and many clients require NetBIOS name resolution to access much of the company's resources, such as file and print services.

Background

Contoso has grown over the past decade to become one of the premier high-end modem manufacturers in the country, selling primarily to large companies and Internet service providers (ISPs).

Geography

In addition to its primary location, Contoso also has two branch offices within the United States—one in Atlanta, Georgia, and one in San Francisco, California.

Network Infrastructure

Each branch office has approximately 1,500 workstations equally distributed between eight subnets: SubnetA, SubnetB, SubnetC, SubnetD, SubnetE, SubnetF, SubnetG, and SubnetH. SubnetD and SubnetE are connected together with a 128Kb frame relay connection. All of the other subnets are connected together over high-speed WAN links. At the branch offices, clients and servers are all connected via 10/100 Mbps connections.

Future Plans

The company will be acquiring a small, Florida-based company, which specializes in the creation of technical/training manuals, within the next several weeks. The office has only nine workstations, all running Windows 95 in a Workgroup environment. The company will need to have access to the resources in the Atlanta branch office.

Questions

Given the previous scenario, answer the following questions.

1. What is the minimum amount of WINS servers needed if fault tolerance, availability, and network latency were not considered in the decision-making process?

   _____

   _____

2. Assuming that Contoso does acquire the Florida-based company, what additional information would you need to obtain? What could be some alternative methods you could implement to enable the workstations in Florida to access NetBIOS resources in the Atlanta branch office?

   _____

   _____

3. There are several non-WINS clients that are configured as B-nodes in a small office that does not have a WINS server available. What can you do to enable these clients to resolve NetBIOS names?

   _____

   _____

4. You need to design a replication strategy between SubnetD and SubnetE. How would you configure the WINS servers in these subnets?

   _____

   _____

Chapter Summary

- WINS is a distributed database that stores NetBIOS names and services. The NetBIOS names are mapped to IP addresses and, like DNS, WINS makes it possible for you to access resources on your network using easy, friendly names instead of hard-to-remember IP addresses.

- NetBIOS name resolution is still necessary in networks that have earlier Windows operating systems running, such as Windows NT, Windows 95/98, and so on. There are three ways NetBIOS name resolution can occur on a Windows Server 2003 network: broadcasts; Lmhosts files; and WINS.

- To improve WINS database performance, transactions are written to transaction log files first, and then later written to the WINS database. This also aids in data recovery in case of a database crash.

- A WINS proxy is a WINS-enabled computer that is configured to register, release, and query NetBIOS names for clients that are non-WINS-enabled. On network segments that do not have a WINS server available, B-node client workstations, which are not WINS-enabled, will contact the WINS proxy through broadcast, which in turn will contact the WINS server across the router on behalf of the non-WINS-enabled client.

- Before a conceptual NetBIOS name-resolution design can be created, a thorough understanding of the present network topology and documentation (network maps, inventory of all servers and workstations, etc.) must be available.

- Even though WINS servers are used to reduce broadcast traffic, network traffic is still generated by WINS-enabled clients as well as by replication data between WINS servers (replication data is discussed in Lesson 3).

- Selecting the server that will run the WINS service should be based on CPU speed, memory, hard disk drive type, and network adapter card. Computers with two CPUs and high-performance disk drives should be selected when scalability is required. Placement of these servers should also be carefully analyzed. Fault tolerance and availability of the WINS service can be obtained through the use of multiple servers and replication.

- Special consideration should be given when designing a WINS infrastructure over a routed network because broadcast packets will not usually pass through a router. Also, the possibility of a router failing should be part of the analysis and may determine if additional WINS servers should be placed on various subnets.

- When gathering information about a Windows NT 4.0 infrastructure, create a diagram showing domains and trust relationships. For each domain, gather information on the domain controllers, users, and resources in the domain.

- In designing your WINS infrastructure, you must take into account the process of replicating your WINS database from one WINS server to another WINS server located on a different subnet. This will ensure that users from either subnet can resolve NetBIOS names.

- WINS servers can be configured as push, pull, and push/pull partners. In designing a replication strategy, bandwidth is one of your most important concerns. For example, you should configure a WINS server as a pull partner if a slow link is used to replicate data. This replication can be set to occur every 12 hours or so. On a LAN, where high-speed bandwidth is available, WINS servers can replicate traffic to each other every 15 minutes without creating a traffic problem.

- As your WINS database grows and replicates its records to other WINS servers, some records become obsolete and need to be deleted from the database. There are two methods used to delete these records: simple deletion and tombstoned deletion.

Exam Highlights

Before taking the exam, review the key points and terms that are presented below to help you identify topics you need to review. Return to the lessons for additional practice, and review the "Further Reading" sections in Part 2 for pointers to more information about topics covering the exam objectives.

Key Points

- There are three ways that NetBIOS names resolution can occur: broadcasts, Lmhosts files, and WINS. Windows Internet Networking System (WINS) is a distributed database that stores NetBIOS names and services. To improve WINS database performance, transactions are written to transaction log files first, and then later written to the WINS database. In the case of non-WINS clients on a network, a WINS proxy may be configured to register, release, and query NetBIOS names.

- Before a conceptual NetBIOS name-resolution design can be created, a thorough understanding of the present network topology and documentation must be available. Special consideration should be given when designing a WINS infrastructure for a routed network because broadcast packets will not usually pass through a router. Selecting the server that will run the WINS service should be based on CPU speed, memory, hard disk drive type, and network adapter card. Placement of these servers should also be carefully analyzed. Fault tolerance and availability of the WINS service can be obtained through the use of multiple servers and replication.

- In designing your WINS infrastructure, you must take into account the process of replicating your WINS database from one WINS server to another WINS server located on a different subnet. This will ensure that users from either subnet can resolve NetBIOS names. WINS servers can be configured as push, pull, and push/ pull partners. You should configure a WINS server as a pull partner if a slow link is used to replicate data. As your WINS database grows and replicates its records to other WINS servers, some records become obsolete and need to be deleted from the database. Simple deletion and tombstoned deletion are two ways to do this.

Key Terms

WINS proxy   A WINS proxy is a WINS-enabled computer that is configured to register, release, and query NetBIOS names for clients that are non-WINS-enabled.

Node types   There are four different node types that determine how NetBIOS resolution will occur on a client workstation: B-node, H-node, P-node and M-node.

Replication partners   The replication process is done by configuring the WINS servers as one of the following: push, pull, or push/pull partners.

Tombstoned deletion   Tombstoning is the marking of records released from active use by the local WINS server. Tombstoned records will be automatically removed from all WINS servers at a specific time set by the administrator to prevent replication of records that have been marked for deletion.

Questions and Answers

Page
7-13

Lesson 1 Review

1. What are the four node types available for NetBIOS name resolution?

   a. B-node, which uses IP broadcast messages

   b. P-node, which uses a NetBIOS name server such as a WINS server

   c. M-node, which uses a mix of B-node and P-node

   d. H-node, which is a hybrid of B-node and P-node

2. A B-node client computer, which is not WINS-enabled, needs to access a resource on your network by using a NetBIOS name. There is no WINS server available on the client's network segment, but a WINS server is available across a router on a different subnet. What possible solutions are available to allow the client to access network resources using the NetBIOS names?

   One option available is to create an Lmhosts file on the client's workstation that has the NetBIOS name-to-IP address mappings for each resource the client needs to access. A more efficient solution would be to configure a WINS-enabled client computer on the segment to be a WINS proxy. The WINS proxy would send the NetBIOS name requested by the non-WINS-enabled client to the WINS server that is located across the router. The WINS server would check its database and return the IP address to the proxy, which would then return the IP address information to the non-WINS-enabled client.

3. WINS database utilizes five different file types for operation. List the five file types and a brief description of their function.

   a. Log files are used to speed up the process of updating the WINS database and may be used to restore a WINS server back to the point of failure.

   b. Checkpoint files are used to indicate which transactions were written to the database file (Wins.mdb).

   c. The WINS server database file (Wins.mdb) contains two tables: IP address-to-Owner ID mappings, and Name-to-IP address mapping.

   d. The WINS temporary database file (Winstmp.mdb) used as a swap file area, or temporary area to aid in index maintenance.

   e. Reserved log files (Res#.log) are used in case of disk space errors where a log file cannot be created because there is not enough disk space available to create the log file.

Lesson 2 Review

1. When deciding which computers (servers) to configure as WINS servers, what are some of the criteria you should use?

Your inventory documentation should indicate the CPU speed and type, memory, disk drives and capacity, and network adapter cards speed available on each server. For optimal scalability, consider using a server that has multiple CPUs and high-speed disk drives.

2. WINS servers in a routed network are sometimes a requirement. Describe why a WINS server or servers may still be required on local non-routed networks.

On local networks without routers configured, B-node client workstations can resolve NetBIOS names using broadcast packets. Hence, a WINS server is not required for the subnet. However, if too many users are resolving NetBIOS names using this method, broadcast traffic over the LAN can affect the overall network performance. To reduce this broadcast traffic, WINS is one of the best solutions. Another solution is configuring all of the workstations with an Lmhosts file that has the NetBIOS names and IP address mappings of all of the network resources. This is also effective, but can be time consuming and fraught with errors.

3. Identify the network traffic that is generated by a WINS-enabled client.

Even though broadcast traffic is reduced when a WINS strategy is implemented, a WINS-enabled client generates the following traffic: NetBIOS name registration, renewal of a NetBIOS name, release of a NetBIOS name, and request for a NetBIOS name resolution.

Lesson 3 Practice

1. Sketch a diagram of the solution you would propose as a WINS replication strategy for Northwind Traders. What are the benefits of this strategy?

Although a number of replication strategies might work, the best solution based on the given scenario is shown in the following diagram. This strategy ensures that each location has two WINS servers, a design that provides a level of fault tolerance in case any single WINS server in a location should fail.

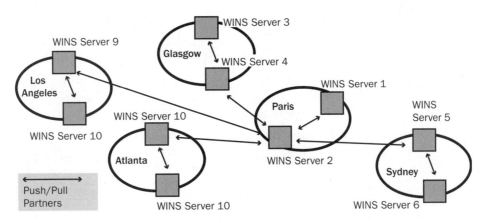

Page
7-26

Lesson 3 Review

1. You are designing a WINS replication strategy for two subnets. What questions should be asked when making a determination of whether or not a WINS server should be a push or a pull partner?

   The most important question to ask when determining the partner type in a replication strategy is the bandwidth available between the subnets in question. If there is a limited bandwidth, you might consider configuring both servers as pull partners, each scheduled to pull information from one another's WINS database at a designated time. This replication could take place late in the evening, when very little traffic is traversing the WAN link.

2. List the three ways a push partner notifies its pull partner to update its WINS database.

   The three ways a push partner notifies its pull partners are: WINS server starts, an IP address change occurs for one of its NetBIOS name-to-address mapping changes, or a certain threshold has been reached, such as a particular amount of changes to the WINS database.

3. You are the administrator of a large enterprise network and receive a phone call from a junior network administrator working at one of your branch offices. The administrator is responsible for several WINS servers and says that he deleted over 25 obsolete records from his database, but that they keep reappearing the next day. How would you explain this occurrence to the administrator? What steps can the administrator take to ensure that the records are permanently removed from all WINS servers?

   Your response to the administrator would be that a simple deletion only deletes records from the local WINS server database. The replication process is replacing the deleted records; he should perform a tombstone delete, which will replicate the deletion to all WINS servers.

Page
7-28

Case Scenario Exercise

1. What is the minimum amount of WINS servers needed if fault tolerance, availability, and network latency were not considered in the decision-making process?

   One. The scenario indicates that there is a total of approximately 8,000 workstations in the Contoso network (4,000 in each branch office). A WINS server with the minimum requirements of 128 MB RAM, 350 MHz processor, IDE disk drive, and so on, can support 10,000 workstations. However, you would never design an infrastructure that did not take into account the possibility of a server becoming unavailable at one time or another. You would most likely configure several WINS servers in this scenario for fault tolerance reasons and load balancing.

2. Assuming that Contoso does acquire the Florida-based company, what additional information would you need to obtain? What could be some alternative methods you could implement to enable the workstations in Florida to access NetBIOS resources in the Atlanta branch office?

   You would need to know how the Florida office would connect to the Atlanta office. That is, your network map would need to include the link connecting these sites. At this time, you can also consider using Lmhosts files for the workstations in Florida, rather than configuring a WINS server at this location, where there are only nine workstations.

3. There are several non-WINS clients that are configured as B-nodes in a small office that does not have a WINS server available. What can you do to enable these clients to resolve NetBIOS names?

One solution would be to configure one workstation as a WINS-enabled, WINS proxy agent. This workstation would forward any NetBIOS broadcast packets received from the non-WINS enabled clients to an assigned WINS server located in a different subnet.

4. You need to design a replication strategy between SubnetD and SubnetE. How would you configure the WINS servers in these subnets?

Because the link connecting these two subnets is rather slow, you might want to configure the servers as pull partners and set a time interval to pull only during times when the link is not being heavily used. For example, you might set the replication to occur during night hours.

8 Designing a Network and Routing Infrastructure

Exam Objectives in this Chapter:

- Design a network and routing topology for a company
  - Design a TCP/IP addressing scheme through the use of IP subnets
  - Specify the placement of routers
  - Design IP address assignment by using DHCP
  - Design a perimeter network
- Design an IP address assignment strategy
  - Specify DHCP integration with DNS infrastructure
  - Specify DHCP interoperability with client types
- Design the network services infrastructure to meet business and technical requirements
  - Create the conceptual design of the DHCP infrastructure

Why This Chapter Matters

Having a good understanding of how your network infrastructure is constructed will help you troubleshoot, maintain your network, and optimize performance. Because Internet Protocol (IP) routers and IP addressing is the foremost technology in use today, you must have the skills and knowledge to configure client computers, servers, and routers to make an efficient network. Also, knowledge of IP addressing and subnetting is crucial if large network segments need to be broken up into smaller, more manageable units. This chapter covers additional skills in IP addressing and subnetting, as well as how Dynamic Host Configuration Protocol (DHCP) services save you time and effort when you are designing your network and routing infrastructure.

This chapter begins with an overview of binary math and IP addressing basics because it would be impossible to design a network and routing infrastructure without competency in these areas.

Lessons in this Chapter:

Before You Begin

To complete this chapter, make sure you are familiar with the concepts described in Chapter 1, "Introduction to Active Directory and Network Infrastructure."

Lesson 1: Creating an IP Addressing Scheme

When you create an IP address scheme for your organization, your first consideration should be whether you will use a private IP address scheme or a public one. This lesson examines both private and public IP addresses and gives a good overview of how IP addressing is used to segment your network for improved performance as well as for security.

This lesson discusses the various classes of IP addresses available for companies and how to create IP subnets to improve performance.

After this lesson, you will be able to

- Describe the various classes of IP addresses.
- Design a TCP/IP addressing scheme using subnets.

Estimated lesson time: 60 minutes

Overview of Binary Numbers

There are three numbering systems you need to be familiar with as a network professional: base 2 (binary), base 10 (decimal), and base 16 (hexadecimal). The base 10 numbering system is what everyone is familiar with because this numbering system relies on decimal numbers. Numbers such as 9876 can be expressed as $9 * 10^3 + 8 * 10^2 + 7 * 10^1 + 6 * 10^0$. As you can see, each column represents the base number 10 with an exponent of 0, 1, 2, 3 and so forth. In base 10, the base number can be any number from 0–9, which is a total of 10 numbers. Hence the name, base 10.

Base 2

Because computers use logic chips that are "on" or "off," "true" or "false," or "yes" or "no," base 2 is the numbering system used. In base 2, the base number is 2 and the exponents, once again, begin with 0 and increase from right to left, as illustrated below. Base 2 allows only two numbers, 0 and 1.

The following is a base 2 number: 1000 0001. The column in which the 0 or 1 is located determines the value of the number, just as with base 10 numbers. In this example, the decimal equivalent of the binary number is 129. Binary numbers are usually represented as eight characters because there are 8 bits in a byte.

128	64	32	16	8	4	2	**1**	**128 + 1 = 129**
$\mathbf{2^7}$	2^6	2^5	2^4	2^3	2^2	2^1	$\mathbf{2^0}$	
1	0	0	0	0	0	0	**1**	

If all the bits are on, or set to 1, the largest number a byte could hold is the decimal number 255.

128	64	32	16	8	4	2	1
2^7	2^6	2^5	2^4	2^3	2^2	2^1	2^0
1	1	1	1	1	1	1	1

128 + 64 + 32 + 16 + 8 + 4 + 2 + 1 = 255

Base 16 (Hexadecimal)

Computers handily work with all of those ones and zeros, but we humans find them to be quite cumbersome. So, base 16 was another numbering system developed to make it easier for us to work with these numbers. Once again, in base 16, our base is 16, and the numbering system can include any number from 0–15. Letters are used to represent numbers because one digit cannot express a number greater than 9. In hexadecimal, A = 10; B = 11; C = 12, and so on. So, a base 16 number could look like the following:

4096	256	16	1
16^3	16^2	16^1	16^0
1	3	A	B

To convert the hexadecimal number 13AB to decimal, you would do exactly the same thing you did to convert a decimal number.

$1 * 16^3 + 3 * 16^2 + 10 * 16^1 + 11 * 16^0 =$

Don't worry. You will probably never have to do such a thing for the rest of your life. However, advanced routing concepts do require knowledge of hexadecimal numbers when creating multicast addresses, which this text does not cover. If you want to see a hexadecimal number in action, just type the command **ipconfig /all** at the command prompt.

The Physical Address field, also called the Media Access Control (MAC) address, of your network adapter card is in hexadecimal format, for example, 00-0B-DB-28-F3-9A. Hexadecimal numbers are usually grouped in two-digit formats, each representing the high- and low-order nibbles of a byte. A nibble, which can also be spelled "nybble," is four bits. A byte, of course, is 8 bits. The hexadecimal number 9A, converted to binary, is 1001 1010. A space was placed between the two nibbles for readability. The hexadecimal number F3, converted to binary, would be 1111 0011. As you see, it's a lot easier to read the numbers F3-9A in a MAC address than to have to look at the binary equivalent of 11110011-10011010. Hex numbers are prefixed with a "0x" as in "0x11."

Good news. The calculator program included with the Microsoft operating system can do the conversions for you. Simply open up the Calculator program and select Scientific from the View menu. In the example given, the Bin option button was selected and the binary number 1111 0011 1001 1010 was entered, followed by clicking on the Hex option button.

That's all you need to know for now about these numbering systems. You'll see how this helps you in the next section when subnetting is discussed. Before that, you need to take a quick look at IP addressing.

IP Addressing

For Windows Server 2003 to function, Transmission Control Protocol/Internet Protocol (TCP/IP) is not an option you can take or leave. It is required. An important part of TCP/IP that you must understand is IP addressing. You need to configure all of your client workstations, printers, servers, and so on, with an IP address, or have a DHCP server do the work for you. In any event, you must issue IP addresses to these hosts, or nodes.

Classes of IP Addresses

IP addresses are made up of four bytes, called octets, which represent both a network address and a host address. Depending on the decimal value of the first byte, you can determine the TCP/IP address class from which the IP address is a member. See Table 8-1 for the various classes of IP addresses that are available.

Table 8-1   Address Classes

Address Class	Description
Class A	The first byte contains a value from 1 to 126 and is the network portion of the IP address. The three bytes following the first byte represent the host (node) addresses. For example, the IP address 12.5.5.3 is a Class A address, with a network identity (ID) of 12 and a host ID of 5.5.3. Class A addresses can support more than 16 million host computers.
Class B	The first byte contains a value from 128 to 191. In a Class B address, the first two bytes represent the network ID and the last two bytes are the host ID. For example, 172.16.32.15 is a Class B address with a network ID of 172.16 and a host ID of 32.15. Class B addresses can support up to 65,000 host IDs.
Class C	The first byte contains a value from 192 to 223. The first three bytes in a Class C address represent the network ID portion of the address, and the last byte is the host ID. For example, 192.16.32.15 is a Class C address with a network ID of 192.16.32 and a host ID of 15. Class C addresses can support only 254 host IDs.

Table 8-1   Address Classes   *(continued)*

Address Class	Description
Class D	The first byte contains a value from 224 to 239. Class D addresses use all four bytes to represent a multicast address.
Class E	The first byte contains a value from 240 to 255. Class E addresses, as Class D, cannot be assigned to host computers. These addresses are experimental in nature.

Note that the first octet cannot contain the value of 127 because this address is reserved for loopback and other testing.

> **Exam Tip**   Be sure you can quickly recognize which class an IP address belongs to from the value of the first byte of the IP address number, especially Class A (1–126), Class B (128–191), Class C (192–223), and Class D (224–239 multicast).

Obtaining an IP Address

To obtain an IP address for your company to use, you can contact InterNIC (the Internet Network Information Center) and purchase one. Most Class A addresses are not available because they were gobbled up by the military and universities when the Internet was first established. If you purchased a Class C address, the first three octets would be the network ID your company would use, and you could then add up to 254 host computers to your network segment. Why 254? Because only one octet is available for you to create addresses, you have only 8 bits to work with. The lowest number that can be represented with 8 bits would be 0000 0000, which is equal to zero.

You are not allowed to give a host or node all zeros for a host ID. The highest number you can produce with 8 bits is all ones: 1111 1111. Converting this to decimal, you discover that the value is equal to 255. You should avoid issuing this number to a host. This is discussed in more detail in the subnetting section later in this chapter. For now, understand that all zeros and all ones are not allowed. So, 8 bits gives us $2^8 - 2$ (256 –2), or 254 possible addresses you can issue to your workstations, servers, and so on, if you purchased a Class C address.

There are also Class A, B, and C addresses that can be used by your company as internal IP addresses. That is, routers across the Internet will not route the packets that use these "private" addresses, but your company can use the addresses to connect its infrastructure. By using a private address strategy, you can save your company money while having an unlimited number of IP addresses available to assign to your network resources. These private IP addresses can also access the Internet when using a network address translator (NAT), which is covered in Chapter 9, "Designing Internet Connectivity." Table 8-2 illustrates the addresses that do not need to be registered with the

InterNIC, but which can be used to network your company's computers and workstations together.

Table 8-2   Private and Reserved IP Addresses

IP Address Range	Description
10.0.0.1–10.255.255.254	This private Class A address allows you to create up to 126 separate networks, each containing more than 16 million hosts.
172.16.0.1–172.31.255.254	This Class B address allows you to create up to 16 Class B network IDs, or you can use up to 20 of the host bits for subnetting, covered later in this chapter.
192.168.0.1–192.168.255.254	This Class C address allows you to create up to 256 separate Class C network IDs, or you can use the 16 host bits to create a subnetting scheme.
169.254.0.1–169.254.255.254	This Class B range of addresses is reserved and issued to computers when a DHCP server is not available and the workstation is configured for dynamic addressing. It is a feature available in Windows 98 and later operating systems, and is called Automatic Private IP Addressing (APIPA). This is covered in more detail in Lesson 3, "Understanding DHCP."

Exam Tip   Memorize these address ranges and be especially aware of how a workstation would be issued an IP address of 169.254.*x.x* if a DHCP server was not available and the workstation was configured as a DHCP-enabled client.

Simple networks can be configured using a single network segment and a Class C address range, as Figure 8-1 illustrates.

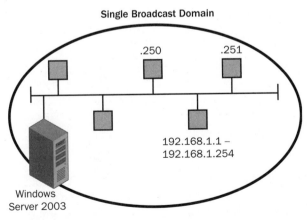

Figure 8-1   Small networks can be built using a single Class C address range.

In Figure 8-1, each node has a network ID of 192.168.1.0 and host IDs ranging from 1–254. Although a single network segment is simple to create, networks that are larger in size or span multiple locations must be divided into multiple network segments. To do this, you need to understand the concept of subnetting because you must now use the network ID portion of your IP address (192.168.8) to create additional network ID addresses called subnet addresses.

Subnet Masks

The subnet mask identifies which portion of the IP address is the network ID and which is the host portion. It does this by using Boolean algebra ANDing, which is discussed briefly in this section.

Each one of the classes you looked at has a default subnet mask, but you'll see later that this number cannot be assumed. Table 8-3 illustrates the default subnet masks for Classes A, B, and C.

Table 8-3   Default Subnet Masks

Class	Default Subnet Mask
A	255.0.0.0
B	255.255.0.0
C	255.255.255.0

When an IP address is entered into a workstation's configuration screen, the subnet mask must also be configured. For example, if your IP address is 10.1.2.3 and you enter a subnet mask of 255.0.0.0, the default subnet mask for a Class A address, the computer would use the following ANDing procedure to calculate the network portion of this IP address.

	00001010.00000001.00000010.00000011	**10.1.2.3**
AND	11111111.00000000.00000000.00000000	**255.0.0.0**
	00001010.00000000.00000000.00000000	**10.0.0.0 (Network ID)**

In Boolean algebra, a 1 AND 1 equals 1. Every other combination is equal to zero. The network portion of a Class A address, using the default subnet mask, is what you learned earlier: the first octet, in this example, 10.

The computer does this to determine if an address it is trying to reach is a "local phone call," meaning it's on the same subnet as itself, or if it's a "long distance phone call," meaning a default gateway (IP router) is needed to get to the address. If the network IDs match, it's local. An IP address without a subnet mask is like a phone number without an area code—useless. If I tell you my phone number is 555-2345 and do not give you the area code, you are missing a critical portion of information. If your IP address is 172.16.12.5 and you need to connect to a computer having an IP address of 172.16.13.5, not knowing the subnet mask associated with these addresses makes it impossible for the systems to communicate. If the default subnet mask in this example were selected, both systems would be on the 172.16.0.0 subnet. This means an IP router would not be needed for these two workstations to communicate because they are both on the same network segment.

Subnetting Your Network

Recall that a Class C address uses the first three octets as the network portion of the address and leaves the remaining 8 bits, the last octet, for host addresses. If you want to split this Class C address into two network addresses, you need to "borrow" some of those host bits. This borrowing of bits from the host portion of an IP address is called subnetting.

How Many Bits Do I Borrow?

How many bits you borrow from the host portion of an IP address is determined by the following:

- How many subnets do you need to create?
- How many hosts are needed on each subnet?

The more bits you borrow from the host portion, the more subnets you create. However, this means fewer hosts on each subnet. Let's look at a very simple example to illustrate this point. If you want to create two subnets from our Class C address 192.168.8.0, you can borrow one of those bits from that last octet. Let's convert your IP address into binary so you can see this more clearly.

1100 0000.1010 1000. 0000 1000. 0000 0000   **192.168.8.0**

1111 1111.1111 1111.1111 1111.**1**000 0000   **255.255.255.128 (Subnet mask)**

Notice the bit we are borrowing in the fourth octet is bolded for clarity. If you use one bit, that bit can be either "on" or "off." That is, it can be a 1 or a 0. Note that the column the bit you borrowed from has the decimal value of 128. This helps us determine the block size of the subnets you are creating. In this example, your block size is 128. So, you just created a 192.168.8.0 subnet and a 192.168.8.128 subnet. If the mask were 255.255.255.192, the block size of the subnets you would create would be 64 because 192 in binary is written as 1100 0000. Note that the second bit is in column 64. This means you would create a 0 subnet, 64 subnet, 128 subnet, and 192 subnet.

In the 255.255.255.128 example, each subnet has 126 host addresses because there are 7 bits left for host addressing. The formula for calculating the number of host addresses available is $2^n - 2$, or $2^7 - 2$, where n represents the number of available host bits. Subnet 1 would have a subnetted network ID of 192.168.8.0, and Subnet 2 would have a network ID of 192.168.8.128. The valid host IDs available for Subnet 1 are 1–126, and the valid host IDs available for Subnet 2 are 129–254. Remember that a host address cannot contain all zeros or all ones. Viewing an IP address in binary, you can see that giving a host computer an IP address of 192.168.8.0/25 would be giving all zeros to the host portion of the address, and the IP address 192.168.8.127 would be all ones in the host ID.

Subnet 1

1100 0000.1010 1000.0000 1000.**0**[000 0000]   192.168.8.0/25

1100 0000.1010 1000.0000 1000.**0**[111 1111]   192.168.8.127/25

The bracket portion of the IP addresses indicates the host bits available for addressing. The bold number represents the subnetted network ID portion.

Subnet 2

1100 0000.1010 1000.0000 1000.**1**[000 0000]   192.168.8.128/25

1100 0000.1010 1000.0000 1000.**1**[111 1111]   192.168.8.255/25

You can easily see that giving a host computer a host ID of 128 or 255 would also be invalid because you would be giving the host all zeros or all ones, respectively.

Note   Windows 2003 does support all-zeros and all-ones subnets, which are permitted by RFC 1812. In the old days, you had to subtract 2 from the total number of subnets created because these subnets were not allowed.

Exam Tip   Be sure you have a good handle on recognizing subnet masks from the Classless Internet Domain Routing (CIDR) notation, such as /8, /16, and so on. Instead of a question being formatted with an IP address followed by a subnet mask, you may see the format: 172.16.8.0/24. This would indicate a subnet mask of 255.255.255.0 because the "24" represents 24 bits (8 * 3), or 3 octets of 8 bits each.

There are calculators and programs on the market that help you determine which subnet masks should be used to create the correct number of subnets/hosts. The following tables illustrate this for Classes A, B, and C.

In the example you looked at earlier, your network segment had a network ID of 192.168.1.0. If you owned a Class C public IP address, and you wanted to break the network into two smaller subnets, you could do this by assigning the subnet mask 255.255.255.128 to all of the workstations and placing a router between the two segments. See Figure 8-2.

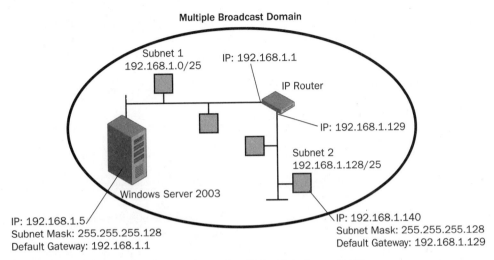

Figure 8-2   A single Class C network can be divided into two subnets.

All of the nodes in Subnet 1 would be assigned IP addresses in the range of 1 through 126. Workstations in Subnet 2 would be assigned IP addresses in the range of 129 through 254. Each of the segments represents its own broadcast domain. Note also that the ports on the router need to be assigned IP addresses that correspond to the default gateway IP address that each node needs configured if that node connects to resources outside its subnet. In Lesson 3 you'll see how DHCP can be configured to assign these parameters to your workstations.

Table 8-4   Class A Subnetted Network ID

Number of Subnets	Borrowed Bits	Resulting Subnet Mask (CIDR Notation)	Number of Hosts per Subnet
1–2	1	255.128.0.0/9	8,388,606
3–4	2	255.192.0.0/10	4,194,302
5–8	3	255.224.0.0/11	2,097,150
9–16	4	255.240.0.0/12	1,048,574
17–32	5	255.248.0.0/13	524,286
33–64	6	255.252.0.0/14	262,142
65–128	7	255.254.0.0/15	131,070
129–256	8	255.255.0.0/16	65,534
257–512	9	255.255.128.0/17	32,766

Table 8-4 Class A Subnetted Network ID *(continued)*

Number of Subnets	Borrowed Bits	Resulting Subnet Mask (CIDR Notation)	Number of Hosts per Subnet
513–1,024	10	255.255.192.0/18	16,382
1,025–2,048	11	255.255.224.0/19	8,190
2,049–4,096	12	255.255.240.0/20	4,094
4,097–8,192	13	255.255.248.0/21	2,046
8,193–16,384	14	255.255.252.0/22	1,022
16,385–32,768	15	255.255.254.0/23	510
32,769–65,536	16	255.255.255.0/24	254
65,537–131,072	17	255.255.255.0/25	126
131,073–262,144	18	255.255.255.192/26	62
262,145–524,288	19	255.255.255.224/27	30
524,289–1,048,576	20	255.255.255.240/28	14
1,048,577–2,097,152	21	255.255.255.248/29	6
2,097,153–4,194,304	22	255.255.255.252/30	2

Table 8-5 Class B Subnetted Network ID

Number of Subnets	Borrowed Bits	Resulting Subnet Mask (CIDR Notation)	Number of Hosts per Subnet
1–2	1	255.255.128.0/17	32,766
3–4	2	255.255.192.0/18	16,382
5–8	3	255.255.224.0/19	8,190
9–16	4	255.255.240.0/20	4,094
17–32	5	255.255.248.0/21	2,046
33–64	6	255.255.252.0/22	1,022
65–128	7	255.255.254.0/23	510
129–256	8	255.255.255.0/24	254
257–512	9	255.255.255.128/25	126
513–1,024	10	255.255.255.192/26	62
1,025–2,048	11	255.255.255.224./27	30
2,049–4,096	12	255.255.255.240/28	14
4,097–8,192	13	255.255.255.248/29	6
8,193–16,384	14	255.255.255.252/30	2

Table 8-6   Class C Subnetted Network ID

Number of Subnets	Borrowed Bits	Resulting Subnet Mask (CIDR Notation)	Number of Hosts per Subnet
1–2	1	255.255.255.128/25	126
3–4	2	255.255.255.192/26	62
5–8	3	255.255.255.224/27	30
9–16	4	255.255.255.240/28	14
17–32	5	255.255.255.248/29	6
33–64	6	255.255.255.252/30	2

Real World   Problems with Incorrect Subnet Masks

In companies that have workstations manually configured with IP address information, there is a good chance that an error will occur while filling out the fields. One of the most common errors is inadvertently entering an incorrect subnet mask for a workstation. For example, if a workstation is configured with a Class C address of 192.16.9.131, it is easy to assume that the default subnet mask of 255.255.255.0 is being used for all workstations.

Let's suppose the other workstations on the subnet are using a 255.255.255.192 mask. Recall that this mask will create four subnets: 192.168.9.0, 192.168.9.64, 192.168.9.128, and 192.168.9.192. If a router separated these networks, and the workstation you configured with an incorrect subnet mask tried to ping a workstation on the 192.168.9.64 network segment, the workstation would receive four Request Timeout messages. This would occur because the workstation you configured would not go to the default gateway, if one were configured, because it would see that its address of 192.168.9.131 was on the same segment as 192.168.9.66. In other words, it would calculate that both addresses were on the 192.168.9.0 subnet and therefore that the address it was trying to reach was a local address and did not require the use of a router. This, of course, is not true.

When manually configuring a workstation with IP information, always verify that subnetting is not being used. A simple way to do this is to look at the configuration of several other workstations in the area and any network topology diagrams available to you.

Practice: Creating an IP Addressing Scheme

In this practice, you create an IP addressing design for a proposed Northwind Traders office in Houston, Texas. If you are unable to answer a question, review the lesson materials and try the question again. You can find answers to the questions in the "Questions and Answers" section at the end of this chapter.

Scenario

Northwind Traders plans to open a new office in Houston. This new office will spread over four office buildings in downtown Houston and will be connected by leased lines as shown in the following diagram.

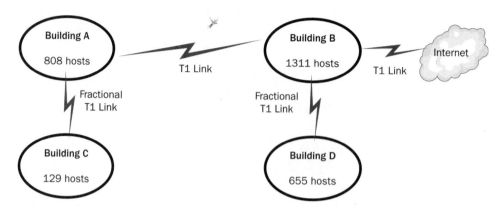

To design a functional TCP/IP solution for connecting networks, you must determine the number of subnets required for each office building and the number of public and private IP addresses required for the design. Your design must meet the following requirements:

- The network will use addresses from the 172.20.0.0/16 private address range for all host addresses in the Houston office.

- The number of hosts per subnet must be limited to 200 or fewer.

Practice Questions

Based on the scenario, create an IP addressing design by answering the following questions.

1. For this design, what is the minimum number of subnets required in each location, based on router performance?

   Building A: _____   Building B: _____

   Building C: _____   Building D: _____

   Total Subnets: _____

2. Choose an appropriate subnet mask for hosts in this design. Choose the correct answer.

   a. /16

   b. /19

   c. /21

   d. /24

3. What is the total number of required private IP addresses? Choose the correct answer.

   a. 7 private IP addresses

   b. 1,204 private IP addresses

   c. 2,903 private IP addresses

   d. 4,032 private IP addresses

4. What is the minimum number of required public IP addresses? Choose the correct answer.

   a. 1 public IP address

   b. 2 public IP addresses

   c. 2,903 public IP addresses

   d. 4,032 public IP addresses

5. At maximum, how many hosts per subnet does the subnet mask in the design provide? Choose the correct answer.

   a. 254 hosts per subnet

   b. 1,022 hosts per subnet

   c. 6,398 hosts per subnet

   d. 65,534 hosts per subnet

6. Management has suggested that a new private address could be chosen. Which of the following private IP network addresses is appropriate for the design? Choose all that apply.

   a. 10.0.0.0/8

   b. 230.120.0.0/16

   c. 69.254.0.0/16

   d. 192.168.0.0/16

Lesson Review

The following questions are intended to reinforce key information presented in this lesson. If you are unable to answer a question, review the lesson materials and try the question again. You can find answers to the questions in the "Questions and Answers" section at the end of this chapter.

1. List the five different address classes and the value of the first octet. Also, list each of the private IP addresses available for internal use by a company.

_____

_____

2. Your company has more than 15,000 workstations spread throughout several towns in the Midwest. As the network administrator, you have been asked to design an IP addressing strategy that will enable the company to access all of its resources using private IP addressing. You determine after careful analysis that you will need to create between 500 and 600 subnets with a maximum of 250 nodes per subnet. What private address will you choose, and what will be the subnet mask be?

_____

_____

3. As the network administrator for a Windows Server 2003 network, you receive a call from one of your users that she is unable to connect to the MS SQL server, which is located on a different subnet. At the user's workstation, you type the command **ipconfig** and receive the following output:

IP Address: 192.168.8.142

Subnet Mask: 255.255.255.128

Default Gateway: 192.168.8.1

What could be the possible reason that the user is unable to connect to the MS SQL database?

_____

_____

Lesson Summary

- TCP/IP is the required protocol for Windows Server 2003. An important part of TCP/IP that must be understood is IP addressing. You need to configure all of your client workstations, printers, servers, and so forth, with unique IP addresses.

- IP addresses are made up of four bytes, called octets, which represent both a network address and a host address. Depending on the decimal value of the first byte, you can determine the TCP/IP address class from which the IP address is a member. Class A addresses allow for the most host addresses, whereas Class C addresses allow for the most subnets.

- Classes A, B, and C have default subnet masks of 255.0.0.0, 255.255.0.0, and 255.255.255.0, respectively. The subnet mask is used to determine the network ID portion of an IP address.

- Borrowing bits from the host portion of an IP address to create additional subnets is called subnetting. You determine the number of bits you need to borrow based on the amount of subnets you need to create and the number of available host addresses you need in each of the subnets.

Lesson 2: Designing a Perimeter Network

Designing a local network that does not connect to the Internet is very simple and certainly much more secure than one that does connect. As soon as you decide to use public IP addresses and host Web servers for outsiders to access, you have opened many doors to intruders and hackers.

In this chapter, you learn how to design a perimeter network, also called a DMZ (Demilitarization Zone), to help protect your company's internal network while still allowing outsiders, such as customers, potential customers, and potential employee candidates applying for positions at your company, and so on, to access your company's servers.

After this lesson, you will be able to

■ Describe a perimeter network's components, such as firewalls, Intrusion Detection Systems (IDS), and Microsoft's Internet Security and Acceleration (ISA) Server.

■ Design and document your company's perimeter network.

Estimated lesson time: 15 minutes

Protecting Your Private Network

In Figure 8-3, your internal network has access to the Internet. This, in itself, also means that Internet users have access to your internal network. This may not be what you were looking for when designing your network infrastructure but, unfortunately, you are stuck with this reality.

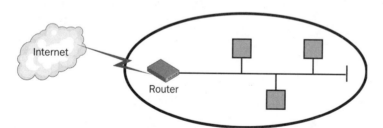

Figure 8-3 Without a firewall, a company's Internet connection is bi-directional.

There are many components you can use to help lessen the risks of intrusion to your network, including firewalls, proxies, and intrusion detection systems.

Figure 8-4 introduces a perimeter firewall into the picture. A firewall can be hardware- or software-based. It acts as a boundary between your network and the outside world. Its job is to filter traffic entering and leaving your network.

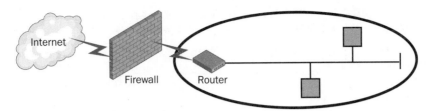

Figure 8-4   A company's connection to the Internet with a firewall protects the internal network.

Routers can also be configured, through the use of access lists, to behave as firewalls. An access list filters traffic based on different criteria, such as the destination or source IP address of a packet; the protocol that is being used, such as User Datagram Protocol (UDP) or TCP; the port ID, such as port 80, port 110 (Post Office Protocol [POP]3); and so on.

There are several different types of firewalls with which you should be familiar:

- Packet filtering firewalls
- Stateful inspection firewalls
- Application-layer firewalls

Packet filtering firewalls do the same thing as that router you just read about, but are more sophisticated. A packet filtering firewall has a set of rules, called a ruleset, and makes decisions on whether to forward the packet, or drop it, based on these rules.

Stateful firewalls take this a step further, and not only look at the packets but the "state" or network transmission, to determine if the packet is valid. For example, if a packet is received by a firewall that is a response, or acknowledgment (ACK) packet, in a TCP three-way TCP handshake, but a SYN packet was never sent, the stateful firewall would suspect that something was not right and drop the packet. Many port scanning programs do just that. An ACK packet is sent to a computer system, even though a SYN packet, which is supposed to be sent before an ACK packet, is sent, thereby revealing information about what is being scanned.

Application-layer firewalls such as Microsoft Proxy Server inspect the contents of a packet, and can choose to forward or drop a packet based on application-specific rules. A common use of application-layer firewalls is to drop browser requests for unauthorized Web sites. A stateful firewall that examined only the headers of a packet would not be capable of making decisions based on the URL of the destination Web site.

Intrusion Detection Systems (IDSs) do more than just filter traffic and drop packets. They detect intrusion and warn an administrator when an intruder is attacking the network or has compromised a server or network resource. There are two types of IDSs:

- **Host-based**   A host-based IDS operates on a particular server and looks at the audit log for any indications that a problem or an attack has occurred.

- **Network-based**   A network-based IDS operates on a network. It looks at data passing through the network and compares it against certain signatures, similar to how an antivirus program works. An alarm is sounded when a signature matches or if something doesn't seem right.

> **Note**   A firewall is not a foolproof way to protect a network. Firewalls add protection but do not guarantee that an intruder will not bypass its security. The only way to ensure a network is impregnable is to unplug the network cable from the wall. As a network administrator, you cannot keep someone from entering your network, but you can use an Intrusion Detection System to warn you when an intruder does enter your network. You can implement a counter-measure after such an occurrence.

Firewalls may be used to protect your internal network from the outside, but suppose you want outsiders to access your company's Web server or email servers? You can place these servers in an area outside your private, internal network. A perimeter network is a small network that is accessible to external users, but does not allow these users to access your internal network. Figure 8-5 illustrates how a perimeter network can do just that.

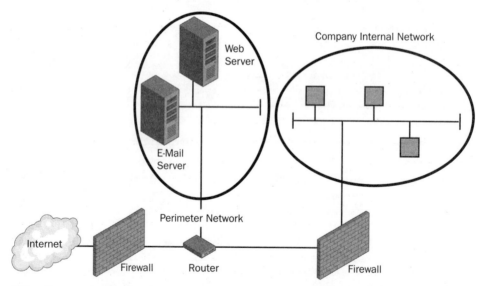

Figure 8-5   A perimeter network is used to separate public services from the internal network.

Notice that the outside users have to go through a firewall to access the Web server and e-mail server, and two firewalls must be entered before accessing the internal private network. The firewalls in the illustration could be Internet Security and Acceleration (ISA) servers or another type of firewall.

Documenting Your Perimeter Network

As you have learned in the previous chapters, documentation of your network infrastructure design is one of the most important aspects of an administrator's job. Documenting your perimeter network infrastructure is no different. In fact, this is probably the most important of all of your documentation because this may affect the security and protection of your company's resources.

As you have learned, the perimeter network contains servers that do not host any critical or proprietary information on them. These servers should be free of Social Security numbers, credit card numbers, marketing plans for the business, and so forth. The perimeter network should house the servers you want outsiders to connect to while limiting access to your company's internal network.

Software and Hardware Components

Your documentation, at a minimum, should include all software, such as antivirus software that is being used, as well as firewalls, IDSs, proxy firewalls, and all of the different operating systems that are in use. For example, you may include such information as:

- Dell Windows 2000 Server running Microsoft Internet Security and Acceleration (ISA) Server—Virtual Private Network (VPN)
- CheckPoint Firewall running on Solaris Server
- Dell Windows Server 2003 running Microsoft Internet Security and Acceleration Server—Firewall

This information, combined with details about how to administer the system, specific software versions, and escalation procedures will help you, or someone else in your absence, maintain the system and troubleshoot any security problems or attacks to your network.

Login Names, Passwords, and IP Addresses

There is nothing worse than being the administrator on duty when your predecessor has left you with little or no documentation. Your documentation should include the login names and passwords for all the servers and routers, or any systems that require a login name. Of course, this information should be locked in a safe or placed in a location that requires a key or lock combination. Your documentation should also include information such as:

- Patching procedures
- Unplanned downtime procedures
- Access methods (Telnet, ssh, rdp)

- Vendor contact information
- Software versions
- Hostnames and IP addresses

Because the perimeter network is never on the same subnet as the company's internal network, be sure to document all IP addresses used by all interfaces and devices and subnet masks as well as the subnet ranges that the perimeter network is using.

This documentation must be locked in a secure place because its release could undermine the security of the company's network infrastructure.

Lesson Review

The following questions are intended to reinforce key information presented in this lesson. If you are unable to answer a question, review the lesson materials and try the question again. You can find answers to the questions in the "Questions and Answers" section at the end of this chapter.

1. You are the network administrator of a large Windows Server 2003 network and have just been tasked to assist the company's Web designer in hosting a "Job Fair" Web site that will list job openings for various positions in the company. The server is located on the same network segment as a confidential database server that contains medical records of all the employees. The IT manager wants you to assure him that you will minimize the additional risk to the confidential database. How would you implement the Web server so that external users could access it without risking access to the database server?

   _____

   _____

2. What network component could be used to warn you of a possible attack on your database server?

   _____

   _____

3. You have completed designing your perimeter network for your company and now need to document the system for improved maintenance and support. What should your documentation include?

   _____

   _____

Lesson Summary

- A perimeter network is a small network that is accessible to external users but does not allow users access to the internal network of a company. Perimeter networks usually contain Web servers and mail servers for external users to access.

- Packet filtering, stateful inspection, and application-layer firewalls may be used to protect your company's internal network from external users.

- Documentation of your perimeter network should include the login names and passwords for all of the servers and routers, or any systems that require a login name. It should also include all of the network components that are used to protect the company's internal network, such as firewalls, proxies, and IDSs.

- Because the perimeter network is never on the same subnet as the company's internal network, document all IP addresses used on all interfaces and devices, as well as subnet masks and subnet ranges used on the perimeter network.

Lesson 3: Understanding DHCP

Manually configuring TCP/IP on workstations is not very complicated. In fact, it is very easy. However, configuring hundreds or even thousands of workstations can prove to be tiring and error prone. It's almost impossible to avoid making a typo, or to enter an incorrect subnet mask when having to sit in front of a user's workstation. Dynamic Host Configuration Protocol is a service that does the work for you. Can mistakes still be made? Yes, but few and far between. Also, DHCP does more than just issue IP addresses, as you'll see in this lesson, which shows you how a DHCP server can dynamically configure computers on your network using a pool of addresses that you have configured it to use.

After this lesson, you will be able to

- Describe how DHCP assigns IP addresses.
- Describe the DHCP IP address-assignment process.
- Identify APIPA (Automatic Private IP addressing).

Estimated lesson time: 25 minutes

Overview of DHCP

Dynamic Host Configuration Protocol (DHCP) is a service that runs on a Windows Server 2003 operating system. A DHCP server is any server that runs this DHCP service. Its function is to automatically allocate IP addresses and other TCP/IP-related information such as Windows Internet Naming Service (WINS) IP addresses, Domain Name System (DNS) IP addresses, default gateway IP addresses, and subnet mask information to DHCP-enabled clients.

Assigning an IP Address

For an IP address to be configured on a DHCP client workstation, four steps take place.

1. When a DHCP client boots up, it sends out a broadcast packet over the network segment requesting that a DHCP server respond. Remember that broadcast traffic does not go over a router unless the router is configured to allow such traffic to be forwarded. This is called the IP Lease Discover phase.

2. All DHCP servers that are configured with a valid range of IP addresses send an offer to the DHCP client. This IP Lease Offer includes the MAC address of the client, an IP address, subnet mask, length of lease, and the IP address of the DHCP server offering the IP address.

3. The DHCP client accepts the offer from the first DHCP server that responded with an offer and sends the server a request to lease the IP address. This request is sent

in a DHCPDISCOVER message and contains the MAC address (hardware address) and the computer name of the DHCP client.

4. The DHCP server that offered the IP address to the client responds to the DHCP-DISCOVER message, and the IP address is assigned to the client. If any other DHCP server offered an IP address to the client, it would now withdraw its offer.

As you see in Figure 8-6, the assignment of an IP address is not very complicated. However, before an IP address can be issued, you must create a range of IP addresses, called a scope, from which the DHCP Server can choose.

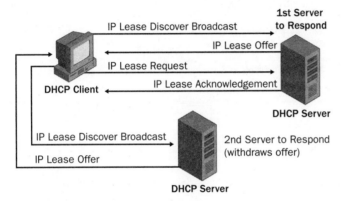

Figure 8-6 Obtaining an IP address using DHCP is a multistep process.

Creating the DHCP Scope

A scope is a range of valid IP addresses that will be leased to DHCP clients. Each DHCP server must be configured with a minimum of one scope, which has the following properties:

- The range of IP addresses that will be leased to DHCP clients.

- The subnet mask.

- The duration of the lease. The recommended time period for smaller networks is the default of eight days.

- DHCP scope options, such as DNS and WINS IP addresses, covered later in this section.

- Reservations, if you want particular DHCP clients to always receive the same IP address and TCP/IP configuration at startup.

For example, if you wanted a DHCP server to issue IP addresses to all of the workstations on the subnet 192.168.1.0/24, your scope of addresses would be 192.168.1.1–192.168.1.254. There is a good chance that a node on that segment, such as a network printer or a server, could have an IP address already statically configured, so you must remember to exclude any IP addresses from your range, or scope.

Assigning IP addresses to workstations and servers on a large network saves the time that would be spent physically visiting each workstation to configure it. If only IP addresses could be issued using DHCP, you would still need to manually assign such things as the IP address of the WINS server, DNS server, or default gateway. Table 8-7 illustrates the additional options you can configure the DHCP server to issue to a DHCP client.

Table 8-7 Additional Configuration Options

Option	Description
003 Router	This option is used to select the default gateway IP address the DHCP client issues.
006 DNS Servers	This option configures the IP address of the DNS server.
015 DNS Domain Name	This option configures the DNS domain name for DHCP client resolutions.
044 WINS/NBNS Servers	This option configures the IP address of the WINS server.
046 WINS/NBT Node Type	This option configures the node type the DHCP client uses for name resolution, e.g., b-node, h-node, p-node, or m-node.
047 NetBIOS Scope ID	This option configures the NetBIOS scope ID, which is seldom used at this time. The NetBIOS scope ID enables an administrator to separate NetBIOS hosts based on this ID, similar to how a subnet mask creates separate subnets.

DHCP Relay Agent

Broadcast traffic, as you might recall from Chapter 7, "Designing a WINS Structure," does not get forwarded by an IP router unless the router is configured to do so. This can be problematic if DHCP clients are located on a subnet that does not contain a DHCP server. See Figure 8-7.

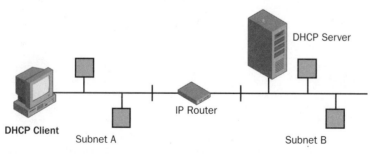

Figure 8-7 Routers block DHCP requests.

When the DHCP client in Subnet A broadcasts a request to locate a DHCP server (IP Lease Discover), the broadcast is heard only on Subnet A. The DHCP server located on Subnet B is not aware of the request. This problem can be easily solved in two ways:

- Configure one or more of the workstations in Subnet A to be a DHCP relay agent.
- Configure the router to be a DHCP relay agent.

By configuring one of the workstations in the subnet to be a relay agent, the workstation hears the broadcast request made by the DHCP client and it forwards the request to a designated DHCP server, using unicast instead of broadcast packets. Sound familiar? This is very similar to how a WINS Proxy Agent, covered in the previous chapter, works. If a router is DHCP/BOOTP (Bootstrap Protocol) compliant (RFC 1542), you don't need to configure a workstation to be a DHCP relay agent.

Automatic Private IP Addressing

Suppose a DHCP-enabled workstation broadcasts for a DHCP server to issue it an IP address, but the DHCP server is down for maintenance. Or the IP router that is configured as a DHCP relay agent was accidentally shut down by a junior administrator so the broadcast packet doesn't reach the DHCP server located in the remote subnet. Would you receive an error that a DHCP server is not available, in these cases? The answer, of course, is no. If a DHCP server does not respond to a client's broadcast, the DHCP client automatically configures itself with an IP address from the range 169.254.0.1–169.254.255.254.

Securing your DHCP Infrastructure

There is always a danger that a careless individual might introduce a rogue DHCP server to your network. If he or she issues bogus IP configuration information to DHCP clients, network clients could be unable to access network resources. When integrating DHCP with Active Directory, you can prevent Windows Server 2003–based rogue DHCP servers from accidentally starting on the network using a DHCP object created in the Active Directory database, which identifies all authorized DHCP servers. Unless the DHCP server is authorized, it's not allowed to issue any configuration information to DHCP clients.

Lesson Review

The following questions are intended to reinforce key information presented in this lesson. If you are unable to answer a question, review the lesson materials and try the question again. You can find answers to the questions in the "Questions and Answers" section at the end of this chapter.

1. On a network segment that contains multiple DHCP servers, which server responds with an offer of an IP address to a DHCP-enabled client?

   _____

   _____

2. Which DHCP options would configure a DHCP client's default gateway and DNS IP address?

   _____

   _____

3. You are the network administrator for a Windows Server 2003 network that has DHCP implemented throughout all of its subnets. You receive a telephone call from a user who says she cannot connect to any network resources. On arriving at her office, you type **ipconfig /all** at her workstation and receive the following output:

   ```
   IP Address: 169.254.112.14
   ```

   ```
   Subnet Mask: 255.255.0.0
   ```

   ```
   Default Gateway:
   ```

   What could be the possible reason that the user is unable to connect to any of the company's network resources?

   _____

   _____

Lesson Summary

- DHCP is a service that runs on a Windows Server 2003 operating system. A DHCP server is any server that runs this DHCP service. DHCP allocates IP addresses and other TCP/IP-related information, such as WINS IP addresses, DNS IP addresses, default gateway IP addresses, and subnet mask information, to DHCP-enabled clients.

- A scope is a range of valid IP addresses that will be leased to DHCP clients. Each DHCP server must be configured with a minimum of one scope.

- In a routed network, a DHCP server located on a remote network segment cannot issue IP addresses to clients across the router unless the router is DHCP/BOOTP compliant (RFC 1542). If the router is not BOOTP compliant, you'll need to configure a workstation on the remote segment to be a DHCP relay agent.

Lesson 4: Creating a DHCP Strategy

In designing a DHCP strategy, you must be aware of how many hosts will be on your network as well as the number of subnets DHCP will need to support. The location of your company's routers, as well as the transmission speed between your network segments, will help you decide on where you place the DHCP servers.

After this lesson, you will be able to

■ Design IP address assignments using DHCP.

■ Describe DHCP integration with DNS.

■ Create the conceptual design of a DHCP infrastructure.

■ Describe DHCP interoperability with various client types.

Estimated lesson time: 25 minutes

Designing a DHCP Addressing Scheme

Designing a DHCP strategy for a nonrouted network will, of course, be different than designing one for a routed network. In a routed network in which routers connect multiple networks, DHCP relay agents must be strategically placed throughout the network, or routers must be RFC-1542/BOOTP compliant so that packets will be forwarded.

How Many DHCP Servers?

When designing your DHCP infrastructure, consider how many servers will be needed. In smaller networks, one DHCP server can service all DHCP-enabled clients. In a routed network, consideration must be given to the transmission speed between the subnets and wide area network (WAN) links, if any are present. You can decide how many DHCP servers are needed based on:

■ Routing configuration

■ Network configuration

■ Server hardware

Placement of DHCP Servers

If you choose to use only one DHCP server in a routed network, you'll need relay agents to forward broadcasts over your routers. You can configure a Windows NT Server, Windows 2000 Server, or a Windows Server 2003 system to use the DHCP Relay Agent component or verify that the routers are BOOTP compliant. You should also place the Windows Server 2003 DHCP Server on the subnet containing the most hosts.

Consider this option if your network configuration includes high-speed connections, which are always available, rather than demand-dialing routers or connections to subnets that are only established when needed.

Server Requirements

In a single-server environment, be sure your hardware can handle the load. A DHCP server running on a computer similar to the one listed below can handle thousands of clients. Microsoft has tested DHCP running on a server with the following hardware and network configurations:

- Two x86 Family 6 Model 7 Stepping 3 GenuineIntel ~500 MHz

- 256 MB RAM

- Three Ethernet 802.3 100 Mbps Network Adapter Cards

- Six subnets, where four of them were separated from the test DHCP server by routers running the DHCP Relay Agent service

- Windows Server 2003, Enterprise Edition Operating System

- Approximately 5,000 scopes

- DHCP database size 2 GB

- Several thousand exclusion ranges, option values, and reservations

The test was conducted over a period of 48 days, and the following services were provided for DHCP clients over that time. Table 8-8 shows the DHCP functions and the volume of transactions processed during this 48-day period.

Table 8-8   DHCP Test Server Functions and Volume Handled

DHCP Service to Client	Total Volume Handled over 48-Day Period
Lease Assignments	68,412,059
DHCP discover messages	20,039,592
DHCP offer messages	20,039,253
DHCP request messages	57,559,426
DHCP acknowledgment messages	57,470,934
DHCP negative acknowledgments sent by the server	484,012
DHCP decline messages	190,901
Lease releases	0

As you can see, a DHCP server can handle an extraordinary volume of functions. In fact, it would be very unusual to have a database this large (2 GB). Most DHCP databases are smaller than 10 MB. This gives you a good benchmark to work with when designing your DHCP infrastructure.

A rule of thumb that may help you select the right server to run the DHCP service is that the performance of a DHCP server increases if the server is configured with:

- Multiple CPUs
- High-performance hard drives
- Multiple network cards or one that has high bandwidth

If you choose to use multiple DHCP servers, you may want to place DHCP servers on subnets that are connected by slow WAN links or dial-up links to avoid sending DHCP requests across the WAN. Your server hardware does not need to be as powerful because you can spread the load over more than one server.

Availability of DHCP Servers Using 80/20 Rule

To increase the availability factor of two DHCP servers located on different subnets, you can distribute the scopes across the two servers. For example, it is recommended that you allocate 80 percent of the IP addresses to the DHCP Server located on the local subnet, and allocate 20 percent of the addresses to the DHCP Server that is located on the remote segment. If the DHCP Server with 80 percent of the IP addresses allocated crashes, DHCP clients are issued new IP addresses from the remote DHCP Server.

DNS Integration

When Windows Server 2003 is installed, it can be configured to perform dynamic updates to a DNS server that supports dynamic updates. The DHCP Server can register the pointer (PTR) and host (A) resource records on behalf of the DHCP-enabled clients as well as discard these records when a client lease is deleted.

Supporting Various DHCP Clients

If your network has only Microsoft-client computers, you can easily configure them to be DHCP clients. But what if your network consists of non-Microsoft workstations that also require automatic IP configuration? Table 8-9 shows these different types of clients.

Table 8-9   Client Support

Type of Client	Description
Non-Microsoft DHCP Clients	May require support for features that are not mandatory and may not support vendor extensions
BOOTP Clients	Requests an IP address each time the client starts. Does not recognize IP leases
Non-DHCP Clients	Addresses for these clients manually configured

Practice: Creating a DHCP Strategy

In this practice, you will design a DHCP infrastructure for the proposed Northwind Traders office in Rio de Janeiro, Brazil. If you are unable to answer a question, review the lesson materials and try the question again. You can find answers to the questions in the "Questions and Answers" section at the end of this chapter.

Scenario

Northwind Traders plans to open an office in Rio de Janeiro. The new office will occupy three different floors of a large office building in the heart of the city. The existing network has several subnets, as shown in the following diagram. All routers can be configured to forward DHCP requests to a DHCP server.

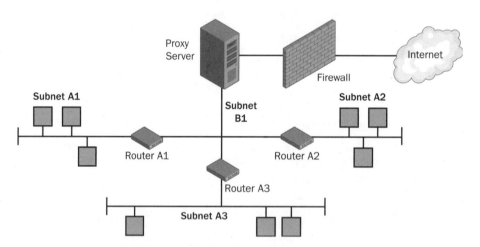

Practice Questions

Based on the scenario, determine how you can plan a DHCP solution for automated host IP configuration in the new office by answering the following questions.

1. Given the scenario, and ignoring reliability considerations, how many DHCP servers are required for a DHCP solution? Why?

   _____

   _____

2. Given the scenario, and ignoring reliability considerations, how many DHCP relay agents are required for a DHCP solution? Why?

   _____

   _____

3. Given the number of subnets, what is the minimum number of DHCP scopes required for a DHCP solution? Why would you make this choice?

_____

_____

4. Senior management wants to avoid paying the service contract on your existing routers by eliminating them from the network. How would you redesign the network with no single point of failure for the network infrastructure while eliminating the routers?

_____

_____

Lesson Review

The following questions are intended to reinforce key information presented in this lesson. If you are unable to answer a question, review the lesson materials and try the question again. You can find answers to the questions in the "Questions and Answers" section at the end of this chapter.

1. You are designing a DHCP strategy for a small network composed of three subnets. Subnets A, B, and C are connected to one router that is RFC-1542 compliant. Subnet B, the largest subnet containing the most DHCP clients, also houses the DHCP Server. The other two subnets do not have a DHCP Server on them. How many DHCP relay agents would you need for all workstations to be able to receive an IP address from the DHCP Server?

_____

_____

2. If you choose to use only one DHCP Server in a routed network, what are some of the things you should consider?

_____

_____

3. List three factors you might want to consider when choosing the computer that will run the DHCP service.

_____

_____

Lesson Summary

- In designing a DHCP strategy, you should be aware of how many hosts will be on the network, the number of subnets DHCP will need to support, the location of the company's routers, and the transmission speed between each of the network segments.

- If you choose to use only one DHCP server in a routed network, you need DHCP Relay Agents on the other subnets. You can configure a Windows NT Server, Windows 2000 Server, or a Windows Server 2003 system to use the DHCP Relay Agent component. Alternatively, you can configure the DHCP/BOOTP-compliant routers in your network to forward DHCP requests.

- The DHCP Server can be configured to register the pointer (PTR) and host (A) resource records on behalf of the DHCP-enabled clients as well as discard these records when a client lease is deleted.

- To increase the availability factor of two DHCP servers located on different subnets, you can distribute the scopes across the two servers. For example, it is recommended that you allocate 80 percent of the IP addresses to the DHCP server on the local subnet, and allocate 20 percent of the addresses to the DHCP server that is located on the remote segment.

Case Scenario Exercise

Review the following scenario and complete the questions.

Scenario

You have been selected to design an IP addressing scheme for a large marketing research company that has just landed a $15 million contract with one of the largest cellular telephone companies in the United States. The company has just purchased all new computer systems; all client systems are running Windows XP Professional, and all servers are running Windows Server 2003.

Background

Trey Research has offices in Chicago, Miami, and New York. The company touts the largest data warehouse storage servers, which have information on the spending and buying habits of more than 200 million people throughout the world.

Network Infrastructure

Jack Moran, the IT manager from Trey Research, has given you a basic sketch of the company's network. (See the diagram that follows.) All of the offices need to communicate with each other over the company's private network. The New York office, however, hosts several Web servers and three Microsoft Exchange 2003 Servers. The IT manager wants users to be able to access these servers from the Internet, but indicates that he is a little concerned about the security ramifications of doing such a thing.

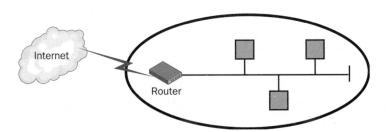

Jack claims that he read an article in a computer journal that said more than two hundred workstations on any one subnet created excessive collision and broadcast traffic. He wants the IP addressing scheme that you design to disallow any more than 300 nodes for each subnet.

Future Plans

The company will be considering purchasing property in Los Angeles, where it plans on opening several offices within a year or so. More than 3,000 workstations will be needed for this location.

Questions

Given the previous scenario, answer the following questions.

1. What private IP address class would you use for this network infrastructure? How many subnets would be required in the Chicago offices?

   _____

   _____

2. How could you design this network so that external users could access the Web server while minimizing the risk of an attack on your company's internal network?

   _____

   _____

3. If a perimeter network were created for the scenario described above, what network components could you use to protect both the perimeter network and the company's internal network?

_____

_____

Chapter Summary

- TCP/IP is the required protocol for Windows Server 2003. An important part of TCP/IP that must be understood is IP addressing. You need to configure all of your client workstations, printers, servers, and so forth, with unique IP addresses.

- IP addresses are made up of four bytes, called octets, which represent both a network address and a host address. Depending on the decimal value of the first byte, you can determine the TCP/IP address class from which the IP address is a member. Class A addresses allow for the most host addresses, whereas Class C addresses allow for the most subnets.

- Classes A, B, and C have default subnet masks of 255.0.0.0, 255.255.0.0, and 255.255.255.0, respectively. The subnet mask is used to determine the network ID portion of an IP address.

- Borrowing bits from the host portion of an IP address to create additional subnets is called subnetting. You determine the number of bits you need to borrow based on the number of subnets you need to create and the number of available host addresses you will need in each of the subnets.

- A perimeter network is a small network that is accessible to external users, but does not allow users to access the internal network of a company. Perimeter networks usually contain Web servers and mail servers for external users to access.

- Packet filtering, stateful inspection, and application-layer firewalls may be used to protect your company's internal network from external users.

- Documentation of your perimeter network should include the login names and passwords for all of the servers and routers, or any systems that require a login name. This information should be placed in a locked safe or location that requires a key or combination. It should also include all of the network components that are used to protect the company's internal network, such as firewalls, proxies, and IDSs.

- Because the perimeter network is never on the same subnet as the company's internal network, document all IP addresses used on all interfaces and devices, as well as subnet masks and subnet ranges used on the perimeter network.

- DHCP is a service that runs on a Windows Server 2003 operating system. A DHCP server is any server that runs this DHCP service. DHCP allocates IP addresses and other TCP/IP-related information, such as WINS IP addresses, DNS IP addresses, default gateway IP addresses, and subnet mask information, to DHCP-enabled clients.

■ A scope is a range of valid IP addresses that will be leased to DHCP clients. Each DHCP server must be configured with a minimum of one scope.

■ In a routed network, a DHCP server located on a remote network segment cannot issue IP addresses to clients across the router, unless the router is DHCP/BOOTP compliant (RFC 1542). If the router is not BOOTP compliant, you'll need to configure a workstation on the remote segment to be a DHCP Relay Agent.

■ In designing a DHCP strategy, you should be aware of how many hosts will be on the network, the number of subnets the DHCP server needs to support, and the location of the company's routers as well as the transmission speed between each of the network segments.

■ If you choose to use only one DHCP server in a routed network, you will need DHCP Relay Agents on the other subnets. You can configure a Windows NT Server, Windows 2000 Server, or a Windows Server 2003 system to use the DHCP Relay Agent component or you can verify that the routers in your network are DHCP/BOOTP compliant.

■ The DHCP Server can be configured to register the pointer (PTR) and host (A) resource records on behalf of the DHCP-enabled clients, as well as discard these records when a client lease is deleted.

■ To increase the availability factor of a DHCP server on a subnet containing DHCP servers, you can distribute the scopes across the two servers. For example, it is recommended that you allocate 80 percent of the IP addresses to the DHCP server located on the local subnet, and allocate 20 percent of the addresses to the DHCP server located on the remote segment.

Exam Highlights

Before taking the exam, review the key topics and terms that are presented in this chapter. You need to know this information.

Key Points

■ TCP/IP is the required protocol for Windows Server 2003. An important part of TCP/IP that must be understood is IP addressing because all nodes on a network must be configured with a unique IP address.

■ A perimeter network is a small network that is accessible to external users, but does not allow users access to the internal network of a company. Perimeter networks usually contain Web servers and mail servers for external users to access. It is crucial that the perimeter network be well documented, and that all login names, passwords, and IP subnet information be accessible to anyone responsible for maintaining or supporting the system.

■ DHCP allocates IP addresses and other TCP/IP-related information, such as WINS IP addresses, DNS IP addresses, default gateway IP address, and subnet mask information, to DHCP-enabled clients. A scope is the range of valid IP addresses that will be leased to DHCP clients. Each DHCP server must be configured with a minimum of one scope.

■ You can configure a Windows NT Server, Windows 2000 Server, or a Windows Server 2003 system to use the DHCP Relay Agent component or you can verify that the routers in your network are DHCP/BOOTP compliant if implementing DHCP in a routed network. The DHCP Server can be configured to register the pointer (PTR) and host (A) resource records on behalf of the DHCP-enabled clients, as well as to discard these records when a client lease is deleted.

Key Terms

Subnetting   Borrowing of bits from the host portion of an IP address to create additional subnets.

Perimeter network   A smaller network segment that hosts servers available to external users. The perimeter network is separated from the company's internal network through the use of firewalls and Intrusion Detection Systems (IDS).

DHCP Relay Agent   A program that forwards DHCP/BOOTP messages to DHCP servers, which are located on different subnets. RFC-1542-compliant routers are routers that behave as DHCP Relay Agents.

80/20 Rule   Recommended method of a DHCP server allocating 80 percent of its IP addresses to DHCP clients on the local subnet, and 20 percent of its IP addresses to the remote DHCP server.

Questions and Answers

Page
8-14

Lesson 1 Practice

1. For this design, what is the minimum number of subnets required in each location, based on router performance?

   Building A: _____Building B: _____

   Building C: _____Building D: _____

   Total Subnets: _____

   Building A: 5 (6 with WAN)

   Building B: 7 (9 with WAN and Internet)

   Building C: 1 (2 with WAN)

   Building D: 4 (5 with WAN)

2. Choose an appropriate subnet mask for hosts in this design. Choose the correct answer.

   a. /16

   b. /19

   c. /21

   d. /24

   The correct answer is d, /24.

3. What is the total number of required private IP addresses? Choose the correct answer.

   a. 7 private IP addresses

   b. 1,204 private IP addresses

   c. 2,903 private IP addresses

   d. 4,032 private IP addresses

   The correct answer is c, 2,903 private IP addresses, which is calculated as follows:

   Building A: 808

   Building B: 1,311

   Building C: 129

   Building D: 655

4. What is the minimum number of required public IP addresses? Choose the correct answer.

   a. 1 public IP address

   b. 2 public IP addresses

   c. 2,903 public IP addresses

   d. 4,032 public IP addresses

   The correct answer is a, 1 public IP address.

5. At maximum, how many hosts per subnet does the subnet mask in the design provide? Choose the correct answer.

   a. 254 hosts per subnet

   b. 1,022 hosts per subnet

   c. 6,398 hosts per subnet

   d. 65,534 hosts per subnet

   The correct answer is a. The subnet mask design allows a maximum of 254 hosts per subnet.

6. Management has suggested that a new private address could be chosen. Which of the following private IP network addresses is appropriate for the design? Choose all that apply.

   a. 10.0.0.0/8

   b. 230.120.0.0/16

   c. 69.254.0.0/16

   d. 192.168.0.0/16

   The correct answers are a and d.

Lesson 1 Review

1. List the five different address classes and the value of the first octet. Also, list each of the private IP addresses available for internal use by a company.

   The five different address classes and the value of the first octet are as follows: A (1–126), B (128–191), C (192–223), D (224–239), and E (240–255). The private addresses available for internal use are: 10.0.0.1–10.255.255.254, 172.16.0.1–172.31.255.254, and 192.168.0.1–192.168.255.254.

2. Your company has more than 15,000 workstations spread throughout several towns in the Midwest. As the network administrator, you have been asked to design an IP addressing strategy that will enable the company to access all of its resources using private IP addressing. You determine after careful analysis that you will need to create between 500 and 600 subnets with a maximum of 250 nodes per subnet. What private address will you choose, and what will the subnet mask be?

Let's begin by eliminating the obvious, the Class C address. In a Class C address, you just about reach the maximum host addresses without even beginning to subnet. That is, a Class C address will give you a maximum of 254 hosts, or nodes, per Class C network ID. If you subnet, you will reduce your host IDs down to 126, 62, 30, and so forth. The Class B address, without subnetting, allows for more than 65,000 host addresses. You see that this address scheme has potential. However, because you will need 500–600 subnets, you see an immediate problem. In a Class B address, the default subnet mask is 255.255.0.0. To create 600 subnets, you need to borrow more than 8 bits (2^8 = 256 subnets), which will take you into the fourth octet. You already saw that all 8 bits would be necessary to allow for 250 node addresses.

The only choice then is a Class A private address. If you use 10.0.0.0 as your network ID and use a subnet mask of 255.255.192.0, you can create up to 1,024 subnets, each one able to house more than 16,000 host addresses. This is a lot more than our requirement, so you have some room for creativity. You can borrow more bits from the third octet, which enables you to create additional subnets when needed, and reduce the number of host IDs available for each subnet. For example, a subnet mask of 255.255.240.0 allows you to create more than 4,000 subnets with approximately 4,000 hosts. A subnet mask of 255.255.248.0 allows you to create up to 8,000 subnets with approximately 2,000 hosts.

3. As the network administrator for a Windows Server 2003 network, you receive a call from one of your users that she is unable to connect to the MS SQL Server, which is located on a different subnet. At the user's workstation, you type the command **ipconfig** and receive the following output:

IP Address: 192.168.8.142

Subnet Mask: 255.255.255.128

Default Gateway: 192.168.8.1

What could be the possible reason that the user is unable to connect to the MS SQL database?

The first thing you should determine is the class of address the workstation is using. This is a Class C address. Because the last octet is not a zero, you can determine that subnetting is taking place on this network. With one bit being borrowed from the fourth octet, you know that two subnets are created, each with a block size of 128. The first subnet would then have host IDs starting with the number 1 (no zero for a host ID) and proceeding to 126 (not 127 because this would be all ones). The next subnet would be 192.168.8.128, and include host IDs ranging from 129 to 254. You quickly notice that the IP address of the workstation is in a different subnet than the default gateway IP address. So, either the IP address is incorrect, the subnet mask is incorrect, or the default gateway is incorrect. An easy way to determine this is to look at any of the other workstations in the same subnet as the user. If all of the other workstations have the default gateway IP address as 192.168.8.1, then the likely culprit is an invalid IP address.

Lesson 2 Review

1. You are the network administrator of a large Windows Server 2003 network and have just been tasked to assist the company's Web designer in hosting a "Job Fair" Web site that will list job openings for various positions in the company. The server is located on the same network segment as a confidential database server that contains medical records of all the employees. The IT manager wants you to assure him that you will minimize the additional risk to the confidential database. How would you implement the Web server so that external users could access it without risking access to the database server?

    The Web server should be placed in a perimeter network, separate from your company's internal network.

2. What network component could be used to warn you of a possible attack on your database server?

    Intrusion Detection Systems are used to warn of a possible attack or intrusion into your network resources. Microsoft's ISA can function as a firewall and as an IDS, with some limitations.

3. You have completed designing your perimeter network for your company and now need to document the system for improved maintenance and support. What should your documentation include?

    At the very least, you should list all of the hardware components, such as routers, firewalls, and any Intrusion Detection Systems. When listing a firewall, you should specify the type (proxy, stateful, etc.), manufacturer, model, and any login names or passwords needed to access the system. This holds true for all devices and servers used on your company network.

Lesson 3 Review

1. On a network segment that contains multiple DHCP servers, which server responds with an offer of an IP address to a DHCP-enabled client?

    All. The broadcast packet (IP lease discover) is received by all DHCP servers. The DHCP client selects the IP address from the first DHCP it receives it from, and all other DHCP servers withdraw their offers.

2. Which DHCP options would configure a DHCP client's default gateway and DNS IP address?

    The 003 Router and 006 DNS Servers options configure the default gateway IP address and the DNS Server IP address.

3. You are the network administrator for a Windows Server 2003 network that has DHCP implemented throughout all of its subnets. You receive a telephone call from a user who says she cannot connect to any network resources. On arriving at her office, you type **ipconfig /all** at her workstation and receive the following output:

IP Address: 169.254.112.14

Subnet Mask: 255.255.0.0

Default Gateway:

What could be the possible reason that the user is unable to connect to any of the company's network resources?

Because DHCP is implemented in this network, the IP address of 169.254.x.x indicates that the DHCP service was not available when the client computer started, and APIPA (Automatic Private IP Addressing) issued an IP address to the client.

Lesson 4 Practice

Page
8-32

1. Given the scenario, and ignoring reliability considerations, how many DHCP Servers are required for a DHCP solution? Why?

Only one server is required. One DHCP server can service up to 10,000 client computers.

2. Given the scenario, and ignoring reliability considerations, how many DHCP relay agents are required for a DHCP solution? Why?

Zero. You do not need any DHCP/BOOTP relay agents because all of the routers will forward DHCP broadcasts.

3. Given the number of subnets, what is the minimum number of DHCP scopes required for a DHCP solution? Why would you make this choice?

Three scopes are required, one for each of the subnets that contain client computers.

4. Senior management wants to avoid paying the service contract on your existing routers by eliminating them from the network. How would you redesign the network with no single point of failure for the network infrastructure while eliminating the routers?

You should set up another server alongside the proxy server, and configure each of the two proxy servers with four NICs. Then, you should connect each proxy server to each of the subnets and configure DHCP redundantly as you previously described. You should also implement two DCHP servers, each with scopes for each subnet. Use the 80/20 design rule for balancing scope distribution of addresses between the two DHCP servers. Finally, you should configure the clients with multiple default gateways.

Lesson 4 Review

1. You are designing a DHCP strategy for a small network composed of three sub-nets. Subnets A, B, and C are connected to one router that is RFC-1542 compliant. Subnet B, the largest subnet containing the most DHCP clients, also houses the DHCP Server. The other two subnets do not have a DHCP server on them. How many DHCP Relay Agents would you need for all workstations to be able to receive an IP address from the DHCP Server?

   None. The IP router is RFC-1542 compliant, which means the router is configured as a DHCP relay agent. Another way to say this is that the router is BOOTP compliant.

2. If you choose to use only one DHCP Server in a routed network, what are some of the things you should consider?

   You should consider either using DHCP relay agents for the various subnets that will not contain the DHCP server, or ensuring that the routers on the network are RFC-1542 compliant. You should also be concerned whether or not the server has the hardware requirements to support its users.

3. List three factors you might want to consider when choosing the computer that will run the DHCP service.

   The three factors to consider are multiple CPUs, high-performance hard drives, and multiple NICs.

Case Scenario Exercise

1. What private IP address class would you use for this network infrastructure? How many subnets would be required in the Chicago offices?

   The Class A and Class B private IP addresses would allow you to create the required number of subnets and host IDs. Chicago needs 1,100 hosts, which breaks down to four subnets with 30s0 host addresses for each. Remember, the IT manager does not want more than 300 hosts per subnet. If you used 10.0.0.0/16 as your IP address/mask, you could create 256 subnets, each having approximately 65,000 host computers. A 10.0.0.0/24 would allow for the creation of up to 65,536 subnets, each containing 254 host addresses.

   If you used the Class B private address 172.16.0.1/24, you could create 256 subnets with each subnet having 254 host IDs. This would leave plenty of room for growth.

2. How could you design this network so that external users could access the Web server while minimizing the risk of an attack on your company's internal network?

   A perimeter network should be created that houses the Web server and e-mail servers.

3. If a perimeter network was created for the scenario described above, what net-work components could you use to protect both the perimeter network and the company's internal network?

   You could place a firewall between the Internet and the perimeter network, as well as a firewall in front of your company's internal network. In this way, an intruder would have to get through two firewalls before reaching your network. Also, an IDS could be placed outside the perimeter network and the company's internal network, which would warn of any intrusions to either system.

9 Designing Internet Connectivity

Exam Objectives in this Chapter:

- Design Internet connectivity for a company

Why This Chapter Matters

In Chapter 8, "Designing a Network and Routing Infrastructure," you recall, many companies chose to use private Internet protocol (IP) addressing for their network to save on the cost of issuing public IP addresses to all of their nodes. Private IP addressing is an efficient and inexpensive solution, but using private IP address network identities (IDs) prevents users from having direct access to the Internet. In these cases, some form of translation must take place in the network that converts the private IP addresses into public IP addresses that are routable and therefore enable Internet connectivity.

This chapter gives you an overview of the technology that translates and maps the private IP addresses a company uses to yield a public address that is routable over the Internet. You'll see how Network Address Translation (NAT) functions and learn how to design a NAT strategy for your company.

Lessons in this Chapter:

Before You Begin

To complete this chapter, make sure you are familiar with the concepts described in Chapter 1, "Introduction to Active Directory and Network Infrastructure."

Lesson 1: Identifying Redundancy Requirements

Just as it is important to have redundancy using Redundant Array of Inexpensive Disks (RAID) to protect your file system and data files, you might need to protect your connectivity to various parts of your network infrastructure. If there is only one way to get to the Internet or to your network resources, this can later prove to be a problem if that one way becomes unavailable.

After this lesson, you will be able to

- Describe the various links that provide redundancy.
- Identify various connection types available.

Estimated lesson time: 20 minutes

Creating a Redundant Infrastructure

When you design a system that gives your company access to the Internet, you might want to consider having more than one way to connect to the Internet, especially if your company relies on this connectivity to do business. However, just as a security professional would not spend $50,000 to protect a company's data that is worth $5,000, you should consider the cost of your redundant system as it relates to the value of downtime or the inability to connect to the Internet.

For example, if a company must wait several hours while the Internet service provider (ISP) repairs a downed Domain Name System (DNS) server, would that downtime create a hardship for the company that could affect its financial viability? Could the company lose Internet connectivity and without losing money to the extent that it would cause a financial hardship?

Companies that do thousands of transactions per minute over the Internet, such as investment trading companies or retail companies that sell large quantities of goods, might warrant the creation of redundant systems. Such a company would not only require the network infrastructure be protected with redundant systems but might also require redundant power systems. Government agencies might require gas-powered generators that would kick in if the public power supply experienced a blackout or brownout. Before designing redundancy into your connectivity design, ask yourself the following questions:

- **Is redundancy required?**   If your company does not require connectivity to the Internet to do its business, you can spend your information technology (IT) budget in other areas. You might need to create redundancy of your hard disks or computer systems (clustering) more than you need to concern yourself with redundant links or routers that will be needed in case of a failure.

- **How long can the company tolerate downtime?**   If your company does require Internet connectivity, how long can the company do without it? Five seconds? Five minutes? Five hours? This is an important question that must be addressed and brought to the table with management. Do not wait until connectivity is unavailable before posing the question to management; it might be too late. Wall Street companies that trade stocks using the Internet might be allowed 1.5 seconds of downtime, whereas a company selling flowers might be able to lose its connectivity for several hours and incur little or no financial loss.

- **What is the cost to the company if downtime occurs?**   It is very important that you can quantify the cost associated with lost Internet connectivity. That is, how much would the company lose for each minute remote users or company employees couldn't connect to the Internet? This can be very difficult to quantify, especially if the company is not selling services using the Internet. If you are using the Internet to sell services, you should be able to get at least a daily average of the company's earning from Internet sales. Of course, the revenue earned might not be from immediate sales, but from future revenue earned from the company's Internet presence.

- **Will downtime cause a loss of customers?**   It definitely can. For example, a company's absence from the Internet for several days can prompt potential clients to remove that company from their Favorites Web page. Most Internet shoppers move on to a new site when they have to wait more than several seconds for a Web page to display. Having to wait several minutes, or even hours, could prove disastrous.

- **What internal network services, if any, rely on the Internet connection?**   For example, do remote users access internal resources across a VPN? If it becomes unavailable, this can essentially prevent employees from doing their jobs.

- **What is the associated cost if there is no redundant system?**   Calculating the hourly wage of each remote employee, including the benefit package costs (health, vacation, sick leave, and so on), shows that lost wages can be considerable. It can be more difficult to quantify the possible loss of sales due to the inability of a sales representative to close a sale because of the downtime. In any event, you must attempt to get as accurate an assessment as possible to help you determine if adding an additional Internet connection is financially prudent.

- **Which connections already offer redundancy?**   If remote users are connecting to your company's resources using the Internet—that is, by a virtual private network (VPN)—is there any other means of connection if the Internet becomes unavailable? (VPNs are covered in detail in Chapter 10, "Designing a Remote Access Strategy.") A VPN uses the Internet as its medium to send and receive data throughout your company's network infrastructure. The question here is, if there were no contingencies in place, and the ISP ceased to provide that connectivity, would there be another way to get to that data? Or, if the company leased a Frame Relay connection, would there be a redundant link if that Frame Relay link became unavailable? In many cases, employees can go home and access the Internet from there. And don't forget, if e-mail is down, a telephone can still be used.

Assessing Internet Service Providers

Many companies rely on their ISP to provide the means of connectivity for all their users. In fact, the ISP, for many small companies, is the only infrastructure in place that enables users and customers to access the company's resources. Virtual private networks (VPNs) are a cost-effective method of making network resources available for outsiders and insiders alike, but there is a hidden cost associated with it: fear of the unknown.

Relying on the uptime of an ISP for sales and electronic communications can be a high risk for any company. At one time, Internet service providers popped up all over the country as quickly as dotcoms. Some disappeared just as quickly as they appeared. This means that you must do your homework when you design your Internet connectivity and put your company's reliance on a particular ISP strategy.

Before selecting an ISP for the implementation of your VPN or connectivity to the Internet, consider the following:

- How is the ISP connected to its peers?

- Does the vendor offer your company any guarantees or service-level agreements? For example, do they guarantee 99 percent uptime? How do they measure this uptime? What is the penalty if they don't meet their guaranteed uptime?

- Does your ISP offer any security features, such as intrusion-detection systems, or firewalls? For example, some ISPs offer only VPNs using Point-to-Point Tunneling Protocol (PPTP) with a lower level of encryption, whereas another might offer Layer 2 Tunneling Protocol (L2TP) with Internet protocol security (IPSec) protection.

- How does the ISP or vendor handling your network connectivity monitor your usage? Are you given reports showing the daily usage or weekly usage of bandwidth or network resources?

- Is more than one vendor involved in the connection to the Internet? For example, is one vendor responsible for the physical link (T-1 link) and an ISP responsible for connecting to the Internet? If so, how do the companies get along? If there are inherent problems between the two companies, your company might well be affected. In some cities, companies are responsible for both the hardware and cabling infrastructure as well as connectivity to the Internet.

There are different connection methods your provider will offer your company: circuit switched, lease line, and packet switched.

Circuit switched connections include:

- Modems, which have a maximum speed of 56 Kbps.

- Integrated Services Digital Network (ISDN), which has connection speeds ranging from 64 Kbps to 2048 Mbps.

Leased lines include:

- Digital Subscriber Line (DSL), which is available in both asynchronous and synchronous options. Asynchronous offers a higher download speed than synchronous. Speeds here range from 144 Kbps to 1.544 Mbps and can go even higher, depending on your company's location.

- T-carrier lines, which are available in North America, are created by combining multiple 64-Kbps channels. A T-1 link consists of 24 64-Kbps channels, for a total link speed of 1.544 Mbps. A T-2 link has a speed of 6.312 Mbps, T-3, has a link speed of 44.736 Mbps, and a T-4 link has a speed of 274.176 Mbps. Your provider can also offer your company a fractional T-1 line, which would be in increments of 64 Kbps.

- E-carrier lines, which are available in Europe, are also created using multiple 64-Kbps channels. A fractional E-1 line would be the same as a fractional T-1 line, except that an E-1 link has a speed of 2.048 Mbps. E-2 links have a speed of 8.448 Mbps.

Packet switched connections include:

- X.25, which was designed for use over unreliable analog telephone connections. Speeds range from 9600 bps to 1.544 Mbps and faster.

- Frame relay, which has available speeds ranging from 56 Kbps to 1.544 Mbps.

- Asynchronous Transfer Mode (ATM), which has available speeds ranging from 25 Mbps to 622 Mbps.

- Virtual Private Network (VPN), which requires an existing routed connection between two private networks.

Many providers will not support all these technologies, so it is important that you choose one that will meet your company's needs.

Lesson Review

The following questions are intended to reinforce key information presented in this lesson. If you are unable to answer a question, review the lesson materials and try the question again. You can find answers to the questions in the "Questions and Answers" section at the end of this chapter.

1. You are the administrator for a medium-sized company that has just begun using the Internet to market its fishing lures. Most of its sales are from catalog orders that are directly mailed to customers who have purchased fishing supplies from various fishing supply stores throughout the United States. Your company uses Digital Subscriber Line (DSL) and Network Address Translation (NAT) to connect to the Internet. You have heard that redundancy should be built into a system connecting to the Internet and that a duplicate server should be installed on the network as well as an alternate way of connecting to the Internet. Prior to implementing redundancy for your network, what steps should you take?

    _____

    _____

2. You are the network administrator for a small software development company. The company relies on its ability to connect to the Internet for more than 95 percent of its business transactions. Your network design consists of one router, one switch, one network access server (NAS) configured as a NAT server, two Microsoft Windows Server 2003 Standard Edition servers, and 32 workstations running Microsoft Windows XP Professional. Employees connect to the Internet by using NAT and a DSL connection. Which network component in this scenario can be a point of failure?

    _____

    _____

3. You are the network administrator for a small real estate company that needs to engage an ISP to implement network services. Your company is also considering implementing a VPN. What criteria would you use in deciding which ISP to choose?

    _____

    _____

Lesson Summary

- When designing a system that enables your company to have access to the Internet, you might want to consider having more than one link to connect to the Internet, especially if your company relies on the connectivity to do business. Relying on the uptime of an ISP for sales and electronic communications can be a high risk for any company.

- Before designing redundancy into your connectivity design, you should verify that redundancy is required. If your company does not require connectivity to the Internet to do its business, you can spend your IT budget in other areas.

- You should determine the cost to the company if downtime occurs. It is very important that you be able to quantify the cost associated with downtime as it relates to Internet connectivity problems. That is, how much could the company afford to lose for each minute remote users or company employees cannot connect to the Internet?

- In designing redundancy into your network, you should identify any hardware components that might become points of failure to your network because they are the only means by which users can do their jobs. For example, if the dial-in server available for remote users to connect to the company's network becomes unavailable, what will happen?

- Before selecting an ISP for the implementation of your VPN or connectivity to the Internet, you should consider how reliable the ISP's Internet uplink is, how stable the vendor is financially, and whether the vendor offers your company any guarantees or service-level agreements, such as 99 percent uptime. You should also determine if your ISP offers any security features, such as intrusion detection systems or firewalls, and if the ISP gives your company reports showing daily or weekly usage of bandwidth that will help you plan for growth.

Lesson 2: Identifying Bandwidth Requirements

Processors seem to be getting faster by the minute. Moore's Law, predicting in 1965 that the clock speed of a central processing unit (CPU) would exponentially increase over the next 20 years, was accurate almost to the megahertz. Memory, another hardware component that has increased at a phenomenal rate, is not the bottleneck in our high-tech world of today. It seems that bandwidth is still our biggest liability; we don't have enough of it. In this lesson, you look at bandwidth and how your design must take into account the bandwidth requirements to make your connectivity to the Internet productive.

After this lesson, you will be able to

- Identify the bandwidth requirements of your network infrastructure.
- Describe the bandwidth usage for various computer technologies.

Estimated lesson time: 20 minutes

Obtaining Bandwidth Requirements

Now that you have designed redundancy into your network infrastructure, you need to be certain that the available bandwidth is enough for your company. After all, if you have the correct amount of servers and links but there is not enough bandwidth to send the data back and forth, you have not properly designed your infrastructure. This section requires some basic math skills, so sharpen those lead pencils.

Bandwidth Requirements for Other Services

It would be nice if all you had to worry about was the bandwidth requirements for the services you need to implement, but in the real world, you will most likely be sharing your company's available bandwidth with other services. For example, there is a good chance that e-mail will also be running across the network link joining those network segments together. Depending on the type of e-mail sent, bandwidth use can vary. Web browsing is one of the biggest hogs of bandwidth, so if bandwidth is an issue, you might want to limit its use.

The average Microsoft Outlook client uses anywhere from 13 MB to 25 MB of bandwidth on a daily basis. If you multiply 20 MB by 100 users and divide the number by 8 for the hours per day, you can see that approximately 2 billion bits of data per hour, or approximately 500,000 bits per second, will traverse your link. If you use a T-1 link to connect the site to the mail server, this would mean that more than 30 percent of the use would be for e-mail alone.

As you can see, it is very important that you make a thorough analysis of the type of traffic that will use any links. There is overhead associated with Ethernet that should also be discussed. A 10-Mbps link does not mean 10 Mbps of data will be able to traverse the wire. In fact, because of the noise and collisions associated with Ethernet, as much as 40 percent of the bandwidth can be lost on non-switched LANs. As a result, most network engineers estimate only 6 Mbps is available for sending data. Similarly, the stated speed of an Internet connection is the theoretical limit, rather than the practical limit. The actual throughput will be lower, though the overhead varies with the connection type. So, you might want to answer the following questions when examining bandwidth requirements for your network infrastructure.

- Will e-mail operate along this link? As previously stated, e-mail can use up much of your available bandwidth. Be sure to account for this usage when determining how much bandwidth is available on a link.

- Will any traffic related to Dynamic Host Configuration Protocol (DHCP) and DNS updating use this link? If so, consider running both of these services on the same server.

- Will Web browsing or other real-time tasks use this link? If your company uses graphical applications or a database application that requires the transferring of large data files, you can expect to use a great deal of your bandwidth. Depending on how these programs create a load on your network, you might see a loss of performance.

- Is Voice over IP (VoIP) using this link? VoIP technology integrates data and voice communication traffic into a single network. This can help reduce the cost of operating two separate network systems: voice and data. However, additional traffic will traverse your current infrastructure and will need to be taken into account when calculating the available bandwidth on your links.

You might consider upgrading the link if too much bandwidth is being used by these additional services running on your network. You might also want to add an additional router at each location in your site so you will be protected in the event of a router failure.

Virtual Private Networks (VPNs)

Virtual private networks (VPNs) are covered in more detail in Chapter 10. Here, however, you look at the bandwidth requirements for using a VPN. When calculating bandwidth, you need to know how many users will need to access the network. You should also determine if the VPN would be used only for certain business transactions and not for general traffic that doesn't require additional security. If remote users do not need to send data over the network securely, consider using another pipe or connection link. Ask yourself the following questions:

- Will other services use this VPN connection?

- Will VoIP, e-mail, or Web servers use any of this VPN bandwidth? If yes, how much bandwidth will these services require?

Just as airlines overbook flights, many ISPs oversubscribe bandwidth. You should verify if your ISP oversubscribes bandwidth so you can get a truer picture of how much bandwidth is available. By overbooking bandwidth, the ISP is counting on customers not using the bandwidth they acquire; in the same way, airlines count on some customers not using their plane tickets.

Increasing Available Bandwidth

Let's face it. Simply stating that upgrading a T-1 link to a T-3 link would solve your bandwidth problems is easier said than done. The cost associated with upgrading your infrastructure might not even be an option. There are some ways you can streamline your current infrastructure so that you can maximize the bandwidth you now have. They are:

- **Combining network services** By combining network services on the same server, you can help reduce some network traffic, thereby giving you more available bandwidth. For example, a Web server will not need to send authentication requests to an Active Directory domain controller located across a VPN if the same server is running both services. Consider this if your links begin to get saturated with too much traffic.

- **Analyzing your network traffic** Look at the traffic your network transmits during peak hours and determine if that traffic can be transmitted when little bandwidth usage occurs. For example, employees can be directed to perform certain transfers of data during nonpeak usage hours.

- **Compressing data on WAN links** You might want to consider compressing data that traverses your company's wide area network (WAN) links and filter unnecessary traffic, such as streaming, file sharing, and non-work-related Web site access. You can also configure your routers to prioritize specific traffic, such as HTTP or Telnet, to be processed before other traffic, such as SMTP and FTP.

Lesson Review

The following questions are intended to reinforce key information presented in this lesson. If you are unable to answer a question, review the lesson materials and try the question again. You can find answers to the questions in the "Questions and Answers" section at the end of this chapter.

1. You are the network administrator for a large retail clothing store that has implemented a remote access strategy. You need to have 100 employees remotely connect to the company's database server to obtain pricing information. The sales representatives will be using 56 Kbps modems to connect over the Internet to the server running a customized Web-based application. What concerns or issues will you need to address before implementing a solution?

   _____

   _____

2. As the network administrator for a medium-sized photography business, you have been receiving numerous calls from users claiming that the network is slow. The only change to the infrastructure is the telephony system recently installed. Your manager has decided to use VoIP to save on the current PBX system. Why would a new phone system slow down your network?

   _____

   _____

3. In designing your network infrastructure, is it important which services run on a particular computer? Explain your answer.

   _____

   _____

Lesson Summary

- Just as airlines overbook flights, most ISPs oversubscribe bandwidth. By oversubscribing bandwidth, the ISP is counting on all of their customers not simultaneously using 100 percent of the bandwidth they are allocated, in the same way airlines count on some customers not using their plane tickets.

- You will most likely be sharing your company's available bandwidth among many network services. It is very important that a thorough analysis be made of the type of traffic that will be using any links.

- When calculating the bandwidth requirements for a VPN, you should know how many users will need to access the network, if VoIP, e-mail, or Web servers will also use the VPN bandwidth, and how much bandwidth these additional services will require.

- You should look at the traffic your network is transmitting during peak hours, and determine if that traffic can be transmitted during periods of low bandwidth usage. For example, employees can be directed to perform certain transfers of data during nonpeak usage hours.

Lesson 3: Understanding NAT

There is no question that the ability of a company of any size to connect to the Internet is mandatory, not optional. For this reason, it's important for a network engineer to be able to design an Internet connectivity solution for a company's network infrastructure. Network Address Translation (NAT) is a protocol that enables a private network to do just that: connect to the Internet. This lesson includes an overview of the NAT protocol and the strategies that might be used to implement a secure NAT solution for this Internet connectivity.

After this lesson, you will be able to

- Describe and understand the function of the NAT protocol.
- Describe the limitations of NAT.

Estimated lesson time: 20 minutes

NAT Overview

Network Address Translation (NAT) protocol makes it possible for smaller companies using a private addressing scheme to connect to resources on the Internet. Remember that the IP addresses in Table 9-1 are routable internally only for a company or home network and are not routable over the Internet.

Table 9-1   Private Network Addressing

Class	Private IP Network ID/Mask	IP Address Range
A	10.0.0.0/8	10.0.0.1–10.255.255.254
B	172.16.0.0/12	172.16.0.1–172.16.31.254
C	192.168.0.0/16	192.168.0.1–192.168.255.254

If any node, or workstation, is configured with one of the IP addresses described here, it will not be able to connect to the outside world—the Internet.

A Windows Server 2003 server configured with Routing and Remote Access or Internet Connection Sharing can act as a NAT server. Internet Connection Sharing is recommended only for very small networks, however, and most organizations should implement NAT using Routing and Remote Access. (See Figure 9-1.)

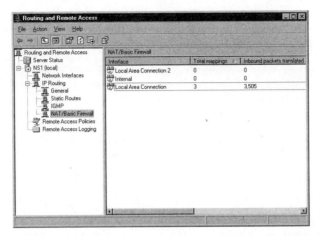

Figure 9-1   Use the Routing and Remote Access console to configure NAT.

NAT translates private IP addresses and the Transmission Control Protocol/User Datagram Protocol (TCP/UDP) port numbers associated with them into public IP addresses. It also assigns a unique port number to the session. Each client computer on the private network is mapped to one public IP address assigned by the Internet Network Information Center (InterNIC) or the company's ISP and assigned a unique port number generated by the NAT server. This mapping enables the NAT server to send packets back to the correct workstations. Lesson 4 examines the possibility of multiple public IP addresses associated with private IP addresses. For now, let's look only at multiple private IP addresses being mapped to one public address.

See Table 9-2 below for all the information stored in the mapping table of a Windows Server 2003 server.

Table 9-2   Network Address Translation Session Mapping Table

Table Value	Description
Protocol	Protocol used to transmit packet. Either TCP or UDP.
Direction	Outbound or inbound traffic.
Private Address	IP address of internal computer.
Private Port	Private port number assigned to the client's session.
Public Address	Public IP address assigned by the ISP or InterNIC that is routable.
Public Port	Public port number assigned to the session.
Remote Address	The remote IP address the client is attempting to access. If the client is connecting to a Web site, this is usually the IP address of the DNS server that services clients on the internal network.
Remote Port	The port number assigned to the session. If this is the connection to the remote DNS server, the port number will be port 53.

Table 9-2 Network Address Translation Session Mapping Table (Continued)

Table Value	Description
Idle Time	Used to keep track of entries in the mapping table. The entry will be removed if no traffic is being sent over the connection for a certain length of time. As new traffic is received by a client, the idle time is reset.

Figure 9-2 illustrates a server running the NAT protocol in a small business environment. The NAT server maps all of the private IP addresses to the public IP address, 66.x.130.77, which can connect to the Internet. The following steps are initiated:

1. The client attempts to connect to a public IP address from the private internal network.

2. The client's IP stack creates an IP packet with a destination IP address the client is attempting to connect to, a source IP address of 192.168.8.2, a destination TCP or UDP port, and a source port.

3. Because the destination IP address is not located on the local subnet, the packet is forwarded to the client's default gateway address, which is the NAT server.

4. NAT translates the source IP address of the client's packet to the external IP address, 66.x.130.77, maps the TCP or UDP source port, places this mapping information in a table, and then sends the packet over the Internet.

5. The responding computer sends a response back to the NAT server, which uses the mapping table to translate the public IP address, and the external port fields, included in the IP header, to the private IP address and internal port of the client.

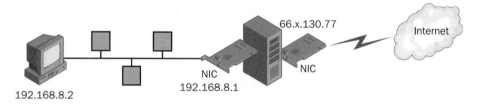

Figure 9-2 NAT forwards packets from a private network to the public Internet.

Shortage of IP Addresses

NAT was created as a temporary solution to a shortage of IP addresses available to handle the large number of users requesting them from the InterNIC. At one time, IP addresses were plentiful. Presently, users are connecting to the Internet by the millions, causing IP addresses to become scarcer. Because most users are using Internet Protocol version 4 (IPv4), NAT is still one of the solutions to the shortage of IP addresses.

Internet Protocol version 6 (IPv6), previously named IPng, short for Internet Protocol Next Generation, will solve this problem by theoretically increasing the 4 billion available addresses in IPv4 to more than one undecillion IP addresses available in IPv6. For those of us who are math illiterates, an undecillion is 1036, which is defined by mathematicians as a "large" number. The format of an IPv6 number is also quite different from what you are used to seeing with IPv4. For example, an IPv6 number could look something like the following:

1AB1:0:0:ABCD:DCBA:1234:5678:9ABC

As you can see, this will take some getting used to, but will make the requirement for NAT and other IP address translating programs unnecessary. Windows Server 2003 Family supports IPv6, and it can be installed by selecting Properties for any local area connection and clicking Install. After selecting Protocol and clicking the Add button, click Microsoft TCP/IP version 6, and select OK.

Enhanced Security

NAT should not be used in place of a firewall, even though it does enhance security of your internal network by hiding the IP address scheme from outsiders. For example, as shown in Figure 9-2, only internal network users will be aware of the 192.168.0.0/24 subnet. Outside users would see only the public IP address if they were to view the header information of an IP packet arriving from the private network. The NAT server forwards packets from Internet-based users to the computers on the company's private network. The NAT server drops packets that do not have a matching port number in the session mapping table. This also enhances the security of the internal network.

Limitations of NAT

The implementation of NAT included with Routing and Remote Access supports the IP protocol only and cannot perform address translation on the following:

- Simple Network Management Protocol (SNMP)
- Lightweight Directory Access Protocol (LDAP)
- Component Object Model (COM)
- Distributed Component Object Model (DCOM)
- Kerberos version 5
- Microsoft Remote Procedure Call (RPC)

Because Active Directory directory service uses Kerberos version 5 protocol, domain controllers cannot replicate through a NAT server. Microsoft Proxy Server can be used in place of NAT where applications not supported by NAT need to be implemented.

NAT Editors

Unlike Microsoft Windows 2000, Windows Server 2003 supports L2TP/IPSec VPN connections to work with NAT. However, if an application, such as the File Transfer Protocol (FTP) Port command, stores IP addresses or port information in its own header, a NAT editor is needed. Windows Server 2003 NAT includes the following NAT editors:

- File Transfer Protocol (FTP)
- Internet Control Message Protocol (ICMP)
- Point-to-Point to the Internet
- Direct Play out to the Internet
- Lightweight Directory Access Protocol (LDAP)-based Internet Locator Service (ILS) registration out to the Internet

NAT Traversal Technology

When a network application uses embedded IP addresses that NAT cannot translate in its headers or requires the use of inbound packets not associated with an existing connection, problems arise. NAT Traversal technology was created so that network applications could detect the presence of a NAT server on a network segment. Once an application detects the presence of a NAT device, it can configure the port mappings and dynamically open and close the ports without user intervention.

Lesson Review

The following questions are intended to reinforce key information presented in this lesson. If you are unable to answer a question, review the lesson materials and try the question again. You can find answers to the questions in the "Questions and Answers" section at the end of this chapter.

1. Several employees from your company who work out of their homes have asked you if it would be possible to have multiple computers share the DSL connections they are using for Internet connectivity. What concerns or issues would you need to address before implementing a NAT solution?

_____

_____

2. You are configuring a client workstation using a private IP address to connect to the Internet. You decide that NAT would be a good solution and are now sitting in front of the user's workstation. Each of the workstations in the subnet uses a static IP address. How would you configure this workstation to connect to a NAT server located on the subnet?

_____

_____

3. After implementing NAT at your organization, a client calls and says she is not able to connect to the Internet but she is still able to run a database application that is located on a NetWare 4.11 server. What could be causing this problem?

_____

_____

Lesson Summary

- Network Address Translation (NAT) is a protocol that enables a private network to connect to the Internet. A mapping table is created on the NAT server that maps all internal IP addresses with port numbers and the external IP address chosen by the company.

- NAT was created as a temporary solution to the problem of a shortage of IP addresses available to handle the large number of users requesting them from the InterNIC.

- The NAT server forwards packets from Internet-based users to the computers on the company's private network. The NAT server drops packets that do not have a matching port number in the session mapping table.

- NAT Traversal technology enables an application to detect that a NAT server is being used on the network, automatically configures the port mappings, and dynamically opens and closes the ports without user intervention.

Lesson 4: Designing a NAT Strategy

This lesson helps you understand the importance of NAT server options and placement and looks at the questions you need to answer prior to designing a NAT strategy. Securing the NAT solution you have chose is also covered.

After this lesson, you will be able to

- Create the conceptual design of a NAT strategy.
- Determine NAT Server options and placement.
- Secure your NAT solution.

Estimated lesson time: 25 minutes

Creating the Conceptual Design

In designing a NAT strategy for your company's network infrastructure, you must consider the following:

- Whether a NAT solution is the right choice for both the size of the business and the needs of the users

- Whether there are any applications or protocols running on the network that will not be supported by NAT

- Which interfaces will be configured with private or public IP addresses

- Whether NAT will be used to issue IP addresses (DHCP allocator) and DNS resolution requests (DNS Proxy)

- Whether your NAT solution will use filters to restrict access to the Internet from your private internal network users

- Whether your NAT solution will enable outside users to access network resources located in your private network

- If your NAT design will contain multiple Internet connections for redundancy

- Which servers will be configured as NAT servers, and if they will be dedicated to perform this function only

NAT is not always the best method for a company to connect to the Internet. In fact, because NAT did not support standards-based network layer security, it was only recommended for small, nonrouted networks that did not have high security requirements. For example, L2TP with IPSec could not pass through a NAT device. Presently, there is an update to IPSec called IPSec NAT-Traversal (IPSec NAT-T), which enables IPSec packets to pass through NAT devices. Also, NAT should be used only on networks using a private IP network ID. After all, if users are configured with public IP addresses, NAT is not needed.

Rather than statically configuring all of the client workstations with private IP addresses or using a separate DHCP server to issue IP addresses, NAT can be configured to issue any DHCP-enabled client a private IP address. (See Figure 9-3.)

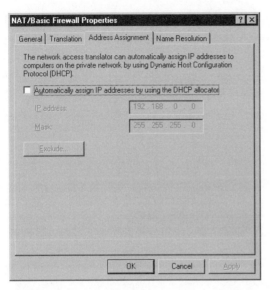

Figure 9-3   NAT can be used to assign DHCP addresses.

You can also configure the client workstations to use the name resolution feature of NAT, DNS proxies, which forwards requests made by the NAT client to a DNS server on the private network or one located across the Internet. Figure 9-4 illustrates the screen used to configure this information.

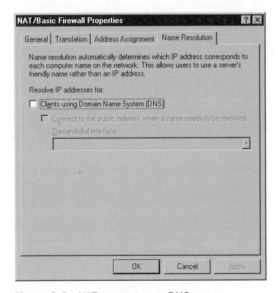

Figure 9-4   NAT can act as a DNS proxy.

NAT Servers

The server you select to be a NAT server is just as important as the one you select to be a Windows Internet Naming Service (WINS) server or a DHCP server. There are many considerations that need to be used in this process. In your design, you should consider

- Server placement.
- Server performance.
- Server interface configuration.

Server Placement

When designing your NAT solution, the NAT server must be placed on the private network and contain two network adapter cards: one configured with the external IP address that connects to the Internet and the other with the internal private IP addresses connecting the internal private network workstations.

Server Performance

For optimal server performance, consider using a dedicated server that does nothing but NAT. This prevents other applications from consuming the system resources and slowing down the system. Also, this reduces the chances of another application causing the system to have to shut down due to programmatic problems.

Server Interface Configuration

Once you have developed the conceptual design, it's time to configure the NAT server's interfaces. If you right-click the NAT server's interfaces while in the Routing and Remote Access console, you can easily configure the adapter cards for your NAT server. Figure 9-5 illustrates the local network interface that is connected to the private network.

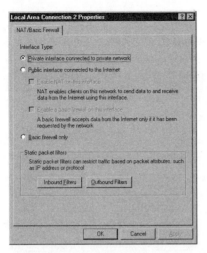

Figure 9-5   To configure NAT, you must specify the internal and external interfaces.

Securing Your NAT Solution

After designing your NAT solution, you should determine if your solution is secure or if some extra precautions should be made. As mentioned in Lesson 3, NAT is not a replacement for a firewall or proxy server. It does, however, offer some features that can add some protection to your internal network.

Inbound Filters

Inbound filters enable an administrator to filter traffic based on the IP address of the workstation that is attempting to enter the internal network. For example, you can enable NAT to only allow traffic that is coming from a designated network.

Outbound Filters

Outbound filters enable an administrator to filter the traffic that is outbound to the Internet. For example, the administrator can restrict traffic originating from a particular IP address from accessing the Internet. Outbound filters are useful for blocking traffic from specific applications, such as instant messaging services.

Access to Private Network Resources

Sometimes you might want outside users to be able to access a Web server located on your private network. Because the private IP network ID is not visible to users connecting from the Internet, an administrator can map external public IP addresses and ports with private IP addresses and private ports. You can implement this through the following.

- **Special Ports**   A special port is a static mapping of a public IP address and port number to a private IP address and port number. Special ports are used to map Internet users to resources located on your private internal network. For example, you can create a Web server on your private network that can be accessed from the Internet. Figure 9-6 shows the Services And Ports dialog box, which is reached by right-clicking the public interface object and selecting Properties from the menu. The Web server must be configured with a static IP address, subnet mask, default gateway, and DNS server IP address, which are selected from the private IP address range of the internal network.

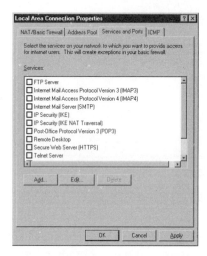

Figure 9-6   Internal services can be shared on the public Internet with NAT.

- **Address Pools**   An address pool is a range of public IP addresses allocated to your company by an ISP. For example, instead of using just one public IP address to access the Internet, you might have a range of IP addresses to choose from. If the range of addresses has a power of 2, such as, 2, 4, 8, 16, and so forth, you can express the range using an IP address and subnet mask. For example, if you are allocated 8 public IP addresses: 192.168.1.32–192.168.1.39, you can express this range as: 192.168.1.32 with a subnet mask of 255.255.255.248. By clicking the Add button in the Address Pool dialog box, as shown in Figure 9-7, you can enter a range of public IP addresses assigned to you by your ISP.

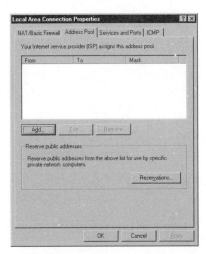

Figure 9-7   NAT can use multiple public IP addresses.

Real World   Too Many Open Ports!

As was discussed in Chapter 8, a perimeter network is a small network segment that is accessible by users outside your network. If you plan on opening ports to make a Web server or mail server available to Internet users, consider placing those servers in a perimeter network. The more ports you open for outsiders to access your company resources, the higher the risks of attack to your network infrastructure. A firewall that has too many ports open can be worse than no firewall at all because having a firewall in place can lead to a false sense of security.

Exam Tip   Be sure you understand that NAT can allow inbound connections to access resources located on your private network segment by using special ports and configuring the resource with a private static IP address, subnet mask, and default gateway.

Practice: Designing a NAT Strategy

In this practice, you will create a NAT Strategy for Northwind Traders. If you are unable to answer a question, review the lesson materials and try the question again. You can find answers to the questions in the "Questions and Answers" section at the end of this chapter.

Scenario

Northwind Traders manufactures a line of network appliances designed to help companies improve their data transmission capabilities. Northwind Traders currently uses a Microsoft Windows NT 4.0 master domain model. In recent years, the company has undergone significant growth and expansion. The company expects substantial growth over the next three years, including growth in market share, revenue, and number of employees. In addition to opening two new offices, executive management has committed to implementing a new Windows Server 2003 Active Directory design to meet the current and future needs of the company.

The following table shows the geographical locations, the departments residing in each location, and the number of users in each of the locations.

Location	Departments Represented	Number of Users
Paris	Headquarters (HQ) Management staff Finance Sales Marketing Production Research Development Information Technology (IT)	2,000
Los Angeles	Sales Marketing Finance IT	1,000
Atlanta	Customer Service Customer Support Training	750
Glasgow, Scotland	Research Development Sustained Engineering IT	750
Sydney, Australia	Consulting Production Sales Finance	500

Practice Questions

Based on the scenario, answer the following questions regarding the NAT strategy for Northwind Traders.

1. The Glasgow office maintains separate domain names and public IP addresses for each of its departments. They are considering implementing NAT. What are their options for securing their NAT solution?

_____

_____

2. The Paris office has just upgraded its servers to Windows Server 2003, its messaging system to Exchange Server 2000, and many of its clients to the mail client Outlook 2003. Outlook 2003 has the ability to connect to an Exchange mail server over RPC. The company needs remote users to be able to use this functionality. Would NAT be capable of performing the address translation for this service? Why or why not?

Lesson Review

The following questions are intended to reinforce key information presented in this lesson. If you are unable to answer a question, review the lesson materials and try the question again. You can find answers to the questions in the "Questions and Answers" section at the end of this chapter.

1. You are the administrator of a small private company that is doing business with the federal government. Security, as well as the need of your users to access sensitive files located in your private network through the Internet, is a major concern. You are presently considering implementing NAT as one of the solutions to this problem. Is NAT a good solution to this problem? Explain.

---

2. As the administrator for a small accounting firm, you have been asked to implement a system that would allow multiple users to access the Internet using one public IP address issued to the company by an ISP. You have decided that NAT would be the perfect solution to the problem at hand. How would you configure the NAT server to allow access to the Internet and also allocate IP addresses to the 25 employees of the company?

---

3. As an administrator of a small company, you want Internet users to be able to access your company's Web server. Because the private IP network ID is not visible to the Internet users, what can you do to enable the Internet users to access your Web server?

Lesson Summary

- In designing a NAT strategy for your company's network infrastructure, you must consider whether or not NAT is the right choice for both the size of the business and needs of the users. You must consider whether preexisting applications or protocols running on the network are supported by NAT.

- Server placement, server performance, and the configuration of the server interfaces are important considerations in your network design. The server you select to be a NAT server must be placed on the private network and contain two network adapter cards. For optimal server performance, consider using a dedicated server that does nothing but NAT.

- Securing a NAT solution can be done through inbound and outbound filters. Access to private network resources by Internet users can be implemented through the use of special ports and address pools.

Case Scenario Exercise

Review the following scenario and complete the questions.

Scenario

Contoso, Ltd., a software engineering company, has approximately 300 software engineers employed in a large office building located in Washington, D.C., and currently has seen drastic increases in its rental costs. Most of the software applications the company creates can be done remotely by its talented staff, and the company had previously experimented with software engineers working from home, with positive results.

Because of this increase in rental space costs, Contoso has decided to close its main office, which required a large retail space and parking facilities for its employees, and to implement home office configurations for its software engineers. Senior software engineers will have two Windows XP Professional workstations and a Windows Server 2003 server located in their residences, and junior software engineers will have one Windows XP Professional workstation with Internet access.

Geography

Contoso has decided to rent 10 smaller offices, which will each house 20 Windows XP Professional workstations and one Windows Server 2003 server, throughout various locations in Washington. These locations will be the hubs where senior software engineers will consolidate the work of all junior software engineers and their subordinates.

Network Infrastructure

The hub offices, which will need to connect to the Internet, should allow only network traffic from senior software engineers to enter the private network. Workstations will need to be configured to connect to the Internet using the DSL connection already connected to the Windows Server 2003 server. Each junior software engineer connects to the Internet using DSL or a cable modem.

Questions

Given the previous scenario, answer the following questions.

1. Several of the junior software engineers, working from home, have attempted to access resources located in one of the hub offices with no success. You check to see if there are any inbound filters configured for the server, and are told there are not. Why can't the junior software engineers access the internal network resources? What can you do to make it possible for them to access these resources?

_____

_____

2. You decide to deploy Active Directory by adding an additional Windows Server 2003 server to the internal network of each hub office. You run dcpromo on one of the servers and create a single forest. When you attempt to upgrade another Windows Server 2003 server located in a different hub office to join this forest, you are unable. Why?

_____

_____

3. After configuring each of the Windows Server 2003 servers as a NAT server, you have decided to make one of the servers, located in one of the hub offices, available only to a user with a private IP address of 10.1.1.112. Is this possible?

_____

_____

Chapter Summary

- When designing a system that enables your company to have access to the Internet, you might want to consider having more than one link to connect to the Internet, especially if your company relies on the connectivity to do business. Relying on the uptime of an ISP for sales and electronic communications can be a high risk for any company.

- Before designing redundancy into your connectivity design, you should verify that redundancy is required. If your company does not require connectivity to the Internet to do its business, you can spend your IT budget in other areas. You should also determine the cost to the company if downtime occurs. It is very important that you be able to quantify the cost associated with the downtime as it relates to Internet connectivity problems. That is, how much could the company afford to lose for each minute company employees cannot connect to the Internet?

- Before selecting an ISP for the implementation of your VPN or connectivity to the Internet, you should consider how reliable the ISP's peering connections are, how stable the vendor is financially, and whether or not the vendor offers your company any guarantees or service-level agreements such as 99 percent uptime. You should also determine if your ISP offers any security features such as intrusion detection systems, or firewalls, and whether the ISP gives your company reports showing the daily usage or weekly usage of bandwidth, so you can plan for growth.

- You will most likely be sharing your company's available bandwidth with other services. It is very important that a thorough analysis be made of the type of traffic that will be using any links.

- When calculating the bandwidth requirements for a VPN, you should know how many users will need to access the network if VoIP, e-mail, or Web servers will also use the VPN bandwidth, and how much bandwidth these additional services will require.

- You should look at the traffic your network is transmitting during peak hours and determine if that traffic can be transmitted during periods of time when little bandwidth usage is occurring. For example, employees can be directed to perform certain transfers of data during nonpeak usage hours.

- Network Address Translation (NAT) is a protocol that enables a private network to connect to the Internet. A mapping table is created on the NAT server that maps all internal IP addresses with port numbers and the external IP address issued by InterNIC or the ISP.

- NAT was created as a temporary solution to the problem of a shortage of IP addresses available to handle the large number of users requesting them from the InterNIC.

■ The NAT server forwards packets from Internet-based users to the computers on the company's private network. The NAT server drops packets that do not have a matching port number in the session mapping table.

■ NAT Traversal technology enables an application to detect that a NAT server is being used on the network, automatically configures the port mappings, and dynamically opens and closes the ports without user intervention.

■ In designing a NAT strategy for your company's network infrastructure, you must consider whether or not NAT is the right choice for both the size of the business and the needs of the users. You must consider whether preexisting applications or protocols running on the network are supported by NAT.

■ Server placement, server performance, and the configuration of the server interfaces are important considerations in your network design. The server you select to be a NAT server must be placed on the private network and must contain two network adapter cards. For optimal server performance, consider using a dedicated server that does nothing but NAT.

■ Securing a NAT solution can be done through inbound and outbound filters. Access to private network resources by Internet users can be implemented through the use of special ports and address pools.

Exam Highlights

Before taking the exam, review the key topics and terms that are presented in this chapter. You need to know this information.

Key Points

■ Before designing redundancy into your connectivity design, you should verify that redundancy is required. You should also determine the cost to the company if downtime occurs, for example, how much the company would lose for each minute company employees could not connect to the Internet.

■ In designing redundancy into your network, you should also identify any hardware components that might be points of failure to your network if they were to become unavailable because they are the only means by which users can do their jobs.

■ Before selecting an ISP for the implementation of your VPN or connectivity to the Internet, you should consider how reliable the ISP's peering connections are, how stable the vendor is financially, and whether or not the ISP offers your company any guarantees or service-level agreements. You should also determine if your ISP offers any security features such as intrusion detection systems or firewalls, and whether the ISP gives your company reports showing the daily usage or weekly usage of bandwidth.

- Just as airlines overbook flights, most ISPs oversubscribe bandwidth. By oversubscribing bandwidth, the ISP is counting on all of their customers not simultaneously using 100 percent of the bandwidth they are allocated, in the same way airlines count on some customers not using their plane tickets.

- When calculating the bandwidth requirements for a VPN, you should know how many users will need to access the network, if VoIP, e-mail, or Web servers will also use the VPN bandwidth, and how much bandwidth these additional services will require.

- Network Address Translation (NAT) is a protocol that enables a private network to connect to the Internet. Private IP network IDs 10.0.0.0 8, 172.16.0.0 /12, and 192.168.0.0 /16 are not able to connect to Internet resources unless they are translated to a public IP network ID.

- The NAT server drops packets that do not have a matching port number in the session mapping table.

- In designing a NAT strategy for your company's network infrastructure, you must consider whether or not NAT is the right choice for both the size of the business and the needs of the users.

- Securing your NAT solution can be done with inbound and outbound filters and the use of special ports and address pools.

Key Terms

Intrusion detection system (IDS)   Software that detects any suspicious network traffic entering or leaving a network and warns the user of a possible intrusion.

Virtual private network (VPN)   A private network that uses a public network as the medium to transfer data. Tunneling protocols are used to encrypt the data as it traverses through the public network.

Bandwidth   The range within a band of frequencies usually expressed in bits per second (bps).

Network Address Translation (NAT)   A Network Address Translation server is a device that translates IP packets and ports as they are forwarded through a network.

NAT Transversal Technology   A technology that enables network applications to detect the presence of NAT devices.

Inbound/Outbound Filters   Filters that can be configured on the NAT interfaces, which allow or disallow inbound or outbound traffic.

Special Port   Maps an inbound connection from an Internet user to a private address located on a private network.

Voice over IP (VoIP)   VoIP technology integrates data and voice communication traffic into a single network, allowing telephone calls to be placed over the Internet.

Questions and Answers

Page
9-6

Lesson 1 Review

1. You are the administrator for a medium-sized company that has just begun using the Internet to market its fishing lures. Most of its sales are from catalog orders that are directly mailed to customers who have purchased fishing supplies from various fishing supply stores throughout the United States. Your company uses Digital Subscriber Line (DSL) and Network Address Translation (NAT) to connect to the Internet. You have heard that redundancy should be built into a system connecting to the Internet and that a duplicate server should be installed on the network as well as an alternate way of connecting to the Internet. Prior to implementing redundancy for your network, what steps should you take?

Prior to implementing redundant links and servers, you should determine if the scenario requires you to implement redundancy. You should determine the cost to the company if downtime occurs and quantify the cost associated with the downtime as it relates to Internet connectivity problems. In the scenario given, the cost of redundancy might exceed the cost of any loss related to connectivity issues.

2. You are the network administrator for a small software development company. The company relies on its ability to connect to the Internet for more than 95 percent of its business transactions. Your network design consists of one router, one switch, one network access server (NAS) configured as a NAT server, two Microsoft Windows Server 2003 Standard Edition servers, and 32 workstations running Microsoft Windows XP Professional. Employees connect to the Internet by using NAT and a DSL connection. Which network component in this scenario can be a point of failure?

In this scenario there are many components that can cause the employees to be unable to work. For example, if the company's router or switch were unavailable, the employees would not be able to access the Internet. The same holds true if the network access server becomes unavailable.

3. You are the network administrator for a small real estate company that needs to engage an ISP to implement network services. Your company is also considering implementing a VPN. What criteria would you use in deciding which ISP to choose?

You might want to ask the ISP if they offer any security features such as intrusion detection systems or firewalls. You should also inquire about how reliable the ISP's Internet uplink is, and whether the ISP offers your company any guarantees or service-level agreements.

Page
9-11

Lesson 2 Review

1. You are the network administrator for a large retail clothing store that has implemented a remote access strategy. You need to have 100 employees remotely connect to the company's database server to obtain pricing information. The sales representatives will be using 56 Kbps modems to connect over the Internet to the server running a customized Web based application. What concerns or issues will you need to address before implementing a solution?

   Before implementing a solution, you must calculate the bandwidth requirements for each of the sales representatives. You need to know the required throughput for the software application as well as the amount of traffic generated by the database program.

2. As the network administrator for a medium-sized photography business, you have been receiving numerous calls from users claiming that the network is slow. The only change to the infrastructure is the telephony system recently installed. Your manager has decided to use Voice over IP to save on the current PBX system. Why would a new phone system slow down your network?

   VoIP uses your current network infrastructure to transmit analog voice messages over your network cables. This prevents companies from having to implement two separate networks: data and voice. The added bandwidth usage might have created additional network traffic, which has slowed down the transmission of all network traffic.

3. In designing your network infrastructure, is it important which services run on a particular computer? Explain your answer.

   Yes. Bandwidth is a very important aspect of creating a system that customers will want to use and be satisfied with. The more bandwidth available for the movement of data across an infrastructure, the better. If you can combine services that must communicate with each other on the same computer, you can reduce the amount of traffic generated by these computers, which will give the customers the needed bandwidth.

Page
9-16

Lesson 3 Review

1. Several employees from your company who work out of their homes have asked you if it would be possible to have multiple computers share the DSL connections they are using for Internet connectivity. What concerns or issues would you need to address before implementing a NAT solution?

   First, make sure the applications that must run on the clients' computers are supported by NAT. Also, the NAT server must have two network interface cards that are properly configured: one connected to the internal private network and the other connected to the DSL line.

2. You are configuring a client workstation using a private IP address to connect to the Internet. You decide that NAT would be a good solution and are now sitting in front of the user's workstation. Each of the workstations in the subnet uses a static IP address. How would you configure this workstation to connect to a NAT server located on the subnet?

If the workstation is already configured with an internal private IP address and subnet mask, you can most likely leave these fields as they are. However, you must change or add the IP address of the NAT server in the default gateway parameter. All NAT client workstations must have the IP address of the NAT server as their default gateway IP address. The NAT server will translate the private IP address of the client's workstation to the company's public IP address, create a unique port number, and forward the packet over the Internet.

3. After implementing NAT at your organization, a client calls and says she is not able to connect to the Internet but she is still able to run a database application that is located on a NetWare 4.11 server. What could be causing this problem?

NAT requires that the client workstation be configured with TCP/IP. Since the client can still connect to the NetWare server, it is possible that the NetWare server is running Internetwork Packet Exchange/Sequenced Packet Exchange (IPX/SPX) protocol, which does not use TCP/IP. To resolve the problem, configure the client's computer with TCP/IP.

Page
9-24

Lesson 4 Practice

1. The Glasgow office maintains separate domain names and public IP addresses for each of its departments. They are considering implementing NAT. What are their options for securing their NAT solution?

Creating Inbound filters would let NAT servers allow connections only for certain IP addresses, a good way of making sure that only valid users can connect to the system.

Creating outbound filters would let administrators govern the traffic outbound to the Internet and block particular types of traffic.

You should also take measures to secure the private services offered on a network from users outside the network who do not need access to them. For example, you might want to let remote users connect to your intranet web server but not to other file servers.

2. The Paris office has just upgraded its servers to Windows Server 2003, its messaging system to Exchange Server 2000, and many of its clients to the mail client Outlook 2003. Outlook 2003 has the ability to connect to an Exchange mail server over RPC. The company needs remote users to be able to use this functionality. Would NAT be capable of performing the address translation for this service? Why or why not?

No, NAT wouldn't be able to perform the address translation. NAT is unable to perform translation for RPC, SNMP, LDAP, COM, DCOM, or Kerberos v5. Exchange 2003 includes the Windows Server 2003 RPC Proxy Service, which allows RPC to work across NAT.

Page
9-25

Lesson 4 Review

1. You are the administrator of a small private company that is doing business with the federal government. Security, as well as the need of your users to access sensitive files located in your private network through the Internet, is a major concern. You are presently considering implementing NAT as one of the solutions to this problem. Is NAT a good solution to this problem? Explain.

    NAT is not a good solution for this problem unless you consider using an updated version of IPSec, called IPSec NAT-Traversal (IPSec NAT-T). IPSec NAT-T enables IPSec packets to pass through NAT devices.

2. As the administrator for a small accounting firm, you have been asked to implement a system that would allow multiple users to access the Internet using one public IP address issued to the company by an ISP. You have decided that NAT would be the perfect solution to the problem at hand. How would you configure the NAT server to allow access to the Internet and also allocate IP addresses to the 25 employees of the company?

    The NAT server must be placed on the internal network with two network adapter cards. One adapter card must be configured with the external public IP address, which connects to the Internet, and the other with the internal private IP address, which is connected to the private internal network. Users on the private network need to have the default gateway configured as the private IP address of the NAT server. Because the scenario requires automatic allocation of IP address information, you should configure the NAT server as a DHCP allocator. The DHCP allocator will issue IP addresses, as well as the subnet masks and default gateway information, to all internal users.

3. As an administrator of a small company, you want Internet users to be able to access your company's Web server. Because the private IP network ID is not visible to the Internet users, what can you do to enable the Internet users to access your Web server?

    Before external users can access the Web server located on your internal network, you must do the following: First, you must issue a static IP address, subnet mask, and default gateway address to the Web server. This IP address must be from your company's private IP network ID range. Second, you need to create a special port, which maps the external public IP address and public port with your company's private IP address and private port.

Case Scenario Exercise

1. Several of the junior software engineers, working from home, have attempted to access resources located in one of the hub offices with no success. You check to see if there are any inbound filters configured for the server, and are told there are not. Why can't the junior software engineers access the internal network resources? What can you do to make it possible for them to access these resources?

The junior software engineers are attempting to access resources that are located on a private internal network through the Internet. Because private network IDs are not visible from the Internet, you must create a special port, mapping the private IP address and private port information with the public IP address and public port number.

2. You decide to deploy Active Directory by adding an additional Windows Server 2003 server to the internal network of each hub office. You run dcpromo on one of the servers and create a single forest. When you attempt to upgrade another Windows Server 2003 server located in a different hub office to join this forest, you are unable. Why?

Active Directory relies on Kerberos version 5 for authentication and replication. NAT does not support Kerberos, and therefore cannot be implemented without forwarding traffic through the NAT server or using IPSec between the domain controllers.

3. After configuring each of the Windows Server 2003 servers as a NAT server, you have decided to make one of the servers, located in one of the hub offices, available only to a user with a private IP address of 10.1.1.112. Is this possible?

Yes. You can create an outbound filter on the network adapter card that is connected to the internal network and designate a specific IP address in the filter.

10 Designing a Remote Access Strategy

Exam Objectives in this Chapter:

- Design the network services infrastructure to meet business and technical requirements
    - Create the conceptual design of the remote access infrastructure
- Design a remote access strategy
    - Specify the remote access method
    - Specify the authentication method for remote access
- Design the remote access infrastructure
    - Plan capacity
    - Ascertain network settings required to access resources
    - Design for availability, redundancy, and survivability
- Design security for remote access users
    - Identify security host requirements
    - Identify the authentication and accounting provider
    - Design remote access policies
    - Specify logging and auditing settings

Why This Chapter Matters

It is important that users have access to your network infrastructure wherever they may be located. Not all users are in the same facility or office building as servers and other network resources. In fact, telecommuting is growing because many companies have discovered that executives, office staff, and others can work just as effectively from home as they can from the office. Salespeople must be able to access network information quickly with the assurance that the data is protected from unauthorized personnel. Remote users need access to the company's resources at all times of the day.

This chapter will help you design a remote access strategy that ensures these company resources are available, protected through redundancy systems, and secured through the use of centralized authentication methodologies and remote access policies. You begin your journey by creating a conceptual design for remote access. Next you learn the details and steps needed to design the remote access infrastructure as well as how to add security to the system.

Before You Begin

To complete this chapter, make sure you are familiar with the concepts described in Chapter 1, "Introduction to Active Directory and Network Infrastructure."

Lesson 1: Designing a Remote Access Strategy

Remote access gives users the ability to connect to your corporate network or to the Internet when they are not on the local network. This lesson includes an overview of remote access and the components and terminology you will need to understand before you can design and implement a remote access strategy for your company.

After this lesson, you will be able to

■ Identify the various components of remote access.

■ Describe the authentication method for remote access.

■ Describe the conceptual design of a remote access infrastructure.

Estimated lesson time: 50 minutes

Remote Access Overview

With the world becoming smaller and smaller through high-speed communication links and satellite communications, customers and employees alike are often located in remote areas, away from the company's resources. Microsoft Windows Server 2003 remote access clients can access these network resources by using dial-up remote access or virtual private network (VPN) remote access. Whichever method is selected, the remote access clients can access these resources just as if they were sitting in front of their computers at their offices.

Components of Dial-Up Remote Access

For a dial-up remote client to be able to access network resources located across a network, sometimes many miles apart, the following components are needed:

■ Network Access Client

■ Network Access Server (NAS)

Network Access Client

A network access client can be any computer running any of the Microsoft Windows operating systems, such as Windows 95, 98, 2000, XP, and so forth, or any other remote access client computers that are capable of running Point-to-Point Protocol (PPP), such as Linux, Macintosh, or NetWare. The remote access client simply runs remote access software and connects to the remote access server. There are three network access client types:

■ Dial-up client

■ VPN client

■ Wireless client

Dial-Up Client

A dial-up client connects to a remote access server through a physical connection to the remote access server. Dial-up clients use the telecommunications infrastructure to create the connection to the remote access server. Dial-up access clients can access network resources, map network drives, share files, and so on, just as if their computers were physically connected to the network. Once a connection is established, clients will not need to reconnect to network resources during a remote session. You can consider using a dial-up client when:

- Accessing the company's private network using the Internet poses an unacceptable risk.

- The cost of modems, phone lines, and multiport adapters is within the company's budget.

- The throughput rate of a dial-up connection is sufficient for the operations the remote clients will need to perform.

- Security requires that a remote client be verified through callback mechanisms or caller identification verification.

When designing a dial-up networking strategy, you must consider the following factors:

- Dial-up networking requires an initial investment in modems, communication hardware, server hardware, and phone line installations.

- Each phone line that is used for remote access increases the cost of dial-up networking.

- The total number of remote access users affects the ongoing support costs for dial-up networking. Users must be trained, and help desk personnel must be available for support and to assist with the deployment of dial-up networking.

The three most popular methods of dial-up networking are:

- **Public Switched Telephone Network (PSTN)**   A client may connect to a physical port on the remote access server by using an analog phone line utilizing the Public Switched Telephone Network. This methodology requires the use of an analog modem for both the remote access server and the remote access client.

- **Integrated Services Digital Network (ISDN)**   ISDN is another methodology that may be implemented to connect the remote access client to the remote access server. ISDN was developed to replace analog, or the PSTN, with a newer, faster, and more efficient digital technology. Basic Rate Interface (BRI) ISDN is composed of two types of channels: B and D. The B channel, or bearer channel, is used to transmit voice or data. There are two B channels in BRI ISDN. Each can transmit 64 Kbps of data, and the channels can be combined to allow for 128 Kbps. The D channel, or data channel, is used for signaling information and has a 16-Kbps capacity.

There is also PRI (Primary Rate Interface) ISDN, which companies requiring higher bandwidth can use. PRI contains 23 64-Kbps B channels and one 64-Kbps D channel. In any case, both the remote access client and the remote access server must be configured with ISDN adapters or connected through an ISDN router. (See Figure 10-1.)

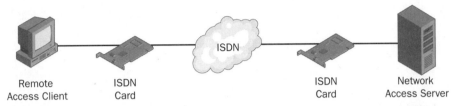

Figure 10-1 Though rarely cost-effective today, ISDN provides a higher bandwidth-on-demand alternative to traditional dial-up.

Larger companies may require the use of third-party modem-pooling equipment, referred to as modem banks. Modem banks are configured to allow multiple clients to participate in dial-up networking. The modem bank adapter contains drivers that are installed on the remote access server so that the modem bank will appear as a multiple-modem port device. Each port in the modem bank is enabled for remote access and is listed separately on the remote access server. The modem bank device and ports can be configured by accessing the Routing and Remote Access interface and selecting Ports.

When configuring a remote access client, you can set permissions on a user's Active Directory service account. Table 10-1 shows the properties you can configure for dial-in accounts.

Table 10-1 User Account Dial-in Permissions

Property	Description
Remote Access Permission (Dial-in or VPN)	You can explicitly restrict a user from accessing your server remotely or require that remote access policies be used to authorize a connection. Remote access policies are covered in Lesson 3.
Verify Caller ID	The remote access server will verify that the caller's phone number matches the one it's configured with. If the phone number doesn't match, the connection is denied.
Callback Options	The remote access server calls back the remote client using the telephone number supplied by the client or the network administrator.
Assign a Static Internet Protocol (IP) Address	Once the connection is made, the remote client can be assigned a static IP address determined by the administrator.
Apply Static Routes	This updates the routing table of the server running Routing and Remote Access service for demand-dial routing.

VPN Client

A VPN client connects to a network using the Internet or public network as its backbone. It uses Transmission Control Protocol/Internet Protocol (TCP/IP) protocols and tunneling, covered later in this lesson, as a means of securing and encrypting the data as it traverses the public network.

Wireless Client

Wireless clients connect to a network by using radio frequencies ranging from 2.4 GHz to 5.0 GHz, depending on which 802.11 wireless standard is being followed (see Table 10-2 for some of the wireless standards). Infrared (IR) frequencies use the frequency a little below visible light and spread-spectrum signals to send data over multiple frequencies. Bluetooth is another popular wireless standard for smaller, short-distance devices such as Personal Digital Assistants (PDAs), and is supported on Microsoft Windows XP service pack 1 and later.

Table 10-2   Wireless Standards

Standard	Frequency Range / Speed
802.11	2.4 GHz / 1–2 Mbps
802.11b	2.4 GHz / Up to 11 Mbps
802.11a	5 GHz / Up to 54 Mbps
802.11g	2.4 GHz / Up to 22 Mbps

For a wireless client to connect to a remote access server, a couple of components are required:

- **Wireless network interface card (NIC) on the client computer**   The wireless NIC translates the workstation's digital signals into radio signals that are sent to a transceiver located in the same area as the wireless client workstation. There can be multiple transceivers spread over a large area, if necessary, as discussed in Lesson 2.

- **Access point (AP)**   The access point is the transceiver that receives signals from the wireless client. The AP is connected to the local area network (LAN) segment, which subsequently sends the data it receives from the wireless client to the remote access server.

In designing your wireless network, you must determine where to locate the wireless APs based on the location of your wireless users. You should create a network diagram that shows the locations within a building that require wireless coverage, or you can enable wireless coverage for an entire building. You should also document any devices that can interfere with your wireless network, such as:

- Microwave ovens

- Cordless phones that use the 2.4- to 2.5-GHz frequency ranges

- Wireless video cameras

- Certain medical equipment, such as X-ray machines

You can also have interference problems with the metal objects that are part of the construction of a building, such as:

- Elevator shafts

- Heating ducts

- Air-conditioning ducts

- Wire mesh used to support drywall or plaster

How Many APs Do I Need?

So far, you have included fault tolerance and redundancy in your network design. Wireless networking should be no exception. Having only one access point in your wireless design is not only risky, it will also have an adverse affect if a wireless remote client is not located close enough to the receiver. The indoor range of most devices is about a 150-foot radius.

You should have an idea of how many wireless clients will be accessing your network. In your design phase you should try to estimate the throughput the average wireless client will use. You can multiply this number by the total number of users and get a good idea of the wireless bandwidth requirement you will need. This will help you determine the total number of APs for your remote access infrastructure. If there are too many users accessing an AP, the effective data transmission rate will be lower and the available bandwidth for each user will be reduced.

Securing Wireless Access

There are some inherent dangers using wireless technologies:

- An unauthorized user who is in close proximity to an AP can intercept data.

- An unauthorized user with a compatible wireless adapter can gain access to a wireless network.

To counter these types of attacks, you can configure the wireless access point as a Remote Authentication Dial-In User Service (RADIUS) client and have it send access requests to a RADIUS server running Internet Authentication Service (IAS). IAS is covered in detail in Lesson 3. You can also encrypt the data so that the unauthorized user who gains access to the wireless network will not be able to read or interpret the encrypted data.

Figure 10-2 illustrates each of the network access clients accessing a network access server that is configured as a remote access server. Remember that a network access server is configured as a remote access server by configuring the Routing and Remote Access service on a Windows Server 2003 server.

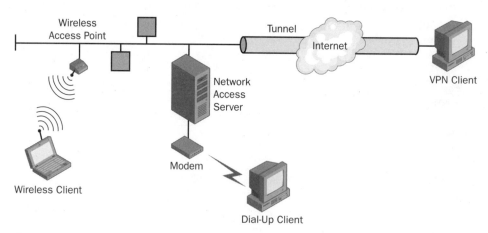

Figure 10-2 Clients can establish a connection to a network access server across a dial-up link, a virtual private network, or a wireless network.

Network Access Server

A network access server is a server that functions as a gateway to a network for remote clients. Routing and Remote Access service can be used to configure a Windows Server 2003 server as a remote access server, which will enable remote clients to create dial-up connections, or as a VPN server.

Remote access servers authenticate clients as they attempt to connect, or a centralized authentication server may be configured if there is a need for multiple remote access servers. IAS Server, which is Microsoft's implementation of RADIUS, is such a server. RADIUS is covered in Lesson 3. In configuring your remote access server, you are able to:

■ Restrict remote clients' access to only the remote access server or to the entire network. With this option, you can allow certain users to access only what is on the remote access server. For example, you can have job announcements listed in a shared folder located on the remote access server that you want potential employees outside of your organization to have access to. However, you do not want these users to be able to access any other resources located on other servers on your network. By restricting users to only the remote access server, you have less chance of an attacker penetrating your local area network.

- Choose the authentication methods that will be used by the server. Authentication is the validation of a user's credentials when he or she attempts to log on to the remote access server. In other words: "Are you who you say you are? Does your password match the one in my database?" A good analogy is the situation of an out-of-towner trying to pay a bill in a fancy restaurant with a personal check. The waiter or manager of the restaurant needs to authenticate the person writing the check, usually by asking for two forms of a picture ID (credentials).

  Authentication should not be confused with authorization. Authorization is the verification of the user's right to be where he or she is. That is: "Yes, you are who you say you are (authentication), but you are not allowed access (authorized) to the CEO's bank account records." Authorization occurs after a user has logged on and has been authenticated.

- Configure Point-to-Point Protocol (PPP) options. Point-to-Point Protocol is an industry-standard protocol that replaced Serial Line Internet Protocol (SLIP) because of SLIP's limitation of only supporting Internet Protocol (IP). PPP works with multiple protocols and also has better security features, such as encryption, mutual authentication, callback, and caller-ID.

- Configure event-logging preferences. A network access server supports three types of logging:

  - Event logging, which is the recording of events in the system event log. There are four levels of event logging available:

    Log errors only

    Log errors and warnings (the default)

    Log the maximum amount of information

    Disable event logging

  - Local Authentication and accounting logging, which enables you to track remote access usage and authentication-attempt information.

  - RADIUS-based authentication and account logging, which enables you to track remote access usage and authentication attempts from multiple remote access servers. RADIUS is a centralized auditing- and accounting-based server usually used by most Internet Service Providers.

Authentication Methods for Remote Access

After the remote client, remote server, and network infrastructure are configured, a method must be implemented to authenticate the clients who will be connecting to the remote access server and gaining access to your company's network resources. After all, you do not want unauthorized access to your company's resources to occur on your network. Table 10-3 illustrates the various methods of authentication available for remote access clients, including wireless access clients.

Table 10-3   Authentication Methods

Authentication Method	Description
Challenge Handshake Authentication Protocol (CHAP)	A challenge-response authentication for PPP connections
Password Authentication Protocol (PAP)	The least secure of all the authentication methods because it uses plain text passwords instead of encryption
Shiva Password Authentication Protocol (SPAP)	More secure than PAP, but uses a simple encrypted password-authentication protocol
Microsoft Challenge Handshake Authentication Protocol (MS-CHAP)	A Microsoft authentication method similar in functionality to CHAP.
Microsoft Challenge Handshake Authentication Protocol version 2 (MS-CHAP v2)	Performs mutual authentication and is installed by default on Windows 2000 and later operating systems
Extensible Authentication Protocol Transport Layer Security (EAP-TLS)	Provides the highest level of authentication security through the use of smart-card certificates and mutual authentication
Protected Extensible Authentication Protocol (PEAP)	Used with 802.1x networks. Increases the security of wireless network encryption; grants access based on the user's identity
MD-5 Challenge	Allows Extensible Authentication Protocol (EAP) authorization using a standard name/password combination. Allows customized authentication to remote access servers

Extensible Authentication Protocol (EAP) provides the framework for such technologies as smart cards and biometric devices. Biometrics uses a person's physical attributes as a means of authentication. Some common biometrics being used by companies today are:

- Voice scan
- Fingerprint scan
- Retinal scan
- Hand scan

Biometrics can be quite costly because the equipment must be installed on every computer a user can log on from to access network resources! Smart cards are more reasonable and offer the strongest form of remote authentication for Windows Server 2003. Microsoft Windows XP and the Windows Server 2003 family support cryptographic smart cards. For more information regarding this level of security, see Microsoft Course 2810, *Fundamentals of Network Security*.

Real World   Training Your Personnel

No matter how sophisticated security systems are, the most important and often neglected piece of the security puzzle is the employee. This is probably true because it does not involve configuring equipment or installing software, tasks at which many network administrators are skilled. Rather, it involves communicating the company's security posture through written policies and memoranda and training employees and customers to refrain from giving any pertinent information over the telephone to someone claiming to be from the help desk or IT staff, even if the information seems mundane or not important. Developing an informed and alert workforce can be more valuable than placing expensive biometrics throughout your company's network infrastructure.

Placement of Network Access Servers

The placement of your network access server in your network topology can affect the network traffic flow and security of your network infrastructure. You should place the server on the network segment that contains the most client-accessible resources.

Another method in which remote connectivity can be accomplished is through virtual private networking.

Virtual Private Networking Remote Access

When companies require a substantial amount of remote access users to access network resources, many implement a VPN solution. Compared to dial-up networking, VPNs reduce remote access expenses by using the existing Internet infrastructure. Some of the benefits of implementing a VPN solution include:

- **A reduction in costs**   Because the Internet is used to connect to the private network, there is considerable savings from not having to make long-distance phone calls, purchase modems and additional hardware, and bear all of the costs associated with a dial-up networking solution.

- **Authentication and encryption capabilities**   Authentication prevents unauthorized users from connecting to the company's private network. Strong encryption methods, such as 3-DES (data encryption standard), make it difficult for an unauthorized user to interpret the data sent across a VPN connection if captured with a network analyzer or sniffer.

In a VPN, clients use tunneling protocols to connect to the VPN server. The advantage to such a technology is that the Internet can be used to send the data. However, since the Internet is a public network, tunneling protocols must be implemented to protect the data from being intercepted along the way. Data in a VPN is encrypted, so even if the data were intercepted as it traversed the Internet, the would-be attacker would also need to decrypt the data to make use of it.

Overview of VPN

A VPN emulates a private point-to-point link between two computers that are actually communicating over a public network. Data from each of the computers is encapsulated with a header that contains the necessary routing information, enabling the data to traverse the public network to reach its destination. Since this data is also encrypted, it cannot be easily interpreted if unauthorized personnel intercept it. This private link, which contains the encapsulated and encrypted data, is called a VPN tunnel. See Figure 10-3.

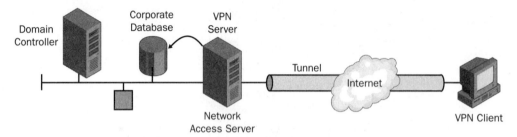

Figure 10-3   VPNs provide privacy for communications across a public network.

On computers running Windows Server 2003, Standard Edition, you can create as many as 1,000 connections using Point-to-Point Tunneling Protocol (PPTP) ports or Layer Two Tunneling Protocol (L2TP) ports. The following steps are initiated when a VPN attempts to connect to resources located across a public network (the Internet):

1. The VPN client creates a connection to the network access server (gateway), which is configured as a VPN server. This is done through the Routing and Remote Access service.

2. The VPN server answers the call, authenticates the caller, and validates if the caller is authorized to connect to the server.

3. The VPN server forwards all data between the VPN client and the corporate network resources. In this case, the VPN client needs access to the corporate database.

As you can see, companies can use the public network as a means to access their private network resources without having to lease telephone lines or having to pay a Frame Relay monthly bill. Some of the other features of using a VPN are:

■ **Enhanced security**   Because the VPN server enforces authentication and encryption, sensitive data is hidden from unauthorized users.

■ **Network protocol support**   VPNs support most of the common network protocols, enabling remote access users to run many different applications.

■ **IP address security**   Because all of the traffic that is transmitted over the Internet is encrypted, a VPN does not expose the company's internal IP address scheme to unauthorized users.

Components of a Virtual Private Network (VPN)

There are many pieces that work together to form the VPN connection just described. The VPN client and VPN server were covered. The following components are also needed for this VPN connection to occur:

- **Transit network**   This is the shared or public network that the encapsulated data traverses to connect to the remote network. This is usually the Internet.

- **Tunneling protocols**   There are two protocols that are used to manage tunnels and encapsulate private data: Point-to-Point Tunneling Protocol (PPTP), and Layer Two Transport Protocol (L2TP). PPTP operates with user-level PPP authentication methods, as well as with Microsoft Point-to-Point Encryption (MPPE) for data encryption. L2TP/IPSec (Internet Protocol Security) used with certificates for authentication is one of the most secure methods of transmitting data over a public network. Both client support and server support for L2TP are built into the Windows XP remote access client and the Windows Server 2003 family.

- **VPN tunnel**   This is the link, or connection, that encapsulates and encrypts the private data.

- **Tunneled data**   This is the data that is sent across the link.

- **Authentication**   The identity of the VPN client and VPN server are authenticated to ensure that neither end-point is being impersonated by a malicious attacker.

- **Address and name server allocation**   The VPN server is responsible for allocating IP addresses from a static pool of addresses or using Dynamic Host Configuration Protocol (DHCP), and assigning Domain Name System (DNS) and Windows Internet Naming Service (WINS) addresses to clients.

Placement of VPN Servers

The placement of your VPN server is once again an important factor when designing your remote access strategy. On one hand you want the VPN server to be available to remote users, but on the other hand you do not want to compromise network security by having the VPN server accessible to unauthorized users.

You can choose between two options for server placement, each requiring a different design:

- The VPN server on the internal network
- VPN server on the perimeter network

When placing the VPN server on the internal network, the firewall protecting the internal network must be configured to allow traffic destined for the VPN server. If you decide to place the VPN server in the perimeter network, you must configure the inbound and outbound filters of the VPN server to allow only VPN traffic to and from the VPN server's Internet interface. Then, you must configure the internal firewall to allow a wide variety of traffic originating from the VPN server. Traffic from the VPN server to the internal network will travel unencrypted toward internal resources. As a result, you must allow a wide variety of protocols and destinations through the internal firewall to ensure VPN users' applications work properly.

Creating the Conceptual Design

Now that you have identified the components of a remote access infrastructure and a VPN network, it's time to create a remote access conceptual design for your company. The conceptual design, if done correctly, can save your company money and you, the administrator, time and aggravation.

Asking the Right Questions

If the right questions are asked during this phase of design, you can avoid hearing yourself later in the design phase saying, "Oh, no! We have employees who access our sales records remotely?" In your conceptual design, you should define the functions of each of the network components covered earlier in this lesson, as well as the total number of users requiring access to your infrastructure. Some of the questions you may ask at this stage are:

- Which users, and how many users, will need to access your company's network resources remotely?

- What levels of authentication and encryption security meet your company's security requirements?

- Which resources on the internal network will be accessible?

- What level of redundancy is required?

- How well will networked applications function across the remote network, given the increased latency when compared to performance on a LAN?

- Will there be a need for wireless clients to access network resources?

- If using a VPN, will the current Internet bandwidth be sufficient for supporting the maximum simultaneous connections?

- If using dial-up networking, will you need a modem bank to handle the dial-up clients?

It is important that your design be flexible enough for any changes that may occur in your network infrastructure over the course of time. For example, if your original design called for 10 users having dial-in capability to your dial-up server, but there are now several offices opening requiring an additional 150 remote users, you should have the flexibility to allow for this increase of usage of your network services. That is, you must be prepared to install a modem bank or reconfigure your network access server to handle the increased load.

You should also consider the bandwidth used by the additional remote access dial-up clients because all dial-up clients pass through the network access server interface and connect to the private network. For example, if your design calls for 256 remote dial-up users who have 56-kilobits-per-second (Kbps) modems, and they all access your network at the same time to execute a hotel reservation application, which requires a throughput of 30 Kbps from the network access server to the client, you can calculate the aggregate bandwidth using the formula:

```
30 Kbps * 256 = 7.680 megabits per second (Mbps)
```

This means that the network access server would use more than 70% of the theoretical limit of a 10 Mbps Ethernet segment, which would saturate the realistic throughput capabilities of that type of network. This is not taking into account the unlikely possibility that any additional services are being used at the time. Even though it is possible that all of your dial-in lines can be used at once, it is unlikely that each will be used at peak capacity. For this reason, ISPs and businesses oversubscribe and allocate less than the theoretical maximum bandwidth to a bank of modems. In any event, you can see how important it is to calculate these numbers before implementing a dial-up solution.

Your design must incorporate methodologies that allow you to monitor or measure any changes on the load of your resources so adjustments can be made. For example, your current remote access service may comply with your original design specifications, but now security issues warrant a change in design that adds servers, routers, firewalls, or Intrusion Detection Systems (IDSs) to the present system. Because any of these components could reduce or increase bandwidth usage, monitoring would help you to be aware of any changes that might occur.

Practice: Designing Wireless Network Access

In this practice, you design a wireless access infrastructure for Northwind Traders. If you are unable to answer a question, review the lesson materials and try the question again. You can find answers to the questions in the "Questions and Answers" section at the end of this chapter.

Scenario

Northwind Traders currently uses Wired Equivalent Protocol (WEP) and Media Access Control (MAC) address restrictions to protect wireless access to the corporate network in Paris. In addition to increasing the security of the wireless network in Paris, management wants to implement wireless connectivity in Glasgow, Sydney, Atlanta, and Los Angeles.

Your new wireless design must meet the following criteria:

- Only employees should be able to connect to the company's wireless infrastructure. Visitors and anyone near any of the company locations should not be able to connect to the wireless network.

- The wireless network must be protected by the most secure method of encryption that is currently available.

Practice Questions

Based on the scenario, design a wireless access infrastructure for Northwind Traders by answering the following questions.

1. Which method of authentication will you recommend for Northwind Traders' wireless implementation in each location? Why?

   _____

   _____

2. Which encryption method will you specify for Northwind Traders' wireless infrastructure? Why would you make this choice?

   _____

   _____

3. What additional types of servers or network services will be required to support the wireless design? Why?

   _____

   _____

Lesson Review

The following questions are intended to reinforce key information presented in this lesson. If you are unable to answer a question, review the lesson materials and try the question again. You can find answers to the questions in the "Questions and Answers" section at the end of this chapter.

1. Describe the difference between authentication and authorization.

   _____

   _____

2. Several software engineers from the IT department want to work remotely from home to meet project deadlines. They all have Internet connectivity and you have been asked to implement a remote access strategy that would allow the software engineers to perform their work from home. One of the managers at work says that it would be too risky and that competitors would easily be able to intercept the proprietary software being developed because the Internet has little or no security. What solution would you recommend to solve this problem and allay the fears of the manager concerned about the Internet vulnerabilities?

_____

_____

3. Your small retail business has grown quickly in the last six months and your sales personnel have complained that it has been difficult to dial in to the network to get updated pricing while they are on the road. Presently, your remote access server is configured with one modem, which is usually busy during working hours. Describe what can be done to solve this problem.

_____

_____

Lesson Summary

- Remote access networking gives users the ability to remotely connect to your corporate network or to the Internet.

- A dial-up client connects to a remote access server through a physical connection to the remote access server. Dial-up clients use the telecommunications infrastructure to create the connection to the remote access server.

- A VPN client connects to a network using the Internet or public network as its backbone. It uses TCP/IP protocols and tunneling protocols such as PPTP and L2TP.

- Wireless clients connect to a network by using radio frequencies ranging from 2.4 GHz to 5 GHz, depending on which 802.1x wireless standard is being followed, infrared (IR), which uses the frequency a little below visible light, or spread-spectrum, which sends data over multiple frequencies.

- Extensible Authentication Protocol (EAP) provides the framework for such technologies as smart cards and biometric devices. Biometrics uses a person's physical attributes as a means of authentication.

Lesson 2: Designing the Remote Access Infrastructure

In designing your remote access infrastructure, you must make sure that the company's network resources are available when needed. As with all network infrastructure designs, you must consider redundancy of network access servers, as well as contingencies for failed routers, data links, and the like.

In this lesson, you learn to plan the capacity of your remote access infrastructure as well as how to design redundancy into your design for optimal availability of remote access services.

After this lesson, you will be able to

- Plan capacity of your remote access infrastructure.
- Describe redundancy methodologies for your company's remote access infrastructure.

Estimated lesson time: 20 minutes

Planning the Capacity of Your Remote Access Infrastructure

After conducting a conceptual design for your company's remote access infrastructure, you now have the answers that will enable you to begin your design of a remote access network solution. You should have a good idea of the design requirements and should be looking for the solutions that will improve the availability of the remote access services and offer redundancy in case of server crashes, router outages, and downed network link connections.

Hardware Requirements for VPN Server

In designing your remote access infrastructure you want to be sure your network access server is performing optimally and that each of the hardware components of the server is also optimized. Let's look at the components and the recommended configurations of each.

- **Network Interface Cards**   If your network requires a 100-Mbps bandwidth, and the Remote Access Server interface is connected to the public network, set all devices to 100 Mbps Full duplex and connect all interfaces on the private network to a high-capacity switch. You should also use network adapters capable of IPSec hardware offload on the public network if you determine that processing capacity will limit performance.

- **Processor**   For optimal performance, it is better to double the processor speed than to double the amount of processors. If you do have a multiprocessor computer, bind one processor to each network adapter card.

- **Random Access Memory (RAM)**   As usual, the more the better. If you do not need to handle more than 1,000 concurrent connections, 512 MB of RAM will suffice. For every 1,000 concurrent calls, provide an extra 128 MB of RAM over the recommended RAM capacity for the server and add an additional base of 128 MB more for remote access and related services. For example, a dedicated remote access server with the recommended RAM capacity of 256 MB, which will need to support 2,000 simultaneous VPN calls, should have 768 MB of RAM:

```
256 MB + (128 MB * 2) + (128 MB * 2)
```

If compression is turned on, each connection uses more nonpaged pool memory and requires more processing. Performance can be improved by turning off compression.

Design Requirements

Before you can decide on the remote access design you will use for your company, you should be able to identify:

- **The needs of the users**   How many users will need to access the company's resources remotely? Where are they currently located? Will the present network infrastructure support any new requirements?

- **The type of connection being used between geographic locations.**   Will you need to upgrade a 56-Kbps line to a T1 line to accommodate increased usage?

- **Current network infrastructure**   What are the locations of the routers, switches and data links? Will newer routers need to be purchased to handle increased loads?

- **The current network traffic patterns**   Are there potential bottlenecks in the current design that can easily be improved upon?

- **Any mission-critical applications running on the remote access network**   If yes, does the speed of the data transmission, or the network protocol used by the application program, affect the successful operation of the applications? For example, if the application was for hotel reservations and it ran on a legacy NetWare 4.11 server that relied on Internetwork Packet Exchange/Sequenced Packet Exchange (IPX/SPX) protocol, would your users be able to continue using the program over a remote connection?

Another major factor is whether the maximum network latency is acceptable to run the mission-critical application. If a user in Boston needs to connect to a VPN server in Redmond to use an application hosted on a server on the internal network in Boston, then the round-trip will have to cross the country four times. This latency may cause the program to fail. Determining the network latency requirements ahead of time allows the designer to specify that a VPN server in the Boston area is necessary.

As you can see, there are many questions that need to be answered before you design your remote access infrastructure. Let's look at the three networking services your design may need to implement:

- Dial-up server
- Virtual private network
- Wireless

Any one of these services may be critical for your company's day-to-day operations, and this is a good starting point to identify any redundancy or contingencies you may want to implement. For example, if remote users rely on running a hotel reservation system and there is only one remote access server configured as a dial-up server, there could be catastrophic consequences if that dial-up server were to crash or shut down. If the reservation clerks had another method of accessing the reservation application, such as by connecting through a VPN using the Internet, this could be a viable backup. Remember, availability of a company's resources to its employees is critical!

Consideration should also be given to the resource usage of each of the networking services that are running on your network access server (NAS) so that the correct server is selected for the job. See Table 10-4.

Table 10-4   Network Access Server Resource Usage

NAS Type	Processor	Memory	Disk	Network
Dial-up server	High	High	None	High
Virtual private network (VPN)	High	Low	None	Low
Internet Authentication Service (IAS)	Medium	High	None	Low

You need to know the answers to the following questions so that you can configure the network access server to handle your remote access requirements.

- How many user accounts will need remote access permission?
- What will be the maximum number of simultaneous connections that can occur at any given time?
- How many dial-up ports, telephone lines, and modems are needed to support the remote dial-up clients?
- How many PPTP ports are needed to support the maximum number of VPN connections?
- How many L2TP ports are needed to support the maximum number of VPN connections?

Knowing which resources are being used the most on the server can help you decide which one should be configured to be an IAS server or a dial-up server.

It should also be noted that the server may be up and running, but a router may be nonoperational. This can cause the same type of problem if the router is the only gateway to the company's network resources. You should always be aware of places in your network infrastructure or design that have one place of failure that could render your network useless. The weakest link in your design is the one that depends solely on one component to make it operational.

Sometimes a network service or component in your design may be operational, but can still cause a problem. A service that is not functional at the speed or level of efficiency that it should be can also bring a company to its knees. A network access server functioning as a dial-up server that has only one modem configured could obviously cause problems if 30 salespersons attempted to connect to the inventory database at the same time. It is critical that you always be aware of the load or maximum number of users who may be connecting to any one of your remote access services.

Creating Redundancy

In most cases, one network access server placed in the correct area of your network infrastructure will be sufficient to support your company's users. However, to ensure that the network access servers are available as much as possible, you should consider having an additional server configured in each subnet servicing the remote access infrastructure for redundancy and survivability. If your company has multiple locations, distribute redundant network access servers throughout your offices. This provides improved redundancy as well as better performance for users who can connect to a local VPN server.

Subnets that have only one router servicing them should be modified to include an additional router. Once again, having only one path in and out of a subnet that has a company's mission-critical applications running on it is playing with fire.

Creating a Dial-Up Solution

If after conducting your conceptual design it was determined that there would be a need for the company to allow dialing capability for over 150 customers, there would now be many considerations to address:

- Where will you place the network access servers?
- To provide for redundancy, will you have multiple network access servers in your design?
- Will the servers be placed on the internal network or the perimeter network?

Dial-up servers provide access to a company's internal network resources and your design must address such issues as:

- The total number of telephone lines, modems, and adapters needed to support the maximum number of remote client connections.

- The names of the user accounts that will be granted remote access.

- Any remote access policy restrictions that may apply to groups of users.

You should also consider having additional phone lines and modems available in case there are changes in the number of remote users needing dial-up access to your network access server or if there are the inevitable equipment failures that occur on all networks.

Creating a VPN Solution

If your design requires that you design a VPN solution for your company, there are issues and questions that must also be addressed:

- Which tunneling protocol will you use for your customers while they are connecting to the network access server, PPTP or L2TP?

- Will you use remote access policies to control access to resources?

- What authentication and encryption methods will you use for VPN clients?

Practice: Designing a Remote Access Infrastructure

In this practice, you design a remote access infrastructure for Northwind Traders. If you are unable to answer a question, review the lesson materials and try the question again. You can find answers to the questions in the "Questions and Answers" section at the end of this chapter.

Scenario

Northwind Traders wants to enable its employees to access the corporate network over the Internet. Northwind Traders' current network infrastructure is illustrated in the following diagram. To protect its product data, Northwind Traders wants to ensure that all connections to the corporate network use the most secure encryption method available. In addition, the company wants to optimize its network traffic to ensure that this additional traffic will have minimal impact on the wide area network (WAN) link connections.

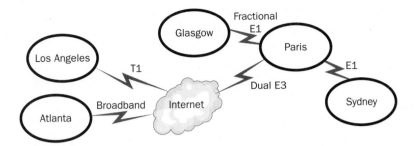

Practice Questions

Based on the scenario, design a remote access infrastructure for Northwind Traders by answering the following questions.

1. Will you include any additional Internet connections in your design? If so, at which locations? Why?

_____

_____

2. Where will you place the VPN servers? Why?

_____

_____

3. Which authentication and encryption methods will you specify in your design? Why?

_____

_____

Lesson Review

The following questions are intended to reinforce key information presented in this lesson. If you are unable to answer a question, review the lesson materials and try the question again. You can find answers to the questions in the "Questions and Answers" section at the end of this chapter.

1. Describe the components needed to design a dial-up access infrastructure.

_____

_____

2. List some of the requirements you need to know before you can decide on the remote access design for your company.

_____

_____

3. As a network administrator for a small electronics company, your manager has hired an outside consultant to assist you in developing a remote access strategy. Many of the sales personnel want to be able to access database files from varied locations throughout the United States. The consultant has mentioned that using a tunneling protocol could offer you more security than simply connecting from the Internet. Explain what the term "tunneling" means. Give two examples of tunneling protocols supported by Microsoft Server 2003.

_____

_____

Lesson Summary

- Before a conceptual remote access design can be created, a thorough understanding of the present network topology and documentation (network maps, inventory of all servers and workstations, etc.) must be available.

- To ensure that the network access servers are available to users, consider having an additional server configured in the same or a different subnet servicing the remote access infrastructure, for both redundancy and survivability.

- Before you can decide on the remote access design you will use for your company, you must identify the needs of the users, current network infrastructure, network traffic patterns, and any mission-critical applications that will run on the system.

Lesson 3: Designing Security for Remote Access Users

Securing network infrastructure for remote users is one of the most critical jobs of a network administrator. With viruses and attacks occurring on thousands of computer systems daily, you must protect your systems. Clients should be authenticated when they attempt to access your remote access infrastructure so that your company data is protected from unauthorized users.

After this lesson, you will be able to

■ Secure remote host computer systems.

■ Design remote access policies.

■ Describe centralized administration through IAS.

Estimated lesson time: 60 minutes

Securing Your Remote Access Infrastructure

As your remote access infrastructure grows, it may become necessary to implement a centralized system to perform authentication and accounting functions. For example, to assist you in planning or to calculate billing, you may want to keep track of the amount of time and bandwidth a customer uses. You may also find it more efficient to create remote access policies that can be applied to an Organizational Unit (OU) or to a domain in your organization, rather than to individual users.

In this lesson, you learn how to use Internet Authentication Service (IAS) to help manage your remote access infrastructure, as well as how to create remote access policies that provide you with a more powerful way of managing remote access permissions than setting permissions for individual accounts.

Creating a Remote Access Policy

A remote access policy is composed of an ordered set of rules, each containing one or more conditions, profile settings, and remote access permission settings. A condition is one or more attributes that are compared to the settings of a connection attempt. See Table 10-5.

Table 10-5   Remote Access Policy Conditions

Attribute	Description
Authentication Type	Authentication type, such as CHAP, MS-CHAP, and so forth that is being used by the remote client.
Called Station ID	The phone number of the network access server (NAS). Windows Server 2003 server, phone line, and hardware driver must support passing the called ID.

Table 10-5   Remote Access Policy Conditions (Continued)

Attribute	Description
Calling Station ID	Phone number used by the caller.
Client-Friendly Name	The name of the RADIUS client requesting authentication.
Client IP Address	The IP address of the RADIUS client.
Client Vendor	The vendor of the network access server (NAS) requesting authentication.
Day and Time Restrictions	Day of week and time of day the connection can be attempted.
Framed Protocol	Used by IAS to determine the framing type (PPP, SLIP, Frame Relay, or X.25) of incoming packets.
MS RAS Vendor	The manufacturer of the RADIUS client machine. This attribute is not commonly used.
NAS Identifier	The name of the network access server.
NAS IP Address	The IP address of the NAS (RADIUS client).
NAS Port Type	The type of media used by the access client, such as ISDN, wireless, or analog phone lines.
Service Type	Type of service, such as PPP connection, Telnet connection, and so on, being requested.
Tunnel Type	Type of tunnel, such as PPTP, L2TP, and so on, that is being created.
Windows Groups	Name of the groups the user or computer is a member of that is attempting a connection.

The rules determine if a connection is authorized or rejected. If the connection is authorized, the policy profile may specify certain connection restrictions. A remote access profile is a set of properties applied to a connection if the connection has been authorized. A profile has the following group of properties:

- **Dial-in constraints** You can set the minutes a server can remain idle before it is disconnected. Routing and Remote Access service does not by default disconnect idle connections. You can also set a maximum amount of time a connection is connected as well as the days of the week and hours each day a connection is allowed. Dial-in constraints can also be based on the type of media being used to create the connection. For example, you can reject all connections from any modem that has a telephone number not matching the configured dial-in number of the remote access server.

- **IP properties**   You can require that the access server supply an IP address, the access client request an IP address, the access server determine an IP address assignment, or that a static IP address is assigned. You can also define IP packet filters that restrict or block traffic (incoming or outgoing) based on the IP address.

- **Multilink properties**   You can set multilink properties that enable multilink and determine the maximum number of ports a multilink connection can use.

- **Authentication properties**   You can enable the various authentication types that are allowed for a connection, such as MS-CHAP, EAP, and so on, and can specify whether users can change their expired passwords using MS-CHAP and MS-CHAP v2.

- **Encryption properties**   You can set encryption properties to various encryption strengths such as No encryption, Basic encryption, Strong encryption, and Strongest encryption, which supports triple DES (160-bit encryption).

- **Advanced properties**   You can set advanced properties to specify which RADIUS attributes are sent back by the IAS server to the RADIUS client.

Remote policies can also be used to specify additional restrictions. After the connection is authorized, remote access policies can restrict connections based on:

- Idle timeout time

- Maximum session time

- Encryption strength

- IP packet filters

- Advanced restrictions such as IP addresses for PPP connections and static routes

Using an Internet Authentication Service Server

In organizations in which more than one network access server is required, centralization of accounting and authentication of connections may be the preferred method of doing business. For example, instead of each NAS being responsible for keeping track of how long users connect to various devices or authenticating the users as they connect to various remote systems, each NAS can redirect these tasks to a centralized server that is running the Internet Authentication Service (IAS).

Before you can understand what IAS is, you must first understand the technology on which it is based, Remote Authentication Dial-In User Service (RADIUS). This is a widely used protocol that enables centralized accounting, authentication, and authorization for remote network access. With RADIUS, you can manage network access for VPN, dial-up, and wireless networks.

How RADIUS Works

There are several components needed to implement RADIUS:

- **RADIUS server** This server authenticates, authorizes, and performs accounting functions when a connection attempt is made from a remote access client. The remote access client can be any of the clients you learned about earlier: dial-in, VPN, and wireless. For example, if a connection request is made, the server compares the attributes of the connection request with a set of rules and any information it has in the user account database. The attributes can be such things as day and time, IP number of the RADIUS client, and so forth. Based on this information, the RADIUS server either accepts or rejects the connection.

- **RADIUS client** A RADIUS client can be a dial-up server, VPN server, or a wireless access point (AP). When a remote access client attempts a connection to any of these servers, the RADIUS client receives the request and forwards it to the RADIUS server. For example, if a connection to a dial-up server were made, the dial-up server (RADIUS client) would not handle the authentication or authorization of the connection, but would send it to the RADIUS server.

- **RADIUS proxy** In very large organizations or when an ISP is outsourced to perform dial-up access for a company, there may be multiple RADIUS servers available to authenticate, authorize, and perform accounting functions. A RADIUS proxy determines which RADIUS server to forward the request to. For example, the RADIUS client would receive a connection request from a remote access client, forward the request to the RADIUS proxy, and the RADIUS proxy would then forward the request to the appropriate RADIUS server. See Figure 10-4.

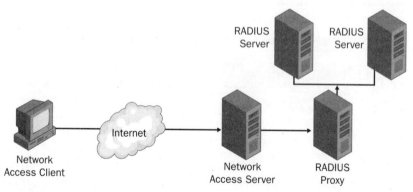

Figure 10-4   RADIUS clients, proxies, and servers work together to authenticate users.

IAS performs the following for dial-up, VPN, and wireless connections:

- **Centralized accounting** IAS collects usage or accounting information from all network access servers.

- **Centralized authentication** IAS supports many of the standard authentication methods such as Challenge Handshake Authentication Protocol (CHAP), Microsoft Challenge Handshake Authentication Protocol (MS-CHAP versions 1 and 2), and Extensible Authentication Protocol (EAP). IAS interoperates with network access devices from different vendors regardless of the access method used. If IAS is configured as a member of an Active Directory domain, the user account database is used to authenticate and authorize access to the network.

- **Centralized auditing** IAS logs all authentication Accepts and Rejects, as well as usage information such as logon and logoff records.

Instead of having your dial-up server or VPN server performing these tasks and storing accounting and auditing information, you can configure them to be RADIUS clients, each forwarding all connection requests to your IAS server. Any remote access policies stored on these RADIUS clients are no longer used. Instead, these policies, which are stored on the IAS server, will be used.

Designing a RADIUS Solution

When you begin your design, you first need to determine the role of your IAS server. That is, will it be a RADIUS server, RADIUS client, or RADIUS proxy? There is a good possibility that your design may require the use of a RADIUS server. As you recall, a network access server running the IAS is a RADIUS server. Instead of having multiple RADIUS clients performing authentication, authorization, accounting and auditing, you can have one server perform all of these functions. As always, you must consider the following when designing a RADIUS strategy:

- Securing your RADIUS solution

- Availability of RADIUS to your remote users

- Improving RADIUS performance

You must once again reference your topology diagrams so you can determine

- The geographic locations of the remote users.

- Number of users at each of the locations.

- The connection type between each geographic location, for instance, T1 line, Frame Relay, and so forth.

Securing Your RADIUS Solution

Because remote access users will have access to your company's internal private network, your RADIUS solution must protect this confidential information. You must secure the connection between the remote access client and the RADIUS client, as well as the connection between the RADIUS client and the RADIUS server. You can use remote access policies that the RADIUS client can use to restrict remote access users. The advantage of applying remote access policies on the RADIUS server, instead of on the RADIUS client, is that the remote access policies of the RADIUS server are applied to all remote access users. All RADIUS clients who are assigned to a RADIUS server use the remote access policies configured on the RADIUS server and ignore any policies configured on the RADIUS client.

Authentication protocols and methods, as well as the encryption algorithms covered previously in this chapter, may also be used to enhance the security of your RADIUS solution. Because a RADIUS server is a network access server, which supports all authentication protocols, RADIUS servers also support all of the authentication protocols covered earlier:

- MS-CHAP v1, v2

- EAP-TLS

- CHAP

- SPAP

- PAP

RADIUS clients support data encryption for remote access clients by using MPPE over PPTP, and IPSec if Layer 2 Transfer Protocol is chosen as the tunneling protocol. IPSec enables you to encrypt up to 160-bit encryption algorithm, called 3-DES (pronounced as "triple-dez").

Availability of a RADIUS Solution

If your remote access design includes state-of-the-art equipment, enhanced security features, and so forth, but is not available for remote users, then you have not accomplished your goal as a network engineer. Once again, availability of the network infrastructure and the company's network resources is probably the most important aspect of your job. The most obvious way to increase the chances of your RADIUS solution being available to your remote users is to include more than one RADIUS client and server. However, it is important that you balance this need for availability with the costs of the hardware needed to duplicate these IAS servers and with the company's need for such a level of availability.

If you do decide that your company should have two IAS servers configured as RADIUS servers, be sure to:

- Configure the RADIUS clients as RADIUS proxies. This will enable load balancing because the RADIUS proxy can forward connection requests to either of the two RADIUS servers configured.

- Copy the configuration of one IAS server computer to the other IAS server. This will allow both servers to perform the same authentication, authorization, accounting, and auditing functions for all of the RADIUS clients.

Ensuring the availability of RADIUS servers and RADIUS clients means that your remote users have access to network resources located on the internal network, and that neither component can become a single point of failure in your remote access strategy.

You may also want to ask management if they want to track accounting information, such as: How long was a connection established by a remote user? or What time did the user log on to the system? A basic rule of thumb for any design is to make sure the features of the service or components you implement do indeed support your company's requirements. For example, you would not implement a RADIUS solution if the company did not require centralized accounting, authentication, authorization, and auditing.

Designing Client Connectivity

There are different ways remote clients can access a RADIUS client. Your design must take into account the various network technologies discussed in Lesson 1:

- Dial-up modems
- Integrated Services Digital Network (ISDN)

Your decision here may be based on the current infrastructure, or on financial constraints placed on you by the company. In any event, your network diagram would show the type of network technologies currently implemented and your recommended changes or additional components. Many companies that have a Frame Relay connection between geographic locations also have an ISDN line in place as a contingency. That way, if the Frame Relay connection became unavailable, the ISDN line can be used to access the company's network resources. You might consider doing the same for connections that rely on an ISP for connectivity. This can be quite risky. If your design only allows access to network resources when an ISP is up and running, you might want to consider having a dial-up server available in case the ISP becomes unavailable. One again, having all of your eggs in one basket is not recommended if the business depends on those eggs to function!

Placement of RADIUS Servers and Clients

In designing your RADIUS solution you must consider how to place the RADIUS servers and RADIUS clients so they will be the most secure and will minimize network traffic over your network infrastructure. You must also decide whether the RADIUS clients will support dial-up and VPN-based remote access clients. At a minimum, your RADIUS design will contain at least one RADIUS server and one RADIUS client. The

RADIUS client should be placed as close as possible to the remote access users. This includes the following advantages:

- Reduces dial-up charges by using localized traffic

- Reduces traffic traversing WAN links

- Reduces the risk of exposing the company's confidential data because you have better control of the security between the RADIUS client and the company's private internal network

The RADIUS server should be placed close to the domain controller (DC), which provides authentication for the remote access clients. The authentication server and the RADIUS server should both be located on the private network, reducing the risk of attack by unauthorized persons.

Practice: Designing Security for Remote Access Users

In this practice, you explore the requirements involved in planning secure remote access. Think of the company you work for now (or have worked for in the past) and describe your experience with network security. Use the following questions to guide your thoughts.

1. Which authentication and encryption methods do you use on your organization's network for remote access authentication? For VPN authentication?

   _____

   _____

2. If your organization has a wireless network, which authentication and encryption mechanisms does it use?

   _____

   _____

3. Does your organization use RADIUS servers for authentication? If so, do you use IAS or another implementation?

   _____

   _____

4. Does your organization use any multifactor authentication methods, such as smart cards? If so, when is their use required?

   _____

   _____

Lesson Review

The following questions are intended to reinforce key information presented in this lesson. If you are unable to answer a question, review the lesson materials and try the question again. You can find answers to the questions in the "Questions and Answers" section at the end of this chapter.

1. You are the network administrator for a marketing computer sales company and have many salespeople who travel away from corporate headquarters. Accounting has stated that the costs of the sales personnel remotely accessing the company's database system from Asia, using dial-in modems, has been extremely high due to the high cost of dialing out from hotels. What possible solutions can you suggest to lower this cost?

_____

_____

2. You are the administrator of a Windows Server 2003 network and have just implemented IAS as a solution. What would be an advantage of applying remote access policies on the RADIUS server?

_____

_____

3. You are the administrator of a large enterprise network and have multiple RADIUS servers spread throughout your organization. What component can be configured to forward a connection request to a particular RADIUS server?

_____

_____

Lesson Summary

- A remote access policy is composed of an ordered set of rules, each containing one or more conditions, profile settings, and remote access permission setting.

- If a connection is authorized, a policy profile may specify certain connection restrictions. A remote access profile is a set of properties that are applied to a connection if the connection has been authorized.

- As your remote access infrastructure grows, it may become necessary to implement a centralized system to perform authentication and accounting functions. IAS Server is Microsoft's implementation of RADIUS.

- IAS performs centralized accounting, authentication, authorization, and auditing for dial-up, VPN, and wireless connections.

- A RADIUS server is a server that authenticates, authorizes, and performs accounting functions when a connection attempt is made from a remote access client.

- A RADIUS client can be a dial-up server, VPN server, or a wireless access point (AP). When a remote access client attempts a connection to any of these servers, the RADIUS client receives the request and forwards it to the RADIUS server.

- A RADIUS proxy determines which RADIUS server to forward a request to. For example, a RADIUS client would receive a connection request from a remote access client, forward the request to the RADIUS proxy, and the RADIUS proxy would then forward the request to the appropriate RADIUS server.

Case Scenario Exercise

Review the following scenario and complete the questions.

Scenario

You have been selected to design a remote access strategy for a Maui property that is managed by Contoso, Ltd., a property management company located in Honolulu, Hawaii. The company relies on its ability to make reservations for its condominium holdings, apartment rentals, and several five-star hotels. Much of Contoso's revenue is earned from golf course fees, golf shops, and restaurants located on hotel properties. Many of the restaurants are running legacy applications that have not been updated for more than ten years and are starting to have problems. The golf shops are located too far from the main computer buildings, which house two Windows 2000 servers, four Windows Server 2003 servers, a NetWare 4.11 server running an application that keeps track of the cleaning staff's room assignments throughout the complexes, and the routers and switches supporting the network infrastructure.

Background

Contoso has acquired many hotels and restaurants during the past 12 years and is expanding to Southeast Asia. Its largest customer base is Japanese travelers, from whom it receives more than $22 million per year.

Geography

In addition to its primary location, Contoso also has branch offices located on Maui, Kauai, and Tokyo, from where most of its customers come. Depending on which island a customer wants to visit, he or she must call an 800 number to make a reservation.

Charge card numbers are given over the telephone and inputted into the systems by reservation clerks.

Network Infrastructure

Each branch office supports the hotel property, which includes the restaurants and golf shops. Fiber-optic cable is run underground to most facilities and is connected to a main dedicated building that houses all of the network's technological equipment such as servers, routers, and switches. There are many small offices throughout the properties, where managers use dial-in services to query several databases for hotel occupancy numbers.

Future Plans

The company is considering developing a Web-based application that would allow customers to make their reservations online. The system would need to securely accept charge card and debit payments from customers.

Questions

Given the previous scenario, answer the following questions.

1. Several of the golf shops located on the Maui complex are too far away from the building that houses the computer infrastructure, including the fiber-optic cable run. These golf shops are running stand-alone applications that require the shop clerk to enter all of the customer information into the system, save it to diskette, and load it on the Windows Server 2003 server later in the evening. This has caused major problems, and you have been asked to come up with a solution to this problem. What would you suggest to management to improve on the current method?

   _____

   _____

2. Managers who are accessing the network using modems are complaining that they always get a busy signal when trying to connect early in the morning. It is critical that all managers can get information regarding occupancy rates any time of day because they must sometimes relay this information to sales staff selling large travel packages. During golf tournaments, occupancy is very high and rooms are scarce. What solution could you offer to help alleviate this problem?

   _____

   _____

3. Because of the time difference in Japan, several managers ask if it would be possible for them to access the internal network from their homes, where they use cable modems to access the Internet. They want to be able to access the company's private network's databases and give information to their partners in Japan. What network service would you recommend to offer a solution to their problem?

_____

_____

4. You need to come up with the various authentication methods remote access clients can use to connect to your NAS. Which method is the least secure? Which method is the most secure?

_____

_____

Chapter Summary

- Remote access networking gives users the ability to remotely connect to a corporate network or to the Internet.

- A dial-up client connects to a remote access server through a physical connection to the remote access server. Dial-up clients use the telecommunications infrastructure to create the connection to the remote access server.

- A VPN client connects to a network using the Internet, or public network, as its backbone. It uses TCP/IP protocols and tunneling protocols such as PPTP and L2TP.

- Wireless clients connect to a network by using radio frequencies from 2.4 GHz to 5.0 GHz, depending on which 802.1x wireless standard is being followed, infrared (IR), which uses the frequency a little below visible light, or spread-spectrum signals, which send data over multiple frequencies.

- Extensible Authentication Protocol (EAP) provides the framework for such technologies as smart cards and biometric devices. Biometrics uses a person's physical attributes as a means of authentication.

- Before a conceptual remote access design can be created, a thorough understanding of the present network topology and documentation (network maps, inventory of all servers and workstations, and so on) must be available.

- To ensure that the network access servers are available to users, you should consider having an additional server configured in each subnet servicing the remote access infrastructure, for both redundancy and survivability.

- Before you can decide on the remote access design you will use for your company, you must identify the needs of the users, current network infrastructure, network traffic patterns, and any mission-critical applications that will run on the system.

- A remote access policy is composed of an ordered set of rules, each containing one or more conditions, profile settings, and a remote access permission setting.

- If a connection is authorized, a policy profile may specify certain connection restrictions. A remote access profile is a set of properties that are applied to a connection if the connection has been authorized.

- As your remote access infrastructure grows, it may become necessary to implement a centralized system to perform authentication and accounting functions. IAS Server is Microsoft's implementation of RADIUS.

- IAS performs centralized accounting, authentication, authorization and auditing for dial-up, VPN, and wireless connections.

- A RADIUS server is a server that authenticates, authorizes, and performs accounting functions when a connection attempt is made from a remote access client.

- A RADIUS client can be a dial-up server, VPN server, or a wireless access point (AP). When a remote access client attempts a connection to any of these servers, the RADIUS client receives the request and forwards it to the RADIUS server.

- A RADIUS proxy determines which RADIUS server to forward a request to. For example, a RADIUS client would receive a connection request from a remote access client, forward the request to the RADIUS proxy, and the RADIUS proxy would then forward the request to the appropriate RADIUS server.

Exam Highlights

Before taking the exam, review the key topics and terms that are presented in this chapter. You need to know this information.

Key Points

- Remote access networking gives users the ability to remotely connect to corporate networks or to the Internet. Clients can be dial-up, VPN, or wireless clients. Dial-up clients use the telecommunications infrastructure to create the connection to the network access server. VPN clients connect to the private network using the Internet, or public network. TCP/IP tunneling protocols, such as Point-to-Point Tunneling Protocol (PPTP) and Layer 2 Tunneling Protocol (L2TP) are used to encapsulate and encrypt the data.

■ Before a conceptual remote access design can be created, a thorough understanding of the present network topology and network technologies must be available. To ensure that network access servers are available to users, you should consider having an additional server configured in the same or a different subnet servicing the remote access infrastructure, for both redundancy and survivability.

■ A remote access policy is composed of an ordered set of rules, each containing one or more conditions, profile settings, and remote access permission setting. If a connection is authorized, a profile policy may specify certain connection restrictions.

■ As your remote access infrastructure grows, it may become necessary to implement a centralized system to perform authentication, authorization, accounting and auditing services. Internet Authentication Service (IAS) Server is Microsoft's implementation of Remote Authentication Dial-In User Service (RADIUS). The minimum components found in a RADIUS solution is one RADIUS server and one RADIUS client.

■ A RADIUS server is a network access server (NAS) that is running IAS. A RADIUS client can be a dial-up server, VPN server, or a wireless access point (AP). A RADIUS proxy determines which RADIUS server connection requests will be forwarded to if there is more than one RADIUS server.

Key Terms

Access point (AP)   The access point is the transceiver that receives signals from a wireless client. The AP is connected to the LAN segment, which subsequently sends the data it receives from the wireless client to the remote access server.

Network Access Serve (NAS)   A network access server is a server that functions as a gateway to a network for remote clients. Routing and Remote Access service can be used to configure a Windows Server 2003 server as a remote access server, which will enable remote clients to create dial-up connections, or as a virtual private network (VPN) server, which will enable VPN clients to connect.

RADIUS Server   A RADIUS server is a network access server (NAS) that authenticates, authorizes, and performs accounting functions when a connection attempt is made from a remote access client.

RADIUS Client   A RADIUS client can be a dial-up server, VPN server, or a wireless access point (AP) that receives requests and forwards it to a RADIUS server.

RADIUS Proxy   A RADIUS proxy determines which RADIUS server to forward a request to after it receives a request from a RADIUS client.

Extensible Authentication Protocol (EAP)   An Extensible Authentication Protocol provides the framework for such technologies as smart cards and biometric devices. Biometrics uses a person's physical attributes as a means of authentication.

Questions and Answers

Page
10-16

Lesson 1 Practice

1. Which method of authentication will you recommend for Northwind Traders' wireless implementation in each location? Why?

   Use 802.1x authentication for all locations because this is the most secure method of authentication available.

2. Which encryption method will you specify for Northwind Traders' wireless infrastructure? Why would you make this choice?

   Use WiFi Protected Access (WPA) encryption for all locations because this is the most secure method of encryption available.

3. What additional types of servers or network services will be required to support the wireless design? Why?

   Because of the size of the company, a public key infrastructure is required to support WPA encryption. Also, a RADIUS server will be required in each location to perform the 802.1x authentication.

Page
10-16

Lesson 1 Review

1. Describe the difference between authentication and authorization.

   Authentication is the validation of the credentials, such as a name and password, a user gives to a remote access server. Authorization is the verification that the authenticated individual does indeed have permission to use the resource he or she is attempting to access.

2. Several software engineers from the IT department want to work remotely from home to meet project deadlines. They all have Internet connectivity and you have been asked to implement a remote access strategy that would allow the software engineers to perform their work from home. One of the managers at work says that it would be too risky and that competitors would easily be able to intercept the proprietary software being developed because the Internet has little or no security. What solution would you recommend to solve this problem and allay the fears of the manager concerned about the Internet vulnerabilities?

   This is a perfect time to create a VPN connection, that you configure using Routing and Remote Access service, from each of the software engineers' home computers to the company's VPN server. The manager can be assured that the tunneling protocol will protect the encrypted data at the same level of protection afforded on a local area network (LAN).

3. Your small retail business has grown quickly in the last six months and your sales personnel have complained that it has been difficult to dial in to the network to get updated pricing while they are on the road. Presently, your remote access server is configured with one modem, which is usually busy during working hours. Describe what can be done to solve this problem.

To allow multiple remote users to connect to a remote access server, it is necessary to configure a bank or pool of modems. The modem bank adapter includes drivers that make the modem bank appear as a device with multiple modem ports.

Page
10-23

Lesson 2 Practice

1. Will you include any additional Internet connections in your design? If so, at which locations? Why?

Create a new Internet connection for the Sydney office. Also consider upgrading the Internet connections for the Atlanta and Los Angeles offices to handle the additional traffic. The Atlanta office's Internet connection, in particular, deserves close attention. Broadband connections are often asymmetrical, and the bandwidth available for traffic leaving the Atlanta office may be much smaller than the bandwidth available for traffic traveling from the Internet to the Atlanta office.

2. Where will you place the VPN servers? Why?

Place a VPN server in each location so that users can connect to their closest office, which will reduce the amount of VPN traffic that traverses the company's WAN links. Configure the firewall that is used to protect the company's network from the Internet in each location as the VPN server for that location.

3. Which authentication and encryption methods will you specify in your design? Why?

Use L2TP/IPSec for all connections because there is now a way for L2TP/IPSec traffic to traverse a Network Address Translation (NAT) server. Issue smart cards to all employees requiring VPN access to the network. Require smart card authentication for VPN access. Use 3-DES IPSec encryption for all VPN access.

4. What hardware and software will be required in addition to the VPN servers?

Because IPSec encryption and smart card authentication will be used, a Public Key Infrastructure (PKI) will have to be implemented to support the VPN solution.

Page
10-23

Lesson 2 Review

1. Describe the components needed to design a dial-up access infrastructure.

You need to determine the total number of telephone lines, modems, and adapters needed to support the maximum number of remote client connections.

2. List some of the requirements you need to know before you can decide on the remote access design for your company.

You should determine the needs of the users and have a good idea of the current network infrastructure, network traffic patterns, and any mission-critical applications the company needs to run. It would also be prudent to find out what the budget constraints are, since this could have a dramatic affect on the course of action you may take.

3. As a network administrator for a small electronics company, your manager has hired an outside consultant to assist you in developing a remote access strategy. Many of the sales personnel want to be able to access database files from varied locations throughout the United States. The consultant has mentioned that using a tunneling protocol could offer you more security than simply connecting from the Internet. Explain what the term "tunneling" means. Give two examples of tunneling protocols supported by Microsoft Server 2003.

Tunneling is another term for encapsulating—or wrapping data with headings—and encrypting the payload. Point-to-Point Tunneling Protocol and Layer 2 Tunneling Protocol are the two tunneling protocols supported by Microsoft.

Page
10-33
Lesson 3 Review

1. You are the network administrator for a marketing computer sales company and have many salespeople who travel away from corporate headquarters. Accounting has stated that the costs of the sales personnel remotely accessing the company's database system from Asia, using dial-in modems, has been extremely high due to the high cost of dialing out from hotels. What possible solutions can you suggest to lower this cost?

You can set the minutes a server can remain idle before it is disconnected. Routing and Remote Access service does not, by default, disconnect idle connections. You can also set a maximum amount of time a connection is connected as well as the days of the week and hours each day a connection is allowed. Dial-in constraints can also be based on the type of media being used to create the connection. For example, you can reject all connections from any modem with a telephone number that doesn't match the configured dial-in number of the remote access server.

2. You are the administrator of a Windows Server 2003 network and have just implemented IAS as a solution. What would be an advantage of applying remote access policies on the RADIUS server?

The advantage of applying remote access policies on the RADIUS server, instead of on the RADIUS client, is that the remote access policies of the RADIUS server are applied to all remote access users. All RADIUS clients that are assigned to a RADIUS server use the remote access policies configured on the RADIUS server and ignore any policies configured on the RADIUS client.

3. You are the administrator of a large enterprise network and have multiple RADIUS servers spread throughout your organization. What component can be configured to forward a connection request to a particular RADIUS server?

In very large organizations, or when an ISP is outsourced to perform dial-up access for a company, there may be multiple RADIUS servers available to authenticate, authorize, and perform accounting functions. A RADIUS proxy determines which RADIUS server to forward the request to.

Page
10-35

Case Scenario Exercise

1. Several of the golf shops located on the Maui complex are too far away from the building that houses the computer infrastructure, including the fiber-optic cable run. These golf shops are running stand-alone applications that require the shop clerk to enter all of the customer information into the system, save it to diskette, and load it on the Windows Server 2003 server later in the evening. This has caused major problems, and you have been asked to come up with a solution to this problem. What would you suggest to management to improve on the current method?

This is a perfect time to implement a wireless solution. Because the golf shop is too far from the network infrastructure, you can implement a wireless solution by installing an access point (AP) close to the remote golf shop and a network access server connected to the Maui internal network. This way, all transactions made at the golf shop can be updated to the database application located on a server that is on the internal network.

2. Managers who are accessing the network using modems are complaining that they always get a busy signal when trying to connect early in the morning. It is critical that all managers can get information regarding occupancy rates any time of day because they must sometimes relay this information to sales staff selling large travel packages. During golf tournaments, occupancy is very high and rooms are scarce. What solution could you offer to help alleviate this problem?

There is a good chance that a modem bank or pool of modems is not being used in this scenario. Verify that a bank of modems is configured for this company. If only one modem is available, it is no wonder that multiple users are having difficulty connecting to the dial-up server. When selecting the hardware for the multiple modem ports, be sure to verify that the hardware is on the Hardware Compatibility List (HCL) and that you properly install it on the network access server.

3. Because of the time difference in Japan, several managers ask if it would be possible for them to access the internal network from their homes, where they use cable modems to access the Internet. They want to be able to access the company's private network's databases and give information to their partners in Japan. What network service would you recommend to offer a solution to their problem?

You can configure a network access server to be a virtual private network (VPN) server. By configuring the NAS to be a VPN server, you can transfer data to and from VPN clients over a secure, tunneled protocol. As long as your users can connect to the Internet, they can connect to your company's private internal network. For example, by using Layer Two Tunneling Protocol (L2TP) with Internet Protocol Security protocol (IPSec), you can protect your company's data while using the public Internet to connect to your private network.

4. You need to come up with the various authentication methods remote access clients can use to connect to your network access server (NAS). Which method is the least secure? Which method is the most secure?

Password Authentication Protocol (PAP) is the least secure of all the authentication methods you can use in your remote access design because it uses plain-text passwords instead of encryption. Extensible Authentication Protocol (EAP) provides the highest level of authentication security through the use of smart card certificates and mutual authentication.

Glossary

A

access control entry (ACE) An entry on an access control list that associates a user or group with a particular permission.

access control list (ACL) A list of security permissions applied to an object. An ACL for an item normally includes membership and the actions that each member can perform on the item.

Active Directory directory service The Microsoft Windows directory service that replaced the Security Accounts Manager in Microsoft Windows NT 4. Active Directory consists of a forest, one or more domains, sites, organizational units, containers, and objects. Various classes of objects can be represented within Active Directory, including users, groups, computers, printers, and applications.

Active Directory integrated zone A zone type that stores a read-write copy of the Domain Name System (DNS) zone resource records in Active Directory. Instead of relying on zone transfers to replicate DNS information between DNS servers, DNS information in an Active Directory integrated zone is replicated along with Active Directory information.

Address Resolution Protocol (ARP) Determines hardware addresses (MAC addresses) that correspond to an Internet Protocol (IP) address on the local subnet.

administrative structure A representation of the functions, divisions, departments, or positions within an organization and their relationships, including the organization's hierarchy and authority structure. The administrative structure reflects how an organization is managed and how it conducts administrative operations.

administrator A person responsible for setting up and managing domain controllers or local computers and their user and group accounts, for assigning passwords and permissions, and for helping users with networking issues.

attribute The individual properties that are assigned to an object.

authentication The process by which the system validates the user's logon information. A user's name and password are compared against the list of authorized users. If the system detects a match, the system considers the user's identity validated. Before the authenticated user can access resources, the user must also be authorized.

authorization The process of granting or denying access to network resources based on the authentication of a user's logon credentials.

available bandwidth The amount of bandwidth that is actually available for use after normal network traffic is handled.

B

backbone The network segment or segments that carry traffic between destination networks.

bandwidth The amount of data that can be transmitted across a communications channel in a specific amount of time. In computer networks, greater bandwidth indicates faster data-transfer capability and is expressed in bits per second (bps).

Berkeley Internet Name Domain (BIND) An implementation of the Domain Name System (DNS) written and ported to most available versions of the UNIX operating system. The Internet Software Consortium maintains the BIND software.

bridgehead server A server that is responsible for transferring directory replication information between sites.

C

caching-only DNS server A DNS server that doesn't contain a local copy of zone information on local disk and only forwards requests. Caching-only DNS servers can reduce network traffic by not requiring DNS zone replication.

Challenge Handshake Authentication Protocol (CHAP) An authentication protocol used by Routing and Remote Access. Using CHAP, a remote access client can send its authentication credentials to a remote access server in an encrypted form.

connection object An Active Directory object representing a replication connection from one domain controller to another. The connection object is a child of the replication destination's NT Directory Services (NTDS) Settings object and identifies the replication source server, contains a replication schedule, and specifies a replication transport.

contact A nonsecurity principal that represents a user outside of the organization. A contact generally has an e-mail address, but cannot log on to a network.

D

default gateway A router that is used by networked devices (including computers) to forward IP packets to remote networks when no other router has a more-specific route to the destination.

DHCP *See* Dynamic Host Configuration Protocol.

DHCP client Clients that receive their IP configuration information automatically from DHCP servers.

DHCP relay agent   Forwards DHCP messages between DHCP clients and DHCP servers on different IP network segments.

DHCP scope   A range of IP addresses to be managed by the DHCP server. DHCP scope options are assigned to a DHCP scope to provide IP configuration options that are particular to a specific IP address range.

DHCP server   Provides automatic IP configuration to other IP devices on the network. DHCP servers are configured with a range of IP addresses and other DCHP scope options. A DHCP server grants a DHCP client a lease for an IP address for a specific length of time.

directory   An authoritative source of information that contains information about people, resources, or other objects.

directory service   Both the directory information database and the services that control the database and make it available across the network.

distinguished name   A name assigned to every object in Active Directory that identifies where the object resides in the overall object hierarchy.

DNS   *See* Domain Name System.

DNS notify list   A list maintained by the primary master for a zone of other Domain Name System (DNS) servers that should be notified when zone changes occur. The notify list is made up of Internet Protocol (IP) addresses for DNS servers configured as secondary masters for the zone. When the listed servers are notified of a change to the zone, they will initiate a zone transfer with another DNS server and update the zone.

DNS server   A computer that runs DNS server programs containing name-to-IP address mappings, IP address-to-name mappings, information about the domain tree structure, and other information. DNS servers also attempt to resolve client queries. A DNS server is also called a DNS name server.

domain   The core unit in Active Directory. A domain is made up of a collection of computers that share a common directory database.

domain controller   A server running Microsoft Windows 2000 Server or Microsoft Windows Server 2003 that has Active Directory installed. Each domain controller is able to authenticate users for its own domain. It holds a complete replica of the domain naming partition for the domain to which it belongs and a complete replica of the configuration and schema naming partitions for the forest.

Domain Name System (DNS)   A widely used standards-based protocol that allows clients and servers to resolve names into IP addresses and vice versa. Windows Server 2003 extends this concept by supplying a dynamic DNS (DDNS) service that enables clients and servers to automatically register themselves in the database without requiring administrators to define records manually.

domain restructure   A migration method that involves the redesign of the Windows NT domain structure, which often results in fewer, consolidated domains.

domain tree   A collection of domains with a contiguous namespace, such as microsoft.com, dog.microsoft.com, and cat.microsoft.com. Domains within the forest that do not have the same hierarchical domain name are located in a different domain tree. When different domain trees exist in a forest, it is referred to as a disjointed namespace.

domain upgrade   The process of upgrading an existing Windows NT domain structure without restructuring the domains.

Dynamic Host Configuration Protocol (DHCP)   A TCP/IP protocol that provides automatic configuration of IP addresses on network devices.

dynamic update   An updated specification to the Domain Name System (DNS) standard that permits hosts that store name information in the DNS to dynamically register and update their records in zones maintained by DNS servers that can accept and process dynamic update messages.

E

Extensible Authentication Protocol (EAP)   An extension of the Point-to-Point Protocol (PPP) that provides remote access user authentication by means of other security devices. These security devices can include smart cards, X509 certificates, Kerberos v5 tickets, and others.

F

fault tolerance   The resistance of a computer or operating system against downtime when a failure occurs.

firewall   A system designed to prevent unauthorized access to or from a private network. A firewall can be made up of hardware, software, or a combination of both. Firewalls can work by blocking certain types of packets or certain applications.

forest   A collection of domains and domain trees. The implicit name of the forest is the name of the first domain installed. All domain controllers within a forest share the same configuration and schema naming partitions. The first domain within the forest cannot be removed.

forest root domain   The first domain created in an Active Directory forest. After the forest root domain has been created, you cannot create a new forest root domain or a parent for the existing forest root domain, and you cannot rename the forest root domain.

forward lookup   In the Domain Name System (DNS), a query process in which the friendly DNS domain name of a host computer is searched to find its Internet Protocol (IP) address.

fully qualified domain name (FQDN)   A DNS domain name that fully and uniquely defines an object's location in the DNS namespace.

full zone transfer (AXFR)   The standard query type supported by all Domain Name System (DNS) servers to update and synchronize zone data when the zone has been changed. When a DNS query is made using AXFR as the specified query type, the entire zone is transferred as the response.

functional level   The mode in which an Active Directory domain or forest is operating. A domain can exist in a number of functional levels, each of which is determined by the versions of Windows Server running in the domain or forest. In Windows 2000 mixed mode (where Windows NT, Windows 2000, and Windows 2003 servers may run), the domain has limitations (such as 40,000 objects) imposed by the Windows NT 4 domain model. However, Windows 2000 domain controllers and Windows NT 4 backup domain controllers can coexist within the domain without problems. Switching to Windows 2000 native mode (which allows Windows 2000 and 2003 servers only) allows the directory to scale up to millions of objects. Windows Server 2003 level provides the full functionality of Windows Server 2003 but requires that all servers run Windows Server 2003.

G

geographical structure   A representation of the physical locations of the functions, divisions, departments, or positions within an organization. It reflects how an organization is structured geographically at a regional, national, or international level.

Global Catalog server   A server that holds a complete replica of the configuration and schema naming contexts for an Active Directory forest, a complete replica of the domain naming context in which the server is installed, and a partial replica of all other domains in the forest. The Global Catalog (GC) knows about every object in the forest and has representations for them in its directory. However, it may not know about all attributes (such as job title and physical address) for objects in other domains.

globally unique identifier (GUID)   An attribute consisting of a 128-bit number that is guaranteed to be unique and is used by applications that need to refer to an object by an identifier that remains constant. A GUID is assigned to an object when it is created, and it never changes, even if the object is moved between containers in the same domain.

group   An object defined in Active Directory that contains other objects such as users, contacts, and possibly other groups. A group can be either a distribution group or a security group, and its scope can be local, domain, or universal.

group policy object (GPO)   A collection of group policy settings that can be applied across an entire site, domain, or organizational unit.

group scopes   A categorization of groups that enables you to use groups in different ways to assign permissions. The scope of a group determines where in the network you are able to use the group to assign permissions to the group. The three group scopes are global, domain local, and universal.

GUID   *See* globally unique identifier.

H

hop   In network routing, the transmission of a data packet through a router.

host ID   A number used to identify a particular interface on a logical subnet.

hostname   The name of a device on a network. For a device on a Windows network, this can be the same as the computer name (the NetBIOS name), but it may not be. The hostname must be in the Hosts file, or it must be known by a DNS server, for that host to be found by another computer attempting to communicate with it.

I

incremental zone transfer (IXFR)   An alternate query type that can be used by some Domain Name System (DNS) servers to update and synchronize zone data when a zone is changed. When IXFR is supported between DNS servers, servers can keep track of and transfer only the incremental resource record changes between each version of the zone.

infrastructure master   The domain controller assigned to update group-to-user references when group membership changes and to replicate these changes to any other domain controllers in the domain. There can be only one infrastructure master in a particular domain at any one time.

InetOrgPerson   An object—similar to a user object—that is used to migrate users from other Lightweight Directory Access Protocol (LDAP) directory services to Active Directory.

Internet Protocol (IP)   The messenger protocol of TCP/IP that is responsible for addressing and sending IP packets over the network. IP provides a best-effort, connectionless delivery system that doesn't guarantee that packets arrive at their destination or in the sequence in which they were sent.

intersite replication   Replication traffic that occurs between sites.

intrasite replication   Replication traffic that occurs within a site.

IP address   A 32-bit address used to identify a node on an IP internetwork. Each node on the IP internetwork must be assigned a unique IP address, which is made up of a network identifier and a host identifier.

K

Kerberos v5   An Internet standard security protocol for handling authentication of user or system identity. With Kerberos v5, passwords that are sent across network lines are encrypted, not sent as plain text. Kerberos v5 includes other security features as well.

Knowledge Consistency Checker (KCC)   A built-in service that runs on all domain controllers and automatically establishes replication connections between domain controllers in the same site and between bridgehead servers in different sites.

L

local area network (LAN)   A group of computers and other devices that are connected by a high-speed communications link.

Lightweight Directory Access Protocol (LDAP)   A standards-based protocol that can be used to interact with conformant directory services. LDAP version 2 allows users and applications to read the contents of a directory database, whereas LDAP version 3 (defined under RFC 2251) allows them to read from and write to a directory database.

M

Microsoft Challenge Handshake Authentication Protocol (MS-CHAP)   An authentication protocol used by Routing and Remote Access that lets clients send authentication credentials to a remote access server in a secure form. This is the Windows-specific variant of CHAP.

multihomed   A computer that has more than one network interface.

multimaster replication   A replication model in which all domain controllers hold an equally authoritative replica of the Active Directory database.

N

namespace   A logical collection of resources that can be managed as a single unit. Within Active Directory, a domain defines a namespace.

naming partition   A self-contained section of a directory hierarchy that has its own properties, such as replication configuration and permissions structure. Active Directory includes the domain, configuration, and schema naming partitions.

NetBIOS   A system of special networking services added to the Basic Input Output System (BIOS) of a computer. Windows-based computers rely on NetBIOS for much of their network functionality, including their NetBIOS-based computer names assigned to the computers.

network access server   A server that controls access to a network. A network access server typically acts as a router, a NAT server, or a remote access server.

Network Address Translation (NAT)   A protocol that maps private IP addresses on an internal network to the public IP addresses accessible externally. In Windows Server 2003, the NAT protocol is provided by both Routing and Remote Access and Internet Connection Sharing.

O

object   An entity that is described by a distinct, named set of attributes. In Active Directory, all network resources are represented as objects that can be centrally administered.

operations master role   A domain controller that has been assigned one or more special roles in an Active Directory domain. The domain controllers assigned these roles perform operations that are not permitted on other domain controllers at the same time.

organizational unit (OU)   An Active Directory container object that is used to organize other objects within a domain for the purposes of delegating administrative authority. An OU can contain user accounts, printers, groups, computers, and other OUs.

P

Password Authentication Protocol (PAP)   An authentication protocol used by Routing and Remote Access Server. PAP has weak security because the user name and password are transmitted in plain text.

path   A sequence of directory (or folder) names that specifies the location of a directory, file, or folder within the directory tree.

PDC emulator master   A domain controller assigned to emulate a Microsoft Windows NT 4 primary domain controller (PDC) to service network clients that do not have Active Directory client software installed and to replicate directory changes to any Windows NT backup domain controllers (BDCs) in the domain.

perimeter network   A special area of a network that contains services typically accessible by the public and is bounded by two firewalls—one preventing unauthorized intrusion from a public interface, such as the Internet, and another firewall with even tighter controls preventing unauthorized access to the private network.

primary DNS server   The authoritative server for a primary zone. A primary zone database file must be administered and maintained on the primary DNS server for the zone.

primary zone database file   The master zone database file. Changes to a zone, such as adding domains or hosts, are performed on the server that contains the primary zone database file.

R

relative distinguished name (RDN)   The part of an object's distinguished name that uniquely identifies it within its parent container.

relative ID master   A domain controller that is assigned to allocate sequences of relative IDs to each domain controller in its domain. Whenever a domain controller creates a security principal (user, group, or computer object), the domain controller assigns the object a unique security ID. The security ID consists of a domain security ID that is the same for all security IDs created in a particular domain and a relative ID that is unique for each security ID created in the domain.

Remote Authentication Dial-In User Service (RADIUS)   RADIUS is commonly used to provide centralized authentication, authorization, and accounting for dial-up, virtual private network, and wireless network access.

remote procedure calls (RPCs)   A reliable synchronous protocol that allows a program on one computer to execute a program on another computer.

replica   In Active Directory replication, a copy of a logical Active Directory partition that is synchronized through replication between domain controllers that hold copies of the same directory partition.

replication   The process of copying data from a data store or file system to multiple computers to synchronize the data. Active Directory provides multimaster replication of the directory between domain controllers within a given domain.

replication interval   The time between scheduled transfers of replication data between sites over a site link. By default, the replication interval in Windows Server 2003 is 180 minutes.

request for comments (RFC)   RFCs are a series of notes about the Internet. Anyone can submit an RFC and, if an RFC gains enough support, it may become an Internet standard. Each RFC is designated by an RFC number. Once published, an RFC never changes. Modifications to an original RFC are assigned a new RFC number.

resource record   A database record used in a DNS zone to associate a particular type of resource to an IP address.

reverse lookup   In the Domain Name System (DNS), a query process by which the Internet Protocol (IP) address of a host computer is searched to find its friendly DNS domain name.

root domain   The domain at the top of the DNS hierarchy, represented as a period (.).

RPC   *See* remote procedure calls.

S

schema   The metadata (data about data) that describes how objects are used within a given structure. The Active Directory schema defines the classes of objects that can be created in Active Directory and the attributes those objects can posses.

schema master   The domain controller assigned to control all updates to the schema within a forest. At any time, there can be only one schema master in the forest.

schema naming partition   A partition of Active Directory that contains all object types and their attributes that can be created in Active Directory. This information is replicated to all domain controllers in the forest.

scope   In DHCP, a pool of IP addresses that a DHCP server is configured to provide to DHCP clients.

secondary DNS server   A backup DNS server that receives the primary zone database files from the primary DNS server in a zone transfer.

secondary master   An authoritative DNS server for a zone that is used as a source for replication of the zone to other servers. Secondary masters update their zone data only by transferring zone data from other DNS servers. They do not have the ability to perform zone updates.

secondary zone database file   A read-only replica of an existing standard primary zone database file stored in a standard text file on a secondary DNS server.

Security Accounts Manager   A service that stores and manages information for user accounts.

security identifier (SID)   A unique number that identifies a user, group, or computer account. Every account on a network is issued a unique SID when the account is first created.

security principal   An Active Directory object, such as a user or group, that defines a security context. A non-security principal is an object represented in Active Directory that cannot access resources within the enterprise.

Shiva Password Authentication Protocol (SPAP)   An authentication protocol implemented in Routing and Remote Access Service. SPAP allows computers running Windows Server 2003 to connect to Shiva-based servers.

shortcut trust   A two-way trust relationship that is explicitly created between two Windows domains that are not directly connected to one another. The purpose of a shortcut trust is to optimize the interdomain authentication process.

Simple Message Transfer Protocol (SMTP)   A widely used standards-based protocol that allows for the transfer of messages between different messaging servers. SMTP is defined under RFC 821 and uses simple command verbs to facilitate message transport over TCP/IP port 25.

site   In Active Directory, a collection of IP subnets. All computers in the same site have high-speed connectivity—LAN speeds—with one another. Multiple sites can exist within a single domain, and, conversely, a single site can span multiple domains.

site link   A link between two sites that allows replication to occur.

site-link bridge   A configuration allowing the transmission of replication information between sites that are not directly linked. Site-link bridges are used when site-link transitivity is disabled.

site-link cost   A value assigned to the site link that indicates the cost of the connection relative to other site links. Lower-cost links are favored over higher-cost links. Higher costs are typically assigned to slow links, lower costs to faster links.

site topology   A logical representation of a physical network using site boundaries.

standard primary zone   A DNS zone type that stores a read-write copy of the DNS zone resource records in an operating system file. Standard primary zones are replicated by using DNS full or incremental zone transfers.

standard secondary zone   A DNS zone type that stores a read-only copy of the DNS zone resource records in an operating system file. Secondary primary zones are replicated from standard primary zones by using DNS full or incremental zone transfers.

Start of Authority (SOA) record   A DNS record that indicates the starting point of authority for information stored in a zone. The SOA resource record is the first resource record created when adding a new zone.

subnet   A portion of a network, which may be a physically independent network segment with a single network ID. Hosts within a subnet can communicate without sending packets through a router.

subnet mask   Allows IP to distinguish the network ID portion of the IP address from the host ID portion.

T

trust relationship   A relationship established between domains to allow pass-through authentication, in which a trusting domain honors the logon authentications of a trusted domain.

U

user   In Active Directory, a security principal (a user who can log on to the domain).

user principal name (UPN)   A name that is generated for each object, in the form username@domainname. A UPN allows the underlying domain structure and complexity to be hidden from users. For example, although many domains may exist within a forest, users would seamlessly log on as if they were in the same domain.

V

virtual private network (VPN)   Provides encapsulated, encrypted, and authenticated virtual connections across public networks. VPN connections can provide secured remote access and routed connections to private networks over the Internet. VPN connections can be created by using Layer Two Tunneling Protocol (L2TP) or Point-to-Point Tunneling Protocol (PPTP) tunnels.

W

wide area network (WAN)   A series of one or more LANs that are geographically separated but connected by telecommunications links.

Windows Internet Naming Service (WINS)   A service that maps IP addresses to computer names (NetBIOS names). This allows users to access resources by name instead of requiring them to use IP addresses that are difficult to recognize and remember.

Z

zone   In a DNS database, a contiguous portion of the DNS tree that is administered as a single entity by a DNS server. The zone contains resource records for all the names within the zone.

zone transfer   The process used by DNS servers to synchronize authoritative name data between servers in a zone.

Index

The practical, portable guides to
Microsoft Windows Server 2003

Microsoft® Windows® Server 2003 Admin Pocket Consultant
ISBN 0-7356-1354-0

The practical, portable guide to Windows Server 2003. Here's the practical, pocket-sized reference for IT professionals who support Windows Server 2003. Designed for quick referencing, it covers all the essentials for performing everyday system-administration tasks. Topics covered include managing workstations and servers, using Active Directory® services, creating and administering user and group accounts, managing files and directories, data security and auditing, data back-up and recovery, administration with TCP/IP, WINS, and DNS, and more.

Microsoft IIS 6.0 Administrator's Pocket Consultant
ISBN 0-7356-1560-8

The practical, portable guide to IIS 6.0. Here's the eminently practical, pocket-sized reference for IT and Web professionals who work with Internet Information Services (IIS) 6.0. Designed for quick referencing and compulsively readable, this portable guide covers all the basics needed for everyday tasks. Topics include Web administration fundamentals, Web server administration, essential services administration, and performance, optimization, and maintenance. It's the fast-answers guide that helps users consistently save time and energy as they administer IIS 6.0.

To learn more about the full line of Microsoft Press® products for IT professionals, please visit:

microsoft.com/mspress/IT

In-depth technical information and tools for
Microsoft Windows Server 2003

Microsoft® Windows Server™ 2003 Deployment Kit: A Microsoft Resource Kit
ISBN 0-7356-1486-5

Plan and deploy a Windows Server 2003 operating system environment with expertise from the team that develops and supports the technology—the Microsoft Windows® team. This multivolume kit delivers in-depth technical information and best practices to automate and customize your installation, configure servers and desktops, design and deploy network services, design and deploy directory and security services, implement Group Policy, create pilot and test plans, and more. You also get more than 125 timesaving tools, deployment job aids, Windows Server 2003 evaluation software, and the entire Windows Server 2003 Help on the CD-ROMs. It everything you need to help ensure a smooth deployment—while minimizing maintenance and support costs.

Internet Information Services (IIS) 6.0 Resource Kit
ISBN 0-7356-1420-2

Deploy and support IIS 6.0, which is included with Windows Server 2003, with expertise direct from the Microsoft IIS product team. This official RESOURCE KIT packs 1200+ pages of in depth deployment, operations, and technical information, including step-by-step instructions for common administrative tasks. Get critical details and guidance on security enhancements, the IIS 6.0 architecture, migration strategies, performance tuning, logging, and troubleshooting—all with timesaving tools, IIS 6.0 product documentation, and a searchable eBook on CD. You get a the resources you need to help maximize the security, reliability, manageability, and performanc of your Web server—while reducing system administration costs.

To learn more about the full line of Microsoft Press® products for IT professionals, please visit

microsoft.com/mspress/IT

Microsoft Press products are available worldwide wherever quality computer books are sold. For more information, contact your book or computer retailer, software reseller, or local Micro Sales Office, or visit our Web site at **microsoft.com/mspress.** To locate your nearest source for Microsoft Press products, or to order directly, call 1-800-MSPRESS in the United States. (Canada, call 1-800-268-2222.)

© 2004 Microsoft Corporation. All rights reserved. Microsoft, Microsoft Press, Windows, and Windows Server are either registered trademarks or trademarks of Microsoft Corporation in United States and/or other countries.

In-depth technical information
for Microsoft Windows Server 2003

ur Windows Server 2003 TECHNICAL REFERENCE series is designed for IT professionals who need in-depth information bout specific topics such as TCP/IP protocols and services supported by Windows Server 2003, Internet Information ervices security, Active Directory Services, and Virtual Private Networks. Written by leading technical experts, these ooks include hands-on examples, best practices, and technical tips. Topics are discussed by presenting real-world cenarios and practical how-to information to help IT professionals deploy, support, maintain, optimize, and oubleshoot Microsoft products and technologies. You start with the fundamentals and build comprehension layer by yer until you understand the subject completely.

Microsoft® Windows® Server 2003 TCP/IP Protocols and Services Technical Reference
SBN: 0-7356-1291-9
U.S.A. $49.99
Canada $76.99

Microsoft Internet Information Services Security Technical Reference
SBN: 0-7356-1572-1
U.S.A. $49.99
Canada $72.99

Active Directory® Services for Microsoft Windows Server 2003 Technical Reference
ISBN: 0-7356-1577-2
U.S.A. $49.99
Canada $76.99

Deploying Virtual Private Networks with Microsoft Windows Server 2003 Technical Reference
ISBN: 0-7356-1576-4
U.S.A. $49.99
Canada $76.99

To learn more about the full line of Microsoft Press® products for IT professionals, please visit:

microsoft.com/mspress/IT

crosoft Press products are available worldwide wherever quality computer books are sold. For more information, contact your book or computer retailer, software reseller, or local crosoft Sales Office, or visit our Web site at **microsoft.com/mspress**. To locate your nearest source for Microsoft Press products, or to order directly, call 1-800-MSPRESS in the United ates. (In Canada, call 1-800-268-2222.)

Get a **Free**
e-mail newsletter, updates,
special offers, links to related books,
and more when you

register online!

Register your Microsoft Press® title on our Web site and you'll get a FREE subscription to our e-mail newsletter, *Microsoft Press Book Connections*. You'll find out about newly released and upcoming books and learning tools, online events, software downloads, special offers and coupons for Microsoft Press customers, and information about major Microsoft® product releases. You can also read useful additional information about all the titles we publish, such as detailed book descriptions, tables of contents and indexes, sample chapters, links to related books and book series, author biographies, and reviews by other customers.

Registration is easy. Just visit this Web page and fill in your information:
http://www.microsoft.com/mspress/register

Microsoft®

Proof of Purchase

Use this page as proof of purchase if participating in a promotion or rebate offer on this title. Proof of purchase must be used in conjunction with other proof(s) of payment such as your dated sales receipt—see offer details.

MCSE Self-Paced Training Kit (Exam 70-297): Designing a Microsoft® Windows Server™ 2003 Active Directory® and Network Infrastructure
0-7356-1970-0

CUSTOMER NAME

Microsoft Press, PO Box 97017, Redmond, WA 98073-9830

MCSA and MCSE for Microsoft Windows Server 2003

The Microsoft Certified Systems Engineer (MCSE) credential is the premier certification for professionals who analyze the business requirements and design and implement the infrastructure for business solutions based on the Microsoft® Windows Server™ 2003 platform and Microsoft Windows Server System. Implementation responsibilities include installing, configuring, and troubleshooting network systems.

The Microsoft Certified Systems Administrator (MCSA) credential proves that you have the skills to successfully implement, manage, and troubleshoot the ongoing needs of Windows Server 2003–based operating environments.

For information on study materials, training, and certification for Microsoft Windows Server 2003, please visit: **www.microsoft.com/traincert**.

MCSA/MCSE Core Requirements

MCSA

Three core exams, including:

- Two Networking System exams
- One Client Operating System exam

MCSE

Six core exams, including:

- Four Networking System exams
- One Client Operating System exam
- One Design exam

Networking System Exams

MCSA (Two Exams Required)	MCSE (Four Exams Required)	Core Exams: Networking System	Microsoft Press® Study Materials	ISBN
✔	✔	Exam 70-290: Managing and Maintaining a Microsoft Windows Server 2003 Environment	MCSA/MCSE Self-Paced Training Kit (Exam 70-290): Managing and Maintaining a Microsoft Windows Server 2003 Environment	0-7356-1437-7
			MCSE Self-Paced Training Kit: Microsoft Windows Server 2003 Core Requirements, Exams 70-290, 70-291, 70-293, 70-294	0-7356-1953-0
✔	✔	Exam 70-291: Implementing, Managing, and Maintaining a Microsoft Windows Server 2003 Network Infrastructure	MCSA/MCSE Self-Paced Training Kit (Exam 70-291): Implementing, Managing and Maintaining a Microsoft Windows Server 2003 Network Infrastructure	0-7356-1439-3
			MCSE Self-Paced Training Kit: Microsoft Windows Server 2003 Core Requirements, Exams 70-290, 70-291, 70-293, 70-294	0-7356-1953-0
N/A	✔	Exam 70-293: Planning and Maintaining a Microsoft Windows Server 2003 Network Infrastructure	MCSE Self-Paced Training Kit (Exam 70-293): Planning and Maintaining a Microsoft Windows Server 2003 Network Infrastructure	0-7356-1893-3
			MCSE Self-Paced Training Kit: Microsoft Windows Server 2003 Core Requirements, Exams 70-290, 70-291, 70-293, 70-294	0-7356-1953-0
N/A	✔	Exam 70-294: Planning, Implementing, and Maintaining a Microsoft Windows Server 2003 Active Directory® Infrastructure	MCSE Self-Paced Training Kit (Exam 70-294): Planning, Implementing, and Maintaining a Microsoft Windows Server 2003 Active Directory Infrastructure	0-7356-1438-5
			MCSE Self-Paced Training Kit: Microsoft Windows Server 2003 Core Requirements, Exams 70-290, 70-291, 70-293, 70-294	0-7356-1953-0

Client Operating System Exams

MCSA (Choose One)	MCSE (Choose One)	Core Exams: Client Operating System	Microsoft Press Study Materials	ISBN
✔	✔	Exam 70-270: Installing, Configuring, and Administering Microsoft Windows® XP Professional	MCSE Training Kit (Exam 70-270): Windows XP Professional	0-7356-1429-6
✔	✔	Exam 70-210[1]: Installing, Configuring, and Administering Microsoft Windows 2000 Professional	MCSA/MCSE Self-Paced Training Kit (Exam 70-210): Microsoft Windows 2000 Professional, Second Edition	0-7356-1766-X

Design Exams

MCSA (Not Applicable)	MCSE (Choose One)	Core Exams: Design	Microsoft Press Study Materials	ISBN
N/A	✔	Exam 70-297[2]: Designing a Microsoft Windows Server 2003 Active Directory and Network Infrastructure	MCSE Self-Paced Training Kit (Exam 70-297): Designing a Microsoft Windows Server 2003 Active Directory and Network Infrastructure	0-7356-1970-0
N/A	✔	Exam 70-298[2]: Designing Security for a Microsoft Windows Server 2003 Network	MCSE Self-Paced Training Kit (Exam 70-298): Designing Security for a Microsoft Windows Server 2003 Network	0-7356-1969-7

1 Candidates who passed Windows NT 4.0 Exams 70-067, 70-068, and 70-073 had the option to take the comprehensive Exam 70-240: Microsoft Windows 2000 Accelerated Exam for MCPs Certified on Microsoft Windows NT 4.0. By passing this exam, candidates met the MCSE exam requirement for 70-210. Exam 70-240 is no longer available.

2 Exams 70-297 and 70-298 may each count once as either one core design exam or one elective exam.

✔ = qualifying exam